Here you are girls! 'Butch' bares his chest and has a cup of tea from a 'strange mug'!

We hear it doesn't happen very often but 'Butch' here helps out watering the flowers at home

Proud Mum and rightly so—'Butch' and Graham with the statuette from the Mini World Cup victory

THE OFFICIAL
CHELSEA FC
PROGRAMME BOOK

Written & Compiled by David Antill

Trinity Mirror Sport Media

Business is brisk for our programme sellers ahead of a match against Arsenal in 1966

Trinity Mirror Sport Media (S)

Written & Compiled by David Antill
Cover by Glen Hind

Production Editor: Harri Aston
Design and production: Roy Gilfoyle, Adam Oldfield

Thanks to:

David Kostis - without whose help, this book would not have been possible - Albert Sewell, Hugh Hastings,
Richard Godden, Andy Jones, Kevin Newman, Martin Williams and Chelsea Football Club museum.

Published by Trinity Mirror Sport Media
Managing Director: Steve Hanrahan
Commercial Director: Will Beedles
Executive Senior Art Editor: Rick Cooke
Executive Editor: Paul Dove
Marketing and Communications Manager: Claire Brown

Published in hardback in Great Britain in 2016.
Published and produced by: Trinity Mirror Sport Media,
PO Box 48, Old Hall Street, Liverpool L69 3EB.
Images: Trinity Mirror, PA pictures

ISBN: 9781910335307

Printed and bound by Bell and Bain Ltd, Glasgow

THE OFFICIAL
CHELSEA FC
PROGRAMME BOOK

CONTENTS

As the editor of the Chelsea matchday programme,
Albert Sewell had a ringside seat witnessing the ups and
downs of life at Stamford Bridge for nearly three decades.
Here, he explains how the publication has helped capture
a unique history of the club

The history of matchday programmes at Chelsea FC stems back to the club's infancy, with the Chronicle produced for every home match following the birth of the Pensioners in 1905. This was a precursor to the modern publications fans continue to adore to this day.

Therein lies the real beauty of the programme, which still retains its popularity amongst match-goers young and old. In the modern era, news on a club of Chelsea's magnitude is available from more sources than I can fathom, yet the appeal of the programme remains.

For well over a century, it has acted as the voice of the club, providing supporters with official information, not to mention a unique memento of matches they have been to. How many fans still have the programme from the first game they ever went to? Perhaps many more have collections which take up far too much valuable storage space in their homes!

To edit the Chelsea programme from 1949 to 1978 was 29 seasons of pride, pleasure… and punishment! During that period the club won the League Championship, the FA Cup, the League Cup and the European Cup Winners' Cup for the first time.

On the down side, we were relegated twice to the old Second Division and, between times, promoted back to the First. It seemed there was always "something" going on – years of jubilation, desperation and exaltation.

Chelsea made football history of sorts on Christmas Day 1948. At home to Portsmouth, we launched the magazine-style programme, its front cover depicting Scotland inside-forward Tommy Walker, on his last Chelsea appearance before returning to Heart of Midlothian.

The London Evening News was hostile, saying it was scandalous that Chelsea were doubling the price of their programme to sixpence (2½p in today's money). But the fans loved it and the programme sold out before kick-off. Arsenal followed the trend next season, and the format quickly spread through the First Division.

It was the idea of the club's assistant-secretary, John Battersby. Billy Birrell was officially titled secretary-manager, but much of the administrative work behind the scenes was done by JB, as he was known. He was also instrumental in Chelsea becoming the first club to introduce colour photography to their programme in the Sixties.

In producing football's first magazine programme, Chelsea replaced a threepenny pamphlet with a 16-page all-football edition, with no advertisements, and trailed it as a "unique publication full of pictures, cartoons, articles by leading soccer writers and the full inside story of what goes on at Stamford Bridge."

Through the Fifties, Sixties and Seventies, the programme continued to develop, but always maintained its position as the official voice of the club, something I was proud to oversee through columns such as The Talk of Stamford Bridge. I also took great pride in bringing the fans closer to the players through the programme. The supporters loved it and the players enjoyed it too – they always wanted to do interviews and I was lucky enough to have a fantastic relationship with many of them, getting on particularly well with the likes of Roy Bentley and John Harris.

Of course, the first-team manager has often put his thoughts across in the programme and I wrote notes for Ted Drake, Tommy Docherty and Dave Sexton. The dynamic Doc couldn't stand "sameness". Going to press with the programme one week, when I asked him what team to print, the XI were the same as the previous game. I mentioned this to him and he said: "Then I'll change the sub!" How the team page has changed since my days. It used to be set out in 2-3-5 order – in front of the goalkeeper two full-backs, three half-backs and five (yes, five!) forwards. Now a squad of 20-plus players is listed.

There were so many fantastic characters during my time at the club and there was also a huge number of talented players who came through the junior ranks to make their names in the Drake's Ducklings and Docherty's Diamonds sides. The one who excited me the most was Jimmy Greaves, no doubt. He was an incredible striker and such a nice guy too – a genuine young man from the East End who gave the impression of knowing how lucky he was to be at Chelsea and, of course, he will go down in history as one of our great players.

The programme has always developed, with full colour and glossy covers becoming the norm, not to mention the number of pages increasing on a regular basis. Progress has continued in recent times as you will be able to see in this book, which provides not only a snapshot of a product with a special place in the hearts of Blues supporters, but also captures the history of the club in a unique fashion.

From its tanner (sixpence) start at Stamford Bridge all those years ago, to a tenner for the Wembley Cup Final programme these days, how the business has changed since that Christmas Day launch by Chelsea.

Albert Sewell MBE
Chelsea Programme Editor: 1949-1978

Ken Armstrong reads the Chelsea programme in the changing room before a match in 1955, while Roy Bentley bandages his shin

EARLY DAYS

Our original programmes shine a fascinating light on the history of Chelsea Football Club, with the cartoons, columns and features still entertaining us all these years later

Chelsea's matchday programme dates back to the earliest days of the club's existence. In fact, the first-ever edition of the modern publication's original ancestor, the Chelsea Chronicle, was produced for a friendly against Liverpool at Stamford Bridge on 4 September 1905, two days after we had played our inaugural competitive game, away to Stockport County.

Writing the content for the Chronicle was among the responsibilities of club co-founder Fred Parker, having already suggested the name Chelsea, gained admission to the Football League and recruited a playing squad.

It is intriguing, over 110 years later, to read the club's first official words in the Daisy Cutters column on the front cover, full of optimism about what the future would hold with a sense of confidence that great things could be achieved. This is tempered by a warning for fans not to expect too much, too soon, although the two-year wait for promotion to the top flight was perhaps shorter than many could have hoped for or expected.

Inside, popular features of matchday programmes for years to come were evident, including a write-up on the referee, details of forthcoming matches and ticket prices.

Of course, programmes wouldn't be adored by fans if it weren't for features on the players they idolise and this first edition profiled a man who has gone down in folklore as one of our biggest characters of all time, the club's first captain William "Fatty" Foulke. Alongside it, the Straight Talk column discussed how the club managed to be elected to the Football League without kicking a ball and also called for a certain decorum from those in the stands as we sought to establish a good reputation both on and off the pitch.

On the back page, of course, the team line-ups were printed, along with a subtle dig at journalists who had clearly taken an anti-Chelsea stance in their reporting. It may only have been a four-page publication but the club's earliest programme set the stall out as being essential reading for the fans.

The CHELSEA F.C. Chronicle

OFFICIAL PROGRAMME of The Chelsea Football & Athletic Company, Limited.

President: THE RIGHT HON. THE EARL OF CADOGAN, K.G.

Vice Presidents:

C. A. WHITMORE, ESQ., M.P.
COLONEL LESLIE POWELL, J.P.
C. B. FRY, ESQ.

W. HAYES FISHER, ESQ., M.P.
MAJOR W. F. WOODS, J.P.
H. VENN, ESQ.

Directors:

W. CLAUDE KIRBY, ESQ., *Chairman.*
H. A. MEARS, ESQ.   J. T. MEARS, ESQ.
A. F. JANES, ESQ.   H. BOYER, ESQ.
G. THOMAS, ESQ.   T. L. KINTON, ESQ.

Manager: MR. JOHN T. ROBERTSON.   *Hon. Financial Sec.* F. W. PARKER, ESQ.   *Secretary:* MR. WILLIAM LEWIS.

Colors: Light Blue and White.

Vol. i. No. 1.]   **MONDAY, SEPTEMBER 4TH, 1905.**   **[One Penny.**

DAISY CUTTERS.

"THEY'RE OFF!"

*   *   *

Racing men talk of "the saddling bell at Lincoln" in March.

*   *   *

Bah! It's at the "bottom of the League" compared with the first trill of the Ref's whistle in September.

*   *   *

Well, now what do you think of our Ground—and the stand—and the terracing? Good enough for SECOND Division Football, is it not?

*   *   *

And it is only a baby as yet. Wait until it is full grown, and then—well, we shall see what we Chel-sea.

*   *   *

Don't be over sanguine and expect *too* much of the teams at the first start. We don't expect to "stroll" into the First Division, but we *shall* get there in time.

*   *   *

One thing, we have a team of genuine triers, who are on the best of terms with themselves and with one another. If they cannot always command success, they will do their level best to deserve it.

*   *   *

Hearty congratulations to our friendly opponents to-day upon their elevation to the "Upper House."

*   *   *

And may we follow in their footsteps!

*   *   *

True, "We've got a long way to go," but we are good stayers, and one of our mottoes is "Excelsior."

Yes, that is one of our mottoes. We have another one, which we owe to (and is typical of) the Father of the Chelsea F.C.—Mr. "Gus" Mears. It is "Don't Worry."

*   *   *

When the baby-Club, a fine healthy child from the first, was scarcely opening its eyes upon the world, it found—like all good children in the fairy tales—an evil genius, which took the form of a Dakoit, seeking an opportunity to destroy it. Good word, Dakoit, look it up in Nuttall's. We had some anxious moments, but the "happy father" merely smiled good humouredly and said "Don't Worry!"

*   *   *

Then we had some more anxious moments. There were many and vexatious delays caused by various formalities with the constructional work, and doubts were freely expressed as to the completion of the Stands, &c., in time for the season. Again the same cheery optimism and emphatic "Don't Worry!"

*   *   *

And so the expression has become our watchword, and you will hear it twenty times a day at Stamford Bridge.

*   *   *

Bye-the-way, one of our most enthusiastic followers is "Count" Schomberg, who states that we can "count" on him to follow the first team wherever they go. We cannot have too many of this class of sportsmen!

*   *   *

Next Saturday we have our longest journey of the League Season—to Breezy Blackpool. We hope and expect to draw the full two points after a tough fight.

The cover of the first-ever edition of the Chelsea Chronicle from 4 September 1905.

STRAIGHT TALK.

Our Thanks. WE desire to tender our most sincere and hearty thanks to the very many friends and well-wishers, including many of the foremost gentlemen in the Football world, for the invaluable assistance, support, and advice which they so freely gave us in the fight to establish ourselves as a leading Club, one worthy of the great Metropolis and of the splendid ground, equal at least, to any in the Kingdom, which is our home. To the Press, also, we are most grateful for the kindly interest they have evinced, and the warm interest they have given to the "little stranger" of Chelsea.

No foul Language. WE have received numerous congratulations upon having achieved a record that is unique, viz. :—that of being elected to *the* League in the first year of the Club's existence, without, in fact, having "kicked the ball" as a club. This success was not secured without a struggle, upon which we have no wish to unduly dwell. A certain amount of opposition was anticipated, but we were not prepared for such almost incredibly insidious and unprincipled tactics as we were called upon to combat. The full extent of these are known perhaps to but few. With less resolute men at the head of affairs the outcome would have been very different. However, " they laugh who win," and we can now very well afford to let the matter drop into oblivion.

Now, there is a matter upon which we want to have a little more Straight Talk. We refer to the very objectionable habit indulged in by a small section of most football crowds—that of using language which is both foul and free upon the smallest provocation, often upon none. Of course we do not for a moment expect to find some thousands of men with the "football fever" on them talking like a congress of Sunday School Teachers. That would be absurd. Still, there is a medium in all things. The man who cannot enjoy a little sport without howling a torrent of invective couched in terms calculated to blister the paint on the steel girders is not wanted at Stamford Bridge. Large as our ground is we have no space for him. We vastly prefer his room to his company.

We have the best ground and *one* of the best teams in London. Let us also be able to boast that we are supported by a crowd that sets a good example to other crowds all over the country, and not merely by having proper regard for the ears of more sensitive neighbours in the crowd, but also by giving due appreciation and recognition to the efforts of our visiting teams. *They* are trying to win, just as our boys are, you may be sure, when away from home. A good old sporting toast is—" May the best side win." Let us act up to it.

SOME OLD PROVERBS IN FOOTBALL DRESS.
Many " hands " make no light work—for the Referee.

* * *

Where there's a Will (Foulke) there's *no* way to the net.

* * *

Many a random shot hits the—fence.

* * *

A ball in the net is worth ten in the hand of the goalkeeper.

CHELSEA'S PLAYERS

And all about them.

———•———

OUR CAPTAIN - WILLIAM FOULKE.

LITTLE WILLIE" was born at Wellington, Shropshire, 29½ years ago. He stands 6 ft. 3 in., weighs 22 st., and is as fine a specimen of manhood as ever stepped on the field. In spite of his bulk he possesses all the activity of a cat, combined with the playfulness of a kitten. Has knocked out our punching-balls, whether hung with rope, stoutest cord or four-strand wire, faster than they can be re-slung. Is the cheeriest of companions, brims over with good humour, and at repartee is as difficult to "score" against as when he is between the posts. He makes a splendid captain, and is certain to become a very great favourite with the crowd. As regards his career, it is almost unnecessary to add that he gained fame as goalkeeper for Sheffield United, his cap against Ireland, and F.A. cup medals (for winning team) on two occasions, and is confident of adding a third before he finishes. Also played against Scotland in International League. As a cricketer he has represented Derbyshire.

Photos with brief sketch of the careers of our team will appear in rotation

---

The first Chelsea Chronicle contained a profile on captain William 'Fatty' Foulke, above, as well as information on the team line-ups, opposite page.

CHELSEA v. LIVERPOOL.

SEPTEMBER 4th, 1905.   KICK OFF 5.15.

CHELSEA (Light Blue)

FOULKE
GOAL.

MACKIE		McEWAN
Right Back		Left Back

KEY	McROBERTS	MILLER
Right Half	Centre Half	Left Half

MORAN	COPELAND	JAMES ROBERTSON	WINDRIDGE	KIRWAN
Outside Right	Inside Right	Centre	Inside Left	Outside Left

O

COX	RAYBOULD	PARKINSON	ROBINSON	GODDARD
Outside Left	Inside Left	Centre	Inside Right	Outside Right

FLEMING	RAISBECK	PARRY
Left Half	Centre Half	Right Half

DUNLOP	WEST
Left Back	Right Back

DOIG
Goal

LIVERPOOL (Red).

REFEREE - MR. J. LEWIS, Blackburn.

LINESMEN—J. J. BENTLEY, ESQ. (President of the Football League) and C. E. SUTCLIFFE, ESQ. (Burnley).

SOME FOOTBALL "INTELLIGENCE."

A WEEK ago a local journal came out with some "exclusive" information, "specially contributed.'

Amongst other items of undoubted "news"—to even the boy in the street, was the statement that "It "was fortunate for Chelsea's application to the Foot- "ball League that it happened to be in the year when "the long-fought-for extension to forty clubs met with "approval, and, being carried * * * the opportunity "was promptly taken to admit both Chelsea and "Clapton Orient." We wonder where the special contributor obtained this wonderful information.

Everyone taking an intelligent interest in League Football is well aware that Chelsea was elected to the League *before* the extension was even formally pro- posed to the meeting. As a matter of fact, Chelsea's representative subsequently voted for the extension, and, between ourselves (for voting is by ballot and you musn't tell anyone how you voted, of course), he also gave a vote to our "neighbours" at Clapton.

The same special contributor also refers to "Hearts" as "a place," and pictures the Directors "dreaming of fat dividends." He probably never heard of the F.A. or their five per cent. maximum rule.

Even more surprising is the following which we cull from a Sunday newspaper with a gigantic circu- lation, and which really ought to know better:—"The "famous left-wing pair of the 'Spurs go to Chelsea, "which is in the Second Division of the Southern "League, as is also the Crystal Palace. Both Clubs "should earn promotion to the First Division next ."year, and we will then probably have eight London "clubs in the League."

Would it not be a good idea for some Fifth Standard schoolboy to start an evening class for back- ward Football Journalists?

Printed and Published for the Proprietors (The Chelsea Football & Athletic Co. Ltd.,) by BARNARD & CRANNIS, 36, Frith St , Soho, W.

In the big league for first time, 1907/08

Having been promoted as runners-up in 1906/07, we were getting our first taste of the big time and the fans loved it. Our first meeting against Arsenal, whose name back then was preceded by Woolwich, came in November 1907 and attracted an official crowd of 55,000, although as the newspaper clipping suggests, there were many more inside the ground. By now, cartoons were commonplace on the front cover, with our very own Pensioner offering a cordial invite to the visiting Gunner.

Delightful start to new year, 1908/09

The dawn of 1909 heralded our first competitive fixture against Liverpool. As the cover indicated, Chelsea's form had been poor during the autumn, but we got the new year off to a positive start with a 3-0 win over the Reds. Programmes at the time were also issued for reserve-team matches held at the Bridge, with this edition doubling up for a South Eastern League fixture against Queens Park Rangers.

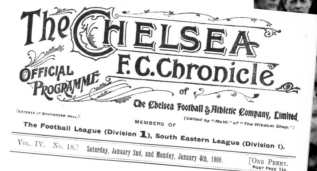

Record crowd at Stamford Bridge

Fast forward to the 1935/36 campaign, and the visit of the Gunners attracted another mammoth crowd, with 82,905 fans packing into the Bridge, pictured above. Back then it was a Football League record and it remains Chelsea's highest official attendance to this day. The Chelsea Chatter column accurately predicted a close encounter, with the match ending 1-1.

"LOVE ME AND THE CUP IS MINE."

Miss English Cup (aside): "Well, of all my many admirers, this old gentleman deserves my encouragement the most."

Derby kicks off run to the semi-final, 1910/11

The importance of the FA Cup during the early part of the 20th century is perfectly captured by the cover illustration of this edition of the Chronicle. In 1910/11, our run in the competition began with a derby against Leyton and we would go on to reach our first semi-final, which we lost 3-0 to Newcastle.

Dreams of cup glory overshadow league encounter, 1914/15

Chelsea's first FA Cup final appearance came in 1915 and the cover for our league game against Blackburn was devoted to the forthcoming semi-final tie against Everton. Having overcome the Toffees 2-0 at Villa Park, the next programme was a jubilant one. Sadly, we lost 3-0 to Sheffield United in the final at Old Trafford.

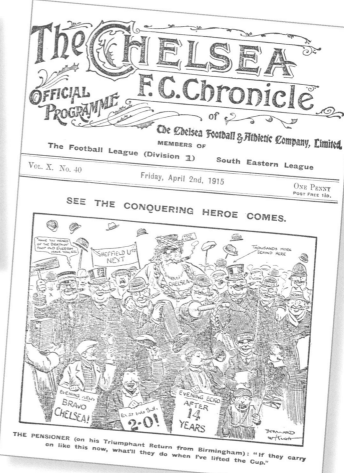

CHELSEA EXPECTS THAT THE OLD MAN THIS DAY WILL DO HIS DUTY.

The Pensioner (as he erects the New Season's Flag): "I'll stick to these colours as long———as they let me."

WHERE THE CHELSEA FOOT-BALLS HAVE GONE.

THE following is a list of the Battalions to which we have sent a football—mainly through the generosity of our followers. It may be added that these footballs are of the very best quality in every way. We could have sent out twice or three times the number of an inferior quality with the same expenditure, but a ball that would get kicked to pieces in a week would be a poor sort of "gift" to our gallant lads who are so freely offering their lives and limbs for England, home and beauty.

Sergt. H. B. Allaway, R.A.M.C., British Expeditionary Force.

Driver J. Broadbridge, 3rd Div. R.A., British Expeditionary Force.

Pte. E. T. J. Owen, 1st Royal Scots Fus., British Expeditionary Force.

Pte. R. Davies, Army Vet. Corps, British Expeditionary Force.

Lieut. H. R. Hood Bars, 4th Siege Battery R.G.A., British Expeditionary Force.

Corpl. A. J. Timoney, 4th Company A.S.C., British Expeditionary Force.

Corpl. T. C. S. Seasbrook, R.A.M.C., British Expeditionary Force.

L.-Corpl. Brooks, No. 2 Company A.O.C., British Expeditionary Force.

Gunner H. A. Jarvis, 2nd Div. Ammunition Column, British Expeditionary Force.

Pte. G. Anderson, No. 1 Field Ambulance, British Expeditionary Force.

Driver Ponman, 3rd Company A.S.C., British Expeditionary Force.

Pte. Catchpole, 1st Div. Ammun. P.K., British Expeditionary Force.

Pte. J. A. Cornell, R.N.V.R., Holland.

Sergt. J. Soan, 1st City of London Regt., Malta.

Pte. Russell, Royal Sussex Regiment, Bexhill.

A. Sub-Section 71st Brigade, R.F.A., Bordon.

H. Trusler, R.N. Div., Crystal Palace.

And many others.

Our show of support for all the brave servicemen fighting on the front line

Following the outbreak of World War One, the Football League ran for the duration of the 1914/15 campaign amidst heated dispute about whether the professional game should continue or not. The message on the front of the Chronicle for our first match of the season signalled Chelsea's intent and the club showed its support for those in action by collecting money in a "Football for Tommies" scheme to dispatch 50 top-quality footballs to servicemen. All had been sent to the field by December 1914 and the Chronicle listed where they had gone. There was even a possibility that one of the balls could have been used in the Christmas Truce match. Pictured below are British and German soldiers standing together on the battlefield.

Back in action after four years of conflict, 1919/20

League football was suspended for four years, with many of our professional players on duty. Matches were limited to the London Combination League – which Chelsea won in 1916. First Division action resumed at the start of the 1919/20 season and the cover cartoon for our first home game of the campaign against Sunderland helped fans get to know some of our players again.

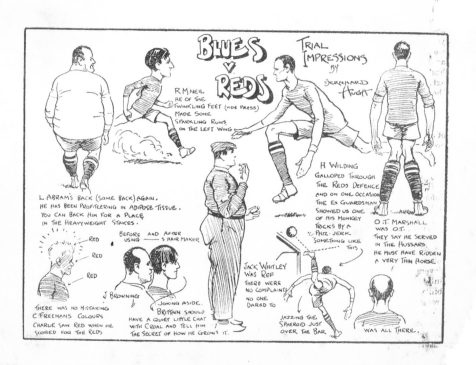

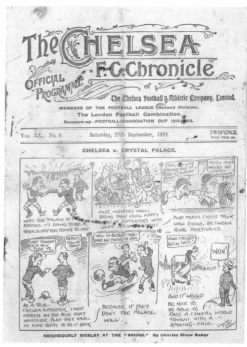

The front cover cartoons were an undoubted highlight of the Chelsea Chronicle, having been commonplace for much of the club's infancy. The incredibly detailed depiction of Blues players was complimented by topical insight into the club's fortunes or simply a sideways glance at another aspect of the game, as these examples from the 1920s demonstrate.

Demolition job brings Easter delight, 1920/21

Easter time has always been a busy period in the football calendar, but spare a thought for the Chelsea players who, when we took on Aston Villa in March 1921, were taking part in their third match in four days. The Chronicle highlighted how fatigue may be a factor, although a 5-1 victory would suggest the players weren't feeling the strain.

Playing for the first time

Meanwhile, FA Cup meetings against sides we had not faced before, in these cases Southampton and Rotherham County, conjured up whimsical discussions on opposition clubs' mascots and nicknames.

Welcome Strangers— ROTHERHAM COUNTY.

If the Rotherham players are all, or practically all, strangers to Stamford Bridge, the same cannot be said of their Manager, Mr. Maurice Parry, for he took part in the first football match ever played at Chelsea. He then played at right-half for Liverpool.

C. S. SUTCLIFFE, who hails from Bradford, is a younger brother of the famous "J. W." of Bolton Wanderers and International fame.

RICHD. JACKSON was formerly with Crook Town, and F. MACKENZIE came from Inverness.

A. EMMETT and W. PICKEN are local born and bred players.

J. EVANS hails from Carmarthen.

J. WILLIAMS is a sort of local "Fanny Walden." He was previously with the local "Town" club. Standing no more than 5 ft. 4 in., and weighing barely 10 st., he is fast, has good ball-control, and knows how to put the ball across at the right moment.

G. COOK is an ex-amateur who is rapidly making a name for himself. His previous club was Bishop Auckland.

A. PAPE is, perhaps, the outstanding figure in the team. Built very much on the lines of Chambers of Liverpool, he is almost equally dangerous in front of goal. Close on 6 ft. in height, and weighing 12½ st., he is not easily dispossessed of the ball, and is one of the best "shots" in the Second Division. This is his third season with the County, and each time he has been their top scorer. He has scored 13 League goals this season.

Opponents anything but Saintly, 1924/25

Come the 1924/25 campaign, cartoon duties had passed to Charles Shaw Baker, who also noted how Southampton's nickname belied their physicality. This cover had added interest as it referred to a friendly against Arsenal which had taken place the week before as a trial for the new offside rule. Rather than three opponents needing to be between an attacking player and the goal, this was reduced to two. There may only have been one goal in the Gunners game, but the new legislation had the desired effect as the number of Football League goals rose from 4,700 to 6,373 in the 1925/26 campaign.

Another of Charles's creations can be seen on the cover of the programme for Chelsea'a FA Cup tie against Accrington Stanley in 1927.

Why not deal direct with the Farmer for
EGGS—BUTTER—CREAM—FOWLS
V. J. WOODWARD,
WELCHES FARM,
St. OSYTH, Nr. CLACTON-ON-SEA.
LONDON DELIVERIES EVERY FRIDAY

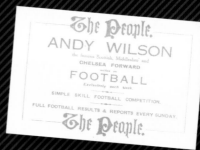

When Football
claims you as a looker-on

You stand or sit in the chilly air, perhaps in drizzling rain—and the game is all that counts.

Forgotten are the risks of chills, cold or influenza. And forget them you can, if you are really fit—if, for instance, you have had your morning dash of ENO regularly.

ENO'S "Fruit Salt" promotes and maintains health in a likeable way. Just a delightful, sparkling drink that aids Nature to keep your system on good terms with itself and more than able to resist Winter's buffetings. First thing every morning drink a glass of water (warm or cold) with a "dash" of

ENO's "FRUIT SALT"
The World-Famed Effervescent Saline
1/9   3/-

The Daily Telegraph
FOOTBALL REPORTS
.. BY ..
B. BENNISON
the acknowledged authority on the game,

contain the fullest accounts of all important matches.

Chelsea spent the latter half of the Twenties in the Second Division, but the crowds still flocked to Stamford Bridge and it was during this period that the commercial benefits of the Chronicle began to be explored, with adverts appearing regularly for the first time. The products advertised included fountain pens, fruit salts, petrol and, perhaps unsurprisingly, beer. The growing coverage of football in newspapers was reflected as well, including a tabloid column for one of our star forwards of the period, Andy Wilson.

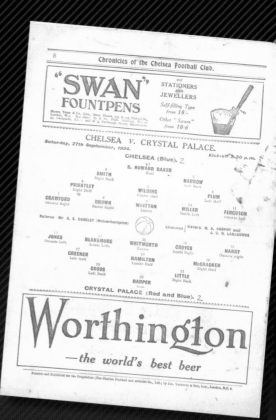

AFTER THE MATCH
VISIT
THE KENSINGTON
LONDON'S LATEST KINEMA

TAKE A BUS TO TOP OF
EARL'S COURT ROAD

Geordie legend joins the Blues, 1930/31

Having been promoted as runners-up in 1929/30, Chelsea signalled our intent with the signing of the hugely prolific striker Hughie Gallacher from Newcastle United. A crowd of nearly 70,000 turned out to see the return of the prodigal son at St James' Park in only his second game with the Pensioners, which the Magpies won 1-0. His home debut came three days later against Manchester United and Gallacher scored a brace in a 6-2 win to confirm what most people already knew – Chelsea had a special goalscorer, even if he was outshone on the day by fellow new signing Alec Cheyne who netted a hat-trick. Chelsea Chatter discussed the arrival of the Scottish internationals and also note the plug for speedway racing, which took place at the Bridge between 1929 and 1932.

Speedway Racing will take place at Stamford Bridge every Wednesday and Saturday during September at 8-15 p.m.

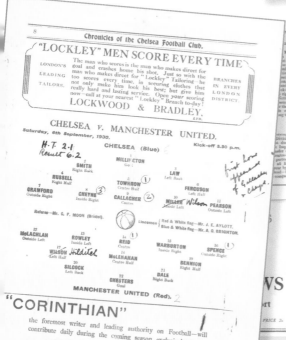

Chronicles of the Chelsea Football Club.   3

CHELSEA CHATTER.

BOWED HEADS.—In common with Britons the whole
world over, irrespective of creed or class,
the sport-loving masses of England bow the head in
profound grief and silent homage to the memory of a
beloved King, who was as truly a king of sport as he
was monarch of his peoples' hearts.

His unfeignedly keen interest in every branch of sport
especially endeared him to the toiling masses no less
than to those of the leisured classes. Ever more than
considerate for the poorest and meanest of his subjects,
King George was one of whom it may truly be said that
he always thought of himself last. Who can name
another man of who that might be said with equal
sincerity ?

　　Each bullet has got its commission,
　　And when our time's come we must go.

That couplet—written by Charles Dibdin, although
often wrongly attributed to Kipling—brings the reflection : Would that we could all, when our time comes to
go, have as little to reproach ourselves with as the most
dearly-loved monarch who ever sat on the throne,
King George V.

Many moving eulogies to his memory have been
spoken and written, but none more roughly eloquent
than the tribute of a working man : " He was our
King, our best friend, and a sportsman and gentleman
to his very finger-tips."

★ ★ ★

FIFTH TIME.—It was a rather curious trick of fate
which pitted Chelsea against two of the
only three Second Division clubs—in successive Cup
ties—whom we have never encountered in League
matches ; first, Norwich City, and now Plymouth
Argyle. The latter ascended to Division II. simultaneously with Chelsea once more regaining the
premier division. On the other hand, this will be the
fifth time Chelsea and Argyle players have faced one
another in a Cup struggle.

★ ★ ★

" POT " PLETHORA.—The opening months of 1921
brought the Chelsea " blues " a plethora
of Cup games. In the First round three meetings
with Reading were necessary before we beat them
3—1. Same week-end went to Swindon to knock the
Signalmen out in Round 2. Paired with Plymouth
Argyle, away, a goalless draw was followed by another
double-blank at Stamford Bridge before we won on
neutral ground at Ashton Gate, Bristol, by the odd goal
in three. Five days later we travelled to Cardiff for
the Fourth Round. Cup staleness and injuries told their
tale ; we lost by one goal, thus being narrowly deprived
of the rare distinction of reaching three semi-finals in

VOL. XXXI. No. 35.   Saturday, 25th January, 1936.

A Treasured Memory

H.M. KING GEORGE V. at our Match v. Leicester City on 21st February, 1920.

Our tribute to King George V, 1935/36

The cover of the Chronicle for our
FA Cup fourth-round tie against
Plymouth in January 1936 featured
a full-page photograph in tribute
to King George V, who had
passed away that week. Chelsea
Chatter reflected the mood of a
nation in mourning. Meanwhile,
advertisements showed how indoor
football, not to mention cricket, was
becoming a popular pastime among
match-goers and the fans were also
being made aware of the growing
number of post-match entertainment
options on the King's Road.

New look for a new campaign, 1936/37

The 1936/37 season saw the first major change to the cover design of the Chronicle, with the introduction of an athletic-looking footballer and the first semblance of a crest in the bottom right featuring, of course, the club's symbolic character the Chelsea Pensioner. Popular features inside remained, with Daisy Cutter continuing its irreverent look at football, focusing on other clubs' fortunes on the opening day of the season. Chelsea Chatter discussed all things blue and, as always, fans could read up on the opposition – on this occasion Grimsby who we beat 3-2.

Mills the hat-trick hero as we thrash Liverpool, 1937/38

The messaging on the front of the Chronicle for our opening game of the 1937/38 season certainly came to fruition as we beat Liverpool 6-1, thanks in no small part to a hat-trick from George Mills.

EMPIRE
STADIUM
WEMBLEY

Managing Director - A. J. ELVIN

SATURDAY, APRIL 15th, 1944

Kick-off 3.0 p.m.

FOOTBALL LEAGUE (SOUTH)

WAR CUP FINAL

CHELSEA

v.

CHARLTON

ATHLETIC

OFFICIAL PROGRAMME SIXPENCE

AIR RAID PRECAUTIONS.
In the event of an Air Raid Alert, if aircraft are reported in the immediate vicinity of the Stadium, spectators will be requested to leave the enclosures and make their way quietly to the Circulating Corridors under the Stands as directed by the Stewards and Officials. Those wishing to leave the Stadium may do so by any of the usual Exits.

TIME TABLE
AND
PROGRAMME of MUSIC

1.45 p.m. to 2.25 p.m.

THE BAND OF THE SCOTS GUARDS

By kind permission of
Colonel W. H. Wynne-Finch, M.C., Lieutenant-Colonel Commanding Scots Guards.

Director of Music : CAPTAIN S. RHODES, MUS. BAC., A.R.C.M.

1.	MARCH MEDLEY	...	"Martial Moments"	...	Arr. Winter
2.	WALTZ	...	"Estudiantina"	...	Waldteufel
3.	SELECTION	...	"The Rose"	...	Arr. Myddleton
4.	MEDLEY OF SONGS FROM 1914-1918—MEDLEY OF SONGS FROM 1939-1944.				
5.	EXCERPTS FROM	...	"Irene" ...	...	Tierney
6.	AIRS FROM	...	"The Lisbon Story"	...	Parr Davies
7.	FANTASIA	...	"Our Empire"	...	Arr. Godfrey

2.30 p.m. to 2.50 p.m.
BAND of Central District U.K. Base of the UNITED STATES ARMY

Leader : CHIEF WARRANT OFFICER F. J. ROSATO.

2.55 p.m.   THE NATIONAL ANTHEM
followed by
RECEPTION OF TEAMS

3.0 p.m.   KICK-OFF

3.45 p.m.   Half-Time

PHYSICAL FITNESS DISPLAY
by detachments of the Army Cadet Force drawn from the six Counties of the London District. The average age of the 250 performers is 16½ years, and all are volunteers. Their training takes many forms, but is designed with only one aim—to produce a happy boy, healthy in mind and body, imbued with the spirit of service.

4.40 p.m.   MATCH ENDS
Presentation of Trophy and Tokens.

THE NATIONAL ANTHEM

If the scores are level after 90 minutes, a further 30 minutes (15 minutes each way) will be played. If no decision has then been reached, play will continue until a goal is scored or a corner-kick is forced. The first side to score a goal or to force a corner will then be declared the winners.

Cup success as Football League matches are put on hold during wartime

The 1938/39 season was the final full campaign before the start of World War Two and there were only three competitive fixtures in 1939/40 before the suspension of the Football League. However, football continued in the form of regional competitions, notably the London War League. Simple one-sheet programmes, complete with air raid warnings, were issued. In 1944 and 1945, Chelsea reached the Football League South Cup final at Wembley Stadium. We lost 3-1 to Charlton in front of 85,000 fans in 1944, but there was joy the following year when we beat Millwall 2-0, this time watched by a crowd of 90,000. That took us through to the Wartime Cup play-off against Bolton Wanderers, who prevailed 2-1.

"Turning out supplies for the forces and turning all our spare cash into War Savings is our way of saying 'thank you' for all they're doing for us"

LET'S SAVE AS HARD AS THEY FIGHT

Issued by the National Savings Committee   Space kindly donated by Wembley Stadium Ltd.

ASSOCIATION FOOTBALL

COMBINED SERVICES XI v. NATIONAL POLICE & C.D.

(In aid of R.A.F. Benevolent Fund ; Red Cross Prisoners of War Fund ; Harrow, Wembley & St. Thomas' Hospitals)

FOOTBALL LEAGUE PROFESSIONALS

At this Stadium — Wednesday, May 9th — Kick-off 7 p.m.

ADMISSION : 5/-, 2/6 and 1/-

Tickets obtainable from Wembley Stadium Box Office (Wembley 1234), any police station in "X" Division, or from usual London ticket agencies.   Admission also at turnstiles on day of match.

Published by Wembley Stadium Ltd.   (Copyright).   Printed by McCorquodale & Co. Ltd., S.E.1. Concessionaires for Programme & Sales :   Betts, Son & Malyon, Wimbledon, S.W.19.

EMPIRE STADIUM
WEMBLEY
Managing Director - A. J. Elvin
SATURDAY, APRIL 7th, 1945
Kick-off 3.0 p.m.

FOOTBALL LEAGUE (SOUTH)

CUP FINAL

CHELSEA

v.

MILLWALL

ATHLETIC

OFFICIAL PROGRAMME SIXPENCE

CHELSEA FOOTBALL CLUB

Official Programme

SATURDAY JANUARY 10th 1942   PRICE ONE PENNY

CHELSEA v. ARSENAL

LONDON WAR LEAGUE.

CHELSEA (Blue)   Kick-off 3.0 p.m.

Next Saturday's Match (January 17th) v. Queen's Park Rangers at Chelsea. KICK-OFF 3.0 p.m.   LONDON WAR LEAGUE

THANK YOU

Any Coupons ?

PLAN OF THE FIELD OF PLAY

Att.–90,000   H.T. 0-0

CHELSEA 2
Colours : Red shirts, white knickers.

Chelsea unchanged.

MILLWALL 0
ATHLETIC
Colours : White shirts, black knickers.

Referee : G. Reader (Southampton)
Linesmen : P. Stevens (Luton) and C. Kearse (Reading)

OFFICIAL PROGRAMME
CHELSEA FOOTBALL & ATHLETIC CO., LTD.

Directors :

Lieut. J. H. MEARS, R.M.   J. E. C. BUDD   C. J. PRATT   H. J. M. BOYER   L. J. MEARS
(Chairman)   (Vice-Chairman)   Manager-Secy.—Wm. BIRRELL

2nd JUNE, 1945.   **Price: ONE PENNY**

FOOTBALL LEAGUE
NORTH v. SOUTH CUP WINNERS

CHELSEA 1
(ROYAL BLUE)

Kick-Off 3 p.m.

1
Cfn. BLACK, I. H.
(Aberdeen)

2
Cpl. COWAN, R.
(Glasgow Rangers)

3
F/Sgt. HARDWICK, G.
(Middlesbrough)

4
Cfn. RUSSELL, R.

5
HARRIS, J. (Capt.)
(Wolves)

6
FOSS, S. R.

7
S/l WARDLE, G.
(Exeter City)

8
Pte. MACHIN, A.

9
Sgt. ROOKE, R.
(Fulham)

10
GOULDEN, L.
(West Ham)

11
L/S. BAIN, J.

Referee—Comdr. G. CLARK (Royal Navy)

Linesmen

C.E.R.A. W. SADLIER (Kent)
Red Flag
Marine W. WEIR (Kent)
Blue Flag

11
MOIR, W.

10
BARRASS, M. W.

9
LOFTHOUSE, N.

8
HUNT, G. S.

7
WOODWARD, T.

6
MURPHY, D.

5
HAMLETT, T. L.

4
TAYLOR, G.

3
HUBBICK, H. (Capt.)

2
THRELFALL J. R.

1
FIELDING

BOLTON WANDERERS 2
(WHITE)

Truscotts, London

FA Cup returns after peace is declared at last, 1945/46

With peace declared in Europe in May 1945, national football officially returned in 1945/46, although only in the form of the FA Cup. Ties were two-legged, with two of Chelsea's three matches attracting crowds in excess of 65,000. Interestingly, it was during the war that the term "programme" was introduced on the cover and, as conflict ended, the public's appetite for the beautiful game was alive and kicking. Those attending games in the years to follow would soon be treated to a major development in the club's official publication.

SPECIAL OCCASIONS

Stamford Bridge has played host to all manner of unique fixtures over the years, from cup finals to internationals, exhibition matches and more besides. Over the next few pages we take a look at the programmes produced for a selection of these encounters, some of which involved the Blues, although many of them didn't...

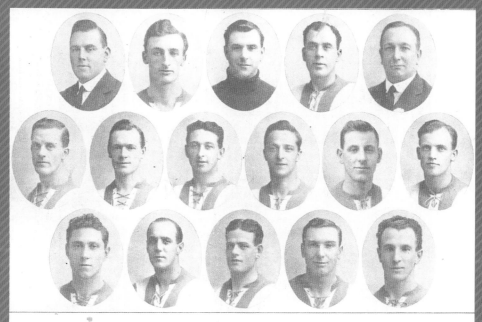

HUDDERSFIELD TOWN.

PRESTON NORTH END.

The FA Cup final took place at the Bridge on three consecutive years between 1920 and 1922, with Aston Villa beating Huddersfield Town 1-0 after extra-time in the first of them. In 1921, Tottenham Hotspur saw off Wolverhampton Wanderers by the same scoreline and a year later it became a hat-trick of 1-0 victories in SW6 cup finals. On that occasion, Huddersfield made amends for the disappointment of losing out to the Villans two seasons previously by overcoming Preston North End, and the two teams are pictured above.

Stamford Bridge has been the home of 10 Charity Shields, including the first four instalments from 1908 to 1911. Our stadium was also the venue for the matches in 1923, 1927, 1930, 1950, 1955 and 1970. The latter two years were notable as Chelsea took part in both of them. In 1955, having claimed our maiden top-flight title three months earlier, we beat FA Cup winners Newcastle 3-0 thanks to goals from Roy Bentley, Frank Blunstone and an own goal by Alf McMichael. However, with the game scheduled for a Wednesday afternoon – and almost a month after the start of the season – a crowd of just 12,802 was present to see the win.

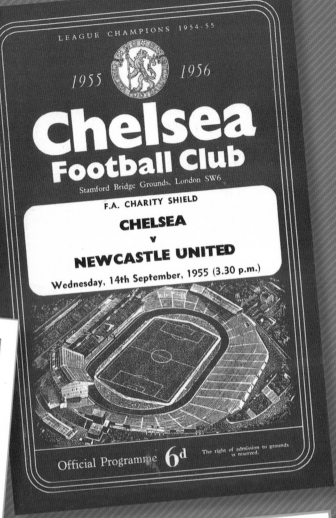

LEAGUE CHAMPIONSHIP FLASHES

The goal that virtually decided the Championship. Peter Sillett beats Williams, of Wolves, from the penalty spot on Easter Saturday.

THE GREATEST CHELSEA PICTURE EVER SEEN
OLD TRAFFORD, APRIL 29, 1970

F.A. Cup Winners for first time

When you're a goal down in the Cup Final, the one thing you must not do is lose your heads. Use them, by all means, as Peter Osgood does here to meet Charlie Cooke's centre and keep up his record of scoring in every round.

A header (Ian Hutchinson's) saved us late in the game at Wembley, another (by "Ossie") brought us level against Leeds at Old Trafford ... and here's yet another—the most important of all. It's the goal that brought the Cup to Chelsea, scored in extra time by David Webb.

4

There was a healthier attendance of 43,547 for the match in 1970, when the Blues were beaten 2-1 by champions Everton, after we had lifted the FA Cup for the first time. Unsurprisingly, the programme was packed full of the jubilant scenes during and after our memorable replay victory over Leeds United.

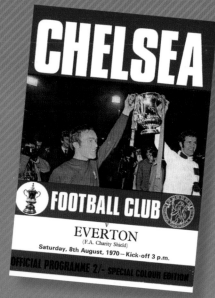

CHELSEA

FOOTBALL CLUB

v
EVERTON
(F.A. Charity Shield)
Saturday, 8th August, 1970—Kick-off 3 p.m.

OFFICIAL PROGRAMME 2/- SPECIAL COLOUR EDITION

THE WORLD AT THEIR FEET

SW6 has seen its fair share of international encounters over the years, from schoolboy matches to Under-23 and senior age groups. We take a look at some of those that have involved Blues players...

Stamford Bridge hosted England's British Home Championship match against Scotland in 1913, when the Three Lions won 1-0. Meanwhile, in 1946, Tommy Lawton was the Chelsea representative for England in a 4-1 win over Switzerland.

THE "YOUNG ENGLAND" WHO VISITED ITALY

This was the team to represent England against Italy in the Intermediate International at Bologna last January. Back row: Wood, Dodgin, Ellis, Gunter, Edwards, Whitefoot. Front: Finney, Broadbent, Leary, Nicholls, Blunstone.

As the introduction to this programme, below, for a match between England and Italy Under-23s demonstrates, Chelsea's commitment to the development of young talent meant fixtures of this nature were always welcome at the Bridge. Frank Blunstone featured in a 5-1 win for the Three Lions.

Welcoming the Young Players of England and Italy to Stamford Bridge

TO-DAY'S match is unique in that nothing of its kind has previously taken place in England, and we, the Chelsea Club, are delighted that our ground should have been selected for this auspicious event.

No club is more vitally concerned with the development of football at Youth and Intermediate levels, which will ultimately lead to British standards being again accepted (as once they were) as the highest in the world, and with that end in view Stamford Bridge will always be available to matches such as we are watching here this afternoon.

Within our own Club, Youth football is blossoming as it has never done before. The Football Association is to be commended for the way in which it is sponsoring the Youth and Intermediate aspects of the game, and obviously the Italian soccer authorities also appr young players in the setting of new standards.

We welcome both sides to Stamford Bridge with will be the forerunner of many similar matches to come

GREAVES

Jimmy Greaves netted a brace and Peter Brabrook scored once during England Under-23s' 6-1 victory against Bulgaria in 1957. Brabrook was also pictured, opposite, in the programme for an England World Cup versus England Under-23 match ahead of the 1958 World Cup finals. He was one of three Chelsea players named in the 40-man squad and would go on to make the cut along with Peter Sillett. Reg Matthews missed out on the final squad and, while there were no appearances for Brabrook, Sillett played three times in Sweden.

PETER BRABROOK (Chelsea). Outside-right. He was discovered by a former Chelsea player, Jimmy Thompson, and became a member of ground staff when 15. By then he had already made a name as a schoolboy, representing East Ham, Essex and London. Youth caps followed against Wales and Scotland before, in March, 1955, eight days after signing professional forms, he made his League debut against Sunderland. When Jim Lewis went to Melbourne with the Olympic party Brabrook was tried on the wing and met with immediate success.

JIMMY GREAVES (Chelsea). Inside-right. The surprise selection for many followers, but not Chelsea fans, or club manager Ted Drake, who maintains: " If a lad's good enough he is old enough." Greaves who is only 17 set the critics raving by the form he displayed on his debut against Tottenham Hotspur at White Hart Lane in August. Another of Jimmy Thompson's discoveries, he has poise and ability far above his years. Hails from Dagenham where he first caused a stir with his cultured footwork as a boy at Kingswood School.

36

PETER BRABROOK

Peter, with Peter Sillett and Reg Matthews, have been selected for the 40 players from which the final England team for the World Cup will be selected.

Published by *Programme Publications Limited*, 39/43 Battersea High Street, London, S.W.11.
Printed by *Welbecson Press Limited*, London, S.W.11.

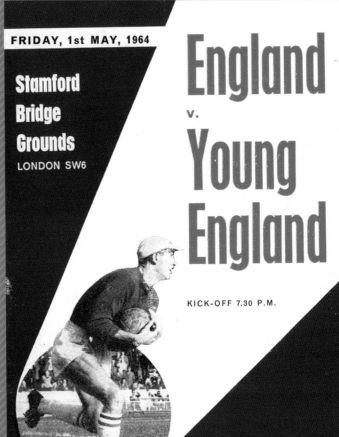

Peter Bonetti, Bobby Tambling and Terry Venables lined up for Young England versus England in 1964.

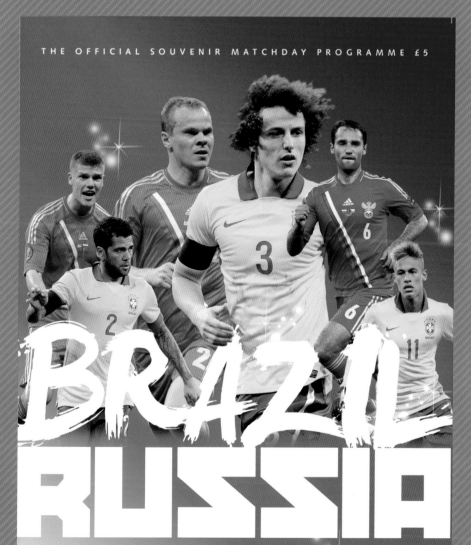

THE OFFICIAL SOUVENIR MATCHDAY PROGRAMME £5

BRAZIL RUSSIA

Three of Chelsea's players featured in the programme for Brazil's 2013 Global Tour fixture with Russia at Stamford Bridge in what was the first senior international at the stadium in nearly 67 years. Ramires, Oscar and David Luiz were interviewed and the latter started the game for the Selecao, with future Blue Diego Costa also coming off the bench for them. The match ended 1-1.

AN EXTRA TOUCH OF GLAMOUR

Before we had our own squad of world-class players from across the globe, exhibition matches gave fans the opportunity to witness club sides from far and wide, with some major stars visiting the Bridge in the process

FOOTBALL IN RUSSIA

Forty - five years ago, football in Russia was in its inception. St. Petersburg (Leningrad), the cradle of Russian football, in those days had two English teams, F.C. Nevsky, and F.C. Neva, a semi-German, F.C. Victoria, and purely Russian teams, F.C. National, F.C. Sport, and F.C. Mercur. Those were the only teams that played organised League matches.

In Moscow, under the able leadership of H. Charnock, the F.C. Morosovtzy and a few others kept the sporting interest high. The league matches were played in the Autumn on **Sunday afternoons,** and always attracted a large following of spectators. The entrance fees were 30 copecks (6d.).

The real progress of the Soccer commenced in 1908 when an enthusiastic footballer, V. Stieble, and an undergraduate of the II St. Petersburg Gymnasium (College) and B. Bratoluboff of the V Gymnasium introduced the football in colleges. To their assistance came Boris Souvorin (a newspaper proprietor), who gave a football cup for the inter-college games. The response was spontaneous and games were organised on a very large scale. In 1908 the chairman of a suburban F.C. Oudelnia

NOT **OXO**
so good to drink...
so easy to make

CHELSEA 3
(RED)
R. WOODLEY, V. L.

2 S/I. WHITE, A.   3 S/I. TENNANT, A.

4 Cfn. RUSSELL, R.   5 HARRIS, J. (Capt.)   6 FOSS, S. R.

8 WILLIAMS, R. F.   9 10 GOULDEN, L. A.
7 Sgt. DOLDING, D. L.   C.S.M.I. LAWTON, T.   11 L/S. BAIN, J. A.

Referee—
Lt. Com. G. CLARK
(London)

BLUE GILLETTE BLADE
MADE IN ENGLAND

Linesmen—
Blue flag Mr. A. T. FORD
Red flag—Mr. W. VINE

11 SOLOVIEV, S.   10 DEMENTIEV, N.   9 BEKSOV, K.   KARTSEV, V.   7 TROFIMOV, V.

6 SOLOVIEV, L.   SEMICHASTNY, M. (Capt.)   4 BLINKOV, S.

3 STANKEVICH, I.   2 RADIKORSKY, V.

KHOMICH, A.

L **DYNAMO F.C. (MOSCOW)** 3 R
(LIGHT BLUE)

THE GRAND
Direction—NAT TENNENS
'Phone—BAT. 3030
Clapham Junc.

Nov. 12th. "FOOLISH THINGS"—THE HIT REVUE OF 1945—featuring JACK FARR—ERIC ... Full Supporting West End Co.
Nov. 19th. " ...
Britain FREDDY M ...
that baffled the B ...
Commencing D ...
" BABES IN ...
HARRIS, Principal ...
Book early to avoi ...

MATINEES a ...

o.ganised a suburban football league and presented a cup. Once again it was a huge success. In the same year, Drs. Lange and Larsen of F.C. Sport (Krestofsky Ostroff) arranged a match with Helsingfors F.C. and later St. Petersburg selected team played against Moscow. In 1912, Russian football was good enough to be represented at the Olympic Games in Stockholm. Later the same year, Czech F.C. Slavia, captained by Benes (centre forward), played against Russia. English Corinthian F.C. also tried its strength against Russia.

The 1914 war slightly interfered with Russian football, but football was already in Russian blood and a ball was kicked about on every barrack square. In winter on Sundays games were played in every available Cavalry school barracks hired to teams for so much per head or so much per hour.

There is no doubt that football in Russia would not have reached its popularity of to-day if it had not been for the support which the present Government has given to sports generally. About 1919, the Government formed the Commissariat (Ministry) for Physical Culture ; the curriculum of that Commissariat included football and thus the Soccer has become a **National sport in Russia** as much as it has with us.

D.A.B.

" BACK PAGE " NOTES

History is being made before our eyes to-day. Our Moscow visitors are the first representatives of Russia to play against a Football League Club in this Country and we as a Club are justifiably proud of the fact that we share in the event.

Football is a summer game in Russia and the season ended last month. Our opponents had a most successful campaign, finishing as Champions of their premier League by winning 19 games in 22—drawing 2 and losing 1—and in the process scoring 73 goals for the loss of 13.

Truly a grand record and one that would put us on our toes if we knew nothing more of their prowess, but some of us have been privileged to see them in their preparations and know at first hand their capabilities.

PEN PICTURES.

Goalkeeper ALEXEI KHOMICH, nicknamed "Tiger" because of his agility. He was a member of Army Team in Iran that won the Shah's Cup two years ago.

Right full-back VSEVOLOD RADIKORSKY is termed a grand defender if on the heavy side. An international who has played in France and in U.S.S.R., and is a bosom pal of

Left full-back IVAN STANKEVICH. On and off the field they are inseparable. Ivan is the smaller and faster.

Right half-back SERGEI BLINKOV is a player of sterling defensive qualities and he is renowned for his ability to stop his opponents.

Centre half and Captain MIKHAIL SEMICHASTNY besides playing in internationals against France has played in Czechoslovakia against a Basque team and a Turkish team. In winter he plays Ice-hockey and is no mean performer on skis.

Left half LEONID SOLOVIEV is a comparative newcomer to the game, but his natural ability and stature have gained him fame as one of his Country's best halves. Is the possessor of a terrific kick and is the "penalty king". He is known to his fans as " Soloviev the White " because of his flaxen locks.

Outside right VASSILI TROFIMOV is short, thick-set and a speed-merchant. This latter quality earned him his place in the Moscow Ice-hockey team. Fans call him "Night-cap" because he once turned out in severe cold wearing a warm cap resembling a night-cap.

Inside right VASSILI KARTSEV is the prime favourite—possessor of two strong feet and a goal getter.

Centre forward KONSTANTIN BEKSOV is a hard-going, spear-head dubbed "the Bombadier", because of his assault methods, but is also a telling force in combination.

Inside left NIKOLAI DEMENTIEV is "the brains" of the attack—small, almost boyish in his set-up, he performs miracles on the field and has unlimited stamina.

Outside left SERGEI SOLOVIEV is very fast, has a strong shot and has the reputation of being a master "rammer".

The Team Coach MIKHAIL YAKUSHIN is a veteran of many matches in Czechoslovakia, Finland, France, Turkey and other countries.

CHE ...
Dir ...

Ground :—STAMFORD BRIDGE, S.W. ...

COMMEMORATING THE FIRST VISIT OF A RUSSIAN CLUB TO ENGLAND.

CHELSEA F.C.
v.
DYNAMO F.C.
(MOSCOW)
(U.S.S.R. CHAMPIONS)

Tuesday, November 13th, 1945
KICK OFF 2.30 P.M.

ДОБРО ПОЖАЛОВАТЬ!

Мы—Директора, игроки-спортсмены и публика футбольного клуба Челси, сердечно приветствуем Вас—персонал и игроков Московского футбольного клуба "Динамо"

Мы приветствуем Вас как членов вашей страны и надеемся, что Ваше пребывание здесь будет для Вас приятным.

WELCOME !

We, the Directors, players supporters of the Chelsea Foo Club, extend a hearty welcom the Officials and players o Moscow Dynamo Football We congratulate you as Cha of your Country and ho your stay in this Island w happy one.

PRICE TWOPENCE

T. W. Pico & c ...

Shortly after the end of World War Two, the club made history when we played Moscow Dynamo in a game which set an unofficial attendance record at the Bridge. The crowd was stated was 82,905, although it is thought more than 100,000 were inside the stadium to witness a thrilling 3-3 draw.

CHELSEA v. MOSCOW DYNAMO in 1945

A mass lock-out, with traffic brought to a halt for miles around Stamford Bridge.

They climbed over railway embankments, scaled walls and fences, broke down gates. Anything to see Britain's first big post-war match.

A multitude packed tight, where the West Stand is now situated.

Support right behind Vic Woodley's goal, as thousands spread from the terraces and surrounded the pitch.

 1945

 The scene in front of the East Stand, with British Servicemen prominent among thousands crammed to the touchline.

1945

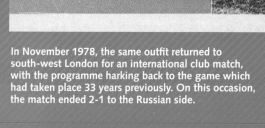

In November 1978, the same outfit returned to south-west London for an international club match, with the programme harking back to the game which had taken place 33 years previously. On this occasion, the match ended 2-1 to the Russian side.

CHELSEA
v
MOSCOW DYNAMO
International Club Match   Season 1978-79   Wednesday November 15 (8 p.m.)

OFFICIAL PROGRAMME 25P
plus SPECIAL SUPPLEMENT inside
recalling the famous
CHELSEA v. DYNAMO MATCH in 1945

INTERNATIONAL CLUB
CHARITY MATCH

PROCEEDS IN AID OF
BRITISH O.R.T. AND
J.N.F. CHARITABLE TRUST

CHELSEA
v
REAL MADRID

EUROPEAN CUP HOLDERS

Tuesday 22nd. November
1966

KICK OFF 7·30 p.m.

at STAMFORD BRIDGE

OFFICIAL PROGRAMME ONE SHILLING

As all-star line-ups go, this 1974 charity match between Great Britain and Europe representative sides in aid of the Goaldiggers takes some beating. Just cast your eye down the two squad lists for some of the most famous names in football.

Five years before Chelsea memorably beat Real Madrid over two matches to lift the European Cup Winners' Cup for the first time, we beat the Spanish giants 2-0 in a charity game, and the front cover of the matchday programme can be seen on the opposite page.

GREAT BRITAIN

Colours: All White

JACK KELSEY (Arsenal & Wales)	1	GYULA GROSICS (Hungary)
GEORGE COHEN (Fulham & England)	2	DEZSO NOVAK (Hungary)
JIMMY ARMFIELD (Blackpool & England)	3	VELIBOR VASOVIC (Yugoslavia)
DANNY BLANCHFLOWER (Tottenham & N. Ireland)	4	KALMAN MESZOLY (Hungary)
BILLY WRIGHT (Wolves & England) Captain	5	WILLI SCHULZ (West Germany)
PAT CRERAND (Man. United & Scotland)	6	ERNST HAPPEL (Austria)
TOM FINNEY (Preston & England)	7	FERENC SIPOS (Hungary)
BRYAN DOUGLAS (Blackburn & England)	8	LADISLAV KUBALA (Spain)
JOHN CHARLES (Leeds & Wales)	9	JUST FONTAINE (France)
JOHNNY HAYNES (Fulham & England)	10	FERENC PUSKAS (Hungary & Spain) Captain
FRANK BLUNSTONE (Chelsea & England)	11	FRANCISCO GENTO (Spain)
MEL HOPKINS (Tottenham & Wales)	12	SANDOR MATRAI (Hungary)
DAVE SEXTON (Chelsea Manager)	13	BRANKO ZEBEC (Yugoslavia)
	14	BENNIE MULLER (Holland)

EUROPE

Colours: All Red

Images on programme spread:

JIMMY HILL

BRYAN FORBES (Chairman)

BRIAN MEARS

GOALDIGGERS' COUNCIL

WILLIS HALL

MICHAEL PARKINSON

DOUGLAS HAYWARD

THE DUKE'S RIGHT-HAND MEN ...

SIR ALF RAMSEY

ERIC MORECAMBE

AMERICAN EXPRESS
FOLLOW THE WORLD CUP IN GERMANY
JUNE 12 – JULY 7 1974

International Challenge Match

Great Britain
(Represented by the Goaldiggers)
v
Europe

A match of 1,000 international caps between teams each of more than 400 years. All proceeds to Charity.

Tuesday 14 November (7.45pm)

Chelsea F.C. Stadium
Stamford Bridge, London SW6

Official Programme

CHELSEA v. OPPONENTS FROM ABROAD

SINCE the last war, we have played hosts in a total of 32 matches against opponents from abroad. These have been both friendly and competitive fixtures, and have resulted in 22 wins for Chelsea, 7 draws and 3 defeats. Tonight New York Cosmos take the total to 33 in a series of games against overseas challengers representing the remarkable number of 21 different countries. Here are the past results (*Fairs Cup, †European Cup-Winners' Cup):

Date	Opponents	Chelsea Goalscorers	Result		Attendance
13.11.45	Moscow Dynamo (Russia)	Williams, Lawton, Goulden	D	3–3	100,000 (Estimated)
28.11.49	A.I.K. Stockholm (Sweden)	Bowie, Bentley	W	2–1	11,000
15.11.50	Lille (France)	Gray, Armstrong, Bentley	W	3–0	9,696
8. 5.51	Floriana (Malta)	Armstrong, Gray, R. Smith 2, Bentley	W	5–1	11,436
15. 5.51	K.B., Copenhagen (Denmark)	Armstrong	W	1–0	11,903
13. 3.54	Racing, Buenos Aires (Argentina)		D	0–0	30,301
15.12.55	Red Banner (Hungary)	Stubbs, Bentley	D	2–2	40,452
19. 3.57	Sparta (Czechoslovakia)	Allen, Gibbs	W	2–0	30,708
2. 4.57	Esporte Bahia (Brazil)	McNichol, Lewis, Allen	W	3–1	34,555
7.11.57	CDSA, Moscow (Russia)	Tindall	L	1–4	41,991
12.11.57	Beogradski (Yugoslavia)	Tindall 2	W	2–1	11,513
25. 3.58	CDNA (Bulgaria)	Greaves	D	1–1	11,000
22. 4.58	Conto do Rio (Brazil)	Sillett (P.) pen., Casey, Allen	W	3–2	15,364
4.11.58	*Frem (Denmark)	Greaves 2, Sillett (P.), Opponent	W	4–1	13,104
29. 4.59	*Ville de Belgrade (Yugoslavia)	Brabrook	W	1–0	25,771
2.12.59	Atletico Bilbao (Spain)	Livesey 2, Greaves 2, Tindall	W	5–3	16,977
11.12.63	MTK (Hungary)	Mortimore, Venables	W	2–0	6,037
7.10.64	Benfica (Portugal)	Bridges 2	L	2–4	23,369
22. 9.65	*AS Roma (Italy)	Venables 3, Graham	W	4–1	32,753
1.12.65	*Wiener (Austria)	Murray, Osgood	W	2–0	28,254
16. 2.66	*AC Milan (Italy)	Graham, Osgood	W	2–1	59,541
29. 3.66	*TSV Munich (W. Germany)	Osgood	W	1–0	42,224
11. 5.66	*CF Barcelona (Spain)	Opponents (2 own goals)	W	2–0	40,073
22.11.66	Real Madrid (Spain)	Hateley, Hollins	W	2–0	32,277
23.10.68	*DWS Amsterdam (Holland)		D	0–0	28,428
30. 9.70	†Aris Salonika (Greece)	Hutchinson 2, Hollins 2, Hinton	W	5–1	40,425
4.11.70	†CSKA Sofia (Bulgaria)	Webb	W	1–0	41,613
24. 3.71	†FC Bruges (Belgium)	Houseman, Osgood 2, Baldwin	W	4–0	45,558
5. 5.71	Standard Liege (Belgium)	Smethurst	L	1–2	18,363
29. 9.71	†Jeunesse Hautcharage (Luxembourg)	Osgood 5, Baldwin 3, Hudson, Hollins (pen.), Webb, Harris, Houseman	W	13–0	27,621
3.11.71	†Atvidaberg (Sweden)	Hudson	D	1–1	28,071
27.10.75	Italy Under-23 XI		D	0–0	9,061

As a page in the programme pointed out, our 1978 fixture against New York Cosmos was the 33rd match Chelsea had played against overseas opposition. With the likes of Carlos Alberto and Franz Beckenbauer turning out for the North American Soccer League champions, it was certainly a glitzy affair, which ended in a 1-1 draw.

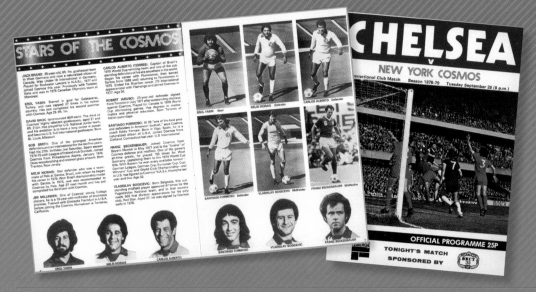

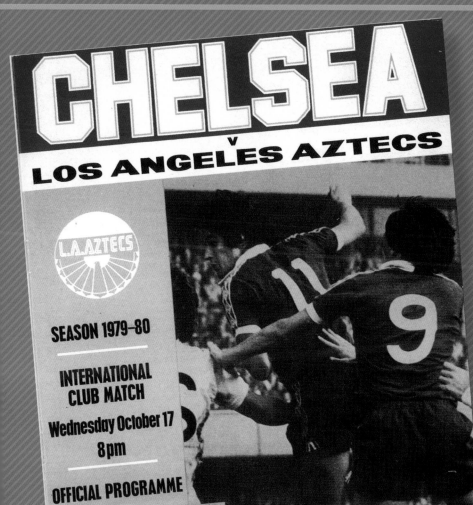

CHELSEA v LOS ANGELES AZTECS

L.A. AZTECS

SEASON 1979-80

INTERNATIONAL CLUB MATCH

Wednesday October 17

8pm

OFFICIAL PROGRAMME

Line - Up

(Names and numbers of selected teams to be announced over the public address system)

CHELSEA 2

COLOURS - Shirts: Royal Blue with White Collar & Cuffs. Shorts: Royal Blue with White Seam. Stockings: White.

Petar BOROTA (un)
Gary LOCKE
Graham WILKINS
John BUMSTEAD (barman) (1)
Micky DROY
Micky NUTTON (chivers)
Ian BRITTON
Mike FILLERY
Tommy LANGLEY (Johnson (Wales))
Gary JOHNSON (Walker)
Clive WALKER Frost (1)
Ron HARRIS
Gary CHIVERS
Bob ILES

AZTECS 0

COLOURS:—Tangerine & Blue.

Colin BOULTON
Mihalj KERI
Bob SIBBALD
Graham DAY
Wolfgang RAUCH
Johan CRUYFF
Jim MILLINDER
Dave SHELTON
Gerry WORAM
Sepp STRASSER
Chris DANGERFIELD
Dave MORRISON
Willem SUURBIER
Billy OLSON
Paul JONES
Thomas RONGEN
Clyde BEST
Neil ROBERTS
Gilbert SMETS
Michel KERI

Referee: Mr. TONY GLASSON (Salisbury)
Linesmen: Mr. K. R. Tilley (Salisbury)—Red Flag
Mr. A. R. Jackson (Salisbury)—Orange Flag

next home matches

Match Sponsored by
...AT MARKETING BOARD

red card or yellow

YES, you can be the ref. at times tonight, because inserted in this programme is a red and yellow card with which you are invited to participate, American-style, in the proceedings.

When referee Tony Glasson blows for a foul, that's the moment when you can join in and give your opinion. If you think it was a sending-off offence, you hold up the red side . . . if you think it was worth a booking, show the yellow.

Mr. Glasson will make his own decisions, of course . . . but as an exercise in crowd participation new to British football, it's an opportunity for you to give your verdict, too. Have fun!

IF TONIGHT'S MATCH IS DRAWN, THERE WILL BE A SHOOT-OUT (ALSO AMERICAN STYLE) TO DECIDE THE WINNERS.

Just over a year later, another US side came to town in the form of the LA Aztecs. Johan Cruyff was making another appearance at the Bridge having turned our for New York Cosmos a year beforehand. The Dutch master could not inspire his team to victory as the Blues won 2-0. As you can see at the bottom of the page, a little American-style razzmatazz was introduced to proceedings.

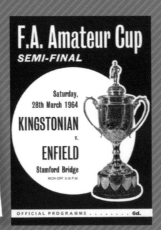

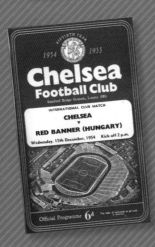

Some Of

TED MAYBANK, GARRY STANLEY, IAN BRITTON,

Our Sunshine Boys...

...HN SPARROW AND 'BUTCH' WILKINS SOAKING-UP SOME PRE-SEASON SUN AT OUR MITCHAM TRAINING GROUND

Design Concept HENLEY AUSTIN   Picture AUBREY TRAUBE   5

A selection of some of the other matches played at Stamford Bridge over the years. We have to say the centre spread from the 1976 Anglo-Scottish Cup programme is an absolute gem!

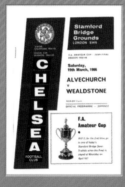

POST-WAR YEARS

Exciting times were ahead following the end of the war. The appointment of Ted Drake as our manager proved a masterstroke as he led us to our first league title, while one of England's greatest-ever strikers made his Blues debut

League football resumed in the 1946/47 season and the style of the programme reverted to that used before the war, although fans were introduced to a new character on the front cover for the opening game of the campaign. A crowd of 62,580 for the match against Bolton demonstrated the public's post-war thirst for football and those in attendance certainly weren't let down as Chelsea won 4-3, with the great Tommy Lawton netting twice on his first league appearance for the club. The former Everton forward had made a goalscoring debut in the historic exhibition match against Moscow Dynamo in November 1945 (see page 40). Although he would move on to Notts County at the end of the campaign, his tally of 30 goals was a major highpoint of a season which saw us finish 15th in Division One under the guidance of Billy Birrell, taking charge of his first full league campaign as Blues manager.

The 1947/48 season saw a great deal of work carried out behind the scenes as manager Birrell persuaded the club to invest in young talent and one of football's most successful youth systems was born. It would be several years until the fruits of that labour would be seen in the first team and this season is perhaps most notable for the arrival of a man who would become a true legend, Roy Bentley. Signed from Newcastle in January 1948, he made his debut against Huddersfield, and was welcomed in the matchday programme, which stated, "We are sure that he will soon make a niche for himself in the hearts of our supporters." How true those words would turn out to be. Also note the club's response to requests for a letters page. It may have been rejected at the time, but it wouldn't be long before this became a staple part of the programme.

PRICE 3D.

THE CHELSEA FOOTBALL CLUB CHRONICLE

GROUND: STAMFORD BRIDGE. S.W.6

Saturday, January 17th, 1948
v
HUDDERSFIELD TOWN
FOOTBALL LEAGUE—DIV. I.   Kick-off 2.30 p.m.

NEXT HOME GAMES

Saturday, January 24th, 1948
v
FULHAM
CUP   Kick-off 2.30 p.m.

Saturday, January 31st, 1948
v
QUEENS PARK RANGERS
CUP   Kick-off 2-30 p.m.

ADMISSION TO GROUNDS IS RESERVED

We have been asked if we can reserve space in our Programme in which to reply to queries on points of interest to our supporters. Much as we should like to adopt this suggestion, we feel that we might be inviting more than we have the time to tackle, and that our mail would be unduly swamped with correspondence on all sorts of topics beyond our capacity to answer correctly. However, perhaps later we may be able to commence something on the lines indicated, but kept within the bounds of Chelsea's own immediate history.

End nigh for old-style programme, 1948/49

Perhaps the biggest-ever evolution in the history of the matchday programme came during the 1948/49 season. The cover for the first game of the campaign, against Middlesbrough, is shown here, along with some pages from the programme for our December fixture with Wolverhampton Wanderers. Fans were far from short-changed before the switch to a new style, with a gatefold-style publication including manager's notes from Billy Birrell, information on our opponents and the Between Ourselves editorial discussing all things Chelsea. There was even a flash of colour on the team line-ups page, but the key inclusion was a short plug for the programme for our next home match, at home to Portsmouth on Christmas Day, which would represent a huge forward shift in the product offered to fans.

BETWEEN OURSELVES

THE VILLA GHOSTS came—and went! That fog experience was a narrow squeak to our point-gathering aspirations—those last five minutes, when the wraith-like figures of the players floated up and down the field, were well-nigh unbearable to some.

TWO POINTS WERE THOROUGHLY EARNED—and the narrow margin did not flatter our boys. The attack opened up the opposing defence repeatedly, only to be met with the indomitable Rutherford.

He was certainly tested to the full and should remember 27th November, 1948, as one of his high-light performances.

THE REAR GUARD were solid and rarely in trouble, the halves had command and the attack enterprising. A surprising Leslie Smith goal was negatived before half-time by a Walker-cum-Campbell-cum-Bentley affair that only emphasized the danger of that fair head in front of goal.

JIMMY MACAULAY, put in possession by the other wee Jimmy, scored the winner after fifteen minutes of the restart. With consummate ease he walloped a low one on the wide side of the helpless Rutherford, from inside the box.

KEN ARMSTRONG deserves mention in despatches for a telling display after an absence since the opening week of the season.

WOLVERHAMPTON WANDERERS have always been what is termed "A popular team," but not for many years have they been able to field a more attractive combination than at the moment. It is a side which has "personality" written all over it, with Billy Wright, at twenty-four years of age England's skipper—possibly the youngest ever—to act as captain and planner-in-chief on the field.

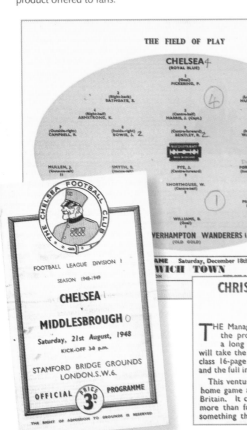

CHRISTMAS DAY WILL MAKE FOOTBALL HISTORY

CHELSEA'S MAGAZINE PROGRAMME

THE Management of the Chelsea Football Club have realised for a long time that the programmes issued for association football, our national winter game, are a long way behind many other sports. Beginning on Christmas Day, Chelsea will take the lead—and a bold one at that—in providing their supporters with a first-class 16-page programme full of pictures, cartoons, articles by leading soccer writers, and the full inside story of what goes on at Stamford Bridge.

This venture is not a special occasion for Christmas. It will be for every First Team home game and will, without doubt, be the finest production of its kind in Great Britain. It cannot be produced at the present programme price of 3d., but at 6d. it will more than fulfil the Management's desire to give the football fan something unique, something that he wants and more than value for his money.

50

START OF AN EXCITING NEW CHAPTER

Although Chelsea had been producing a programme since the club's infancy, it was this new publication which really paved the way for the modern editions fans are able to purchase nowadays

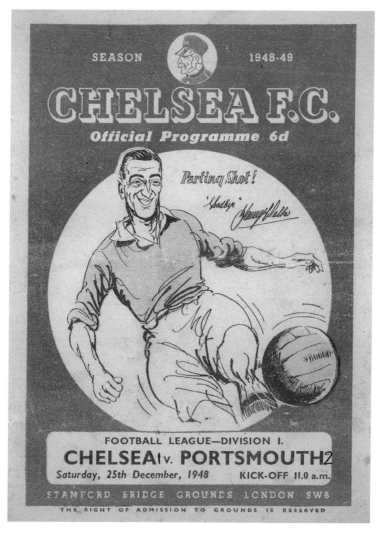

As former programme editor Albert Sewell explains in the foreword of this book, "Chelsea made football history of sorts on Christmas Day 1948, with the launch of the first magazine-style programme." Despite the fact all 16 pages were packed full of content – and notably no advertisements – there were doubters who felt that the increase in price would deter the punters. How wrong they were, with the programme for the Portsmouth game selling out before kick-off and many other clubs imitating this style in the years that followed. The cover paid tribute to Tommy Walker, who would be departing the club after 105 appearances and 24 goals. You can read more content from this trend-setting programme over the following pages.

There is much talk surrounding fixture congestion over the festive period nowadays, but it was much tougher in the Forties and Fifties. Not only did this match against Pompey kick off at 11am on Christmas Day, an away fixture against the same side was scheduled for 27 December, meaning the players could hardly enjoy themselves as the cartoon on page two depicted. As well as kind words for the departing Walker, Billy Birrell dedicated much of his notes to the brand new programme.

A major addition to the programme was extensive match action photography, which in this edition was from our away game against Middlesbrough a week earlier. Long before the days of television coverage, these were the only snapshots fans got of the key moments from our games.

6   CHELSEA F.C. OFFICIAL PROGRAMME   25th December, 1948

Guest Writer

THE SOARING TRANSFER FEES

Chelsea Have A Remedy

By BERNARD JOY
(The Star)

A guest column from The Star's Bernard Joy spoke of the excellent work being carried out by Chelsea with regards the recruitment of talented young footballers, under the guidance of former players Albert Tennant and Dickie Foss. A full shot of the squad and backroom staff was another treat for supporters.

Local Schoolboys

At one time last season, the twenty-two players in the first and second teams of Stoke were former local schoolboys. Since then, they have had to import one or two stars, but a regular supply of newcomers is assured by the understanding the club have with the local schoolmasters.

Chelsea, however, are making the most revolutionary attempt to groom boys for future soccer stardom in their youth side, Tudor Rose. They are providing the model I should like all clubs to adopt. The boys are hand-picked from thousands of applicants, attend Stamford Bridge twice a week, and are coached by Albert Tennant and Dickie Foss. English and maths lessons are given by qualified instructors. Team spirit and character training are secured by the tone and rules of the club.

Giving Something

In a word, Chelsea are giving something as well as taking. They provide a club, the aspiration of all boys in the area, and they send these young men out improved in mind and body by an all-round education.

Clubs on the Continent give full scope to young players. The wartime Chelsea guest, Reg Mountford, who is coaching Frem Club, in Copenhagen, has sixteen teams under his care, ranging from sides of 11-year-olds upwards. All teams are in leagues, competing against players of their own age or quality. From an early age club spirit is instilled, there is a smooth development of the young player, few drop out of the game at the age of 14—16, as they do here, and the senior side has a continuous flow of recruits.

CHELSEA FOOTBALL CLUB 1948-9

Great Incentive

What a grand thing it would be for the youth of London if all the 11 professional sides in the metropolis had teams like Tudor Rose. I should like to see the London F.A. encourage the extension by setting up a league or cup competition for such junior sides. It would be a great incentive for them, especially if some matches were played on the grounds of their senior colleagues.

I do not pretend that these talent-producing methods would eliminate the transfer system. You would probably find, even under the happiest circumstances, that one or two men would have to be acquired to complete the team. But, demand for players would be reduced, and fees in consequence would be brought down to a more reasonable level.

8   CHELSEA F.C. OFFICIAL PROGRAMME   26th December, 1948

OUR VISITORS TO-DAY

BUTLER, E., Goalkeeper 6ft. 0ins.

HARRIS, P., Outside-right 5ft. 6ins.

ROOKES, P., Right-back 5ft. 10ins.

BARLOW, H., Inside-right 5ft. 7ins.

FERRIER H., Left-back 5ft. 9½ins.

CLARKE, I., Centre-forward 6ft. 0½ins.

SCOULAR, J., Right-half 5ft. 7ins.

PHILLIPS, L., Inside-left 5ft. 6ins.

FLEWIN, R., Centre-half 6ft. 0ins.

FROGGATT J., Outside-left 5ft. 8ins.

DICKINSON, J., Left-half 5ft. 10ins.

Headshots of the opposition helped readers identify the Pompey players, alongside line-ups of each side.

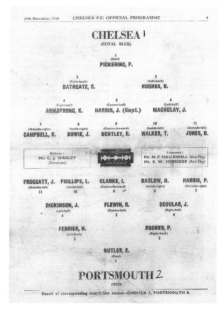

27th December, 1948   CHELSEA F.C. OFFICIAL PROGRAMME   9

CHELSEA 1
(ROYAL BLUE)

1
(Goal)
PICKERING, P.

2 (Right-back)
BATHGATE, S.

3 (Left-back)
HUGHES, B.

4 (Right-half)
ARMSTRONG, K.

5 (Centre-half)
HARRIS, J. (Capt.)

6 (Left-half)
MACAULAY, J.

7 (Outside-right)
CAMPBELL, R.

8 (Inside-right)
BOWIE, J.

9 (Centre-forward)
BENTLEY, R.

10 (Inside-left)
WALKER, T.

11 (Outside-left)
JONES, B.

Referee :
Mr. C. J. WAKLEY
(Somerset)

Linesmen :
Mr. H. F. MAUXWELL (Blue Flag)
Mr. E. W. HERRIDGE (Red Flag)

FROGGATT, J. (Outside-left) 11

PHILLIPS, L. (Inside-left) 10

CLARKE, I. (Centre-forward) 9

BARLOW, H. (Inside-right) 8

HARRIS, P. (Outside-right) 7

DICKINSON, J. (Left-half) 6

FLEWIN, R. (Centre-half) 5

SCOULAR, J. (Right-half) 4

FERRIER, H. (Left-back) 3

ROOKES, P. (Right-back) 2

BUTLER, E. (Goal) 1

PORTSMOUTH 2
(RED)

Result of corresponding match last season—CHELSEA 1, PORTSMOUTH 0.

OUR WELSH INTERNATIONAL
—BILLY HUGHES

*B*ILLY HUGHES *very nearly wasn't an association footballer, and but for a strange twist of fate he might have been better known at Cardiff Arms Park, Twickenham and Murrayfield, where international rugby is played. Billy hails from Llanelly, a stronghold of Welsh rugby. He went to a rugby school, played at centre three-quarter, and as a small boy was always taken to rugby internationals by his father.*

At the age of fourteen he was chosen as reserve for the Welsh schoolboys' rugby fifteen, and then he left school. That was the end of his rugby career. Billy started to play association, and joined Swansea Town as an amateur. At the age of seventeen he signed professional forms. In the summer of 1935 he was transferred to Birmingham; in the season 1936/7, at the age of eighteen, he was capped for Wales—a remarkable record—reserve for schoolboy rugby international aged fourteen—capped for Welsh soccer team aged eighteen.

Billy played against England, Ireland and Scotland in 1936/7 and again in 1937/8. In May of 1939 he played against France in Paris. So he had seven caps before joining the R.A.F. At the end of the war he represented Great Britain against the rest of Europe.

In June, 1947, he left Birmingham to join Luton Town, where he stayed eight months. In March, 1948, Billy became a Pensioner, and it is not necessary to tell Chelsea supporters what a good footballer he is.

Question and Answer

Question : Who are the two most dangerous wingers you have ever played against?

Answer (without hesitation) : Stan Matthews and Willie Waddell.

The new Picture Parade series began with full-back Billy Hughes, who answered a quickfire question in a precursor to the player features which would follow in years to come. Another guest columnist, John Graydon, discussed a wide range of footballing matters.

John Graydon *says* . . . .

TRAVELLING with Stanley Matthews the other day I chanced to ask him what crowd he considers the best to play before. " There are quite a number, John," replied Matthews, " but Chelsea, to my mind, take some beating. They're always ready to cheer the visiting side for a neat piece of play just as much as the home side."

Step forward, Chelsea supporters, and take a bow !

EVER HEARD of a manager taking a coaching course ? I spoke to one during the week—Ivor Broadis, 24-year-old player-manager of Carlisle United. Ivor, a Londoner, is very keen on coaching the many youngsters he has on his staff. " To make sure they get the best possible coaching I intend myself taking an F.A. Course in the summer to fit me for this work," explained Manager Broadis. At 24 years of age the ex-Spur is soccer's youngest manager.

AFTER every Chelsea match, home or away, you will find wee Jimmy Bowie in the opposing side's dressing-room. Jimmy, you see, is collecting the autographs of every First Division team. Even takes in a couple of books from youthful Scottish admirers, in addition to his own !

CHARLIE WAYMAN, who has scored so many goals for Southampton this season, does not wear football boots. Oh, no ! " Cheerful Charlie " is cracking them in wearing a pair of FOOTBALL SHOES presented to him when visiting Brazil with his club last summer. They are approximately half the weight of an ordinary football boot. " Help me run faster, too," said Wayman, with a smile.

TOMMY WALKER, who makes his last appearance for Chelsea today, before returning to Scotland, will never forget the moment he became a professional. Until Tommy signed a pro. form, and was handed the usual £10 signing-on fee, he had never possessed a pound note of his own ! That fact came out when Tommy and I were talking the other morning in the Chelsea office.

963,586 People Have Seen Our First Team This Season
The following attendance figures make interesting reading :

	At Home					Away	
Middlesbrough	...	...	...	57,885	Newcastle	...	65,000
Newcastle	...	...	...	50,207	Birmingham	...	48,000
Bolton	...	...	...	42,971	Charlton	...	38,000
Everton	...	...	...	43,736	Preston North End	...	31,000
Charlton	...	...	...	45,357	Stoke	...	30,000
Burnley	...	...	...	53,193	Liverpool	...	42,709
Blackpool	...	...	...	77,696	Derby County	...	31,000
Arsenal	...	...	...	56,476	Huddersfield	...	18,963
Manchester United	...	...	62,542	Sheffield United	...	25,000
Aston Villa	...	...	...	32,920	Sunderland	...	38,934
Wolverhampton	...	...	43,997	Middlesbrough	...	28,000
				566,980			396,606

25th December, 1948   CHELSEA F.C. OFFICIAL PROGRAMME   ·13

WELCOME, PORTSMOUTH !

THIS IS THE JUBILEE YEAR OF PORTSMOUTH FOOTBALL CLUB, and, as a glance at the First Division table proves, their players are trying very hard to make it a memorable season for the Hampshire club, by winning the League Championship. This Christmas Morning you can be sure they will try their hardest to take over Chelsea's colours, and take back to Fratton Park two precious points, but, for all that, they are assured of a most warm and hearty welcome.

Although known as the " Sailors' Team," Portsmouth, whose President is Field-Marshal Viscount Montgomery, were founded, among others, by men associated with the Royal Artillery.

Way back in 1898 the R.A. side, drawn from soldiers stationed in the town, made a big reputation for themselves, attracted large crowds, and local townsfolk appreciated there was a big opportunity for League football in the district. A meeting was called in April, 1898, to which Sergeant-Major Windrum and Sergeant Bonney, two of the most prominent R.A. officials, were invited. Outcome of this discussion was the formation of Portsmouth F.C., a ground

was acquired and named Fratton Park and Fred Brettell, from the Spurs, was appointed manager.

Several of the early Portsmouth players were drawn from the Royal Artillery, including the goalkeeper, Matt Reilly, who even trained a pet parrot to call out " Play Up, Pompey ! "

Like so many other prominent Southern teams, Portsmouth made their early reputation in the Southern League, which they joined in 1899, and three seasons later became Champions.

When the Southern League developed into the Southern Section of the Third Division, Portsmouth headed the competition in 1924, and gained promotion to the Second Division. Three seasons later the club gained First Division status, beating Manchester City for promotion by one two-hundredth part of a goal !

On three occasions have Portsmouth reached the F.A. Cup Final, winning the trophy in 1939, by defeating Wolves, and being defeated in 1929 and 1934.

Mr. Bob Jackson, who has succeeded Mr. Jack Tinn as manager, is recognised as one of the finest judges of a footballer in the game and his present side, I feel, is a tribute to his blending ability.

Make a note, by the way, of right-half Scoular, left-half Dickinson, and right-winger Harris. In my opinion they are young players destined for honours.

Meanwhile, Pompey, a Merry Christmas from everyone at Stamford Bridge !

DO YOU KNOW ?

1. Jimmy Easson, Portsmouth's trainer, visiting Stamford Bridge to-day, had a very unusual experience during his playing days, also with Portsmouth. Do you know what it was ?

2. Can you name the year a referee first used a whistle ?

3. Think before answering this one. Name a team that has not competed for the F.A. Cup after winning it.

4. Can a substitute called into an England team during an international be awarded a cap ?

5. When Moscow Dynamos visited this country, and played at Chelsea, they called upon a magnificent goalkeeper. Remember his name ?

6. Name the men who form the Football League Management Committee.

(Answers on page 15.)

A review of our recent matches also focused on the attendances at Chelsea games so far that season. The facing page welcomed Portsmouth, looked ahead to our FA Cup third-round tie with Bristol City and provided a brief quiz.

ON THE SLOPES OF HILL BARN GOLF COURSE
—THEN FOUR GOALS

WORTHING TIT-BITS. How much had sunny Worthing to do with our second-half rampage against the Wolves ? Certainly tonic was written all over those 45 minutes, and some credit at least is due to Worthing for its benefits during our short holiday there.

Many enjoyable hours were spent on the slopes of Hill Barn Golf Course under the guiding eye and at times, terse tongue, of genial Arthur Harrison.

Hugh Billington must have derived some inspiration when he walked away with the GOLF HANDICAP off the 10-handicap mark.

JIMMIE BOWIE, too, must have supped well before winning the FLYING SNOOKER HANDICAP at the Sailing Club. Jimmie's "colour bursts" in the semi-final and the final (when he beat Mr. Birrell and partner) will be long spoken of.

● ● ●

THE PEERLESS TOMMY WALKER appears to-day on our famed sward for the last time in our colours.

A cold, bald statement of fact that evokes warm sentiment and inspires deep feeling of regret—and love ; for what other word can express those profound stirrings towards the man and the performer at this time of separation ?

WE OF STAMFORD BRIDGE have been proud to claim him as ours over the last two years, and there can be no doubt that we have shared in the reflected glory of the man who has inspired more "superlatives" than any contemporary.

We, too, have delighted in his skill, and without question will be the poorer for his absence.

NEXT SATURDAY he hopes to reappear in the maroon jersey of his first love—The Heart of Midlothian F.C., and to gratify a life-long desire to finish his playing days in their service. His main concern is to help guide the destinies of that famous club, now as assistant manager and ultimately as manager.

HIS MANY FRIENDS at Stamford Bridge—and who amongst us isn't ?—will watch his efforts with interest, and in saying "Thank you, Tommy ! for your example, and the joys you have given us" wish him every success and happiness in his new sphere.

DURING THE WEEK there was a little farewell gathering for Mr. and Mrs. Tommy Walker, when the Chelsea Football Club Corps of Honorary Stewards presented Tommy with a Parker pen and pencil, and a vellum scroll with all their names inscribed upon it. Mrs. Walker received a bouquet. It was all very informal and a gesture by the stewards that was very much appreciated. Tommy and his wife are sad to leave us, of that there is no doubt.

Tommy Walker

Inside Stamford Bridge heaped more praise on Tommy Walker along with full fixtures, results and stats, which continued on the back cover.

Missing trio bound for Rio, 1949/50

When the Blues hosted Wolves towards the end of 1949/50, attentions were turning towards the World Cup finals in Brazil, with three star players who would have been involved in the game – our own Roy Bentley and the visitors' Billy Wright and Bert Williams – on international duty for England against Scotland. All three would go on to make the squad for the Three Lions. The programme had undergone another redesign, with action shots now appearing on the cover as well as prominently inside. As the season reached its climax, fans were encouraged to give feedback on the features they enjoyed the most.

THE INTERNATIONAL at Hampden Park takes some of the colour from our game this afternoon, for Wolves are shorn of Wright and Williams, and for the first time this season Roy Bentley misses a home match. Barring injury, the Wolverhampton pair are certain to play for England in the World Cup tournament in June; Bentley's Rio place will depend largely on his performance to-day, so here's wishing him a successful Hampden debut.

I have been to many football grounds throughout the country and confirm that Chelsea's programme is among the best. The photographs are an excellent feature and must be continued. If anything has to go, then perhaps the refereeing article—but only if it gives place to more news of the background, style, career, welfare, etc., of the players, including promising reserves and the great ones of the past. A chart showing all First Division results might be worth including next season.

Capt. F. W. WOOD, R.E.,
" Kelvin,"
Upshire Road,
Waltham Abbey,
Essex.

WHAT THE CAMERA SAW

This goal, directly before the interval, put Aston Villa in command last Saturday. Willem covers Medhurst on the line, and Armstrong and Harris move across, but Powell's flying head eludes them all.

Medhurst fists out as Ford goes in. Harris is behind our 'keeper, with Armstrong in the cen-

4

Your Chance to Tell Us

The season's end approaches—there is only one home League game after to-day —and we must think of the next football year.

So far as programmes are concerned, Chelsea's official bulletin is the most informative in soccer and, to assist us in planning the 1950-51 programme, we invite you to voice an opinion on the three features which have interested you most.

Which do you like best—Photographs of the previous week's match ? The refereeing article ? Inside Information ? John Graydon's page ? The Action Shot series ? Something else, perhaps. Anyway, list them 1, 2, 3.

Also which feature would you drop, what other criticisms and suggestions have you ?

See Page 11 for some of the comments already received, then send us *your* views, on a postcard, please, addressed to Mr. Birrell and marked " Programme."

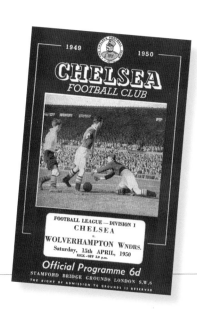

1949   1950

CHELSEA
FOOTBALL CLUB

FOOTBALL LEAGUE — DIVISION 1
CHELSEA
v.
WOLVERHAMPTON WNDRS.
Saturday, 15th APRIL, 1950
KICK-OFF 3.0 p.m.

Official Programme 6d
STAMFORD BRIDGE GROUNDS LONDON S.W.6
THE RIGHT OF ADMISSION TO GROUNDS IS RESERVED

CHELSEA F.C. OFFICIAL PROGRAMME   15th April, 1950

AT OUR EASTER GAMES

Dancing shadows. Bobby Campbell claims a Good Friday corner which Hanson, the Bolton goalkeeper, tries hard to prevent. All in line are Billington, Barrass, Gillies and Howe—an unusual player-formation

r only goal and only point of the holiday. Reg Williams stabs the ball into the net off the far post. Bentley is in the background.

5

ROY'S RELEGATION-SAVING GOALS

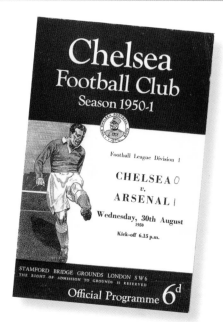

Chelsea
Football Club
Season 1950-1

Football League Division I

CHELSEA 0
v.
ARSENAL 1

Wednesday, 30th August
1950
Kick-off 6.15 p.m.

STAMFORD BRIDGE GROUNDS LONDON SW6
THE RIGHT OF ADMISSION TO GROUNDS IS RESERVED

Official Programme 6d

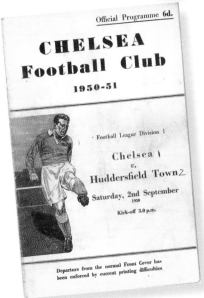

Official Programme 6d.

CHELSEA
Football Club
1950-51

Football League Division I

Chelsea 1
v.
Huddersfield Town 2

Saturday, 2nd September
1950
Kick-off 3.0 p.m.

Departure from the normal Front Cover has
been enforced by current printing difficulties

Bentley saves us from drop, 1950/51

Seasonal changes to the programme, particularly the cover, were now commonplace, but there was disruption to production through the autumn of 1950 owing to a printers' dispute, as you can see from the Huddersfield edition. The 1950/51 campaign was not one to write home about as the Pensioners just avoided dropping to Division Two, with the match action pictures from our Festival of Britain programme against KB Copenhagen showing Roy Bentley's relegation-saving goals on the final day against Bolton.

Drake's arrival excites fans but progress takes time, 1952/53

The 1951/52 season was another disappointing one, leading to Billy Birrell's departure from the club. Our opening programme of 1952/53 dedicated much of its content to the arrival of new manager Ted Drake. A prolific centre-forward during his playing days with Southampton, Arsenal and England, he expressed his admiration for the club in his opening manager's notes, but added how he felt Chelsea had always slightly under-performed. The relationship he hoped for with fans was evident from the column's title Heart to Heart and his desire for positivity from the stands. "Let's have more people eating, drinking and sleeping Chelsea," he declared. With the success he would bring to the club, that would not prove to be an issue. You can read these notes in the Classic Columns section from page 166.

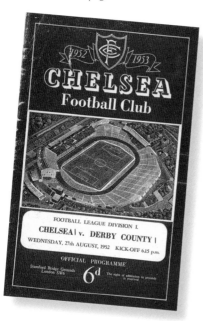

The programme featured a snapshot of Drake's playing career – including a picture of him in action for Hampshire County Cricket Club – and images of his first pre-season at the helm. There was also an interesting article on former players, in this case Hughie Gallacher, and a full rundown of players for the new season. Also take note of the cover, where the Chelsea Pensioner no longer appeared. The Drake factor did not take long to have an impact on crowds, with nearly 20,000 more attending his second home game at the helm – a 2-0 win over Portsmouth. Despite a positive start, it was a campaign of inconsistencies as Drake stamped his mark on the club and for the third season running, we just escaped the drop. However, much better was to follow…

CHELSEA MEN OF MEMORY
No. 1—Wee Hughie Gallacher

FELLOWS of varying shape, size, skill —and temperament have come into and gone out of football. As yet, however, there has been only one Hughie Gallacher and, having a fancy for spice with my play, I regret this quite a lot. Wee Hughie was no copyist. He had ideas of his own —had to have—was a law unto himself, and at times even broke his own laws. Most important, however, was that he very properly stood at the head of the centre-forwards of his time, and part of that time was spent with Chelsea. Everybody bubbled when he was in the team; Hughie himself bubbled most when he was out.

Joining up at Stamford Bridge in 1930, he scored 72 goals in League games in the four seasons and a bit before becoming the most expensive player of his time when transferred to Derby County. Maybe he wasn't at his consistent best in the Chelsea colours, but old-timers remember matches in which his genius and his eccentricity were fully displayed.

Of course, Hughie shouldn't have been a centre-forward at all—only five feet five, and carrying less than eleven stone. But what a footballer. Four times he scored five in a match, one quintette being for Scotland against Ireland. There have been many faster runners, but he had springs in his heels, and was able to get up to the high ones and win battles in the air with fellows who usually looked down on him.

Primarily, though, Hughie wanted to play with the ball close to the turf, and expected others to keep it there. He got the goals, not by barging through, but by helping his pals with good service and getting into position for the return pass. The bullets which went home were let loose from time to time, but the shots which gave him most pleasure were the cutely placed ones so simple that goal-keepers wondered how they had been beaten.

Throughout his career (and this should make the critics of his time admire him the more in retrospect) wee Hughie had not only to play his opponents. He had to play himself. Quick-rising, hot temper was in his temperament. There was the day when he asked to go off the field for a few minutes—wanted to cool down lest he should lose his head. There was also the day when he was picked up hurt and then sent off for telling the referee—the actual wording doesn't matter—what he thought of a decision. Nor does it matter now whether he was more sinned against than sinning. The truth is that opponents were quick to twig that they were less likely to be beaten if, literally or metaphorically, they got Hughie's shirt out.

I have suggested that everybody didn't take to him. But when he left Newcastle there were supporters who swore they would never watch the team again. On his first return to St. James's Park to play in a Chelsea shirt 68,386 people turned up—still a record for the ground—to see the "little blue devil." On nineteen occasions he was the little blue devil in Scotland's attack: the centre-forward who didn't get a goal when Scotland ran England's team giddy to a five-to-one tune at Wembley. But with Hughie doing his stuff in the middle Alec Jackson got three, and Alex James two.

TRUE BLUE

"A law unto himself."

12

JOHN McNICHOL

While at Reading, Ted Drake became a great admirer of McNichol's style with the result that Johnny is now realising his ambition to play First Division football. That desire might have been fulfilled with Newcastle, whom he joined from the Scottish junior side, Hurlford, in 1946, but two years at St. James's Park failed to bring a first-team place and McNichol moved to Brighton. During his stay there, he played 158 out of a possible 176 Third Division games and scored 37 goals apart from the dozens he snapped with clever approach work. A native of Kilmarnock, Johnny is married and has a son and daughter. He signed for Chelsea on August 2nd —four years to the day after joining Brighton.

OUR PLAYERS FOR THE NEW SEASON

GOALKEEPERS

Player's Name	Height	Weight	Birthplace	Previous Club	Date Signed
BREWSTER	W.	5ft 10in	11st 9lbs	Kinghorn	Dundonald Bluebell	July 1951
COLLINS	R.	5ft 11ins	11st 7lbs	Bedlor	Belcor Albion	Nov 1951
MEDHURST	H.	5ft 9in	10st 9lbs	Byfleet	West Ham United	Dec 1946
ROBERTSON	W.	6ft	12st 10lbs	Glasgow	Airburtle	July 1946

FULL-BACKS

BATHGATE	S.	5ft 9ins	11st 9lbs	Aberdeen	Parkvale	Sept 1946
BELL	R.	5ft 11ins	11st 7lbs	Chelsea	Chelsea Youth	Nov 1951
DOUGLASS	R.	5ft 11ins	12st 2lbs	Sunderland	Crook Town	Mar 1952
LEE	J.	6ft	12st 2lbs	Rotherham	Halifax Town	Oct 1951
LEWIS	F.	5ft 8ins	10st 10lbs	Broughton Gifford (Wilts)	Royal Navy	Mar 1946
MITCHELL	L.	5ft 10ins	11st 9lbs	Balclootrie (South Africa)	Marles Brothers	July 1951
TENNANT	A.	5ft 10ins	11st 9lbs	Tilecoon	Scennon Ironworks	Nov 1934
TICKRIDGE	S.	5ft 10ins	11st 7lbs	Stepney	Tottenham Hotspur	Mar 1951
WHITTAKER	R.	5ft 8in	11st	Dublin	Chelsea Youth	May 1952
WILLEMSE	S.	5ft 10ins	12st	Hove	Brighton & Hove A.	July 1949

HALF-BACKS

ALLISTER	J.	5ft 9in	11st 3lbs	Edinburgh	Tranent Juniors	July 1949
ARMSTRONG	K.	5ft 8ins	10st 10lbs	Bradford	Bradford Rovers	Dec 1946
BAVERSTOCK	J.	5ft 10ins	11st 2lbs	West Ham	Chelsea Youth	Oct 1951
BOWMAN	A.	5ft 8ins	11st	Plumstead	Chelsea Youth	June 1951
DICKS	A.	5ft 11ins	11st 13lbs	Kensington	Rainham	Aug 1951
DICKSON	W.	5ft 10ins	11st 7lbs	Lurgan	Notts County	Nov 1947
HARRIS	J.	5ft 10ins	11st 4lbs	Glasgow	Wolverhampton Wdrs.	Aug 1945
McKNIGHT	P.	5ft 8ins	11st	Cambuslie	Albn Athletic	Jan 1947
OKLOPSE	R.	5ft 11ins	12st 4lbs	Johannesburg	Berea Park	Oct 1951
SAUNDERS	J.	6ft	11st 12lbs	Middlesbrough	Darlington	May 1948

FORWARDS

BENTLEY	R.	5ft 10ins	12st 8lbs	Bristol	Newcastle United	Jan 1948
CAMPBELL	R.	5ft 9ins	10st 11lbs	Glasgow	Falkirk	May 1947
D'ARCY	S.	6ft	12st	Newry	Charlton Athletic	Nov 1951
EDWARDS	R.	5ft 11ins	11st 10lbs	Guildford	Woking	Nov 1951
GRAY	W.	5ft 6ins	10st 3lb	Arbington	Leyton Orient	Mar 1949
JACKSON	A.	5ft 10ins	11st 7lbs	Ballymena	Shettleston Juniors	April 1952
JONES	R.	5ft 9ins	11st 6lbs	Ellesmere Port	Tranmere Rovers	Oct 1947
KELL	R.	5ft 8ins	10st 7lbs	Billingham	Chelsea Youth	Mar 1952
McNICHOL	J.	5ft 6ins	11st	Kilmarnock	Brighton & Hove A.	Aug 1952
PARSONS	R.	5ft 7ins	10st 7lbs	Worthing	West Ham United	Nov 1950
RANDALL	R.	6ft	12st 4lb	Bognor	Bognor	Dec 1950
SMITH	J.	5ft 7ins	10st	Sheffield	Shildon	April 1951
SMITH	R.	5ft 10ins	11st 8lbs	Lingdale	Chelsea Youth	May 1950
TUCK	P.	5ft 8ins	11st 12lbs	East Ham	Chelsea Youth	May 1951

13

TURNING THE PICTURE PAGES IN THE GOLDEN CAREER OF

Ted Drake

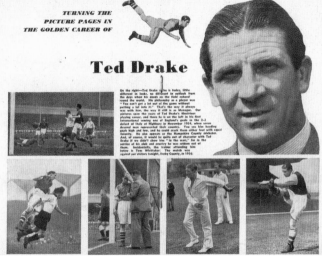

On the right—Ted Drake as he is today, little different in looks, no different in outlook from those who kept his deeds on the field enduring round the world. His philosophy as a player was "You can't get a lot out of the game without putting a lot into it." That's the way it always was with him, the way it still is as Manager. Our picture spans the years of Ted Drake's illustrious playing career, and those he is on the left in his first international meeting one of England's goals in the 3-2 defeat of Italy at Highbury in November 1934, when seven Arsenal men represented their country. You see him heading goals high and low, and he could crash the ball with equal ferocity. He also appears as the Hampshire County cricketer. And, of course, it would be quite out of character with Ted Drake if we didn't show him "in the nest," in the service of his club and country he was seldom out of them. Incidentally, the trainer attending him below is Tom Whittaker. The match was against our visitors tonight, Derby County, in 1936.

Team's improvement is clear to see, 1953/54

Chelsea had suffered an 8-1 humbling away to Wolves in September 1953, but by the time of our home match against Preston in November, Drake was hailing his team's powers of recovery and it was clear a shift in mentality was occurring as we went on to finish in eighth place, teeing us up for what would turn out to be one of our greatest seasons of all time. The appearance of a regular double-page column devoted to our juniors was more evidence of the growing importance of homegrown talent.

The Manager's Notes

FOLLOWING our home win against Burnley, we gained a well-merited draw at Bolton last Saturday just as we had done in the corresponding game last season.

This latest point was won only after a terrific battle, and once again it showed up our splendid grit and enthusiasm when we turned arrears of 0-2 into a two-all result.

The game was fairly even in the first half, with perhaps Bolton showing slightly the more determination, yet our defence stood rock-like with Bill Robertson commanding everything in the goalmouth. The second half opened with a bit of a shock, for within the space of twelve minutes Bolton put two into our net.

After this our lads were seen at their best. Rallying as we know they can, they went at Bolton with everything they had, and it was the proud distinction of Johnny McNichol to score both of our goals. You will wish to join me in a tribute to them all, and I hope we continue our improvement against Preston this afternoon, when victory would give us a run of five points from three consecutive matches and our best sequence of the season.

The second and third elevens gained encouraging wins over Leicester City and Horsham respectively, making last Saturday a good day all round. Although we are not so concerned with injuries as we were a fortnight ago, it was most unfortunate to lose Jimmy Smith, who is in St. Stephen's Hospital under observation for a severe ankle injury. We wish Jimmy well and hope it will not be long before he is back with us.

A reminder about the London Challenge Cup Final. I beat my old club, Arsenal, in the toss for venue and we shall meet them in the decider at Stamford Bridge on Monday week, December 7th (kick-off 2.15 p.m.). I hope as many of you as possible will be able to get along and see what promises to be a rousing final between such old and doughty rivals.

HOW WE WON FIRST LEAGUE TITLE

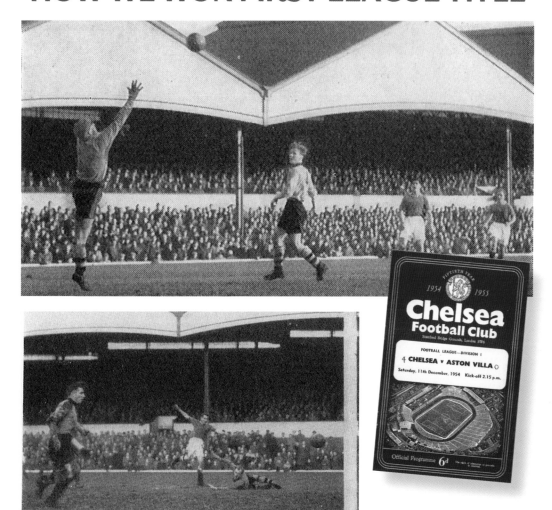

The cover design of the programme may barely have changed in 1954/55, but there was one notable addition to the masthead signalling the club's 50th year in existence. This edition against Aston Villa in December had match action from our recent trip to face champions Wolves, a thrilling fixture which ended in a 4-3 win and took us to within two points of the Black Country side at the top of the table. The importance of that result would not be fully reallised until the climax of a season which would go down in history as we won the title for the first time.

THE GOAL THAT TOOK US TO THE TOP

Our home game against Sunderland in March 1955 came a week after an away win at Cardiff took us top of the table. There was little doubt we were building up a head of steam at exactly the right time and Ted Drake spoke of the fantastic spirit within the team. The back page gave a full rundown of home and away attendances that season and goalkeeper Chic Thompson was profiled on the Star Page.

STAR*PAGE

GOALKEEPING as well as goalscoring has spurred our challenge for the League Championship, with **Charlie Thomson** playing so effectively between the uprights since Bill Robertson was injured in Jan-

uary that Big Bill has been unable to regain his place.

Born at Perth, Thomson spent three seasons with Clyde, mostly in their reserve side, before joining Chelsea in October, 1952. In his first season

here he played fifteen League and seven Cup matches, and in 1953-54 he deputised in seven League games and one Cup-tie while Robertson was injured.

Charlie is now playing better than ever before, earning the full confidence of colleagues and crowd alike. His most obvious improvement is in dealing with the high ball; down below he is nearly invincible. All of which suggests that from the goalkeeping point of view our Championship hopes are in very sound hands.

THREE wins and a draw in the last four matches have put us right there in the challenge for the League Championship in this fiftieth year of the Club. It is a chance that has been created largely by team spirit, but, of course, team spirit alone is not enough—ability of the players individually and as a team is an equally important factor.

TED DRAKE CALLING . . .

WHEN the season's fixtures were prepared, no one could have imagined that, come Easter Saturday, the meeting of Chelsea and Wolverhampton Wanderers at Stamford Bridge would bring together the clubs running first and second in the League Championship.

Chelsea with hopes of their first Championship ever, Wolves seeking to retain the title they won for the first time a year ago—well, there could have been no greater attraction if it had been possible to arrange these things in advance.

FINE RECOVERY AT TOTTENHAM

Having overcome Wolves away from home in December, our home fixture against them in April was effectively a title decider. More than 75,000 fans watched as Peter Sillett settled a tight encounter from the penalty spot. Drake harked back to the victory at Molineux, with action shots from that game and a 4-2 victory at Tottenham a week previously.

The Talk of Stamford Bridge in our programme for the final home game of 1954/55 spoke of how this could be our "day of days" and that is how it transpired with a 3-0 win over Sheffield Wednesday thanks to two goals from Eric "The Rabbit" Parsons and another Peter Sillett penalty. His spot-kick from the vital win over Wolves was pictured inside and on the back cover. You can see Ted Drake's notes from this historic match on page 174.

THE PENALTY THAT BEAT WOLVES

With no score after 75 minutes, Seamus O'Connell's shot beats Williams and is fisted away from under the bar by Billy Wright.

THIS can be our day of days! Victory would mean that we cannot be passed on points and only Portsmouth by winning their last four games, could equal our total. So if we win and Portsmouth so much as drop a point today our name will go at last on the Championship trophy. Everyone will be eagerly awaiting the Cardiff-Portsmouth result and we shall announce it as soon as possible after the match. While naturally hoping to clinch the title this afternoon, we know too much about the fortunes of football to forget that there can be "many a slip," so in case later reference is necessary, these are Portsmouth's fixtures after to-day:—Aston Villa at home next Wednesday, Arsenal at home next Saturday, and Sheffield United away on 2nd May.

... and the penalty thus conceded by England's captain is hammered home by Young England's skipper, Peter Sillett.

Epic cup duel lights up bleak season, 1955/56

Chelsea's title defence fell someway short in 1955/56 as we finished in a disappointing 16th place. We did not take our rightful place in the inaugural European Cup after the Football League rejected it on the grounds of it detracting from domestic competitions. One of the most interesting aspects of the season was an epic FA Cup fourth-round tussle with Burnley, which incredibly took five matches to be settled. Here we feature the covers from all of the games, beginning with a 1-1 draw at Turf Moor. The same scoreline was repeated in the replay at Stamford Bridge and, long before the days of penalty shootouts, a second replay was required at Birmingham City's St Andrews. This time the match finished 2-2, so it was off to Highbury. On this occasion there were no goals and the Blues finally prevailed with a 2-0 win at White Hart Lane. After all that, just three days later, we were beaten in round five at Everton!

BURNLEY LEAD AFTER SIX MINUTES: WE REPLY SIX MINUTES FROM TIME

Parsons again, and this time it's jubilation! Stan Willemse and Roy Bentley are first to congratulate him on the equaliser six minutes from the end. Bentley provided the pass behind the score.

F.A. CUP
FOURTH ROUND—2nd REPLAY
ST. ANDREW'S BIRMINGHAM
MONDAY, FEBRUARY 6th 1956
BURNLEY v CHELSEA

EVERTON'S VISITORS

GOOD AFTERNOON — F.A. Cup talk is the fashion in this region, and in welcoming Burnley and Chelsea to St. Andrew's for their second replay, we do so with the knowledge that both teams are capable of causing a lot of trouble once they settle their fourth round argument.

Already they have figured in two hard battles in which football craft has not been entirely lost in the traditional excitement of the Cup tournament. A crowd of 44,897 (receipts £5,815) saw the first game at Burnley where the Lancashire side had a first half advantage through a goal by McKay. Chelsea's fighting spirit pulled them through after the interval, and Parsons got the goal that earned a replay at Stamford Bridge.

The second meeting on the frost bound Chelsea ground last Wednesday drew 26,661 (receipts £4,218) and it was Chelsea who scored first on this occasion, Blunstone netting ten minutes after the interval. It looked like the winner, but not to Burnley, and Pilkington levelled the score to ensure a hectic session of extra time in which both attacks were further handicapped in their eagerness by the slippery turf.

This is Burnley's fifth Cup match since January 7th when their original third round tie with Bury at Gigg Lane was abandoned with the score at 2-2. Burnley won the second meeting by the only goal, scored by McKay.

Chelsea's fourth round ticket was earned by a 1-0 success at Hartlepools.

For today's victors the prize is great for a visit to Everton is something worthwhile whether it be a Cup or League engagement. —may the better team win.

The work starts and the foundations at the scoreboard end of the ground are laid.

THE new permanent floodlighting scheme—the largest stadium flood-lighting installation in Britain—specially designed and supplied by the G.E.C., will be inaugurated at our ground this evening, when we meet Spartak in an international club match.

The 228 floodlights will consume nearly half a million watts, enough to light 10,000 five-roomed houses, and they are mounted approximately 170 feet high on six tubular steel towers. A man standing on top of the lights would be as high above the ground as the statue of Lord Nelson in Trafalgar Square.

The towers are among the highest to be installed in Britain for floodlighting a football ground.

To avoid obstructing the view of spectators at daylight matches, and to allow for future extensions to the spectators' stands, the floodlights are situated at the back of the main terraces and behind the stands, and are consequently about 200 ft. from the edge of the playing area. High towers are necessary because of this abnormal offset distance.

Mr. Drake, Stan Wicks, Peter Sillett and Mr. Battersby inspect one of the lighting units

The finished work—the three pylons on one side of the ground.

First match under the lights, 1956/57

March 1957 saw the first floodlit match take place at Stamford Bridge, with Sparta Prague the visitors for a friendly fixture. The outcome of the game may not have been the most important thing – with the testing of our ground's new additions the main point – but nevertheless there was a Chelsea victory to cheer as we won 2-0.

Greaves bursts onto the scene, 1957/58

The late-Fifties was the period when Chelsea really began to reap the rewards of the investment in youth which had been in place for around a decade and the 1957/58 season saw the emergence of one of our greatest homegrown talents. Jimmy Greaves made his debut on the opening day of the season – a 1-1 draw away to Tottenham. Pictures of his exploits featured in the second home programme, against Manchester City, when he hit the target twice and the scene was set for the next four seasons, during each of which Greaves finished as our top scorer. Perhaps Ted Drake was purposely under-playing our young talent as Greaves did not receive a mention in his column, but there was a brief note of congratulation in Talk of Stamford Bridge. Programme readers got a full rundown on the club 's professional staff and a squad picture.

Congratulations to Jimmy Greaves who played his first League match for us against Tottenham Hotspur last Saturday and scored the goal in the last few minutes of the game which gained us a valuable point.

CHELSEA 1957-58

Standing: A. Dicks, J. Mortimore, R. Matthews, S. Wicks, I. MacFarlane, W. Robertson, P. Sillett, D. Saunders.   Seated: R. Tindall, J. McNichol, P. Brabrook, L. Stubbs, F. Blunstone, J. Greaves.

SEASONAL GREETINGS from CHELSEA FOOTBALL CLUB—1957

Greaves' highest return in a single game in 1957/58 came during an incredible 7-4 win over Portsmouth on Christmas Day, when he netted four times, with photos of all his goals pictured in a later edition. The players were pictured as caricatures in a festive centre spread. Another match of note at the Bridge was the final of the Inter-Cities Fairs Cup between Barcelona and a London XI, with Greaves unsurprisingly appearing for the latter, along with our right-back Peter Sillett. After a 2-2 draw at the Bridge, the Spaniards comprehensively won the second leg at Camp Nou by six goals to nil.

JIMMY GREAVES GETS FOUR — AGAINST PORTSMOUTH ON XMAS DAY

No. 1—Upitchard dives in a vain attempt to stop Greaves' first goal.

No. 3—see how Greaves has slidden off the defender to leave room to shoot.

No. 2—alone and unmarked Greaves makes it two.

No. 4—Jimmy Greaves completes a memorable Christmas morning.

I SHOULD like to add my personal good wishes to those of the Club to you all for Christmas. May you have happiness and peace in the New Year to come.

On this festive occasion we welcome our old friends and foes from Portsmouth. "Pompey" as they are widely known, have proved themselves one of the most attractive sides in the many clashes the two teams have had over the years.

JIMMY GREAVES (Chelsea—Inside-right): Undoubtedly the discovery of the present season. Narrowly missed selection for the England team after only half a dozen games for Chelsea, but his turn will inevitably come. Just 18, he is a complete master of the inside-forward craft, and can take chances as well as make them He is Chelsea's leading scorer this season, and has found the net on each of his appearances for Young England. His performance tonight will be watched with extreme interest, since on previous occasions Greaves had proved the perfect foil to England's Johnny Haynes.

PETER SILLETT (Chelsea — Right-back): Sillett's father played in the same Southampton team as Ted Drake and so the Chelsea manager took more than a passing interest when Sillett junior made his debut for the Saints at 18. Chelsea signed him for a five figure fee in 1953, but it was some time before he won a regular place in the league side. He played for Young England against Young Italy and Young Scotland in 1954-55; Young Denmark in 1955-56; and England "B" against Scotland in 1956-57.

LEAGUE CHAMPIONS 1954-55

Chelsea Football Club

Stamford Bridge Grounds, London SW6

INTERNATIONAL INDUSTRIES FAIRS INTER-CITIES CUP
FINAL TIE—FIRST LEG   SEASON 1957-58

LONDON
v
BARCELONA

Wednesday, 5th March, 1958   Kick-off 7.15 p.m.

Official Programme 3d

LONDON

Colours—Shirts: White. Knickers: Black. Stockings: Black and White.

1. (Goal)
Kelsey
(Arsenal)

2. (Right-back)   3. (Left-back)
Sillett (P.)   **Langley**
(Chelsea)   (Fulham)

4. (Right-half)   5. (Centre-half)   6. (Left-half)
Blanchflower   **Norman**   **Coote**
(Tottenham Hotspur)   (Tottenham Hotspur)   (Brentford)

7. (Outside-right) 8. (Inside-right) 9. (Centre-forward) 10. (Inside-left) 11. (Outside-left)
Groves   **Greaves**   **Smith**   **Haynes**   **Robb**
(Arsenal)   (Chelsea)   (Tottenham Hotspur) (Fulham)   (Tottenham Hotspur)

Referee:
Herr A. DUSCH
(Western Germany)

Linesmen:
Mr. G. A. SMOKER
(London)
[Red Flag]
Mr. C. A. R. WOAN
(London)
[Yellow Flag]

11. (Outside-left) 8. (Inside-left) 9. (Centre-forward) 10. (Inside-right) 7. (Outside-right)
Tejada   **Villeverde**   **Martinez**   **Evaristo**   **Basora**

4. (Left-half)   5. (Centre-half)   3. (Right-half)
Ribelles   **Biosca**   **Gracia**

6. (Left-back)   2. (Right-back)
Gensana   **Olivella**

1. (Goal)
Estrems

BARCELONA

Colours—Shirts: Blue. Knickers: White. Stockings: White.

Blues win in Denmark on Euro bow, 1958/59

Having hosted the Fairs Cup final towards the end of the previous season, the Blues made our debut in Europe in the same competition – a forerunner to the UEFA Cup and Europa League – in 1958/59. We hosted Danish side Frem at the Bridge in November, winning 4-1 after a 3-1 victory in the first leg in Copenhagen. That earned us a place in the second round against Ville de Belgrade, with the games played after the finale of the domestic season and the Yugoslavian club prevailing 4-2 on aggregate.

BACK HOME FROM COPENHAGEN

Our touring party arrive back at London after our 3-1 win against Frem. Left to right: Mr. J. H. Mears, Tony Nicholas, Mr. J. Battersby, Peter Sillett, Mr. E. J. Drake, Ron Tindall, Cliff Huxford, Bill Robertson, John Sillett, Mr. J. Oxberry, Reg Matthews, Les Stubbs, Jimmy Greaves, Colin Court, Michael Harrison, Melvyn Scott and Derek Saunders.

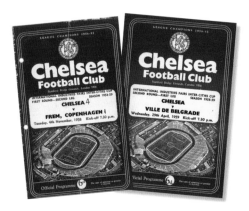

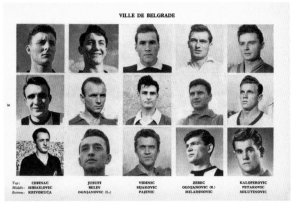

VILLE DE BELGRADE

Top: CERINAC   JUSUFI   VIDINIC   ZEBEC   KALOPEROVIC
Middle: MIHAILOVIC   BELIN   SIJAKOVIC   OGNJANOVIC (R.)   PETAKOVIC
Bottom: KRIVOKUCA   OGNJANOVIC (L.)   PAJEVIC   MILADINOVIC   MILUTINOVIC

TODAY we welcome West Ham United. Newly promoted to the First Division, they have reason to be proud of their achievements to date and, although like ourselves, they are out of the Cup, I feel that they will finish this season well up the Table. Managed by Ted Fenton, whose "F" plan took Colchester for one of the most remarkable Cup runs in the history of the game, our match today should be worth watching.

WEST HAM UNITED 1958-59

Standing: K. Brown, V. Keeble, J. Bond, E. Gregory, N. Cantwell, A. Malcolm. Seated: M. Grice, J. Smith, W. Dare, J. Dick, M. Musgrove. Inset: P. Woosnam.

Following the emergence of Greaves – who notched 37 goals in all competitions in his second season in the first team – this campaign saw more young talent come through the ranks, with Bobby Tambling and Barry Bridges notably making goalscoring debuts in a 3-2 win over West Ham in February 1959.

(Bonetti's Debut)

SEEN

CHELSEA 3

Colours—Shirts: Royal Blue (White Collars). Shorts: White.
Stockings: Navy Blue, Blue and White Tops.

1. (Goal)
Robertson
Bonetti

2. (Right-back)   3. (Left-back)
Sillett (J.)   Sillett (P.)

4. (Right-half)   5. (Centre-half)   6. (Left-half)
Anderton   Mortimore   Crowther

7. (Outside-right) 8. (Inside-right) 9. (Centre-forward) 10. (Inside-left) 11. (Outside-left)
Brabrook   Brooks   Tindall   Greaves   Blunstone
                   openues   Brooks

Referee: Linesmen:
Mr. L. CALLAGHAN   Mr. J. T. W. BIBBEY
(Merthyr Tydfil)   (Porchester, Hants)
                                      [Red Flag]
                                      Mr. W. T. CASTLE
                                      (Colchester)
                                      [Yellow Flag]

Colbridge   Hayes   McAdams   Law   Barlow
11. (Outside-left) 10. (Inside-left) 9. (Centre-forward) 8. (Inside-right) 7. (Outside-right)

Oakes   McTavish   Barnes
6. (Left-half) 5. (Centre-half) 4. (Right-half)

Branagan   Leivers
3. (Left-back)   2. (Right-back)

Trautmann
1. (Goal)

MANCHESTER CITY O

Colours—Shirts: Sky Blue. Shorts: White: Stockings: Sky Blue and White Hoops.

9

ATTENDANCE: 34,044

MANCHESTER CITY 1959-60 Standing: C. Barlow, K. Barnes, W. Leivers, B. Trautmann, D. Shawcross, A. Kerr, C. Sear. Seated: R. Johnstone, W. McAdams, J. Hayes, R. Sambrook.

First glimpse of Bonetti in action, 1959/60

The next season, a young man who would go on to establish himself as the greatest Chelsea goalkeeper of the 20th Century made his senior bow. Peter Bonetti kept the first of his 208 clean sheets in a 3-0 win over Manchester City. As you can see, the proud owner of this programme has "The Cat's" autograph on the team line-ups page. Sadly, the Sixties did not get off to a swinging start for the Blues as we finished 18th in Division One.

Through the years Manchester City have had a fair share of the limelight which shines so fiercely on the doings of football clubs and on the players of the game. In the middle of last month the club made a move which set the newspaper people looking round for the biggest type they could find. They wanted it to announce what I believe can be described as a fact—that Manchester City had paid fifty-three thousand pounds to secure from Huddersfield Town the services of a young forward named Denis Law.

That amount, as everybody interested in the game is well aware surpasses by quite a lot the amount which has changed hands between British clubs for any one player. Just how long the deal will occupy the top line in the record books so far as transfer fees are concerned is anybody's guess. What we do know is that the ceiling has been raised higher and higher in the fifty-five years since Middlesbrough paid an "unheard of" fee of one thousand pounds for another inside forward—Alf Common.

I won't stop here to speculate how much higher the price will go for some player in the years to come. Nor do we need to hang around trying to reply to the oft-asked question: can one player be worth so much money? The obvious answer is that the officials of Manchester City thought so, and they will get some assurance that they are right if he brings quick relief from anxiety by helping to lift the club to a position in the League table free from worry about the possibility of relegation.

1

TESTIMONIALS

They may not be so common in football nowadays but, over the years, testimonials have given fans the opportunity to pay tribute to club legends, traditionally those to have played in the first team for a decade. The matches are some of the most intriguing to have been held at the Bridge, and the programmes often followed suit, as you will see over the next few pages

THE CHELSEA FOOTBALL & ATHLETIC CO. LTD.

FOUNDED 1905

CLUB COLOURS:
Shirts: Royal Blue (White Collars). Knickers: White Stockings: Black, Blue and White Tops

Registered Address: STAMFORD BRIDGE GROUNDS, FULHAM ROAD, LONDON, S.W.6. [FUL 5545]

PRESIDENT: The Right Hon. Earl Cadogan, M.C.

BOARD OF DIRECTORS:
J. H. Mears (CHAIRMAN), C. J. Pratt (VICE-CHAIRMAN), L. J. Mears, L. R. Withey, J. G. Bennett.

MANAGER: E. J. Drake, SECRETARY: J. Battersby, TRAINER: J. Oxberry

League Champions 1955

THIS evening we welcome Leicester City to Stamford Bridge to play a Testimonial match for Ken Armstrong, who is retiring at the end of a long career with Chelsea. This season Leicester City have ended as champions of the Second Division and we congratulate them on their return to the First Division after a period of two years.

Ken is a one-club player, joining us direct from Army service in December, 1946. He made his first League appearance for us in the opening game of the 1947-48 season and played in all 42 League matches that winter. The 1948-49 season saw him play 25 matches, and then, in 1949-50 he began a run of appearances that gave him little rest for six seasons. He missed only one League match in 1949-50, two in 1950-51, five in 1951-52, one in 1952-53, two in 1953-54 and three in 1954-55. A serious illness laid him low in January, 1956, but he returned in August, 1956 and, when Stan Wicks was injured early in the season, captained Chelsea for the greater part of the campaign. Ken has appeared in 362 League matches for us: more than any other player.

Ken's happiest moments must have been in April, 1955, when he not only helped us to our first League Championship, but also gained a place in the England team against Scotland at Wembley: a match that England won 7-2.

Now, Ken has decided that the time

has come for him to retire and seek a new life in New Zealand, where the climate is more friendly to those who have been affected with chest trouble.

We all wish him well in the future and assure him that he leaves many happy memories with his team mates, club officials and Chelsea supporters. The Chelsea Supporters Club are to make a presentation to John Harris and Ken Armstrong at their dance at Caxton Hall tomorrow evening, 3rd May.

And a Farewell from Ken Armstrong himself:

This is a sad evening for me, as it is the last time that I will wear the Chelsea blue shirt. I have enjoyed the years I have spent at Stamford Bridge and thank you all very much for the encouragement that you have given me over the years.

It is hard to break with my career as a professional footballer, but there comes a time when one must retire and I have, reluctantly, decided that the time is now.

I have the offer of a job in New Zealand and will leave, together with my wife and four kiddies, at the end of this month. This time last year I was recovering from pleurisy and I feel that the change of climate will be beneficial for my health.

I would like to take this opportunity of thanking those of you who have sent donations to my testimonial fund and all of you for supporting my match this evening.
Ken Armstrong.

REMAINING MATCHES AT THIS GROUND

Saturday, 4th May	Monday, 6th May
CHARLTON ATHLETIC	Sporting Celebrities v. Famous Fools
(Kick-off 10.30 a.m.)	(Kick-off 7 p.m.)
South East Counties League—Cup Final	The Craziest Charity Match ever

KEN ARMSTRONG leads Chelsea into the field in one of his last matches for Chelsea. He has captained the first team for most of the season, taking over after Stan Wicks had been seriously injured with the campaign only a month old.

Ken Armstrong was the first player to reach 400 appearances for Chelsea and the one-club man's Blues career came to an end in 1957 after a total of 402 first-team games. Leicester were our opponents for his testimonial which ended in a 2-1 Blues victory.

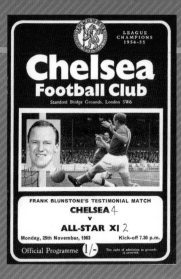

LEAGUE CHAMPIONS 1954-55

Chelsea
Football Club
Stamford Bridge Grounds, London SW6

FRANK BLUNSTONE'S TESTIMONIAL MATCH

CHELSEA 4
v
ALL-STAR XI 2

Monday, 25th November, 1963   Kick-off 7.30 p.m.

Official Programme 1/-   The right of admission to grounds is reserved

My Thanks
to you All

SAYS FRANK

THIS is an evening I shall never forget, and I cannot let it pass without some attempt to acknowledge the efforts of all concerned towards the success of my Testimonial.

When, as a lad of 18, I left my family and Crewe Alexandra for a life in London and football with Chelsea, I could never have imagined that ten years would pass so quickly and so happily. Now, as I reach this milestone, I say a sincere "Thank you".

To Chelsea, first and foremost, for granting me this Testimonial and for doing everything any club could possibly do to make it a success.

To the Testimonial Committee for all their efforts through 1963 in the various functions and enterprises that have been staged on my behalf. To the Supporters Club, who have given tremendous help.

To the Players on both sides—also the Match Officials, Gatemen and Stewards—who are honouring me with their presence tonight. And, of course, to you Supporters who have come along on this my big night.

In short, my thanks to everyone who has contributed in any way to my Testimonial—and, indeed, to all who have given me such wonderful support and encouragement throughout my career with Chelsea.

I look back on ten years which I have been proud to spend among you all. At 29, I hope I can look forward to spending many more seasons in what, to me, will always be the best blue of all—Chelsea blue.

Sincerely yours,

FRANK BLUNSTONE.

HIS OLD FRIENDS SAY . . .

ROY BENTLEY, Manager of Reading:

I was never more pleased to read of a player being granted a testimonial. Knowing Frank from his first days at Chelsea, the amount of effort he has put into the game, and the grit and determination he has shown in getting over two broken legs, I am sure everyone in football will want to wish him a bumper testimonial. Good luck, Frank.

JOHNNY HARRIS, Manager, Sheffield United:

It was my pleasure and privilege to take Frank Blunstone under my wing when he first moved to Chelsea from Crewe Alexandra. Frank was a good boy, eager to learn, and loved his football, and has proved a credit to himself, to the Chelsea Football Club, and football in general.

Frank Blunstone attracted an All-Star XI side including the great Tom Finney for his 1963 testimonial. As well as a glowing thank you from Blunstone – who was on the scoresheet in a 4-2 win for Chelsea – there was praise from two of his old team-mates who had since turned to management, Roy Bentley and Johnny Harris.

Ken Shellito—by our Medical Room "Team"

SUCH COURAGE
says Trainer Harry Medhurst

THERE ought to be a plaque placed on one of the benches in the Treatment Room with the inscription "Ken Shellito Recovered Here". It would serve as a permanent reminder of one of the most courageous battles any footballer has staged in order to stay actively in the game.

I keep a card-index of the injuries and treatment of every Chelsea player. Ken's file records that his first operation was in October 1963, the second in November 1964, the third in December 1965 and the fourth in July 1966 (when, as fellow patients, we watched the World Cup together on TV in the same hospital ward).

Ken now has no cartilages in the left knee. The various periods he has spent in hospital add up to only a fraction of the time occupied in rehabilitation and, going back nearly two years to just before his last "op", we had all but given up hope of his playing career. But, at the final medical consultation, it was decided that Ken had been through so much that he must be given one more chance, however slight, to play again.

At first, Ken himself was against it. We talked him round. Now, two years later, having played in practically every Reserve game this season, he appears tonight in his own big match. I've never known a player go through so much, work so hard to get fit, or show such dedication and guts as Ken has done. Believe me, it wasn't us who kept him going – he kept "Doc" Boyne, Norman and me going. For if he refused to give up the fight, how could we possibly do so?

Good luck, Ken. It's terrific to see you out there tonight. I know it must be a thrill to you. It's a joy and a thrill to me, too.

Dr. Paul Boyne, Hon. Medical Officer to Chelsea F.C. writes: Within three months of becoming Chelsea F.C.'s Hon. Medical Officer in 1963, the first problem with which I was involved was Ken Shellito's left knee. It is common knowledge that Ken has had four operations because of cartilage injury and, although this is not the place to go into medical details, it is worth pointing out that among the after-effects of such an operation are the collection of injury fluid in the joint and muscle-wastage above and below the joint due to disuse.

These Ken had to a great extent. It is necessary in the rehabilitation of a knee with these disabilities to get rid of the fluid and build up the muscles. The treatment is not fundamentally difficult, but 90 per cent depends on the patient, and when he is a man of Ken's calibre the treatment becomes easy – from the doctor's point of view.

Ken's determination and absolute dedication to get back into football was shown in the hours, days and weeks of lonely, patient, boring exercises under the watchful eye of Harry Medhurst. He really was quite fantastic in his approach to his injury, and I would suggest, with no disrespect, that many a player would long since have thrown in the sponge.

We all know now that Ken has won through, and has played regularly for the Combination side this season, showing his old skills. For him, the countless hours of honest endeavour have paid off. The Treatment Room will never seem the same again!

7

KEN SHELLITO OPENS — **HIS PICTURE ALBUM**

There was a touching tribute from trainer Norman Medhurst in Ken Shellito's 1968 testimonial programme, praising the full-back's courage after his playing days were plagued by injury. The match against QPR ended in a 6-3 win for the Blues.

CHELSEA
FOOTBALL CLUB

It's His Big Night!

KEN SHELLITO
★
Welcomed back to first-team football after being absent since December 1965.

STAMFORD BRIDGE GROUNDS London SW6

KEN SHELLITO TESTIMONIAL MATCH
SEASON 1967-68

Monday, 6th May

v

QUEEN'S PARK

Bobby Tambling

Chelsea's all-time leading goalscorer – before Frank Lampard broke his record – was Bobby Tambling, and the Blues hosted Charlton for his testimonial at the end of the 1968/69 season, a year before he departed the club. The affection in which the man who netted 202 goals for the club was demonstrated in both the foreword and a heartfelt letter from a fan. The inclusion of a colour poster was rare at the time, and showed Bobby in his sports shop in Havant, near Portsmouth.

ON BEHALF OF CHELSEA FANS . . .

A letter that says it all about Bobby Tambling

MANY people have expressed the pity it is that there are not many players in the game of the Bobby Charlton mould; a man whose loyalty and fair sense of play have made his a household name. But I believe that we at Chelsea do not have far to look for another such gifted player – Bobby Tambling.

It was in October 1957 that I first saw Bobby, and what an impression he made on me. The match was an F.A. Youth Cup first round tie at Stamford Bridge against Woodford Youth Centre which Chelsea won 14-0. Bobby's personal goal haul that day was three and several "assists" to the six scored by Barry Bridges. I still remember how he put everything into that match even when it had long been won. Bobby has never given up since. I did not see him again until he made his League debut on February 7, 1959, in the 3-2 home victory against West Ham. He capped a fine first performance with the first of his record number of goals for Chelsea.

The matches I remember best, in which Bobby's goals have given me most pleasure, are headed by that memorable game at Villa Park on September 17, 1966. Chelsea beat Aston Villa 6-2 and Bobby scored five. All of us who travelled to Villa Park that day were really proud to be seen with our club colours, and when we reached Paddington in the evening everyone on the station knew about Tambling. It seemed as though they all wanted to congratulate Bobby personally. He showed then what a great fellow he is by thanking all those of us near enough to hear for travelling and giving our support at the match.

Another big goal haul was the four he scored in Chelsea's 7-0 defeat of Portsmouth to put Chelsea back in the First Division in May 1963. Club captain at the time, Bobby set an example to all and led the team to promotion with remarkable maturity. But probably the goal that no Chelsea supporter will forget, will be Bobby's F.A. Cup Final goal that had me biting my finger nails for those last hectic minutes at Wembley two years ago.

That 2-1 defeat to Spurs was not Bobby's first disappointment at Chelsea, and it says a lot of a player who stays with one Club, yet whose only Club honours have been that F.A. Cup finalist's medal, a Football League Cup-Winner's medal and an F.A. Youth Cup-Winner's medal. I know I was in tears all the way down Wembley Way, so goodness knows how Bobby and the rest of the players felt. It is just like him, however, to forget the last match and get on with the next, always looking for a goal chance.

His loyalty has been second to none and his courage unbeatable. I have seen him, before the introduction of substitutes, refuse the requests of Harry Medhurst on the touchline to come off when injured, but this is typical of the man, knowing he would never forgive himself if he went off and left his team mates to struggle without him.

It will be a sad day for Chelsea when Bobby gives up playing, but let us hope that will not be for many years to come. Finally let me, on behalf of all true Chelsea supporters, thank Bobby sincerely for all the wonderful entertainment he has given us and wish him every success in his Testimonial.

R. N. Billinghurst,
2 The Cedars,
Reigate, Surrey.

A few words to you all from Bobby himself . . .

SOMETIMES it seems only yesterday that I came to Chelsea as a junior. In fact, it was July 1957, and the thought of being awarded a Testimonial some 12 years later no more entered my mind at that time than the likelihood that over the seasons I would find myself at the top of the Club's list of goalscorers.

Yet both these things have happened and tonight, on the occasion of this Testimonial Match, there are so many people I would like to thank for the successful career I have had (and will, I hope, continue to have) with Chelsea.

Goalscorers get a lot of the glory, but like everyone else they depend on the help of ten others out there on the field, so I would say a sincere "thanks" to all the Chelsea players I have been privileged to line up with since I came to Stamford Bridge.

My thanks also to the Chelsea Board for awarding me this Testimonial; to Dave Sexton and the lads for their support, not only tonight, but at the various events and functions they have attended for me through the season – cricket last summer, my Testimonial Dance, darts matches, last Sunday's football match at Tooting, to name some of them.

I thank Charlton Athletic for coming here to play for me, and wish Brian Kinsey a very successful Testimonial when we reciprocate with a visit to The Valley on Friday night.

I thank most sincerely my Testimonial Committee for all their work on my behalf over the past year; also the Supporters' Club, tonight's match officials, stewards and match staff; the programme sellers and supervisors; the advertisers who have taken space in this programme.

I thank Harry Medhurst for his part, in the Medical Room, in getting me over the bumps and bruises, sometimes worse, that have to be part and parcel of this great game; and Mr. Edgar Bonvin, of the Montana Hotel, for his kind hospitality.

And, most of all, I realise how much I owe to you fans on the terraces and in the stands, for your magnificent support over the seasons and for your presence here again tonight. A goal to mark the occasion is, no doubt, a hope we share. I'll be even happier if I can be "on target" next season and helping Chelsea to win one of the game's top prizes. Thank you all.

Sincerely,

Bobby Tambling

Monday, 21st April (7.30 p.m.)

CHELSEA
v
CHARLTON ATHLETIC
Bobby Tambling Testimonial Match

OFFICIAL PROGRAMME 9½

SEASON 1968-69

John Mortimore says thank you...

I WOULD like to welcome you to Stamford Bridge tonight for my Testimonial Match and hope you will have a thoroughly enjoyable evening.

The Directors of Chelsea F.C. promised me, when I was transferred to Q.P.R. just over a year ago, that a Testimonial Match would be staged to mark the completion of ten years with the Club. This evening has seen that promise fulfilled and I sincerely appreciate their generosity.

It has not been easy to arrange this match, because of the heavy commitments that face clubs each season, and I sincerely thank the players of the London XI for appearing, also the managers of their respective clubs for enabling them to do so.

To Tommy Docherty and the Chelsea team, thank you for playing, not only tonight but also in the game at Woking last December. I sincerely hope that you will go on to further success this season.

Ever since the Directors granted me a Testimonial, a small committee has worked tremendously hard to organise my Testimonial Fund. I am indebted to them for their efforts and assistance. Miss Christine Mathews has acted as Secretary and has done a wonderful job. Mr. A. Bennett, Mr. T. Beattie-Edwards, Mr. E. Bonvin and Mr. A. Meadows have also worked hard to help promote the Testimonial. My sincere thanks to you all.

Thanks also to tonight's match officials and match staff, and the team of trampolinists from the Army School of Physical Training, who are providing the half-time entertainment. And, of course, to all you Supporters who have come along.

6

Chelsea 9 — London XI 7

Colours:
Shirts: Royal Blue.
Shorts: Royal Blue.
Stockings: White.

Colours:
Shirts: Red.
Shorts: White.
Stockings: Red.

Chelsea		London XI
PETER BONETTI	1	RON SPRINGETT
JOE KIRKUP	2	GEORGE COHEN (06)
EDDIE McCREADIE	3	JIM LANGLEY HOWE
JOHN HOLLINS	4	BOBBY ROBSON
JIM THOMSON	5	JOHN MORTIMORE (Captain)
RON HARRIS (Captain)	6	FRANK UPTON (1)
JOHN BOYLE	7	GRAHAM LEGGAT (2)
PETER HOUSEMAN	8	TERRY VENABLES (2)
TONY HATELEY (4)	9	GEORGE GRAHAM
CHARLIE COOKE (1)	10	JOHNNY HAYNES
BOBBY TAMBLING (3)	11	GEORGE EASTHAM (2)

(Subject to alteration)

Referee: Mr. KEN ASTON (Ilford)
Linesmen: Mr. S. F. LOVER (London, S.E. 18) Red Flag
Mr. J. A. FINN (Chigwell Row, Essex) Yellow Flag

7

BEST WISHES

J. P. Greaves

Tottenham Hotspur F.C. and England

TRIO PACKING MATERIALS LTD.
Southend Arterial Road
Harold Park, Romford, Essex

CHELSEA FOOTBALL CLUB

LEAGUE CHAMPIONS 1954-55
LEAGUE CUP WINNERS 1964-65

STAMFORD BRIDGE GROUNDS
London SW6

JOHN MORTIMORE TESTIMONIAL MATCH
Tuesday 29th November
v
LONDON XI

KICK-OFF 7.30 P.M.

John Mortimore
in action in one of the 279 competitive first-team matches he played for Chelsea between 1956 and 1965.

OFFICIAL PROGRAMME 1/-

HIS CAREER RECORD WITH CHELSEA

(Goals scored in brackets)

Season	Football League	F.A. Cup	Football League Cup	Inter-Cities Fairs Cup	Total
1955-56	1	—	—	—	1
1956-57	2	—	—	—	2
1957-58	39 (1)	3	—	3	42 (1)
1958-59	37 (1)	1 (1)	—	—	41 (2)
1959-60	33	—	—	—	33
1960-61	12 (1)	—	3 (1)	—	15 (2)
1961-62	14	—	—	—	14
1962-63	42 (1)	4	—	—	46 (1)
1963-64	41 (2)	3	—	—	44 (2)
1964-65	28 (2)	5	8	—	41 (2)
	249 (8)	16 (1)	11 (1)	3	279 (10)

11

If ever you're going to get a 9-7 scoreline in football, it's likely to be in a testimonial fixture, and that was the case in the match dedicated to John Mortimore in 1966, when Chelsea took on a London XI. Mortimore lined up for the London team, following his switch to QPR the year before, but it was the Blues who came out on top, Tony Hateley top-scoring with four goals. Former team-mate Jimmy Greaves did not feature in the fixture, but he did take the opportunity to advertise one of his business pursuits while offering congratulations.

DOUBLE CELEBRATION

You know you have reached true legendary status when you receive two testimonials and two Chelsea players fit into that category, Peter Bonetti and Ron Harris. Bonetti's first was in May 1971, just a fortnight before our European Cup Winners' Cup final against Real Madrid. Standard Liege were the visitors and it is totally understandable that the Blues were on the end of a 2-1 defeat, given the magnitude of the game that was to follow.

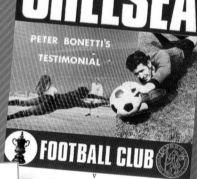

CHELSEA

PETER BONETTI'S - TESTIMONIAL -

FOOTBALL CLUB

v

STANDARD LIEGE
(Belgian League Champions 1970-71)

Wednesday, 5th May, 1971—Kick-off 7.30 p.m.

OFFICIAL PROGRAMME 10p (2/-)

PETER BONETTI *writes...*

DURING my time at Stamford Bridge, it has been my pleasure to play in Testimonial and Benefit matches for a number of fellow-professionals with Chelsea and other clubs. My own Testimonial tonight brings me an opportunity to thank so many people for the help I have received since the start of my career.

My thanks go first to this wonderful Chelsea Football Club for all they have done for me from the day I arrived as a boy fresh from school . . . to my Team-mates over the years, the Directors, Management and Staff . . . and to you, the Fans, for your magnificent support. Believe me, when Chelsea won the Cup last year I was as pleased for our marvellous Supporters as I was for myself that at last this great prize had come to Stamford Bridge.

Coming to tonight's match, I would like to thank in particular *Esso* for the sponsorship and advertising they have given to my Testimonial; Standard Liege of Belgium for providing such attractive opposition; also the Match Officials, Stewards and Match Staff; the Advertisers who have given their support in this Programme; and, most of all, you the Fans for coming along.

I would like publicly to thank my wife Frances for the tremendous help she has given me in my career, similarly my Family for their intense support and, going right back to the beginning, my Mother and Father. I often wonder how my life would have turned out if Mother had not written to Chelsea in 1957 and asked Ted Drake if he would give a trial to her boy who was just leaving school. Thanks, Mum . . . and thanks, Ted, for signing me on—I hope I have the pleasure of seeing Ted as well as all my Family here tonight.

I want also to thank my Testimonial Committee who, during the past year, have given so much time and thought towards promoting this and other functions on my behalf; also Mr. Edgar Bonvin for his great friendship and hospitality over the years. To the Chelsea Pools Office Staff and the Supporters' Club, again my thanks.

At 29, I would like to think I still have several seasons' football in front of me. Meanwhile, to all my friends in the game, on and off the field, my very sincere thanks for all you have done to help make my career so happy and successful.

TOP 'KEEPER ...'TOP CAT'

TONIGHT we honour a player whose service to Chelsea has exceeded that of all others in our history and may never be equalled. As someone who has completed 500 first-team matches for the Club, Peter Bonetti is out on his own and, combining this record number of appearances with his distinguished goalkeeping and consistent high standard of performance, it is not surprising that our Supporters should have voted him "Chelsea's Greatest-ever Player."

To emphasise the value of a forward—or, in the modern idiom "striker"—one can produce figures representing the number of goals scored and the victories they won. With a goalkeeper it is rather different; no-one keeps a record of the number of saves he makes in his career. What we can say, statistically, about Peter is that he has kept his goal intact in something approaching one-third of those 500-plus senior games for Chelsea—as well as in five of his seven full Internationals for England.

To his great ability, coolness and daring is added a degree of courage that was shown to the full in last season's F.A. Cup Final. In the first match against Leeds at Wembley Peter Bonetti performed almost miraculously to save the day. Then, up at Old Trafford, his own finest hour, under the severe handicap of a knee injury, became Chelsea's also as we won the Cup for the first time.

Peter Bonetti's loyalty to Chelsea is reflected in the award of this Testimonial, in which we wish him all the success that a player, and a man, of his calibre deserves. Yet another "clean sheet" in this his own special match, from the goalkeeper who has thrilled football fans wherever he has played in a first-class career spanning twelve seasons, would be particularly well received by the legion of admirers who are here to salute him tonight.

Chelsea 1		Standard 2
Colours : Shirts : Royal Blue Shorts : Royal Blue with White Seam Stockings : White		Colours : Shirts : Red Shorts : White Stockings : Red
PETER BONETTI	*1*	CHRISTIAN PIOT
PADDY MULLIGAN	*2*	JACQUES BEURLET
RON HARRIS *(Captain)*	*3*	JEAN THISSEN
CHARLIE COOKE	*4*	NICO DEWALQUE
JOHN DEMPSEY	*5*	LEON JECK
DAVID WEBB	*6*	LOUIS PILOT
KEITH WELLER	*7*	LEON SEMMELING
ALAN HUDSON	*8*	WILFRIED VAN MOER
DEREK SMETHURST	*9*	ERWIN KOSTEDE
JOHN BOYLE	*10*	LUDOVIT CVETLER
PETER HOUSEMAN	*11*	SYLVESTRE TAKAC
	Substitute	

Stamford Bridge Grounds, Fulham Road, S.W.

Linesman (Red Flag) :
Mr. D. V. Reeves
(Uxbridge)

**Referee :
Mr. B. J. HOMEWOOD**
(Sunbury-on-Thames)

2

Linesman (Orange)
Mr. B. K. Robinson
(Shepperton)

THE STARS PAY TRIBUTE TO PETER BONETTI

GORDON BANKS I have great respect for Peter as both

a man and a goalkeeper, and hope his Testimonial Match is a tremendous success. He has given Chelsea years of top-class service and has been a favourite of football crowds everywhere. He is a master of the reflex save . . . more agile than I am . . . and I have to make up for that with positioning—I'm too big to fling myself about at the speed Peter does. Although we have been rivals for the England jersey, we are great friends, and I was honoured to be the opposing captain that day last November when Stoke came to Stamford Bridge and he played his 400th League game. Good luck, Peter, and may you long continue to thrill football fans all over the country.

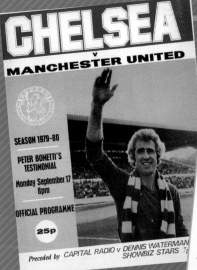

CHELSEA
v
MANCHESTER UNITED

SEASON 1979-80

PETER BONETTI'S
TESTIMONIAL

Monday September 17
8pm

OFFICIAL PROGRAMME

25p

Preceded by CAPITAL RADIO v DENNIS WATERMAN'S SHOWBIZ STARS 7p

The last of Bonetti's 729 competitive appearances for the Blues came at the end of the 1978/79 season and his second testimonial was not long after the start of the following campaign, when Chelsea beat Manchester United 5-2. The Cat received an "illuminated address" on his big night, as was shown in our programme for the friendly against LA Aztecs a month later.

MY THANKS TO YOU ALL
By Peter Bonetti

It's wonderful to be back beneath the crossbar at Stamford Bridge tonight for just one more time. Twenty-one years ago I was starting out on my career as a Chelsea junior; now I am making my farewell appearance before the people who have always been so marvellous to me—the CHELSEA FANS, and among them so many good friends I have made over the years.

My sincere thanks to them for all the encouragement and support during my time here. My thanks to CHELSEA FOOTBALL CLUB for awarding me this Testimonial . . . to MANCHESTER UNITED for providing such illustrious opposition . . . to EVERYONE who has helped with tonight's arrangements—particularly Capital Radio.

As you know, the Bonetti family are now living in Scotland on the Isle of Mull, and settling down fast in our new surroundings. The guest house has kept my wife Frances and me very busy since we moved in May—in fact, I'm working harder now than ever I did as a player!

But I've managed to find time and opportunity to extend my playing career a season or two with Dundee United, and am still enjoying my football each week-end when I ferry across to the mainland and pull on the 'keeper's jersey again.

The memories will come flooding back to me tonight. My first day here as a Chelsea junior . . . winning a Youth Cup medal in 1960 . . . my League debut the same season . . . playing in three major Cup-winning teams—the League Cup in 1965, the F.A. Cup in 1970, the European Cup-Winners' Cup in 1971—in the promotion sides of 1963 and 1977. And seven full England caps.

Oh, yes, there have been one or two bleak times, too. But you have to experience those to enjoy the good days to the full, and I certainly had plenty of those with Chelsea.

Though it will be "goodbye" to the fans tonight, it will only be au revoir to Stamford Bridge, because whenever I come down to London in the future I shall always want to look up the place that was "home" to me for so long and to greet old friends again.

Meanwhile, on behalf of my family and myself, thanks again to all who helped make my career here so happy and successful. My truest wish for Chelsea Football Club is that the good times soon return to Stamford Bridge, and stay.

WE SALUTE
ONE OF FOOTBALL'S GREATS

To those of us long associated with Chelsea, it seems more like yesterday than 21 years ago that a 16-year-old goalkeeper named Peter Bonetti joined us as a junior. We very quickly knew that here was a player with something extra special to offer in ability, courage and temperament.

Against Arsenal here last May, Peter made his 600th League appearance for Chelsea. In all competitions that was his 729th first-team game for our Club—two Chelsea totals that are exceeded only by those of Ron Harris, a career-long friend of Peter and another wonderful servant in our colours.

Peter Bonetti's achievements for Chelsea are shown on other pages of this programme, but figures do not reveal the warmth and character of the man we honour tonight. For on the field and off it, he has always been the model club-man—a man for Chelsea and for professional football to be proud of.

We are delighted to see Peter back at Stamford Bridge on the occasion of this Testimonial which Chelsea F.C. is proud to have awarded him.

To Peter, his wife Frances and their family of four now living in Scotland, we extend warmest wishes for every future happiness in new surroundings, and may Peter continue to thrill Scottish fans with his goalkeeping for Dundee United, through this season and beyond, in the way he thrilled Chelsea supporters for so long.

Peter's "Address"

Our last midweek game at Stamford Bridge was Peter Bonetti's Testimonial a month ago, when we beat Manchester United 5-3. This was the scene just before kick-off, with players and crowd applauding Peter as he displays the illuminated address presented to him by Chairman Brian Mears in recognition of his wonderful career with Chelsea.

(Photograph by Dawn West)

RON HARRIS —
CUP CAPTAIN EXTRAORDINARY

SOME players are born to collect caps. Others, like Ron Harris, make cups their speciality. These pictures, from his own football album, show how, from schooldays to the present time, he has grown accustomed to being photographed, trophy in hand, on the shoulders of cup-winning teams. We hope it continues, Ron, and that we shall see you posing for the cameras in similar style at Wembley in 1972—either at the League Cup Final on March 4 or the F.A. Cup Final on May 6. Or maybe both! After all, somebody, some day will be the first to win both big Wembley Finals in the same season. We'd like to think it could be us . . . and YOU!

1970
It's Chelsea's F.A. Cup at last! After a 2-2 draw against Leeds at Wembley, the replay is staged 18 days later at Old Trafford and we win 2-1 after extra time.

1955
Ron Harris captains Hackney & District Schools to victory in the Batchelor Cup. They beat Southall 3-0 on the Southall F.C. ground and, remembers Ron, Rodney Marsh scored all three goals.

1963
A great night at Wembley. Skipper Ron is chaired by the England team and cheered by a 35,000 crowd after the 4-0 triumph in the International Youth Tournament Final against Northern Ireland.

Our Great Regard for Ron Harris

OVER the years it has been Chelsea's policy to award a Testimonial to players who have served the Club with distinction for ten seasons or more, and now we are proud to do our Captain, Ron Harris, this honour with the visit of Glasgow Rangers, whom we are delighted to welcome to Stamford Bridge.

In the past two seasons Testimonials have been staged here for two of the most distinguished players in our history: Bobby Tambling, the highest goalscorer we have ever had, and goalkeeper Peter Bonetti, who has played more games than anyone else for Chelsea.

There is a special glamour and excitement about goalscoring and goalkeeping yet, in what is becoming more than ever a team game demanding all-round application, the less spectacular but vital jobs must be done equally well in midfield and at the back if a club is to gain distinction.

That we have achieved major successes in recent seasons is due in no small measure to what Ron Harris has given as both Captain and defender. He is a player who has never offered less than 100 per cent effort, and his dedication, determination and loyalty to Chelsea place him among the very finest club-men ever to serve at Stamford Bridge.

As captain of our teams which have won the F.A. Cup and the European Cup-Winners' Cup, Ron has achieved greater success than any previous skipper here. And now, in thanking him for all that he has contributed to the ever-growing reputation of Chelsea Football Club, we wish him continued success on and far beyond his Testimonial night.

Ron Harris' Chelsea appearance record stands at a staggering 795 and it seems conceivable that the mark may never be beaten. His first testimonial came in November 1971, when Rangers were the visitors and won 1-0. Unsurprisingly, the programme was full of imagery of two of our most famous triumphs – the 1970 FA Cup final and 1971 Cup Winners' Cup – not to mention some earlier achievements which Chopper had been captain for. One of the most intriguing entries is the school picture featuring Ron and the person he says he owes his career to.

Winners of European Cup-Winners' Cup 1971

Chelsea

Ron Harris's Testimonial - Season 1971/72

Tuesday, 23rd November
RANGERS
Kick-off 7.30 p.m.

'I OWE IT ALL TO HER' SAYS RON

This is the Craven Park, Stamford Hill, Primary School team in season 1953-54. The captain, holding the ball, is Allan Harris and next to him is brother Ron. On the left is the headmaster . . . on the right the football teacher—Miss Hubert. Says Ron: "In a way, all I've achieved in football I owe to her for what she taught me at the very beginning. She is married now and is still teaching but at another school. As a sort of 'thank you' I've sent her a Cup Final ticket each time we've go to Wembley. I'll always be grateful to her. She was the best teacher I ever had!"

Ron Harris: The Chelsea View

Loyal, dedicated and supremely professional. These are the words that probably sum up Ron Harris best. Loyal? Well, he has been with Chelsea, man and boy, for 20 years and is approaching his 800th first-team game for us. Only a few months ago he turned down what would have been for him a very lucrative move to Luton.

Dedicated? At an age when a good many players are taking things a little easy and, indeed, most have given up playing at top level, Ron still trains as hard as when he came to us as a boy of 15 in the days when Ted Drake was our manager. Through every game, Ron still gives 100 per cent effort. As part of his duty to the Club, he has always looked after himself well, and his fitness and continued ability are shown by the fact that last season and this – two of the most demanding of his career – he has missed only a handful of matches.

Professional? Ron has always been the model club man, has always done his best for Chelsea, and you measure his commitment to football as much by the sweat on his shirt after every game as by the all-time record number of matches he has played for Chelsea.

It is a record that is never likely to be beaten. Ron has played in every jersey for Chelsea except the goalkeeper's – he wore eight different shirt-numbers last season. He has been the most successful captain in Chelsea's history, leading our F.A. Cup-winning team ten years ago and receiving the European Cup-Winners' Cup a year later. He was also in our League Cup-winning side in 1965 at the age of twenty.

Ron, born at Hackney and as down-to-earth a Londoner as they come, has been a member of two promotion-winning Chelsea teams, and we all hope he is about to complete that particular hat-trick in less than two weeks from now. That would be quite a way for him, and us, to celebrate his 20th season as a Chelsea professional.

Ron Harris, dedicated footballer and devoted family man, never seems to look any older or play with any less commitment. He is Chelsea's Peter Pan. Few are those of today's supporters who can remember the time when he was not at Chelsea, and we cannot imagine a future time when he is not still part of our Club.

We thank you most sincerely, Ron, for your wonderful service to Chelsea Football Club, and we wish you the reward you deserve from your Testimonial season.

All the Best, Ron.

Fast forward to April 1980 and Chopper's second tribute match. This time, a Chelsea Past XI – who Ron lined up for – won 1-0 thanks to a Jimmy Greaves goal.

RON HARRIS Testimonial

Official Programme 50p

CHELSEA V. CHELSEA PAST XI

Monday, April 21st, 1980 (7.45 p.m.)

RON THE FAMILY MAN With his wife Lee, their sons Paul (9), Mark (7) and daughter Claire (2 in June).

Thanks – from Ron

I have spent more than half my life playing football for Chelsea's first team, seen a great many changes during my time at Stamford Bridge and made a lot of good friends. Tonight I realise how lucky I've been when I try to thank all those who have combined to make this match possible.

Top of the list are the hard-working members of my Testimonial Committee – I don't know how I'd have managed without them. Thanks, too, to the Players who are taking part and the Referee and Linesmen. There are not many footballers in the League who know referees as well as I do.

I'm grateful to the Chelsea Directors and Officials, and equally to people like the Groundsmen and Programme Sellers who are just as important on such an occasion.

I've been fortunate in having so many star footballers as club-mates at Chelsea, and in having a wife and parents who have been such a help throughout my career.

But all those I've mentioned will understand when I say that I owe the biggest debt of all to you, the Fans, who have never given me a bad time even when I had the kind of off-day which every player dreads but can't avoid.

It's easy to praise Supporters – but I can honestly claim that I've never wanted to play for any club other than Chelsea, and the simple reason is the encouragement I've always received from the terraces and stands which has made me feel at home.

Thanks 700 and more times over. In fact, thanks a million!

From

BATTERSEA BOY

to

CHELSEA STAR!

"Nobby"—aged 7.

Captain of Spencer Park, Wandsworth, school team, 1951.

Chelsea Youth win the 1963 Cannes Easter Festival—Peter Houseman left, John Hollins right.

Wembley 1970—presented to H.R.H. Princess Margaret before the F.A. Cup Final against Leeds.

Peter scores our first equaliser in that Final—to the delight of Tommy Baldwin and all Chelsea.

PETER HOUSEMAN'S PICTURE ALBUM

THANK YOU ALL says Peter Houseman

THERE are so many people I want to thank for making possible the match that is being staged here tonight on my behalf. First, the Chairman and Directors of Chelsea Football Club for awarding me this Testimonial, and Dave Sexton and my Chelsea team-mates for all they have done to help me in my career—as well as for playing for me this evening.

Sincere thanks also to Fulham for so readily agreeing to provide the opposition . . . to tonight's match officials . . . to my Testimonial Committee for all their work on my behalf . . . to the Chelsea ground and match staff . . . to the Victoria Sporting Club for arranging the reception to tonight's teams and special guests after the game . . . and to everyone who has helped in any way towards my Testimonial.

And, particularly, you Supporters of Chelsea and Fulham who have come along tonight. I thank you most sincerely, one and all.

Season 1973-74

CHELSEA

The mid-Seventies were something of a peak time for Chelsea testimonials. In November 1974, Peter Houseman – who played 343 times for the Blues – brought Fulham to the Bridge, with Chelsea winning 4-1. The local lad done good expressed his thanks to the fans, who would be shocked by his tragic death in a car crash less then three years later.

Tuesday 6 November

Fulham

Peter Houseman's Testimonial
Kick-off 7.45 pm

OFFICIAL PROGRAMME

10p

March 1965: As a one-night Cup Final centre-forward, Eddie McCreadie scores one of the finest solo goals ever seen at Stamford Bridge. At the end of an 80-yard run he pushes the ball past Leicester City goalkeeper Gordon Banks—and it's the goal that brought the League Cup to Chelsea.

Season 1973-74

CHELSEA

Wednesday 1 May

Manchester United

Kick-off 7 p.m.

OFFICIAL PROGRAMME

10p

EDDIE McCREADIE—THIS IS YOUR LIFE

CAPTAIN OF CHELSEA, EDDIE LEADS OUT THE BLUES.

CHELSEA'S MOST-CAPPED PLAYER —23 TIMES BY SCOTLAND.

THE DAY IN APRIL 1970 WHEN WE BROUGHT HOME THE F.A. CUP.

EDDIE'S 400th FIRST-TEAM GAME FOR CHELSEA—AT NORWICH LAST APRIL.

The following May, Eddie McCreadie's testimonial was against Manchester United at the Bridge, and it was the visitors who won 2-1. A fine full-back, one of his most famous moments as a player came when he played as an emergency forward and scored a wonder goal against Leicester to win us the League Cup in 1965. A year after his tribute match, he returned for an all-too-short stint as manager.

MY THANKS TO YOU ALL

By Eddie McCreadie

I WOULD like to thank everyone who has helped me in my career as a Chelsea player, and especially the Club for awarding me a Testimonial which began last season and is completed with the playing of tonight's match.

I thank Manager Dave Sexton and the Chelsea Players, past and present, who have contributed so much to the success I have achieved in the game—and here I must also mention Trainers Harry and Norman Medhurst and the Club Doctors for giving McCreadie so much of their time, patience and understanding in the treatment room.

To Tommy Docherty and Manchester United my special thanks for coming to play for me at Stamford Bridge tonight. I often wonder how, and where, my career would have developed if Tommy had not brought me down from Scottish football to Chelsea twelve years ago. I shall always be grateful to him for that first big step up the ladder.

Sincere thanks also to my Testimonial Committee for all they have done on my behalf. And to Chelsea fans I would like to say a very special "thank you" for your support all the time I have been with the Club, and particularly for coming along tonight.

Thank You All

says John

SINCE I came into football, I have always felt it a privilege and pleasure to play in Testimonial matches, both here and on other grounds, but I find it hard to realise that tonight others are playing for me. Hard, because it seems only a short time ago that I was a little lad of fifteen reporting, white-faced and nervous, at the training ground on my first day as a Chelsea junior.

Hundreds of people — no, I should say thousands because they must include the Chelsea fans—have helped shape my career since that day, and here I would like to mention a few names. First, my **Father**, always a source of good advice and encouragement from the time I first put foot to ball. There was **Dick Foss**, then Chelsea's Youth Manager, who took over from Dad when I arrived here and did a great "moulding" job on me. He decided I would never make a winger and switched me to the middle of the field. **Tommy Docherty** gave my teenage confidence a mighty boost when he blooded me in the first team at seventeen, and when Tommy left Stamford Bridge his successor, **Dave Sexton**, produced a team that was to achieve more than any previous Chelsea side.

I am grateful to them all for the varying influences they had on my career, and at the same time I would like to thank everyone at The Bridge —**Directors, Players, Training Staff, Office and Ground Staff, and Supporters**— for the help they have given me over the years.

With tonight's proceedings very much in mind, my special thanks go to **Arsenal Football Club**, their Manager, **Bertie Mee**, and their **Players** for so promptly accepting the invitation to provide the opposition in the main match, and to the **Top Ten** and **London Broadcasting** teams, who are presenting a novel "warm-up" match.

I would like to express sincere appreciation to the members of my **Testimonial Committee** for their efforts towards tonight's match and other events on my behalf. In fact, my thanks to everyone who has helped to promote my Testimonial, and particularly to you Supporters for coming along this evening.

After helping Chelsea to win the League Cup, the F.A. Cup and the European Cup-Winners' Cup, I can look back on the most successful times in the Club's history. I am proud to have played a part in those achievements, but I believe it is more important to look forward than back. I have always said my biggest aim is to play in a Chelsea side that wins the League Championship, and as long as I am kicking a football for a living, that will remain my No. 1 ambition.

At present, I know, we are in a state of team rebuilding, but I believe that within a season or two we can figure among the League challengers. And in thanking **Chelsea Football Club** for all they have done for John Hollins since he came here as a boy from school, I would like to wish our new Manager, **Ron Suart**, Coach Eddie **McCreadie** and the lads the best of fortune in our combined efforts to bring fresh success to the Club.

IT'S ALL SMILES AT 'CHUCKLES' OF COURSE

John and his wife Linda have recently opened a baby-and-children's wear shop in Sidcup High Street.

As you can see from our picture below, it's got style—like the owners. There are smiles, too (right), that match the name of the shop . . . from Linda, John and three-year-old son Christopher, who looks the perfect model for a business like this.

Among the most loyal and consistent players in Chelsea history, John Hollins – who sits fifth on our all-time appearances list with 592 – received a thoroughly deserved testimonial in November 1974. Arsenal were the visitors and the match ended 1-1. Commonly regarded as one of the nicest men in football, it came as no surprise to see the midfielder sing the praises of a long list of people in the programme.

Chelsea Footballers in Full Song. Chelsea football team, League Cup finalists, are seen recording a disc, "Blue is the colour."
Seen from left (front row) are: Steve Kember, Tommy Baldwin, Ron Harris, Mickey Droy (half hidden), John Dempsey, Alan Hudson, John Phillips and Peter Houseman; (back row) Paddy Mulligan, Charlie Cooke, John Hollins, Marvin Hinton, David Webb, Peter Osgood, Chris Garland and Eddie McCreadie.

Football at Old Trafford. F.A. Cup Final, Replay. Chelsea v Leeds. Jubilation from Chelsea's Peter Osgood after scoring the equalising Goal.

Peter Osgood
Born Feb 20th 1947 at Windsor, he was recommended to Chelsea by his uncle who is Bob Snashalli. He was signed as an amateur in March 1964 and he was signed as a pro on Sept. 1964. His first team debut was Dec 16th 1964 against Workington. He scored both goals in a 2 nil victory. (League Cup 5th round replay).
His League debut was Sept. 28th 1966 verses Newcastle. He broke his right leg at Blackpool on Oct 6th 1966. Which was the 3rd round League Cup.
England Caps, 4. Youth, 6. Under 23, 4. Full England, 3. Football League.
Chelsea appearance figures. Football League, 276 plus 3 subs. The F.A. Cup, 33. Charity Shield, 1. League Cup, 30. European Football, 25 plus 1 sub. Total 365 plus 4.
Goals. Football League, 103. F.A. Cup, 19. Charity Shield, 0. League Cup, 10. European Football, 16.

The 1970 F.A. Cup Final at Wembley: Chelsea v Leeds. Princess Margaret shakes hands with Peter Osgood (Chelsea) as she meets the team at Wembley.

Blues heroes do not come much bigger than Peter Osgood so it's little wonder an impressive crowd of more than 25,000 attended his testimonial in November 1975. The King of Stamford Bridge had departed the club midway through the 1973/74 campaign and turned out for a Chelsea Past XI featuring a certain George Best. We have to credit Playboy Bookmakers for an excellent piece of marketing in the programme dedicated to one of the original King's Road swingers. Incidentally, it was the current Chelsea team which won 4-3.

CHELSEA

OFFICIAL PROGRAMME 15p

SEASON 75-76

The Peter Osgood Testimonial Match Chelsea Past v Chelsea Present
Monday 24th November. Kick-off 7.45pm.

CHELSEA PAST

George Best – probably one of the world's best known footballing personalities. A tremendous crowd puller who it is hoped will make a successful return to British football. He played 361 league games (137 goals) for Manchester United and won 32 full caps (9 goals) for Northern Ireland.

HUTCH WRITES THE WORDS ABOUT HOSPITAL, HARRY, HUD.... AND HAPPINESS!

This time it's an arm that's in plaster... and Alan Hudson finds it just the place to sign his autograph.

A young visitor helps me pass the time in hospital.

Ian Hutchinson was the perfect foil for Osgood, who lined up alongside his good friend in an International XI which beat Chelsea 6-3 in November 1976. Injuries had brought Hutch's playing days to a premature end, but one of the shots from the treatment room showed it wasn't always so bad to be out of action!

HUTCH
MY GREAT TIMES AT CHELSEA

Maybe I'll last only ten minutes out there this afternoon. Perhaps I'll manage half a game. But I've promised myself I'd put in an appearance of some sort on the field—I owe it as a gesture to all the fellers who are playing for me here today and, most of all, I owe it to the Chelsea fans. They have always been tremendous to me, even at times when I've come back from one injury or another and been struggling.

When I look back on my seven seasons' football for Chelsea, I suppose everyone expects me to choose the 1970 F.A. Cup Final as the occasion I remember best. After all, getting a goal at Wembley and then having a part in the replay winner at Old Trafford was a bit special.

But the warmest glow is brought by the memory of the Chelsea crowd on a December day in 1972. The match was against Norwich and I was back in the first team after 22 months. The fans chanted my name all through the first half, when I was diabolical. Then I got a couple of goals in a 3-1 win and they chanted it for the rest of the game. I was practically in tears because of those supporters, and that was the game I shall always remember above all others.

I have no regrets about the way things have turned out. I have loved my years with Chelsea and the many great moments—set against every injury, every hour spent on the treatment table and every spell in hospital—have made it all worthwhile. To the club doctors, to former Trainer Harry Medhurst and his son Norman, my sincere thanks for all you did for me. I am only sorry I took up so much of your time in the treatment room.

I want to thank Chelsea for putting on today's game for me—the Directors, Manager Eddie McCreadie and this great new Chelsea team. I am so thrilled to see them heading back towards the First Division.

My thanks, too, to the Internationals XI, including many old Chelsea team-mates. It's great to see them all again. Thanks also to Tommy Docherty, today's "visiting manager"....and for his offer to bring Manchester United to The Bridge later this season to play another Testimonial for me.

It was Dave Sexton, of course, who brought me to Chelsea, and really I owe everything to him. Now I'll let you into a secret. Some months before Dave left Stamford Bridge, Tommy Docherty offered something like £200,000 for me to go to Old Trafford. Chelsea turned it down, but Tommy has remained a good pal, and I am very pleased to see him here today among many other familiar faces.

My thanks also to everyone who supported my Racenight held at Stamford Bridge recently....and may I mention that there are still a few tickets left for a stag night being run on my behalf at the Saxon Tavern, Bellingham, Kent on Monday night.

Ten days from now I will be back in hospital. It's a two-week, general tidying-up job on the right knee—they'll give it a good service—and when that's over I can start organising a new life away from football. Perhaps I'll take a pub somewhere in Surrey or Sussex; it would have to be one with a restaurant, because I love cooking.

That's for the future. Meanwhile, thanks again to everyone who has helped in any way towards today's Testimonial. It's one more Chelsea occasion I'll never forget.

Ian Hutchinson was talking to Albert Sewell, Chelsea Programme Editor.

But it isn't all agony—not when model Stephanie is around. You must admit she's better looking than Harry and Hud!

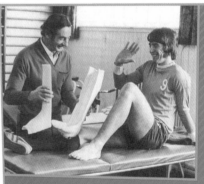

Ian Hutchinson TESTIMONIAL

OFFICIAL PROGRAMME 15p

CHELSEA V. INTERNATIONAL XI

Saturday, November 13th 1976. Kick-off 3 p.m.

Chelsea Testimonial Match for MARVIN HINTON

CHELSEA v CRYSTAL PALACE

FRIDAY, 7 MAY 1976
OFFICIAL PROGRAMME 10p
Kick-off 7.45 p.m.
SEASON 75-76

PRECEDED BY A MATCH (35 minutes each way)

MITCHAM ROYALS (Shirley & District League) Under 13 Game V REPRESENTATIVE SIDE (from the Independent League)

Kick-off 6.15 p.m.

JOHN BUMSTEAD TESTIMONIAL

CHELSEA v. REAL SOCIEDAD
TUESDAY, 25th AUGUST 1987
STAMFORD BRIDGE
KICK-OFF 7.45 p.m.
Souvenir Programme £1

From Everyone at Stamford Bridge . . . . .

GOOD LUCK, HUTCH

If football awarded medals for courage against adversity, Ian Hutchinson would have a showcase full of them. Words and pictures on other pages of this programme portray the career of one of the bravest players in the game's history, and after the years he spent battling for fitness—during which he underwent five operations and with another to come later this month—it was the saddest of days when, last February, Ian was told that because of the arthritic condition of his right knee his first-class career was over. For the same reason his attempt this season to carry on part-time with Dartford, in the Southern League, ended a few weeks ago.

As soon as it became known that Hutch's career at Stamford Bridge was over, Chelsea Football Club promised to do everything possible to stage a Testimonial worthy of the man. Being without a League fixture today has afforded us the opportunity to do so now, and we are delighted to make the stadium available to Ian for this afternoon's match. For Chelsea and our supporters it is a nostalgic occasion on which we welcome a number of our former stars back to Stamford Bridge together with other players who also readily agreed to give up a "day off" to turn out for Hutch.

Chelsea Football Club extend the warmest of welcomes to everyone associated with this Testimonial and, in thanking Ian Hutchinson for all he did on the field during his career here and acknowledging his particular example of courage that must serve as a beacon to everyone, we add sincere wishes for every success in the future he is now planning.

Tributes to John . . .

GEOFF HURST
'During my two years at Chelsea it was a great pleasure working with the players and particularly with John, as he is a terrific person to know. I wish him the very best for tonight — he really deserves a successful testimonial.'

JOHN NEAL
'I had the pleasure and privilege of managing John during my years in charge at Chelsea and it is a great honour for me to pay my personal tribute to him. He is what is commonly known as a "player's man" and a manager's dream. John was never given the credit he deserved and I hope that he will be rewarded tonight. The mind boggles at the thought of the midfield trio of John, Nigel Spackman and Michael Thomas and if one reflects the number of games they played together as a midfield trio, the results were amazing. Finally, from me personally, a big thank you to you, John, for the wonderful service you gave me and Chelsea overall. Good luck tonight.'

JOHN HOLLINS
'John Bumstead has been a great servant to Chelsea Football Club, both on and off the field. He is what we consider the quiet man of the team, always in the action, even though he has taken a lot of kicks through the years.

'If anyone sums up the revival of Chelsea, it's John Bumstead — he gives 100% and has a never-say-die attitude about his football. I do hope the supporters will come and support him this evening because he certainly deserves it.'

COLIN PATES
' "Bunners" and I have been mates since our first days at the Bridge and I must say I've enjoyed every minute of playing alongside him. He really is a great character — serious on the field, but always willing to look on the bright side and share a joke after the match.

'I can't imagine a Chelsea set-up without John — he is part-and-parcel of the set-up at the Bridge and I really hope that he gets the support he deserves for his testimonial.

'On behalf of the other players — have a good testimonial, John.'

Earlier that year, Blues stalwart Marvin Hinton's 344 appearances were recognised in a fixture against Crystal Palace which ended in a 1-1 draw. In 1987, John Bumstead – who with 409 appearances is our 11th-highest appearance-maker of all time – was equally deserving of a testimonial, with Real Sociedad the visitors in a 1-0 win for Chelsea.

" KERRY ALWAYS HAD A LOT OF TIME FOR FANS.

That's why he was so popular. That goes a long way. So many players these days don't care about the fans, but he always did. He's a smashing fella.

He did brilliantly for Chelsea, especially when we won the Second Division. His goals and his partnership with David Speedie were a main factor. He fully deserved his place in the England squad.

I'd love to be there tonight but I'm away with Wales Under 21s in Bulgaria. I'd love to play for Kerry and pull on the shirt again.

He was good in the air, had great strength and speed. He could make goals out of nothing in the box. He held defenders off. It was a pleasure to play in the same team. "

Joey Jones

In March 1995, the programme for Kerry Dixon's testimonial pictured some memorable moments from his Chelsea career and the tributes came from far and wide, including the man he shared the First Division Golden Boot with in the 1984/85 season, Gary Lineker. Also, things just wouldn't be right if Dennis Wise didn't take the opportunity to rib his former team-mate! Unsurprisingly, Dixon netted in a 5-1 win over Tottenham, something he had become very accustomed to over the years at Chelsea with a tally of 193 competitive goals.

" THE WIG!

When we used to go on away trips he would have the biggest suit carrier of anybody. It had all his awful gear in it.

The tie would be one colour, the jacket another, the trousers a third. Nothing matched. Everything was just thrown in. Then there was all his wigs. Kel was more worried about his hair than anything.

Not many people know this, but he had more hair on his chest than on his head. I know because I was his room partner.

We were Little and Large. He was a good room partner. We always had a good laugh. No-one messed about with us. They didn't dare, not after a couple of young lads tried it once. It was Damian and Jason, and when we found out we made sure that no-one would ever try it again. I'm afraid it's unrepeatable what we did on that occasion!

It was great playing with the Wig. I enjoyed every minute, as a player and as a friend. It's a pity he didn't go on just a bit longer because I'm sure he'd have broken Bobby Tambling's goalscoring record.

It's lovely to see him back tonight. He deserves a great turn out. "

Dennis Wise
Captain

KERRY DIXON
BENEFIT MATCH

Monday March 27, 1995   £1.50

Match Sponsors
WINDOWS
BY
Design

The Coral B...
Hotel & Re...
Trophy

Chelsea v Tottenham Hotspur

" KERRY DIXON WAS ONE OF THE TOP STRIKERS OF HIS GENERATION

I first remember hearing of him at Reading, but at Chelsea he quickly became part of a successful team and partnership with David Speedie, and was obviously very popular at the club.

We played together for England, and he scored some good goals, and I got to know him then.

He was a nice guy, typical striker, lived to score goals. For two or three years we were always fighting to be top scorer, and we shared the Golden Boot in my last season at Leicester. I was very pleased that they gave us one each, so we didn't have to cut it in half.

I'm delighted to be here tonight to support him, and just sad that the state of my foot stops me from playing. "

Gary Lineker

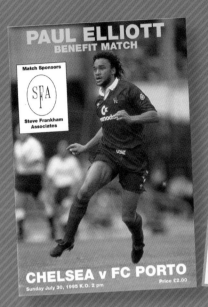

PAUL ELLIOTT
BENEFIT MATCH

Match Sponsors

SFA

Steve Frankham
Associates

CHELSEA v FC PORTO
Sunday July 30, 1995 K.O. 2 pm   Price £2.00

Letter from Downing Street

Dear Paul

I was extremely disappointed to learn of your terrible injury and understand the frustration you must feel at not being able to take a full part in Chelsea's progress this season.

I am sure I join all your colleagues and fans in wishing you best wishes for a full and speedy recovery.

Yours sincerely

John Major, September 1992

Later that year, Porto came to the Bridge for Paul Elliott's benefit match after his career was brought to a premature end through injury. It was just over a year after he had announced his retirement and he was full of praise for the club. As for tributes to the talented defender – well, they don't come from any higher than the Prime Minister, with Blues fan John Major penning a brief letter.

Paul's debut goal against Wimbledon (17/8/91) and his last goal against Oldham (21/12/91)

RESPECT

"NO AMOUNT OF words can justify my appreciation of your support since I stepped into Chelsea Football Club in July 1991, especially in the midst of my adversity on suffering my injury.

I've been in professional football for the best part of 14 years, and I know you judge people in adversity, not when things are going well. Your continual support has really touched me in a big way.

Playing for Chelsea has probably been the real highlight of my career. I played with a lot of pride. I hope that showed.

The day to day aspect of football is something that fills a massive void in anyone's life, and despite losing that I've been very fortunate to have still a very big involvement in the club. I'm extremely grateful.

So many people have been very good to me. I need more than a page here to express all my thanks.

But that is all I have. I must start with Ken Bates and Colin Hutchinson for their loyalty and for granting me this match. Glenn Hoddle has been fabulous to me. He's shown compassion and understanding, and is responsible for keeping me involved on the footballing side.

The Chelsea staff, Thresa Conneely, Carole Phair, Keith Lacy, Doug Johnson and everyone, too numerous to mention, have been hard working and supportive throughout. The stewards giving their services today I also thank.

I have had a great rapport with the players. Their loyalty has always been appreciated.

I hope everyone enjoys the day because we have fantastic opponents in FC Porto. They are the Portuguese champions and European Cup Winners Cup quarter-finalists. Had fate been kinder we would have met each other in the final. A warm welcome to them and a great deal of thanks to Bobby Robson for recognising the cause and making the great effort to bring his team over.

My Benefit committee including my old friend Melvyn Hartog has worked wonderfully for me. Steve Frankham has been the catalyst for all the superb organisation of my year. I am deeply indebted to him for his massive contribution. The highest praise I can pay him is that amongst so many great Chelsea supporters he stands head held high.

Nobody can do without families. I'm very fortunate to have the one I was born into. My mum, my brothers and sisters, they've all kept with me throughout the hardest times, and on this very special day I give a special welcome to my dad, Milton, who has come all the way from America to support me, and to Brian and June Little, wonderful parents of one of my best friends Barry Little, a former professional footballer who sadly died from a brain tumour less than a year ago at the tender age of 29.

David Dandy, one of the world's leading knee specialists, he described as the worst footballing injury he had ever seen. It forced my retirement, he has enabled me to regain the mobility at least to give me good quality of life. Thanks to him and to all the medical people at the various hospitals and here at the club who have treated me.

Then there's my old friend Mike Dove, my mentor since he was my coach when I was ten, and now coach at my Academy.

My old mate, The Spy, I could never forget him. Thanks for organising this superb programme.

Finally, a special woman who's been important to my rehabilitation. Eileen, thank you for your continuous support.

To all of you here today, be proud to be a part of Chelsea, the same as I am. A new era dawns, Ruud Gullit, Mark Hughes and a smashing new season. Keep supporting the boys.

Respect. *"*

Paul Elliott

3

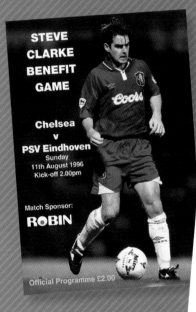

STEVE CLARKE BENEFIT GAME

Chelsea v PSV Eindhoven
Sunday
11th August 1996
Kick-off 2.00pm

Match Sponsor:

ROBIN

Official Programme £2.00

Another mid-Nineties testimonial was for Steve Clarke, with PSV Eindhoven the opponents in August 1996. The reliable full-back had joined the Blues in 1987 and would still have a key role to play in some of our cup triumphs during the latter part of the 20th century, finishing his Chelsea career with 421 appearances, which puts him eighth on our all-time list.

It was January 1987 and the only thing that felt like home was the weather! It was cold and snowing — if anyone had told me then, as I walked into a cold, damp portakabin to meet the players of Chelsea Football Club for the first time, that I would stay ten years and be rewarded with a testimonial match against a top European side, I would have laughed!

If they had then proceeded to tell me my team mates would include international players from Russia, Romania, Norway, Scotland Denmark, Eire, Wales, France, Italy and England, not forgetting a player-manager from Holland, I would have told them to seriously consider visiting a psychiatrist. However, here I am at the start of my testimonial season about to take part in such a game.

Having experienced the ups and downs of the last ten years with you, the supporters, I now consider myself to be in a position where I can say that I have Chelsea in my blood and no matter what the future holds for me, Chelsea Football Club will always be close to my heart.

There have been a few times in the last decade when things haven't gone as well as I would have liked, but I can honestly say that I never once felt as though the Chelsea support was turning against me. In fact the support I received when things were not going my way was the reason that I found the strength to dig deeper and find a way back to form, first team player and Player of the Year 1993/94. So from me, my wife Karen and children, Emma, John and Joseph to all you Chelsea supporters — THANK YOU for the last ten years, and for coming today to support my testimonial match.

I would like to take this opportunity to thank the board, Ken Bates, Matthew Harding, Colin Hutchinson and Yvonne Todd for allowing me to use the stadium for this match and for all the help and support they have given me in my Chelsea career.

Also, my sincere thanks to the Chelsea staff who have, voluntarily worked above heir duties to help organise my match even though they have had a busy summer coping with an increased workload, Carole, Michelle, Kim, Keith Lacey, Doug Johnson and everyone else who has helped in any way. A special mention for Thresa Conneely and

Gwyn Williams who have both been at the club longer than I have and who have always been there to help, advise and keep me on the right track over the past ten years.

Thank you to my Benefit Committee, Graham Bell for his drive and enthusiasm, Steve Frankham for his experience and guidance, Len Montague for his financial advise, Phil Smith — chairman — for putting it all together as if he had been doing it all his life, and to Sarah Bathard for being a great secretary because without her efficiency, all the work put in by my committee would have been wasted. Thanks also to Neil Barnett and Thruxton Press for doing an excellent job in putting this programme together.

I would also like to take this opportunity to welcome the players, officials and supporters of PSV Eindhoven and to thank them for their help in putting this game on today, especially Frank Arnesen and Ingrid van Osch. I hope PSV have a successful season both domestically and in Europe.

Finally, I hope you enjoy today's game and we, the players and management of Chelsea Football Club will endeavour to give you what you want from the coming season — stylish football, and a piece of silverware.

Best Wishes

Steve Clarke

Steve Clarke is the perfect professional in an age when loyalty is not encouraged by the structures within the game. The structures encourage you to move around. But Steve has put ten years into Chelsea Football Club. There can be few players around more loyal or more professional.

As the PFA delegate he has always acted with dignity, being able to see the club side of any argument as well as the players'. I must say, though, that he hasn't been to see me lately! He's obviously been thinking about today! And I bet he reckons he's won the football pools. It's only going to cost you a lemonade, Steve. The very best of luck to you and you family.

Colin Hutchinson
Managing Director

I don't understand. The way Steve played last year, I thought he should have been chosen to play in the Scotland national team. He is the kind of player that every coach needs, reliable, works hard. He gives 200 per cent.

I wish him a very nice day today, a lot of crowd, a nice evening, and then a very good season.

Ruud Gullit
Chelsea player-manager
Chelsea 1995-now and Holland

Steve with wife Karen and children Emma, John and Joe.

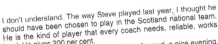

ZOLA MESSAGE

After all the great moments we've been through together, it was not the right thing to leave the way I did. But that is football. I couldn't give Chelsea fans your proper farewell, and you supporters couldn't do the same to me.

When I left, it happened quite suddenly. I wasn't expecting it, and I've had so many fans coming over to watch the games in Cagliari it's been astonishing.

This game means so much to me. What Chelsea is doing is fantastic because they've got a very busy schedule, and to find the time to organise a game like this is wonderful. I won't be able to say thank you enough.

I've had a lot of fun and a lot of good fortune with Chelsea. The best way I can say hello again, and goodbye properly, is to play in front of you one more time, and hopefully give you some magic.

Gianfranco Zola.

WHEN YOU READ THIS FRANCO, DON'T START CRYING!'

CHELSEA GREATS REMEMBER GIANFRANCO

It feels appropriate to end our section on testimonial programmes with one of the most popular players ever to have worn the Blues shirt. Gianfranco Zola was, quite simply, a genius and what he meant to Chelsea supporters was evident from the mammoth crowd of over 38,000 for his tribute match in August 2004. By far the glossiest of any of the publications reproduced here, there simply isn't room to include all the tributes that were printed in the A4 programme for a man who will forever be remembered fondly by those who saw him play.

JOHN TERRY

Hitchy [Kevin Hitchcock] used to look after me when I was a kid coming through, and as he and Franco were good mates, I started playing golf with Zola.

I always used to say publicly I beat him, but to be honest there were times when he was all over me – he was such a perfectionist. He took three hours more than anyone to play his round. If he sliced his drive, he'd be there for ten minutes practicing his swing. He'd take 15 minutes for every putt. I've never met anyone like him.

As I came through, he took an interest in me. I was often marking him in training and if the ball went dead, he'd always spend two or three minutes with me, laughing or joking. He's the best I've played with. Everyday the guy was unbelievable. Obviously there were so many special moments in games and goals everyone can remember, but working with him everyday was a lesson because he was such a perfectionist. It wasn't just the free-kicks he used to practice that are always mentioned, it was things like bringing the ball down time and again, perfecting his touch. And he had the best touch ever. That's what I learnt most from him.

Zola always had time for people. Seeing how he did that, and how people responded, has helped make me the way I am with fans. You only hear good things about Franco. But for all of us who worked with him he's still a midget! The best one ever.

ZOLA taught John Terry skills both on and off the pitch

RUUD never imagined Zola would bring so much to the club

RUUD GULLIT

I knew Gianfranco's qualities, but I never expected so much. I expected him to do well, but to become a legend like he has is a real – and welcome – surprise.

It's always difficult for foreigners to adapt in new countries, especially for Italians who don't have a history of going abroad to play. Other nations, like the Dutch, are used to it.

So, at the beginning it was like: let's see how he adapts himself. And he did it remarkably well. I think it was important there were other Italians there for him, Luca (Gianluca Vialli) and Roberto (Di Matteo), while Dan Petrescu and myself had played in Italy.

The Mark Hughes and Gianfranco Zola partnership was incredible. At the beginning I thought it was Luca who must play, but Luca was not in good condition – he kept getting injured. Mark and Franco made a great partnership.

It was a great time. We won things and learnt things. For foreigners it is always amazing to see how the English celebrate. I remember one Christmas when Dennis and everyone insisted that Franco take his first alcohol, and tried to force it down him. It is always a culture shock to celebrate with the English. Franco coped very well. He just said no!

To him I'd like to say 'thank you' for the great moments we had with each other. I wish you well with your family, and I hope to see you in football management one day.

THE *SIXTIES*

A decade of ups and downs led to one of the club's most memorable achievements. While star players like Greaves, Tambling and Osgood were making names for themselves, the quality of the programme was getting attention too...

There were no discernible changes to the matchday programme in the 1960/61 season, a campaign marked by one young man's incredible achievement. Jimmy Greaves scored a club-record 43 goals in all competitions, 41 of them coming in the league. And all this in a campaign during which he turned just 21 years of age having already become the youngest player to reach 100 league goals. Standout games were frequent as he scored three hat-tricks and two four-goal hauls, as well as netting five in a 7-1 win over West Brom at the Bridge. Sadly, his Chelsea playing days finished at the end of the season, with his final game a 4-3 win over Nottingham Forest. The victory was a bittersweet one for fans who saw Greaves net all four goals before his move to AC Milan. In spite of the loss of such a hugely talented player, there were more bright, young stars making their mark in the first team, including Terry Venables whose efforts were recognised in the programme. At the start of the following campaign, Ted Drake devoted the majority of his column to Greaves.

THE CHELSEA FOOTBALL & ATHLETIC CO. LTD.

FOUNDED 1905

CLUB COLOURS:
Shirts: Royal Blue (White Collars), Shorts: White,
Stockings; White; Red, White and Blue Tops.

Registered Address:
STAMFORD BRIDGE GROUNDS, FULHAM ROAD, LONDON, S.W.6
[FUL 5545]

PRESIDENT: The Right Hon. Earl Cadogan, M.C.

BOARD OF DIRECTORS:
J. H. Mears (CHAIRMAN), C. J. Pratt (VICE-CHAIRMAN),
L. J. Mears, L. R. Withey, J. B. Mears.

MANAGER: E. J. Drake.

SECRETARY: J. Battersby   TRAINER: H. Medhurst

League Champions
1955

F.A. Youth
Cup 1960 and 1961

TED DRAKE CALLING . . .

THIS is the first opportunity I have had of speaking to you this season and I want you to know that, as always, I shall be perfectly frank in these articles.

During the summer this Club suffered the misfortune of losing one of the greatest players England has known for a decade, Jimmie Greaves. You can imagine our feelings when this lad, whom we had brought along from his earliest days, was likely to go from us. Everything that we could possibly do within the rules was done, but after a very anxious time for all parties concerned, Jimmie made his final decision. I am sure you will all join me in wishing him well in his new life. This great little fellow will always remain in our hearts and there will always be a place for him here should he wish to return to us.

We are now, therefore, in a position of having to find a replacement. How does one find a substitute for perfection? I think even England will find this a difficult matter. Having found and trained this lad, I now have to set about the task of finding another, whether ready-made or otherwise. Efforts to obtain class players who would fill the gap are being made and we shall continue our quest.

We extend a welcome to Frank Upton, who joined us before the season commenced. I know that he and all the other lads can count on your support throughout the months to come.

3

A MESSAGE FROM THE CHAIRMAN

SINCE our last Home Match, I am sure you all know that Ted Drake, our Manager for nine years has left us. First let me say how grateful everyone at Stamford Bridge, and I am sure this includes all of you, is to Ted for the honours he has brought us in the past, especially in our Jubilee Year when, besides winning the Football League Championship, all our other teams won League honours and many Cup competitions besides.

But since then, although our Football Combination and Youth Teams have continued to collect honours our First XI has had no success and that is what we want to remedy now. This means that we all have to make a very great effort and when I say " all " I include you, our loyal supporters.

The Directors are all taking on more responsibility and you may not see all of us at Home Matches in the future.

We intend to appoint a full-time Chief Scout who will organize an efficient scouting system. Tom Docherty has been given full authority to control the playing side of our Club and I appeal to all of you to do as you did in our Championship Year, that is to give our players your full support, particularly vocally, in both home and away matches.

Your support means everything to all of us and I know I can rely on you to help us to get our Club out of its present precarious position.

JOE MEARS.

3

The first managerial change in over a decade took place not long into the 1961/62 campaign. After a slow start, and the arrival of Tommy Docherty as player-coach in September, Ted Drake parted company with the club a month later with Docherty stepping into the hotseat. The influence of the new arrival was evident from his playing debut, as the Blues romped to a 6-1 victory over Sheffield United. Chairman Joe Mears addressed the fans in the programme for our home game against Leicester City in October, thanking Drake for his service and urging the fans to get behind Docherty. However, as the Doc imposed his character on the squad as manager, fortunes on the pitch dwindled and we were relegated after finishing bottom.

SHEFFIELD UNITED 1961-62

Standing: B. Richardson, G. Summers, A. Hodgkinson, T. Hoyland. Back: D. Shiels, W. Hodgson, K. Kettleborough, J. Simpson, G. Shaw. Seated: L. Allchurch, W. Russell, C. Coldwell, J. Shaw, D. Pace, R. Simpson.

8

scew

CHELSEA 6

Colours: Shirts: Royal Blue (White Collars). Shorts: White.
Stockings: White: Red, White and Blue Tops.

1. (Goal)
Bonetti

2. (Right-back)   3. (Left-back)
Sillett (J.)   **Harris**

4. (Right-half)   5. (Centre-half)   6. (Left-half)
Venables   **Scott**   **Mortimore**
MORTIMORE   DOCHERTY

7. (Outside-right) 8. (Inside-right) 9. (Centre-forward) 10. (Inside-left) 11. (Outside-left)
Brabrook   **Cliss**   **Bridges**   **Tambling**   **Harrison**
(1)   BLUNSTONE   (2)   (3)

Referee: Linesmen:
Mr. H. G. NEW   Mr. F. E. BURLING
(Havant, Hants.)   (Cambridge)
                                   [Red Flag]
                                   Mr. W. J. PARADISE
                                   (Frome)
                                   [Yellow Flag]

HODGSON   KETTLEBOROUGH (1)
Simpson   **Hodgson**   **Pace**   **Russell**   **Allchurch**
11. (Outside-left) 10. (Inside-left) 9. (Centre-forward) 8. (Inside-right) 7. (Outside-right)

Summers   **Shaw (J.)**   **Richardson**
6. (Left-half)   5. (Centre-half)   4. (Right-half)

Shaw (G.)   **Coldwell**
3. (Left-back)   2. (Right-back)

Hodgkinson
1. (Goal)

SHEFFIELD UNITED 1

Colours—Shirts: Red and White Vertical Stripes. Shorts: Black.
Stockings: Black with Red and White tops.

9

ATTENDANCE: 22,026

The Doc's boys bounce back up, 1962/63

For all the disappointment of the previous campaign, the new style of flowing football introduced by Tommy Docherty meant the Blues had too much for Division Two opponents and we bounced back to the top flight at the first time of asking. Bobby Tambling was proving more than capable of filling the hole left by Jimmy Greaves as he netted 37 goals in all competitions. Docherty's eye for a player was also evident as he signed Eddie McCreadie from East Stirling and the stylish left-back became an integral cog in the Chelsea machine, complementing Ken Shellito in the other full-back position perfectly. The matchday programme for the November win over Norwich welcomed McCreadie, along with Tommy Knox and Jimmy Mulholland from the same club. The cover was now featuring match action shots which were explained inside.

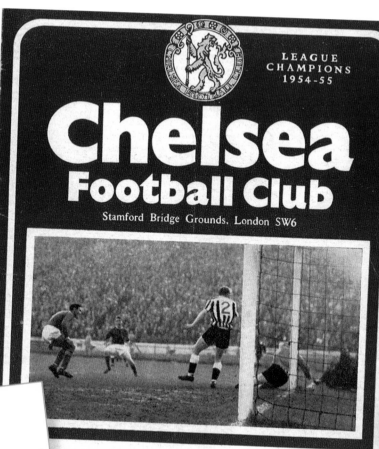

Chelsea
Football Club
Stamford Bridge Grounds, London SW6

LEAGUE CHAMPIONS 1954-55

TBALL LEAGUE—DIVISION II   SEASON 1962-63

CHELSEA 2

v

NORWICH CITY 0

lay, 17th November, 1962   Kick-off 3 p.m.

al Programme **6**D   The right of admission to grounds is reserved.

Three from East Stirling

EDDIE McCREADIE was the first of our three recent signings from East Stirling. Born in Glasgow, he joined us just before the end of last season and filled the regular spot of left-back in our League team from the start of this campaign until his injury a month ago.

During the close season TOMMY KNOX, who also hails from Glasgow, made the same journey. Still on National Service in Germany, he had his first League game in our colours against Swansea Town on September 22nd.

The third player to make the journey was JIMMY MULHOLLAND a month ago. A hat-trick from centre-forward in a friendly game against Hendon followed, and he had his League baptism a fortnight ago against Newcastle United.

8

OUR FRONT COVER

Albert Murray heads our third goal in the game against Newcastle United.

Come May, all was still to play for at the top of Division Two, with Stoke and Sunderland our closest rivals for one of the two promotion spots. We hosted the Potters in our third-from-last game, but it was the visitors who prevailed by a goal to nil to put themselves in pole position with two matches left. The programme would certainly have been a big seller, with 48-year-old Stanley Matthews in the Stoke team. As editor at the time Albert Sewell explained, "I would phone up the club in the week and if Matthews was playing I would add up to 10,000 on the print run." A huge crowd of over 66,000 – our biggest of the season by more than 20,000 up to that point – turned out. Unsurprisingly, Matthews was pictured on the opposition pages and the programme also featured action shots from a 2-2 draw at Leeds, while The Talk of Stamford Bridge discussed the various permutations as the season reached a climax. There was also a novel behind-the-scenes feature, helping fans feel closer to the club.

Behind the Scenes at STAMFORD BRIDGE

Photographs by RICHARD TRAUBE

Below: "Track-suit Manager" Tommy Docherty comes straight in from training to discuss the next day's Combination match with reserve-team trainer Dave Sexton. Then for a shower with the lads . . .

Above: Trainer Harry Medhurst marks up the latest injury on his medical-room wall chart. He records every player's injuries, treatment, vaccinations, jabs, etc.

Below: Youth-team Manager Dick Foss congratulates one of our up-and-coming lads—John Cowen—on keeping his goal intact throughout England's recent International Youth Tournament triumph.

Top: Who's for win bonus this week? Secretary John Battersby (standing) and Assistant-secretary Alan Bennett cast an eye over the players' pay ledger.

JUST THE TONIC WE NEEDED!

TOMMY HARMER

After that win at Sunderland, we join Bobby Tambling and Frank Upton (back to camera) in the toast: "Here's to the First Division".

STANLEY MATTHEWS
The "Prince of the Potteries".

WHO GOES UP?

Three games to go, six clubs still chasing two promotion places . . . and we kick off today with only one thing certain: if we take five points from these remaining matches — yes, a tall order but what a target to aim at! — we must go up.

Four could be enough; five would leave no doubts. These are the games to come for the clubs concerned, as at the start of today's programme:—

CHELSEA (3)
Home (2): *v.* Stoke and Portsmouth.
Away (1): *v.* Sunderland.

OUR BIGGEST CROWD (66,199) SINCE APRIL 1960 . . .

Chelsea Football Club
Stamford Bridge Grounds, London S.W.6
FOOTBALL LEAGUE—DIVISION II   SEASON 1962-63
CHELSEA 7
v
PORTSMOUTH 0
Tuesday, 21st May, 1963   Kick-off 7.30 p.m.
Official Programme   6d

IT'S SEVEN AND UP!

Promotion was sealed in emphatic style with a 7-0 thrashing of Portsmouth at the Bridge, Bobby Tambling scoring four of our goals. Quite aptly, the striker featured on the cover of the programme, in action during the vital 1-0 win over Sunderland four days previously. The goal-scoring hero of that game was Tommy Harmer, who was pictured on The Talk of Stamford Bridge and there was also an image of Tambling and Frank Upton celebrating after the victory.

PEN PICTURES OF WORKINGTON

IAN OWER (Goalkeeper): Signed by Workington from St. Johnstone in February 1963. Has never missed a game since. Height 6 ft.; weight 12st.

JOHN OGILVIE (Right-back): Local boy who had a spell with Blackpool. Began as centre-forward, but switched to the defence last season. Height 6 ft.; weight 11st. 9lbs.

JOHN LUMSDEN (Left-back): Signed in February 1962 from Aston Villa as a centre-half, but switched effectively to full-back by Ken Furphy. English Youth International. Height 6 ft.; weight 12st. 2lbs.

DIXIE HALE (Right-half): Signed during the close season from Barrow where he spent two seasons. Previously with Swansea Town who signed him from Shamrock Rovers. Born Waterford. Height 5 ft. 8 ins.; weight 11st.

THE MATCH AT WORKINGTON

Wednesday, 25th November.
Drew with WORKINGTON 2-2. Half-time: winning 2-1.

Workington—Ower; Ogilvie, Lumsden; Hale, Brown, Burkinshaw; Lowes, Carr, Napier, Moran, Martin.
Scorers: Carr, Napier.

Chelsea—Bonetti; Hinton, McCreadie; Watson, Mortimore, Harris (R.); Fascione, Graham, Bridges, McCalliog, Houseman.

Scorer: Bridges 2.
Referee: Mr. K. Dagnall (Bolton).
Attendance: 18,000.

BOBBY BROWN (Centre-half): Longest serving player with Workington, having joined them from Motherwell in 1956. Began as a full-back. Holds the club's appearance record. Height 5 ft. 11 ins.; weight 11st.

KEITH BURKINSHAW (Left-half): Another long-serving player who joined Workington from Liverpool in 1957. At £3,000 he is the club's costliest player. A fully qualified F.A. coach. Height 6 ft.; weight 12st. 4lbs.

BARRY LOWES (Outside-right): Began his career with Barrow and was with Blackpool before Workington signed him. A speedy raider with 11 goals in 21 games last season. Height 5 ft. 7 ins.; weight 11st. 7lbs.

DAVE CARR (Inside-right): Signed from Darlington with Ken Furphy two seasons ago and has led the goalscoring list each season. Height 5 ft. 9 ins.; weight 11st. 7lbs.

KIT NAPIER (Centre-half): Went straight from school to Blackpool where he spent three seasons. Transferred to Preston, from whom Workington signed him during the close season. At 20 is the youngest player in the side. Height 6 ft.; weight 12st.

JIMMY MORAN (Inside-left): Clever ball player with an eye for an opening. Played previously for Leicester City, Northampton, Norwich and Darlington. Joined Workington at the beginning of last season. Height 5 ft. 7 ins.; weight 10st. 10lbs.

GEOFF MARTIN (Outside-left): Strong, go-ahead winger who went to Borough Park from Carlisle plus £3,000 in exchange for Frank Kirkup. Previously served Chesterfield, Leeds and Darlington. Height 5 ft. 10 ins.; weight 11st. 7lbs.

FOOTBALL LEAGUE—DIVISION III
(Up to and including Saturday, 12th December)

		HOME						AWAY					Goals		
	P	W	D	L	F	A	W	D	L	F	A	Pts		F	A
Grimsby	23	9	4	0	25	11	3	4	3	16	15	32			
Bristol R.	23	9	3	0	34	11	2	6	4	15	21	31			
Mansfield	24	8	3	2	32	19	5	5	1	17	20	30			
Bristol City	24	7	3	2	32	11	4	4	4	21	23	29			
Brentford	24	9	2	1	27	10	3	1	6	18	23	27			
Carlisle	24	6	3	2	23	11	4	5	4	14	15	28			
Gillingham	24	8	4	0	27	5	3	2	7	11	22	28			
WORK'T'N	22	7	4	1	20	8	3	3	4	18	26	27			
Peterboro'	24	8	2	3	37	24	3	2	6	13	23	26			
Hull City	23	6	3	3	23	13	3	5	5	16	18	24			
Bournem'th	23	6	4	2	22	12	2	4	5	17	22	24			
Shrewsbury	23	7	3	1	28	12	3	3	7	13	24	24			
Reading	24	7	4	1	27	14	2	8	11	22	24				
Q.P.R.	22	8	2	2	26	14	1	4	5	9	22	24			
Southend	24	7	3	1	22	11	3	0	10	12	24	23			
Scunthorpe	24	4	5	2	21	14	3	3	7	13	20	22			
Watford	22	5	4	1	20	8	3	1	8	15	22	22			
Oldham	24	5	2	5	20	20	2	4	6	8	20	20			
Exeter	22	4	3	4	14	9	2	4	6	14	19	19			
Luton	24	6	4	1	14	16	3	3	6	11	26	19			
Port Vale	23	1	4	6	10	16	2	5	5	12	17	14			
Barnsley	24	3	4	3	15	10	0	2	10	12	37	14			
Colchester	24	3	3	7	13	20	2	3	7	12	37	14			
Walsall	24	5	1	6	18	20	1	1	10	8	31	14			

6

CHELSEA 2

Colours—Shirts: Royal Blue. Shorts: Royal Blue. Stockings: White.

(Goal)
BONETTI
1

(Right-back)   (Left-back)
HINTON   **McCREADIE**
2   3

(Right-half)   (Centre-half)   (Left-half)
VENABLES   **MORTIMORE**   **UPTON**
4   5   6

(Outside-right) (Inside-right) (Centre-forward) (Inside-left) (Outside-left)
MURRAY   **GRAHAM**   **OSGOOD**   **McCALLIOG**   **KNOX**
7   8   (2) 9   10   11

Referee:
Mr. H. G. NEW
(Havant)

Linesmen:
Mr. P. K. BYFORD
(Witham)
(Red Flag)

Mr. E. L. PRESS
(Staines)
(Yellow Flag)

11   10   9   8   7
MARTIN   **MORAN**   **NAPIER**   **CARR**   **LOWES**
(Outside-left)   (Inside-left)   (Centre-forward)   (Inside-right)   (Outside-right)

6   5   4
BURKINSHAW   **BROWN**   **HALE**
(Left-half)   (Centre-half)   (Right-half)

3   2
LUMSDEN   **OGILVIE**
(Left-back)   (Right-back)

1
OWER
(Goal)

WORKINGTON 0

Colours—Shirts: Red. Shorts: White. Stockings: Red and White.

7

ATTENDANCE: 7,936

IN OFF THE POST

Your letters should be of not more than 150 words and addressed to "In off the Post", Chelsea F.C., Fulham Road, London, S.W.6.

LETTERS OPENED BY PROGRAMME EDITOR, ALBERT SEWELL

LEAGUE CUP "GHOSTS"

I WOULD like to say how disgusted I was with the two League Cup attendances at the Bridge this season.

Surely it is not worth the club entering the competition if the home ties are going to be so poorly supported, and also it cannot be very encouraging for the players to perform in the ghost-like atmosphere of these games.

What about it, you Chelsea fans who did not turn up for these games? If you want the boys to win the trophies, COME AND SUPPORT THEM!

R. Creese.
7, Lidding Road,
Kenton, Middx.

SO POOR . . .

AS the attendances at the League Cup games at Stamford Bridge have been so poor, why not a 3 p.m. kick-off on Wednesdays? I am sure that this would at least double the attendance.

A. Sturton.
3, Crossways,
Thorpe Lea, Egham,
Surrey.

TIME CHECK

SPURS and Arsenal have clocks installed at their grounds, and we would like to see one on our ground as a most modern club should have one.

Ray & Steve.
21, Glenrosa Street,
Fulham, S.W.6

● Something else for us to bear in mind when the new stand is built.

LOUDER SUPPORT AWAY

I HAVE found more vocal support away from home because there is not the atmosphere at the Bridge for shouting for the Blues.

If everyone capable of cheering would shout powerfully at every home match (especially early on in the game), then Chelsea will know they have supporters on the terraces and Chelsea would be inspired by such support.

Mick Greenaway.
77, Evans Road,
Grove Park, London, S.E.6

COULD you print the official attendance for the League Cup game at Millwall in 1960-61?

G. Thompson.
13, Paragon Bldgs.,
Rodney Road,
London, S.E.17

● Answer: 15,007 and we won 7-1.

COMMENT FROM CUMBERLAND

MY friends and I went to see Chelsea play Workington in the League Cup, and we were very impressed with Peter Bonetti's performance. He surely must be in line for a full cap soon, and with youngsters of the calibre of George Graham, Jimmy McCalliog and Peter Houseman, the club can look forward to a fine future.

Brian Hay.
14, Rydal Street,
Carlisle.

CUP CHARGES

HAVING been a season-ticket holder for the past four years, I feel it is iniquitous that I should have to pay extra to watch reserve and Youth Cup matches.

Being a season-ticket holder, one should be entitled to the privilege of watching matches like the Southern Junior Floodlight Cup and perhaps Junior Cup matches.

This concession would, I'm sure, attract more potential season-ticket holders to these minor games.

A. C. McElroy.
74, Kingsbury Drive,
Old Windsor,
Windsor, Berks.

● Season-tickets admit to all league games (i.e. Football League and Football Combination) played at Stamford Bridge. In accordance with the regulations of Cup competitions, season-tickets do not apply and in addition clubs share the "gate" receipts, usually on a 50/50 basis.

JUNIOR SONGWRITERS

ALL the people who write to you have been Grown-ups, and we think the children should get a chance.

So here is a song which should be easy to pick up for everybody, sung to the tune of "Hello Dolly":—

Come on, Chelsea,
Well come on, Chelsea,
It's so nice to have you back in
scoring form,
You're looking swell, Chelsea,
We can tell, Chelsea,
You're still scoring, we're still roaring,
You're still going strong,
Don't make us sad, Chelsea,
Make us glad, Chelsea,
We still like your Royal Blue and
your White,
So score some goals, Chelsea,
Make the net full of holes, Chelsea,
Chelsea don't you ever lose a game,
HOORAY.

M. Winnett & P. Slattery.
17, Wontner Road,
Upper Tooting, S.W.17

TALE FROM VIENNA

I AM a life-long Chelsea supporter back to the days of George Hilsdon, Ben Warren and company, and a regular at Stamford Bridge until my removal to the West Country. You may therefore be interested to hear of an incident in Vienna while I was on holiday.

I happened to be buying the English newspapers at a time kiosk when I was asked by another English visitor whether I knew the Chelsea result of the previous Saturday. It was the only result I did remember — Chelsea 2, Leeds 0 — and then found myself talking to another Chelsea supporter of many years' standing. Once Chelsea, always Chelsea. My only regret is that I cannot watch you these days.

W. Tubb.
"Apple Tree Inn,"
West Pennard,
Glastonbury, Somerset.

OUR BEST 22?

OUR recent fine win over Everton set me thinking of the best players we have seen down the years at Chelsea since I have been a regular supporter since the 1948-49 season during which time I've missed only two home first team matches of all types — so I pick from this period two teams)

How about these teams:—

1: Bonetti; Shellito, McCreadie; Armstrong, Harris, Mitchell; Parsons, Bentley, Lawton, Venables, Blunstone.

2: Robertson (W. G.); Hinton, Hughes; Hollins, Wicks, Harris (R.); Brabrook, Greaves, Smith (R.) or Bridges, Walker, Tambling.

S. R. Rhodes.
8, Shrubland Grove,
Worcester Park, Surrey.

Keep this Coupon

It may help you to obtain a ticket for the F.A. Cup Final.
5

10   11

Juniors aid quest for cup glory, 1964/65

The 1963/64 campaign saw the club fully reaping the rewards of its long-term investment in the Chelsea Juniors scheme, with no less than 15 homegrown products playing for the side known as Docherty's Diamonds. A fifth-place finish in our first season back in the top flight was hugely impressive and better was to follow next term as we won our first major cup competition, triumphing in the League Cup in 1965. It was en route to lifting the trophy that a true Blues legend made his debut. Peter Osgood scored two goals in his senior bow in a quarter-final replay against Workington Town at the Bridge and a star was born. As you can see in the programme from that match, fans were now interacting with the club through a regular letters page, and a full rundown of players was given in the opposition pages.

Our place in the final came courtesy of a 4-3 aggregate win over Aston Villa in the semis. The programme for the second leg contained match action from the first encounter at Villa Park, played in sub-zero conditions, while Johnny Boyle received credit for an impressive debut.

LET'S HOPE FOR BETTER CONDITIONS TONIGHT

Snow . . . sand . . . mud. These pictures show the treacherous surface on which the first leg of this League Cup semi-final was played at Villa Park. Above: John Hollins at full stretch in an effort to block a centre by Villa outside-left MacLeod.

(*Photographs by courtesy of the "Birmingham Post".*)

An over-the-bar header by Hateley from a corner. Chelsea men (in the all-white strip) are, from left to right, Bobby Tambling, John Hollins, John Mortimore and Ron Harris.

5

A DEBUT TO REMEMBER

John Boyle, our 18-year-old Youth team captain, made his first-team debut in the League Cup semi-final at Villa Park – and marked it with a 25-yard shot that gave us a 3-2 lead on the first leg.

Boyle, a Scot from Motherwell, joined our junior section in August, 1962, and signed as a professional last September.

LEAGUE CHAMPIONS 1954-55

CHELSEA

FOOTBALL CLUB

Stamford Bridge Grounds
LONDON SW6

FOOTBALL LEAGUE CUP FINAL - FIRST LEG SEASON 1964-65

Monday, 15th March, 1965

CHELSEA 3
v
LEICESTER CITY 2
(HOLDERS)

KICK-OFF 7.30 p.m.

OFFICIAL PROGRAMME — SIXPENCE

THE FOOTBALL LEAGUE CUP
® Winners
1960-61 Aston Villa
1961-62 Norwich City
1962-63 Birmingham City
1963-64 Leicester City

NO GOALS FOR HOLDERS IN SECOND LEG:

We went into the second leg of last week's League Cup Final at Leicester leading 3-2, and this was one of the saves by Peter Bonetti that prevented City, the holders, getting the goal they desperately needed.

BLUES' TITLE DOUBLE

The 1965 League Cup final pitched us against Leicester City, who we beat 3-2 in a thrilling first leg at the Bridge. The programme for that match featured some interesting behind-the-scenes imagery and also showcased Bobby Tambling's goal-scoring exploits in the competition. However, neither Tambling or any of his team-mates found the target in the second leg as a goalless draw was enough to win us the trophy.

A goalless night means the trophy is ours. Mr. Joe Richards, President of the Football League, greets Terry Venables as our captain leads the team forward to receive the Cup and presentation tankards.

4

TOP CUP-TIE SHOT

With nine goals – five in the League Cup, four in the F.A. Cup – BOBBY TAMBLING is our leading scorer this season in Cup football, followed by Barry Bridges whose seven comprise four in the F.A. Cup and three in the League Cup.

McCREADIE & BRIDGES DO THE WAITING

Manager Tommy Docherty times Marvin Hinton over sprint distance in special training at Blackpool. Eddie McCreadie looks on . . . awaiting his turn.

Whether the talk is of the F.A. Cup, League Cup or tea-cups, Barry Bridges is the man for the job. Our hotelier centre-forward serves Ron Harris, Marvin Hinton and Tommy McColl.

5

LEAGUE CHAMPIONS 1954-55

C
HE

Stamford Bridge Grounds
LONDON SW6

FOOTBALL LEAGUE - DIVISION 1 SEASON 1964-65

Saturday, 20th March, 1965

CHELSEA 3
v
SHEFFIELD UNITED 0

KICK-OFF 3 p.m.

OFFICIAL PROGRAMME — SIXPENCE

LEICESTER HAND OVER THE LEAGUE CUP

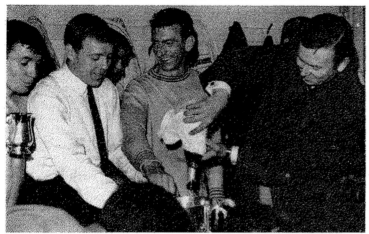

Ken Shellito holds the Cup steady while Mr. Brian Mears, Director, pours the after-match champagne. John Boyle (left) and John Mortimore are ready to lead the "celebration party".

Cheers! Left to right: Barry Bridges, Eddie McCreadie, Terry Venables, Frank Upton, John Boyle, John Mortimore, Peter Bonetti and, in front, Bert Murray.

5

'BRITAIN'S TOP FOOTBALL PROGRAMME'

FOOTBALL'S weekly magazine, "Soccer Star," has been running a competition to discover the "best programme in the country." This is their verdict :—

We have been inundated with entries from all regions of the British Isles. Despite receiving many hundreds, the task of selecting the winner was not as difficult as one might have presumed.

The field was quickly narrowed down to two—Chelsea and Arsenal. In our opinion, these two excellently-produced programmes stand out like a beacon on a bleak winter's day.

In many respects they are similar. But after much discussion, it was decided to name the Chelsea edition as Britain's Top Football Programme.

Sifting the other entries to complete our Top Ten was a long process, but the hit parade finally decided upon was as follows:

1 Chelsea
2 Arsenal
3 Manchester United
4 Sheffield Wednesday
5 Manchester City
6 Sheffield United
7 Tottenham Hotspur
8 Sunderland
9 Middlesbrough
10 Yeovil Town

● We're proud to be top-of-the- table off the field as well as on it.
—Editor.

Our programme for the league match against Sheffield United came after the League Cup final first leg and pictured Eddie McCreadie's wonder goal against the Foxes. This is one of the very few images of the stunning 80-yard run and chip over Gordon Banks, which lasts only in the memories of those lucky enough to be there to see it. There was reason to celebrate off the pitch as the Chelsea programme was voted the best in the country by weekly football magazine Soccer Star. Our programme against West Brom also featured celebratory shots from the League Cup final both on the cover and inside.

EDDIE'S 'GOAL OF A LIFETIME' WINS LEAGUE CUP FINAL FIRST LEG

PREPARING FOR ANOTHER 'SPIN'

THE spin of a coin twice played a decisive part in our third round Fairs Cup-tie against Milan A.C. When the teams were level at 3-3 on aggregate after the second leg, our captain RON HARRIS lost the toss for the right to stage the play-off. When we were still all-square after extra time in the third game in Milan, Ron correctly called "heads" and won us a quarter-final place against T.S.V. München 1860. Our photograph shows him putting in some more coin-tossing practice in case another spin is necessary tonight!

10

Barca blow to Euro hopes, 1965/66

Chelsea's second excursion into European competition came in the 1965/66 season, when we reached the semi-finals of the Fairs Cup. After overcoming Roma, Wiener Sportklub, AC Milan and TSV Munich 1860, we came up against Barcelona. We lost the first leg 2-0 in Camp Nou before levelling things up with the same scoreline at the Bridge. It meant the tie needed to be decided on a play-off which ended in a disappointing 5-0 defeat at the home of the Spanish giants. That match was beamed back to fans watching inside our stadium and a programme was produced for the occasion.

Chelsea Have Always Set the Pace in Programmes

● **CHELSEA WERE FIRST** to introduce the 6d. magazine-type programme (WITHOUT ADVERTISEMENTS) into League football. The first such programme was published for Chelsea's game with Portsmouth on Christmas Day, 1948. Gordon Ross, who edited that first programme eighteen years ago, is still connected with the publishing of our programme. Albert Sewell, our current Editor, first edited Chelsea programmes in the 1949-50 season.

● **CHELSEA WERE FIRST** to sell over 50,000 programmes on a single day. Against Tottenham Hotspur on 20th February, 1965, the sale of programmes reached the massive figure of 54,750. Harry Hitchcock, who is responsible for the selling organisation here, was also at Stamford Bridge on Christmas Day, 1948, watching 6d. programmes being sold for the first time.

● **CHELSEA WERE FIRST** when "Soccer Star" ran a poll in March, 1965 to determine the best soccer programme in the country. The result was:— 1. Chelsea, 2. Arsenal, 3. Manchester United.

● **CHELSEA ARE AGAIN FIRST** to introduce full-colour pictures into a football programme. They are proud to do so tonight. This is just part of our ambitious plan to make our team, our ground, and our administration the envy of the football world.

What Europe Means to Chelsea

By TOMMY DOCHERTY

PARTICIPATION in European competitive football is a must for any top-level British club today. This has been shown to us by the Inter-Cities Fairs Cup tournament this season. For the CLUB it has meant a growing reputation throughout world soccer; big money, too, with receipts at a new record level and greater than any domestic competition can bring.

Going into Europe has enabled our PLAYERS to improve and mature more quickly than would otherwise have been possible. I would say, for instance, that our three games against Milan were equal to a whole season's Football League experience for youngsters like John Boyle and Peter Osgood. Our players have also learned the need for self-discipline on the field, and all the travel involved has broadened their general outlook.

It has given you SUPPORTERS the opportunity to see and appreciate foreign clubs and players who, to many, were only names until this season — as well as the pleasure of following us to this quarter-final stage and, we hope, beyond.

To ME it has provided a fresh insight into match planning and tactics, learning from world-class coaches like Nils Liedholm (Milan) and Max Merkel (Munich). Watching our opponents beforehand has had even greater benefits than in our home competitions. When I went to see T.S.V. Munich before the first leg tie, I noticed something about their defensive play which I thought we might turn to advantage. On the night it helped to bring one of our goals — and could do so again tonight.

3

WHEN BARCELONA WERE HERE IN   THE SECOND LEG TWO WEEKS AGO

Reina makes a magnificent first-half save from Bobby Tambling, third from right.

Ron Harris has put the ball in the net early in the second half. It did not count . . .

Police protection for referee Huber after he has sent off Barcelona left-back Eladio.

14

. . . but this one did. Torres puts into his own net. Then Reina did it again.

15

England's heroes take centre stage, 1966/67

World Cup fever gripped the nation over the summer of 1966 as England won the tournament for the first time. On the opening day of 1966/67, Chelsea beat a West Ham side which included Three Lions heroes Bobby Moore, Martin Peters and Geoff Hurst at Upton Park. Unsurprisingly, the Hammers' programme contained a lengthy World Cup review with pictures of their jubilant players.

Our second home game of the campaign brought Sheffield Wednesday to the Bridge, with the cover of the new-look programme featuring a team photo. The Talk of Stamford Bridge explained how our win against the Hammers was our first-ever in the league at the Boleyn Ground. There was also a column for new Chairman Charles Pratt who had taken over the position from the long-serving Joe Mears who had passed away in the summer. The new Personal Files helped fans get to know the players better and incorporated an autograph.

Introducing our new Chairman

Mr. C. J. PRATT

Mr. CHARLES JAMES PRATT, successor to the late Mr. Joe Mears as Chairman of Chelsea Football Club, has been a Director of our Club since November 1935 and a follower of Chelsea's fortunes for as long as he can remember.

A Londoner, born on March 27, 1899, Mr. Pratt remembers Stamford Bridge from the days when it was better known as the headquarters of London Athletic Club than as the home of Chelsea F.C.

CHELSEA F.C. PROGRAMME
27th August, 1966

Personal File

MARVIN HINTON

BORN February 2, 1940, at Croydon. Joined Charlton Athletic as junior from school (Croydon and Surrey schoolboy honours); captained Charlton's Youth side; League debut October 1957 at right-back away to West Ham.

England Under-23 caps (3): 1961-62 v. Scotland and Turkey; 1962-63 v. Belgium.

Made 129 League appearances for Charlton over seven seasons.

Transferred to Chelsea August 26, 1963. Played his early games for us at right-back.

Made 100th League appearance for Chelsea at West Ham last Saturday.

His Chelsea goals: v. Sheff. Utd. (h) Dec. 21, 1964; v. Liverpool (h) Apr. 16, 1965.

Present contract: To end of season 1968-69, then three-year option. Married; he and his wife Pat have two-year-old son Kevin, and live at Horsham.

Height 5 ft. 10¼ in. Weight 11 st. 11 lb.

HIS CHELSEA RECORD AT START OF THIS SEASON
(Goals scored in brackets)

Season				Football League	F.A. Cup	Football League Cup	Inter-Cities Fairs Cup	Total
1963-64	...	...	...	21 (1)	3	1	—	25 (1)
1964-65	...	...	...	40 (1)	5	6	—	51 (1)
1965-66	...	...	...	38	6	—	11	55
				99 (2)	14	7	11	131 (2)

THE CHELSEA FOOTBALL & ATHLETIC CO. LTD.

FOUNDED 1905

CLUB COLOURS:
Shirts: Royal Blue.
Shorts: Royal Blue.
Stockings: White.

REGISTERED
ADDRESS:
STAMFORD BRIDGE
GROUNDS,
FULHAM ROAD,
LONDON S.W.6.
(FUL 5545)

League Cup Winners 1965

League Champions 1955

F.A. Youth Cup Winners 1960, 1961

PRESIDENT: The Right Hon. Earl Cadogan, M.C., D.L.
VICE-PRESIDENT: R. Attenborough
BOARD OF DIRECTORS:
C. J. Pratt *(Chairman)*, L. R. Withey *(Vice-Chairman)*
J. B. Mears, Viscount Chelsea, L. J. Mears.
SECRETARY: J. Battersby
TEAM MANAGER: T. Docherty   TRAINER: H. Medhurst
HON. MEDICAL OFFICER:
Dr. P. S. Boyne, M.B., B.S. (Lond.), M.R.C.S., L.R.C.P.

THE TALK OF STAMFORD BRIDGE

TODAY'S Football League fixtures mark the half-way stage in the season's programme, being the "return halves" to matches played on the opening day, August 20. There is a first time for most things in soccer—for example, we hope today to score more than one goal in a home League game for the first time since Spurs were here on October 26, the last occasion when we won both points at Stamford Bridge—and this visit of West Ham United provides us with the opportunity of another "first".

The fact that we won 2-1 at Upton Park in August (our first League victory there) means that today we have the chance to complete our very first League double against West Ham. That is something we have been trying to do since season 1923-24. Yes, it's been a long, long time. . . . Can it be that the long-awaited day is here at last? We'll leave that hopefully to these next 90 minutes.

*   *   *

Late goals: Our unbeaten away record was extended at Newcastle last Saturday. Indeed, we were within seconds of winning both points. So, in three out of four consecutive drawn matches — Sheffield United at home and Stoke away were the others—we have lost a goal and a point in the closing minutes. Like our so-far puzzling home performances, one more example of the "ifs and buts" which add fascination to the game.

*   *   *

150 Up: Skipper Ron Harris makes his 150th League appearance this afternoon. Do you remember in which game he made his debut? Answer is at home to Sheffield Wednesday in February 1962, a match we won 1-0.

*   *   *

The home game against West Ham was a standout fixture for other reasons as the sides battled out an incredible 5-5 draw. Bobby Tambling was the Personal File in this game and fans were given the opportunity to collect coupons which could help them get hold of an FA Cup final ticket. Indeed, the Blues reached that stage of the competition but sadly lost 2-1 to Tottenham. However, our wait for FA Cup glory would not be long. Later in the season, the cover of the programme for our game against Southampton was dedicated to Peter Bonetti, who was making a landmark appearance.

KEEP THIS COUPON
It may help you to obtain a ticket for the F.A. Cup Final.

7

CHELSEA F.C. PROGRAMME
17th December, 1966

Personal File
BOBBY TAMBLING

BORN September 18, 1941, at Storrington, Sussex. Joined Chelsea Juniors summer 1957, and signed professional September 1958.

Scored on League debut v. West Ham (a) on February 7, 1959, and completed century of League goals away to West Ham on November 13, 1965.

His total of 154 goals in competitive first-team matches is the highest by any player in our history. Needs one to equal the Chelsea individual record in League football of 128 by Roy Bentley (1948-56).

Scored five in our 6-2 win away to Aston Villa on September 17 last, and four in three other League games: v. Charlton (a) Dec. 1962; Portsmouth (h) May 1963; Arsenal (a) March 1964.

His England honours: Schoolboy caps, seven; Under-23's, 13 (11 goals) 1962-65; full Internationals, three (v. Wales and France 1962-63, Yugoslavia 1965-66).

Present contract: To end of June 1967, then one-year option.

Married, lives at Motspur Park. He and his wife Kathleen have a three-year-old son Gary.

Height 5 ft. 8½ in., weight 12 st.

HIS FIRST-TEAM RECORD TO DATE
(Goals scored in brackets)

Season	Football League	F.A. Cup	Football League Cup	Inter-Cities Fairs Cup	Total
1958-59	1 (1)	—	—	----	1 (1)
1959-60	4 (1)	----	—	----	4 (1)
1960-61	24 (9)	1	3 (3)	—	28 (12)
1961-62	34 (20)	1 (2)	—	—	35 (22)
1962-63	40 (35)	4 (2)	—	—	44 (37)
1963-64	35 (17)	2 (2)	1	—	38 (19)
1964-65	33 (15)	5 (4)	7 (6)	—	45 (25)
1965-66	26 (16)	6 (5)	—	10 (2)	42 (23)
1966-67	20 (13)	—	3 (1)	—	23 (14)
Total	217 (127)	19 (15)	14 (10)	10 (2)	260 (154)

CHELSEA FOOTBALL CLUB

LEAGUE CHAMPIONS 1954-55
LEAGUE CUP WINNERS 1964-65

LEAGUE DIVISION 1
SEASON 1966-67

STAMFORD BRIDGE GROUNDS
London SW6

Saturday
7th January
v
SOUTHAMPTON

KICK-OFF 3 P.M.

PETER BONETTI
Back between the posts today and playing the 250th League game of his career. His first was at home to Manchester City on April 2, 1960.

OFFICIAL PROGRAMME **6d**

OUR FIRST *wembley* F.A. CUP FINAL

Pre-match greetings for John Hollins from well-wishers on the way into Wembley Stadium.

Ron Harris, youngest Cup Final captain on record, at full stretch to stop Jimmy Greaves.

A stunning blow, right on half-time, as Robertson (right) puts Spurs one up.

The big parade — one of the great moments in Chelsea history as Tommy Docherty leads us into the arena alongside Bill Nicholson and his Spurs team.

NOW HERE'S TO THE NEXT !

Oh, dear! . . . now it's 0-2. Peter Bonetti, unsighted, is beaten by Saul's swivel shot.

10

Near miss here by Bobby Tambling. But from a similar situation five minutes from the end he put us back with a chance.

Time has run out . . . we leave the field to a "well played" salute from the crowd. Thanks fans. Hope we'll all be there again soon!

11

THE TALK OF STAMFORD BRIDGE

WELCOME, new season. Welcome to Stamford Bridge, Supporters old and new. Much has happened since we gathered for last season's final home game before we went to Wembley. Now we go forward into 1967-68, believing that not very much advance is required on our form of recent years for this 63rd Chelsea season to be the most successful in the Club's history.

What most certainly IS necessary for the good of our new-season prospects is a substantial improvement in results at Stamford Bridge, about which we hope to do something, starting tonight. The Ticket Office reports that we have sold a record number of season-tickets; such encouragement around the ground well merits the "goods" being delivered out in the middle, and, while no club can *command* success you can be assured of 100 per cent effort on the part of everyone in the Chelsea camp aimed at bringing home one or more of the game's biggest prizes.

Though the close season seems ever-shortening, the summer remains the period of principal change in League club personnel, and Chelsea is no exception. The newest recruit to our first-team pool is 19-year-old defender **Colin Waldron**, signed from Bury; centre-forward **Roy**

Summers, 20, who was with assistant-manager Ron Suart as an amateur with Blackpool, has also come South to Stamford Bridge and signed professional; likewise inside-forward **Brian Goodwin**, 17, from Scottish junior football, and 17-year-old Scottish centre-half **Paul McMillan**, who has switched from amateur to full professional.

While welcoming the new boys and wishing them every success in Chelsea blue, we also extend best wishes for the future to those players who have left us since the end of last season. They include two members of our F.A. Cup Final side, **Tony Hateley**, who has moved to Liverpool, and **Allan Harris**, now with Queen's Park Rangers. Other departures have been **Roger Wosahlo** to Ipswich, **Pat Purcell**

FRONT COVER SHOT

THE pre-season picture with the "great to be back" feeling . . . and among the front-runners none are happier than Peter Osgood and Ken Shellito, both recovered from serious injury.

3

FRANK BLUNSTONE'S
COACHING
CLASS

BOYS! If you have a problem about football technique or tactics, this is your chance to find the answer. You can ask Frank Blunstone, who is in charge of Chelsea's Youth Section. Questions can only be answered through the medium of the club programme, and if you have one please send it by post to: **Frank Blunstone's Coaching Class, Chelsea F.C., Stamford Bridge Grounds, Fulham Road, London, S.W.6.**

Today's question, about centre-half play, is in two parts: (1) **In schoolboy football, should the centre-half ever leave his defensive position and go upfield? (2) What do you do when you find two opponents coming at you in a situation in which the odds are on a goal if they get past you?**

Frank's answers: (1) *At all levels of football, the centre-half's principal job is to stop the opposition and I would advise schoolboys almost invariably to "stay put". If you think that by going upfield you can save or win the match—when, for example, your side get a corner-kick—make sure someone drops back to cover you against a possible break by the opposition. (2) In a two-to-one situation like this, the centre-half should hold off as long as possible. By "playing for time" in this way, he gives his side a double-chance—in the next few vital seconds a team-mate may be able to get back and provide extra cover or the opponent in possession may be forced into error. You should not retreat deeper than the edge of the penalty-area; once the play has advanced that far, you must commit yourself and tackle the man in possession. To let him get any nearer will only increase the danger to your goal.*

DAVE SEXTON:
His Background in Brief

Born Islington, April 6, 1930.
Played inside-forward for Chelmsford City, Luton Town, West Ham United, Leyton Orient, Brighton & Hove Albion and Crystal Palace.

A cartilage injury to the right knee ended his playing career at Selhurst Park. That decision was taken on medical advice in January 1962, and a month later he joined Chelsea as Assistant-Coach.

January 1965: Left Stamford Bridge to manage Leyton Orient.

December 1965: Resigned from Orient.

February 1966: Appointed Coach by Fulham.

August 1966: Moved from Fulham to Arsenal as Coach and, at the start of this season, appointed Assistant-Manager at Highbury.

Monday, October 23, 1967: Appointed Team Manager of Chelsea.

Dave and his wife, Thea, have three children, Anne (9), David (8) and Michael (2), and the Sexton family live at Hove.

All change for Blues and programme, 1967/68

The 1967/68 season was another campaign of change for the Blues in a managerial sense, as Tommy Docherty's reign came to an end, with Dave Sexton appointed our new gaffer in October. There was also a significantly different look to the matchday programme cover, as you can see from the edition produced for our first home match of the campaign against Newcastle. Inside was a poster looking back to the FA Cup final the previous season, with the messaging along with the comment in The Talk of Stamford Bridge making it perfectly clear that the attitude within the club was a positive one. There was also a "Double Look" at Peter Bonetti. An interesting piece from former Blue Frank Blunstone, who was now coaching the juniors, saw him answer questions from aspiring young footballers.

DOUBLE LOOK
AT
THE BLUES

Peter Bonetti

15

The growing pool of talent, 1968/69

Dave Sexton's first full campaign in charge began with a home game against Nottingham Forest and a cover redesign each season was common practice by now. Ian Hutchinson was given a warm welcome after joining the Blues from Cambridge United in the summer and a striker reaching the other end of his Chelsea career, Bobby Tambling, was embarking on his testimonial season. Off the pitch, the first rumblings of the stadium issues which would plague the club for some time were starting to become evident in the Chairman's column.

On Sale Tonight—Bobby Tambling's Own Story

AS most of you will know, this is Bobby Tambling's Testimonial season, which will include, among events being organised on his behalf, a special match at Stamford Bridge (date and opponents to be announced).

Also, published in connection with his Testimonial, is "The Bobby Tambling Story", in which Bobby takes you behind the scenes – in one feature even into the dressing-room on match-days – talks about his career with Chelsea . . . the goals he remembers best in his record club total of 183 . . . names his "top ten" list of goalkeepers . . . picks his best-ever Chelsea XI . . . and tells ambitious boy players how to go about joining a big club like Chelsea.

There is also a special selection of photographs, and a complete analysis of Bobby's games and goals for Chelsea.

You can buy "The Bobby Tambling Story" – price 2/6d. – here tonight, from the Supporters' Club stall at the approach to the East Stand, or by post (2/10d. postage paid) from: Bobby Tambling c/o Chelsea F.C., Fulham Road, London, S.W.6.

CHELSEA F.C. PLAYING STAFF, 1968-69

(As at August 1 1968)

Player	Height	Weight	Place of Birth	Previous Club	Date Signed (as professional or transferred to Club)
GOALKEEPERS					
BONETTI, PETER	5ft. 10¾in.	11st. 2lb.	Putney	Chelsea Juniors	Apr. 1959
HUGHES, TOMMY	6ft. 0½in.	12st. 2lb.	Dalmuir	Clydebank Juniors	July 1965
FULL-BACKS					
HINTON, MARVIN	5ft. 10½in.	12st. 2lb.	Croydon	Charlton Athletic	Aug. 1963
McCREADIE, EDDIE	5ft. 8½in.	10st. 9½lb.	Glasgow	East Stirling	Apr. 1962
SHELLITO, KEN	5ft. 9¼in.	12st. 9lb.	Ea...	... Juniors	Apr. 1957
THOMSON, JIM	5ft. 10¾in.	11st. 11lb.	Gl...		
HALF-BACKS					
BOYLE, JOHN	5ft. 8in.	11st. 9lb.	M...		
HARRIS, RON	5ft. 8in.	11st. 12lb.	H...		
HOLLINS, JOHN	5ft. 7½in.	11st. 1lb.	G...		
HOUSTON, STEWART	5ft. 10½in.	12st. 1lb.	A...		
LUKE, GEORGE	5ft. 10½in.	11st. 7lb.	S...		
WEBB, DAVID	5ft. 11½in.	12st. 12lb.	S...		
YOUNG, ALLAN	6ft.	12st. 1lb.			
FORWARD...					
BALDWIN, TOMMY	5ft. 8½in.	11st. 5½lb.			
BIBBY, DAVID	5ft. 6¾in.	10st. 4lb.			
BIRCHENALL, ALAN	5ft. 11½in.	13st. 1lb.			
COOKE, CHARLIE	5ft. 8in.	11st. 6½lb.			
FASCIONE, JOE	5ft. 5in.	10st. 8lb.			
HALLIDAY, KEN	5ft. 6½in.	10st. 7lb.			
HAMILTON, IAN	5ft. 9½in.	10st. 6lb.			
HOUSEMAN, PETER	5ft. 8½in.	11st. 8lb.			
HUDSON, ALAN	5ft. 10in.	11st. 2lb.			
HUTCHINSON, IAN	6ft.	12st.			
LLOYD, BARRY	5ft. 8in.	10st. 11lb.			
OSGOOD, PETER	6ft. 1½in.	12st. 13lb.			
TAMBLING, BOBBY	5ft. 8in.	11st. 1lb.			
TURNER, BRIAN	6ft.	12st. 10lb.	East Ham	Eden F.C...	May 196...

Name	Age	Position	
COCKS, Alan	17	CF	Orn...
CORFIELD, Paul	15	OR	Edg...
DOVEY, Alan	16	G	Step...
FREWIN, Tony	16	CH	Ilfo...
HAWKINS, Roger	15	CF	Oxf...
CRUICKSHANK, Joe	16	WH	Ab...

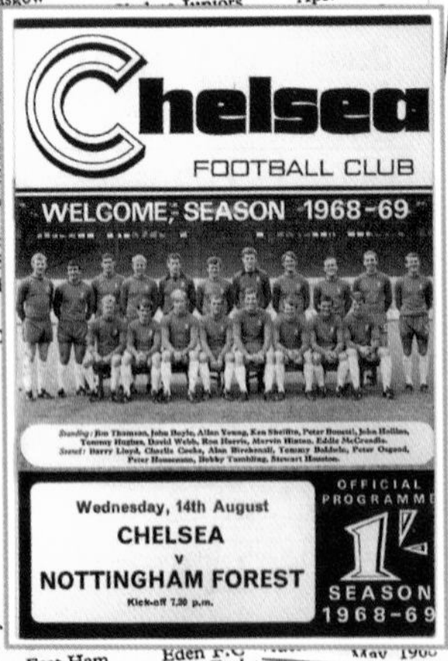

THE CHAIRMAN WRITES . . .

IT is with great pride that, as Chairman of Chelsea Football Club, I welcome all our Supporters at the beginning of the 1968-69 season. In particular (and I know you are with me here) I wish Dave Sexton and our Players a very successful season in all competitions in this country, also in the Inter-Cities Fairs Cup.

Regarding our occupancy of Stamford Bridge Grounds, progress is being made, if somewhat slowly. It must be remembered that in the future, as sole tenants, now that greyhound racing no longer takes place here, our outgoings will increase considerably.

It follows, therefore, that improvements to the Grounds that we, and you, desire cannot be carried out as speedily as one would wish, and must be related to the tenure of the new lease.

You will be kept informed of progress as it is made in this direction and, meanwhile, I would ask you to bear with us during the period of continued negotiation.

L. R. WITHEY

11

EDDIE McCREADIE

New Faces at Stamford Bridge

IAN HUTCHINSON
Signed in July from Southern League club Cambrid...

EDDIE HEATH
Has joined our staff...

Back row: John Boyle, Ron Harris, Stewart Houston, Charlie Morrison, Joe Cruickshank, Stephen Kiff, Derek Vaughan.
Middle row: David Webb, Peter Osgood, Peter Bonetti, John Dempsey, Alan Birchenall, Harry Medhurst (Head Trainer), Dick Spence (Youth Trainer), Joe Larkin, Alan Dovey, Stephen Hipwell, Tony Potrac, Michael Maskell.
Front row: Eddie McCreadie, Peter Houseman, Bobby Tambling, Charlie Cooke, Dave Sexton (Manager), Frank Blunstone (Youth Manager), Dave Bibby, Alan Cocks, Alan Hudson, Tony Frewin.

F.A. CHALLENGE CUP

CHELSEA F.C. 1968-69
DOUBLE QUARTER-FINALISTS

F.A. YOUTH CUP

Congratulations to our Seniors and Juniors on reaching the last eight of their respective National Cup competitions.

Our Sunderland programme in February showed the conveyor belt of homegrown talent was as prolific as ever, after Alan Hudson had made his debut at Southampton along with new signing John Dempsey. Backroom staff were pictured dealing with the rush for tickets for our forthcoming FA Cup quarter-final against West Brom. Sadly, a crowd of over 52,000 watched us lose to the Baggies. The programme for that fixture explained how it was our 200th game in the competition and there was also a treat for fans in the form of a large colour poster of the team.

NEW FACES IN OUR LEAGUE SIDE THIS MONTH

JOHN DEMPSEY
Republic of Ireland centre-half signed last month from Fulham.

ALAN HUDSON
Seventeen-year-old Chelsea Youth captain and inside-forward.

The Great Flood of Cup Ticket Applications...

"Evening News" photograph

OUR 200th F.A. CUP MATCH

TODAY'S game is the 200th we have played in our history in the F.A. Cup . . . and wouldn't it be nice to celebrate in the way we marked our 100th post-war Cup match in the last round against Stoke!

The first, in the first qualifying round of season 1905-06, was against the 1st Grenadiers at Stamford Bridge and resulted in a 6-1 Chelsea win.

Here is our complete F.A. Cup record from that day up to date:

	P	W	D	L	F	A
Stamford Bridge	94	57	24	13	197	81
Away Ties	83	28	22	33	99	113
Neutral Grounds	22	8	5	9	30	30
Total	199	93	51	55	326	224

This season's fourth round first replay against Preston is not included as, being abandoned, it did not count as an official match.

Our farthest F.A. Cup progress: Runners-up season 1914-15 (beaten 0-3 by Sheffield United in Final at Old Trafford) and 1966-67 (beaten 1-2 by Tottenham at Wembley).

Our highest F.A. Cup score: 9-1 (h) v. Worksop in first round, 1907-08.

Heaviest defeat in F.A. Cup: 1-7 (a) v. Crystal Palace in third qualifying round, 1905-06.

Exciting season for Boys in Blue, 1969/70

As the Sixties ticked over into the Seventies, the Blues enjoyed one of our most memorable seasons of all time and there were some exciting additions to the programme as well. Our first home game of 1969/70 saw Ipswich Town visit the Bridge, with a behind-the-scenes shot of the team photo adorning the cover. There was also a shot of Ron Harris on his wedding day and a full page of player autographs. Also note the plug for our next matchday programme when West Ham came to town, with the new Boys in Blue feature shown here.

Boys in blue
David Webb

THERE is no finer or more inspiring sight to Chelsea eyes than David Webb roaring out of defence at one end to reinforce attack at the other.

Eight goals last season are evidence of his all-round purpose. Voted Chelsea's "Player of the Year", he was also our only ever-present player in 1968-69 (54 games) . . . which made his absence through injury from this season's opening matches felt all the more.

Born Stratford on April 9, 1946. Previous clubs: Orient and Southampton, from whom he joined us in February 1968. 5 ft. 11½ in., 12 st. 12 lb.

© sportsgraphic

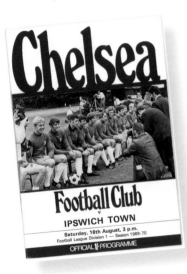

CFC

The Match of Ron's Life!

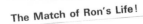

Chelsea Autographs 1969-70

SATURDAY, May 3rd, was "something special" for our captain, Ron Harris, and Miss Linda Joan (Lee) Perry. It was their wedding day, and here they are after the ceremony at the Church of St. Peter and St. Paul, Dagenham.

Our congratulations and best wishes to Ron and Lee, and good luck in the home they have set up at Ewell.

10

NEXT WEDNESDAY'S PROGRAMME

IN our Programme when we meet West Ham United here on Wednesday night, look out for:

● Boys in Blue . . . the first in a brilliant new colour series on the Chelsea players.

● Ron Harris . . . a special interview with our captain.

● Coaching Class . . . the feature in which Chelsea players pass on hints to young fans.

Yes, you'll find plenty that's new in Wednesday's Programme . . . and we hope you enjoy today's special 40-page edition containing the pull-out Chelsea Handbook for 1969-70, all at the usual price, one shilling.

Q&A

**ALBERT SEWELL
Programme Editor
puts the Questions
to the Season's Busiest
Man at the 'Bridge', Trainer
HARRY MEDHURST**

Q. You are once again working "double time", Harry, after a new crop of injuries last weekend just when it seemed the worst was over. Do you regard so many casualties simply as bad luck . . . or what?

A. Times like this come to a club. People say when you're doing well you don't get injuries – and Derby County just now are an example of that – but we've been getting them though not doing badly. Over recent weeks it's been the worst I've known since I joined the training staff 16 years ago, but about four years ago I had 18 in for treatment in one week. It's certainly not due to lack of training.

Q. Is the game getting dirtier, then?

A. Dirtier, no . . . harder, yes. In top-level football today players are more toned up and keyed up than ever before. As I see it, there are more injuries because the game is now so much more competitive in spirit, the tension greater than ever before.

Q. Are Southern players "softer" than those from the North, as Don Revie gives as one reason for the dominance of Northern clubs in modern football?

A. I believe that a hungry footballer is a better footballer, and from the time I came into the game before the war most of those came from the North. It's still true. They have a harder upbringing as boys, and it shows through in their football character later. Of course we have players with tremendous guts and spirit down here – Ron Harris and David Webb to name but two – but your Liverpools, Leeds and Evertons have whole teams of them . . . and how many Southerners play in those sides? There are too many distractions down here which, I think, helps to give the North that vital edge in concentration and overall greater dedication, and as a Southerner myself, it hurts to have to recognise this. Having said that, let me add how satisfying it was to see us come through the way we did at Leeds on Wednesday night. They give nowt away up there!

Q. In what ways has the job of trainer changed since you came back to Chelsea in 1953?

A. In the old days the trainer did the boots, the dressing-rooms, took the actual training as well as dealing with injuries. Now, at the big clubs, he is a full-time physiotherapist in a white coat, involved only on the medical side. From one match until the next, I seldom see the players on the field, unless one of them is having a fitness test or is set a particular

14

Chelsea 3		Arsenal 0
BONETTI	1	WEBSTER
HINTON (boyle)	2	STOREY
McCREADIE (Capt.)	3	McNAB
HOLLINS	4	COURT
DEMPSEY	5	McLINTOCK (Capt.)
HOUSTON	6	SIMPSON
BOYLE COOKE	7	ROBERTSON
HOUSEMAN	8	SAMMELS
BALDWIN (1)	9	RADFORD
BIRCHENALL(1)	10	GRAHAM
OSGOOD	11	ARMSTRONG

Referee: Mr. P. PARTRIDGE

The Talk of Stamford Bridge

ON Wednesday night, when once again having to field a depleted side, we achieved one of our best performances of the season by drawing with the Champions, Leeds United, on their ground in the third round of the Football League Cup four days after losing to them there in the First Division. Even better than a draw appeared in prospect when Alan Birchenall gave us the lead in the second half, but at the last gasp Leeds saved the night and we meet them here in the replay on Tuesday (7.30 p.m.) to continue our battle for a place in the last 16 of the League Cup.

* * *

The injured: Another spate of injuries last week-end has meant that the Treatment Room has been over-populated again this week. At the time of writing the latest information on the players concerned is as follows: **David Webb** – damaged shoulder ligament, probably out for a month; **Ron Harris** – badly bruised shin, absent on Wednesday and doubtful for today; **Ian Hutchinson** – he collected three injuries in last Saturday's reserve match with Southampton (right knee, hamstring and tendon, leg put in compression bandage); **Alan Birchenall** – another casualty at Leeds last Saturday with a bruised shin and again on Wednesday; **Alan Hudson** still under treatment for a leg injury received in the last home game against Burnley; reserve **Derek Smethurst** – Achilles tendon and ankle injuries, hopes to resume training next week; **Bobby Tambling** – cartilage operation last Sunday, progress satisfactory but not expected to play again before December.

So, after less than two months of the new season we are left with only four players who have appeared in every match – Peter Bonetti, John Dempsey, John Hollins and Peter Houseman. As a point of comparison, at the corresponding stage last season, after eleven First Division matches, we had **nine** ever-present players.

**Boys in blue
John Hollins**

After a slow start to the campaign, losing our first two matches, by the time Arsenal visited the Bridge at the end of September, we had lost just once in our last nine league fixtures, not bad when you consider the growing injury list detailed in The Talk of Stamford Bridge. John Hollins – who would go on to join the Gunners later in his career – starred in Boys in Blue, while trainer and physio Harry Medhurst took the hotseat for the Q&A. We beat our London rivals 3-0 to continue our good form in the league, although this season would soon become one where the FA Cup took centre stage...

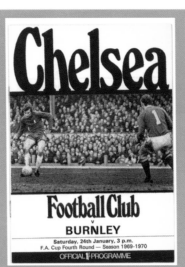

ALL THE GOALS IN WEMBLEY'S FIRST DRAWN F.A. CUP FINAL

PROGRAMMED FOR CUP SUCCESS

Our triumphant 1970 FA Cup run began with a home tie against Birmingham in the third round. In every round after that, the Blues had to win matches away from Stamford Bridge to go on and lift the trophy. After a draw in SW6 in round four against Burnley, we prevailed in a replay at Turf Moor, before away wins against Crystal Palace and QPR and a thumping 5-1 victory over Watford in the semi-final at White Hart Lane. Here are some extracts from each programme issued in the competition that season, up to and including the memorable final against Leeds United. We lifted the trophy for the first time after a 2-1 victory in a replay at Old Trafford following a 2-2 draw at Wembley. Our league game against Liverpool took place between the original final and replay, with plenty of match action from Wembley on the cover and inside.

Football Association Cup

5th Round

v.

CHELSEA

SATURDAY, 7th FEBRUARY 1970

Kick Off 3.00 p.m.

OFFICIAL PROGRAMME - 1/-

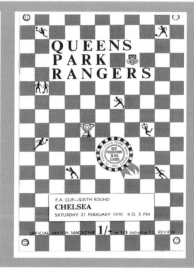

QUEENS
PARK
RANGERS

F.A. CUP—SIXTH ROUND

CHELSEA

SATURDAY 21 FEBRUARY 1970 K.O. 3 PM

OFFICIAL MATCH MAGAZINE 1/- or 1/3 including F.A. REVIEW

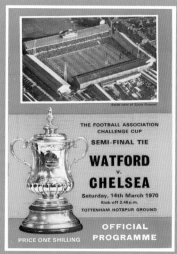

THE FOOTBALL ASSOCIATION
CHALLENGE CUP

SEMI-FINAL TIE

WATFORD
v.
CHELSEA

Saturday, 14th March 1970
Kick-off 2.45 p.m.
TOTTENHAM HOTSPUR GROUND

PRICE ONE SHILLING

**OFFICIAL
PROGRAMME**

Boys in blue
Dave Sexton

FA CUP FINAL REPLAY
OLD TRAFFORD · MANCHESTER

2/-

Chelsea

Leeds
UNITED

April 29th 1970 Kick Off 7·30pm
OFFICIAL PROGRAMME
Published by Manchester United Football Club

QUESTION TIME

The question-and-answer piece with first-team players has been a hugely popular – and often amusing – feature of the matchday programme since the Sixties. Here we bring you a selection from over the years

QUESTION & ANSWER

Our subject tonight in the series of interviews by Albert Sewell with the personalities of Chelsea F.C. could only be:

FRANK BLUNSTONE

LOOKING back, Frank, over your ten years here, which of the 300-odd first-team games you have played for Chelsea stand out most?

Three right at the end of last season. They were so important to the future of the Club. There was that 2-2 draw here with Leeds — I still give a sigh of relief at the thought of our equaliser, one of the most valuable goals I'll ever score. Then after losing at home to Stoke, came the other two I'll never forget — our 1-0 win at Sunderland and finally the 7-0 promotion clincher against Portsmouth.

When you first came to Chelsea, what were your feelings as a lad leaving behind all the warmth of family life at Crewe (where you were one of nine boys, with five sisters) and becoming a stranger in a vast city?

I was very lonely at the start, but Ted Drake, who brought me here, was most helpful. He'd let me nip home at week-ends, and after three months I was called up for the Army. That ended my home-sickness.

Were you always an outside-left?

No. I played inside-left at school and also for Crewe Alexandra.

Were you a schoolboy International?

No, only reserve. But I was to play for England at all other levels — Youth, Under-23's and full International.

In 1957 you broke your left leg twice in seven months — in the Cup at Tottenham and again in your "come-

back" match on the eve of the following season, against Dutch champions Ajax in Holland. Did you fear then that your career might be over?

I never felt I was finished, and hearing it suggested by other people only made me more determined to prove them wrong. It was a grim prospect, though, having to start the long road to recovery again when my leg went a second time, but by November 1958 I'd made it . . . I was back in League football.

Were there any after-effects?

Not really. Even now the leg sometimes aches a little in very cold weather, but a few quick sprints and it's gone.

Did the risk of further injury worry you after that second break?

No. I came back convinced that the bone had mended completely, and I feel I have been able to play as hard since as ever I did before those injuries.

As a winger yourself, who are the best wingers you've seen?

Stanley Matthews and Tom Finney, without any doubt. I watched Stan a lot when I was a boy — Stoke is only 18 miles from Crewe, and they were "my team" back in the days of Frank Soo, Freddie Steele and Neil Franklin.

And the best right-backs, you have played against?

Jimmy Armfield now and, going back a few years, Stan Rickaby, of West Brom.

Continued on page 7

5

Apart from painting, I'm hopeless at do-it-yourself. Couldn't mend a fuse. Ask Doreen! Every man to his trade, I say.

Is tonight's match the last of your Testimonial events?

No, there's a match on Sunday between St. Helen's F.C., of Clapham (I'm their president) and the TV All-Stars. It's on the *News of the World* ground at Mitcham, kick-off 2.15. Tommy Docherty and Tommy Steele are among the players, linesmen are Bobby Tambling and Ken Shellito, and I'm referee.

Lastly, Frank, have you any unful-filled ambition?

Yes, to win an F.A. Cup medal with Chelsea . . . and to get that F.A. coaching certificate.

7

108

DAVID WEBB

QUICKIES

Wife's name? Jackie. **Any family?** Not yet. **Pets?** Yes, Cobbie, our alsatian ... he's about 3½ now ... great chap. **Are you a handyman at home?** No. Jackie is the handy one at our place. I'm a good starter of jobs like decorating or knocking a nail in. Then I lose interest and phone the builder to come and finish it. **Best pal?** At Chelsea, Eddie McCreadie—I room with him on away trips. Anyway, he's everyone's friend, isn't he? Away from football, Alan Ingram—he's a mate who's done well in business—and a friend of us both is Marty Feldman ... he's a lovely fella. **Dislikes?** Teams that beat Chelsea. **Biggest thrill of your career?** Being voted "Player of the Year" here last season.

Frank Blunstone reflected on his 10 years with the Blues during an interview in the 1963/64 season, while Peter Osgood spoke about his rapid progress during the 1965/66 campaign. Also featured here are Q&A sessions with David Webb from 1969/70 and Ian Britton from 1973/74.

20 Chelsea Questions

Answered today by

IAN BRITTON

Moment in my career I've enjoyed most: Scoring against Southampton here in November—my first goal for the Seniors. At 5 ft. 5 in. I felt 10 ft. 10 in. when that one went in.

The day I'll never forget: Signing as a Chelsea professional in July 1971 after two seasons as a junior.

Biggest influences on my career so far: Youth manager Ken Shellito and Dario Gradi, who is in charge of the Combination side here.

Where I live: I'm in "digs" at Mitcham. In the summer I go home to Dundee.

My Chelsea room-mate on away trips: Gary Locke.

Favourite away ground: Arsenal. I felt I'd had one of my best games when we played there in November.

The star I've always admired: Denis Law.

My secret dread: I realise I've hardly started in the game yet ... but I hate the thought of one day having to stop playing football.

My most memorable match so far: Against Manchester United here at the end of last season—Bobby Charlton's last game.

Teams I most like Chelsea to beat: Arsenal and Leeds.

Usual meal before a game: Boiled eggs.

The team I watched as a boy: Dundee United.

Best country visited: France.

Favourite TV programme: The Two Ronnies.

The programme I always switch off: Documentaries.

Clubs to win honours in 1974: Leeds the League, Chelsea the Cup.

This year's World Cup winners: Scotland.

Personal ambition: To gain a regular place in Chelsea's first team.

Tip to junior players: Listen and learn, and always try your hardest.

The headline I'd most like to read: "Chelsea do the Double."

14

QUESTION & ANSWER

Programme Editor Albert Sewell talks to

PETER OSGOOD

IN six months since making your First Division début, Peter, you have probably progressed faster than any other player this season. Going back beyond that, what brought you to Chelsea in the first place?

I left school at 15 and was invited for a trial by Arsenal, who were "my team" as a boy. But I didn't have enough confidence in myself to turn up. I took a job in a factory at Slough, then went into the building trade with my father. At that time I was playing inside-right for Spital Old Boys, Windsor, on Saturdays, and left-half for Windsor Corinthians on Sundays. In February 1964 my uncle, Bob Snashell, a Chelsea supporter, wrote in asking for a trial for me. This time I did show up — one of about 50 boys all hoping to do well at the Hendon training ground that day. I scored a goal and was signed on amateur forms when I came off the field by Youth team manager Dick Foss. I gave up the building job straight away to concentrate on football, and the Boss (Tommy Docherty) signed me as a professional in September 1964.

What was your first big game?

The Football League Cup fifth round replay against Workington last season. It was my lucky night — we won 2-0 and I managed to get both goals. The rest of the season I was in the Combination and Youth teams, but I went on the tour of Australia last summer. I came into the side again this season in the Fairs Cup first round tie at home to Roma in September, and three days later had my first League game, at home to Newcastle.

Was it easy, coming into the side as the "new boy"?

Right from the start, the Boss and the boys have given me tremendous help and encouragement, but I found it hard at first. I remember in the home game with Leicester in October, the crowd gave me some stick. Barry was substitute that day, and while I was struggling, they were chanting "Bridges, Bridges" for him to come on, which he did when Eddie McCreadie was injured. Barry and I are good pals, and things have worked out with a place for both of us, but I felt embarrassed at the time, particularly as he was England's centre-forward.

You have already worn an England shirt — four Youth games in the "Little World Cup" in Germany last Easter, and a full England practice match here in September when you stood in for Alan Peacock and scored two goals. What are your feelings on what you read, as you must have done often in the past few months, of yourself being tipped as England's World Cup centre-forward this summer?

I've gained a lot of experience and maturity these past six months, and I still have a long way to go. I'd be delighted if I could make the Under-23 team in my first full season. There's another World Cup in Mexico in 1970, and when the one after that is held in 1974 I'll still be only 27.

What about all the Press and TV ballyhoo, the "Wizard of Oz" tag, the hero-worship? Do you find it easy to live with?

It was a bit frightening at first, but it's something you've got to be prepared for, I suppose, at a top-level club like Chelsea. Yes, I can take it, because really it means Chelsea are becoming more and more successful ... and you wouldn't be human if you didn't enjoy success, would you?

What does earning big money mean to you?

Apart from paying big Income Tax, it means I can afford things for my wife Rosemary, my baby son Anthony and myself that would not otherwise have been possible—like the new house we are shortly moving into at Windsor. I'm no spendthrift, though.

Of your games and goals so far, do any stand out above the rest?

The match at Burnley in January, when we won 2-1 after being one down. I scored both, and the winner was from one of those long runs that look so good when they come off. It began just inside our own half, and I just kept going ... and going ... and going.

What have you learned most from this season's big European games?

Experience against players of the class we have been meeting in the Fairs Cup is bound to improve your game, as a team and individually. It has taught me to pace myself to last 90 minutes and more.

You started in the side as spearhead, but now more often "come from the back." Why the change?

It was an experiment, and one that has suited me. Playing deep, I can see the game opening out, and I find it easier to

"break" from midfield. I went back to the spearhead style at Newcastle recently, and didn't feel half as comfortable.

Chelsea's training schedule demands as much effort as the toughest match. Do you enjoy it?

To be honest, no. I find training very hard — to me it is all work, whereas I relish matches because they are work and play combined. But I realise that you can't have one without the other, so I've got to learn to like training if I am to go on improving my game. Frankly, I'm staggered at the way things have gone for me these past six months, but it's up to me to keep going. And even training is not as hard as bricklaying!

16

17

CHELSEA PLAYER FOCUS No. 1
RAY 'BUTCH' WILKINS

Born: Hillingdon   Age: 18   Height: 5' 7"   Weight 10st

Appearances 26 (3 as Substitute)   Goals 2

1. Who was your favourite player when you were a schoolboy?
   Bobby Charlton.

2. Which match has given you the most enjoyment in your career so far, and why?
   v Tottenham April 1974—when we had to win to get ourselves out of trouble and it was my first full game for Chelsea.

3. Which player in the Football League who plays in your position do you most admire?
   Johnny Giles.

4. Which Club do you most enjoy playing against?
   Tottenham.

5. Who are the best eleven players (in a 4-3-3 formation) that you have ever watched, played with or played against?

   Banks

   Madeley   McFarland   Moore   Beattie
   Giles   Charlton   Bremner
   Greaves   Osgood   Best

' bares his chest and has a mug'!

We hear it doesn't happen very often but 'Butch' here helps out watering the flowers at home

' and Graham with the statuette from the Mini World Cup victory

15

Down at the Mitcham training ground 'Butch' obliges some young supporters by signing their autograph books

The topic of conversation? Soccer of course. 'Butch', Graham and Stephen keep the subject going

14

JOHN DEMPSEY

My time with Chelsea: The three big things in my ten seasons here all happened at the start of the Seventies—winners' medals in the F.A. Cup in 1970 and Cup-Winners' Cup in 1971, and playing in the League Cup Final at Wembley in 1972. I'm proud to have been part of the best team Chelsea have ever had.

The future: Now it's time to move on, and I've been given a free transfer to help me find a new club before the end of the season. It looks like America—I've had offers from Eddie McCreadie at Memphis, from Los Angeles Aztecs, Philadelphia Furies (Ossie's club) and Vancouver Whitecaps. I expect to decide within a week or two. Like my wife, Margaret, and two young children I'm looking forward to spending maybe two years in America; then I'd like to come back to England and coach youngsters.

My fitness: The chipped ankle bone at the start of this season and the hamstring injury that followed are now way behind me. After playing the last 11 Reserve games, I feel really fit again and know I'm back to what I can do on the field.

Most-prized football possession: My F.A. Cup-winners' medal.

Best moment of career: Scoring in the Cup-Winners' Cup Final against Real Madrid in Athens.

Shock of my life: When playing for Eire in an International in Denmark. I fouled the local hero, and a women ran on the field and hit me with her handbag. I was amazed . . . and relieved when the police took her off.

Young Chelsea players to watch for: Two have particularly impressed me in the Reserves: Lee Frost, a quick, skilful winger who takes people on, and John Bumstead, lightly built but always involved in an attacking midfield role.

My wish for Chelsea's future: For Ken Shellito to be successful as manager. He has come through well from a difficult start, and if two or three more class players can be added to the squad this can become a really great Chelsea side.

John Dempsey

 PUBLISHED BY CHELSEA FOOTBALL CLUB, STAMFORD BRIDGE GROUNDS, FULHAM ROAD, LONDON SW6 1HS.
PROGRAMME EDITOR: ALBERT SEWELL. DESIGN BY JOHN ELVIN. PRINTED BY SAMUEL SIDDERS & SON LTD., LONDON NW6.

Ray Wilkins showed off his bare chest for a 'player focus' feature in 1975/76, while John Dempsey revealed his most prized possessions during the 1977/78 season and Paul Canoville spoke about life as a professional footballer in 1984/85.

CHELSEA SPOTLIGHT

PAUL CANOVILLE *talks to Hugh Hastings*

Q: The last time I interviewed you Paul, was shortly after you joined Chelsea on trial. Has being a professional footballer been everything you expected?

P: Yes. I'm not disappointed. I'd looked forward to being a professional since I was a kid. Luck played a big part in putting me where I am today and I'm very grateful. I hope that I'm accepted by the Chelsea fans now. There was a time when I felt like an outsider. I failed to understand why some people took a stand against me. I thought about it a lot but could find no logical reason for their actions. I had to solve the problems for myself; no-one else could do it for me. Football is quite a hard life but everyone at Chelsea is always ready to give encouragement, which is a great help. It's a tough old world but I've learnt to look after myself.

Q: Are you pleased with your game?

P: Quite, but I'd like to be more consistent. I think my best game was at Sheffield Wednesday this season when I saw a lot of the ball. And the hat-trick against Swansea City last season gave me a lot of satisfaction, but that's all history. I like to think I've got even better things to come. Another aspect of my game that I need to work on is my goalscoring. I lack the killer instinct. I've always been the same ever since my junior days — I'd get through to the goalkeeper then, with only him to beat, I'd suddenly become nervous, like a learner-driver. I would go round the 'keeper but then hit the post. It happened all the time. I think I'm still going through it. I've really got to try and become more confident in front of goal and have been working on it in training but there's no way that compares to being out on the pitch on a match day. You see I can be a nervous character — but I wouldn't show it to anybody. I go away on my own somewhere. Even after a good performance I worry about the things I've done wrong. How I should have done certain things differently. No-one is too sure of their place in this team, so I know I have to play well every match.

Q: Do you enjoy that kind of pressure?

P: It's vital. I need it to make sure I try my hardest. Not only during a match but in training also. You must train hard to ensure you are at your best on a matchday and not knowing if you're playing or not is the most effective incentive to do your best at all times.

Q: How would you feel if asked to take a penalty?

P: Well, I've been asking for them, but with quite a lot of nerve! It's an easy way to get on the goal sheet!

Q: Who is your all-time hero?

P: A hero? My mum — she's given me plenty to think about in my life; made me think twice about decisions. She keeps me on my toes still, telling me I should be scoring more goals. She keeps on at me to buy the Pele video and to make myself watch it twice a day to improve my game.

As for heroes in sport, I know my answer won't be a popular one at Chelsea, but my heroes were the Leeds team of the 1970's. I thought they were a class side with good players in every position. They were a great, professional side.

Q: You were quite a sportsman at school, being a good runner and very promising young cricketer. Did a career as a cricketer appeal to you?

P: Well, I got as far as going to a trial match with Middlesex CCC. I never actually took part in it as my habit of keeping my watch 15 minutes fast backfired on me. I turned up for the rendevous and thought I had missed my contact. When I got home my mother told me what the real time was — I dashed back to the meeting place, but I just missed them. I guess it was fate.

Q: Do you have a message for our supporters?

P: Yes, please give a player a chance. Give him a cheer and he'll reward you.

Out of the Blue
DAVID SPEEDIE

"We're in a happy position at the moment as we're third in the League and we all believe that we can play better, both individually and as a team.

Although we've not won for a couple of matches, I think we're gradually improving with every game. For instance with a bit more luck in front of goal we could have at least drawn at Watford on Saturday. Mind you, they're a fair side and I can't see many teams coming away from Vicarage Road with points in the bag.

As far as my own game is concerned, I'm just trying to improve all the time and become more consistent. That means no more suspensions if I can help it. (Thank goodness no-one took up my offer of a bet that I wouldn't get suspended this season!) With Chelsea poised to win something and the World Cup next summer there's too much at stake for me to miss any games and I'm looking forward to just getting my head down and playing good football."

What are your most prized possessions?
My Scotland Caps (Which I'm still waiting to receive) last season's Chelsea Player of the Year trophy and a picture of Kerry buying a round of drinks.

If you had the opportunity to help people less fortunate than yourself, who would you assist.
I would put money into the Save The Children Fund.

If you could invent something to improve your life, or make it easier, what would it be?
I would like to be able to hypnotise Ernie Walley into playing five-a-sides every day.

What specialised subject would you choose on 'Mastermind'?
Typhoo Book of Coaching.

Tell a joke.
Big Joe's Dress sense.

What is your hidden talent?
An uncanny knack of getting into refs bad books.

If you were a football manager, which Chelsea player would you like to buy?
Eddie — With a backside that big it's nearly impossible to score past him!

On a 1-to-10 basis, how do you rate your performances this season (?) 1 2 3 4 5 6 7 8 9 10

If you won a lot of money would you buy:
(a) A big house and a small car, or
(b) A medium-sized house and a medium-sized car, or
(c) A small house and a flash car, or
(d) A football club.
A football club, and I'd want Ken Bates to do all my negotiating on contracts — he'd save me a fortune!

What would you do if you were asked to play football in the League for expenses only?
Only the Chairman could think of this one!

How would you improve today's society?
Change the present Government.

What kind of pictures do you hang on your walls at home?
I don't but I've got one of Dougie on the Mantlepiece that keeps the kids away from the fire.

What two books, two records and one luxury item would you take to a desert island?
Book One 'Beano',
Book Two 'Dandy'.
Record One 'Monster Mash' (Dougie's favourite).
Record Two 'Hey, Hey its The Monkees'.
Luxury Item. Anything or anyone looking like Angie Dickenson.

Football superstitions.
I'm always last onto the field.

How do you relax away from the pressure of football?
At the Imperial Arms, Farnborough.

If you had the opportunity to change places with a well-known public figure or another sportsman, who would you choose and what advice would you give him as he stepped into your shoes?
Ken Bates — and I'd advise him to not hold his breath for a contract!

David Speedie revealed his most prized possessions during the 1985/86 season, while Dennis Wise was amused by Ruud Gullit in 1995/96. Opposite, Dan Petrescu and George Weah speaking to the matchday programme during the 1996/97 and 1997/98 campaigns.

N THE BALL . . . *with* DENNIS WISE

What's your goal of the month?
I've got to say my goal against Kingstonian, the overhead kick. That was a good goal. I get a couple like that a year — I scored against Rangers the same way — but I miss a lot too.

A message to you Ruudi?
It's nice to have you here. You and Hughesy have set the gaff alight! A serious note, that.

What's the best joke you've heard?
Ruud gave us a joke about this — oh, I can't even say it. He knows a few good ones, Ruud.

On the ball......

DAN PETRESCU

What's your goal of the month?
Zola against West Ham was too long ago. Ah, today, Paul Hughes. I was very happy for him because he has been injured for a year maybe and I told him to go to Italy and see the same specialist as me because I had the same problem. Now he is all the time okay. When he came in I was sure he would do well. People didn't know him, but I know him very well.

And your mug of the month?
I go for Dennis Wise in training because when he went to take a corner, he slipped and the ball just goes one yard. He did it in a game this season, and he did again in the training ground. He has a special signal now, he points to the floor when he is to kick it one yard!

If you were to write a message on your T-shirt for when you scored, what would it say?
I'd write to all the guys on the bench, because I know it is difficult to get in the team at the moment and they are all very good players. I'd say: "Don't be angry, stay happy, because Chelsea will be a great team and you can be part of it." I will have to have a bigger chest to write that of course.

What would wake you from a coma?
Roberto and Luca, they all the time put something between their fingers. You can't stay in the dressing room. All the players hate this because it is killer. I think that would wake me from a coma.

bought the Spice Girls CD and I want to drive round Bucharest listening to it loud on the speakers because I love this music.

How will the England cricket team do in the Test match against New Zealand?
Ha! I don't know. When I came here I didn't know it's existing. When I saw the game I followed it because all the time you see it here. But England seem to lose every match don't they? Maybe if Romania start to play we could beat them.

What qualities do you admire in ot...
If they are amb...
down. Like if...
player, if you...
are not in the...
hard. If you...
dream will c...

**Who is yo...
Chelsea?**
I go for G...
always the...
All the tim...
need a vis...
for my he...
come ov...
at anoth...

**What...
player...
sign fo...**
I think...
come...
have...
the cl...
here...
not l...

wife. Maybe every week. All sorts of films.

Which Chelsea player would you have next to you in the trenches?
Frode, because he is very big, very strong, and I think he would protect me.

What is your view of pay-per-view TV?
In England all the time the crowd is full when we play. In Italy it's not going very well, people stay home. Tickets are expensive. But if in England the crowds stay, I think it is okay.

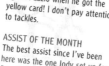

Brain Of Liberia

George Weah

GOAL OF THE MONTH
Poyet against Wimbledon. It was a good goal. He followed the play, he knew he was going to get the come back, and when the ball came it was just how he expected it, how he made it go to goal – that was a good shot.

SAVE OF THE MONTH
The save Ed made at Tottenham where he kicked the ball away. It was a beautiful save because it was very important.

TACKLE OF THE MONTH
Bad tackles? Didier Deschamps against Lazio when he got the yellow card! I don't pay attention to tackles.

ASSIST OF THE MONTH
The best assist since I've been here was the one Jody set up for Dennis Wise in the FA Cup (against Nottingham Forest).

MUG OF THE MONTH
Chris. He's stupid! He's never serious, always joking. I invited him to the Fellowship where we speak about gospel and things, and instead of going there he went to buy pigs – pigs and goats. That was the excuse he gave me. Stupid! And he named one of the pigs George!

BUSIEST PERSON AT THE CLUB
Antonio is always busy looking for something to do even if he hasn't got something.

FUNNIEST PLAYER EVER
Gus. He's always talking. Always.

MOST SERIOUS PLAYER EVER
Not serious, but easy. Flo. He doesn't talk much.

LAST TIME YOU TOOK PUBLIC TRANSPORT
Two weeks ago I took a taxi. That's public transport.

BEST WIND-UP
Dennis Wise always calls Chris Sutton 'Big Nose'. I don't know why, it's just so funny. Chris just looks at him like this (looks down his nose).

RECORD THAT GOT YOU DANCING AT THE SCHOOL DISCO
'Get Down On It' from Kool & The Gang. I was very happy in school because the first time I had a cuddle with a girl to that I was getting down on it.

WHEN DID YOU LAST DOUBT YOUR SANITY?
The last time I was in Portugal when I got sent off because of Jorge Costa.

WHO WOULD YOU LIKE AS A FRIEND?
Terry (Byrne). He's cool, he understands me and he talks sense. He knows how to bring about conversation. He's cool.

LAST EVENT YOU WALKED OUT ON
Nowhere. I went out to a club after I play against Tottenham for my first game. I went out to celebrate to an African club in Tottenham. That was good.

IF YOU COULD DO A GOOD DEED TOMORROW
The same as I do for UNICEF and the kids. I do public speeches to raise awareness, a lot of things.

WHICH OF OUR PLAYERS WOULD YOU ENTER IN AN EVENT FOR THIS YEAR'S OLYMPICS?
I would take Chris to run, 'cause I'm going to run with him and I know I'm going to beat him. I'd take him because I want to win.

THE PERFECT PLAYER
Wisey. He struggles for the team, passes a good ball and he's a real captain. I'm a captain too for the national team, but Wisey shows he's a captain all the time with total determination and a lot of captains don't do that. I saw that against Milan.

THE WORST PLAYER
Anywhere? Probably – Didier Deschamps! For him he's the best player, but he's always making mistakes! So he's the worst. (George adds: "Joke!" for any journalists who might be reading this).

CHAMPAGNE MOMENT OF THE MONTH
I didn't have one. I don't drink champagne, but I shall tell you my Guinness moment. When we had my child, I drank a couple of Guinness. I love Guinness. I don't like champagne. So I had a couple of pints in New York.

Goal of the month

Tore's first at Aston Villa. It was important for him and for us and he left Southgate for dead which is always fun.

Save of the month

Ed from Paul Scholes at Old Trafford when he was running through and he tipped it over the bar. Superb.

Tackle of the month

Hitchy's. He'll know what I mean!

Assist of the month

Jody's for Tore. Great ball. Great vision.

Celebration of the month

Jody's celebration against Blackburn when he reminded Duberry he had a head like the Millennium Dome.

Mug of the month

Mark Nicholls without a shadow. He was in the gym the other day and he was telling me he's just bought a new three-piece for his house. And he goes to me: "I got it half price. Well, not really half price, I got it 50 per cent off, though."

Best dressing room talk ever

Ted Dale's at Crystal Palace last year when we got smashed 4-1, or was it 4-0? At half-time Ted said we had to be stronger and his assistant Andy Ritchie was beside him and Ted just grabbed him and started throwing him about the room. Andy just fell over. No-one knew whether to laugh or not but in the end a couple did. We were about 3-0 down. Andy's no longer with us!

Room mate

Mark Nicholls. He loves having a little bet on the dogs. I know all about dogs now 'cause he's always got it up on the Text and he always wins!

JOHN

terry

Gianluca Vialli spoke to the matchday programme after taking over as player-manager in 1998, while a young John Terry answered our questions during the 1998/99 campaign.

Last opponent you socialised with

Kemy Izzet, Muzzy's brother from Charlton. Me, Paul Nicholls and him went out to a club a few weekends ago. He's a top man. He'll be a good player, even better than Muzzy.

Players' boots you cleaned as a trainee

Wisey, Dave Lee, Eddie Newton. They all produced for me as well. Loads of kit. Oners each at Christmas. I was happy.

Last book you bought

The Guv'nor by Lenny McLean. A quality book by a legend from the East End.

Favourite Simpson

Homer 'cause he's fat, eats anything and is a lazy ******* just like our kit man Aaron.

First kiss

Ohh, the other week! No, I don't know. I didn't see her much after nursery though.

A good night out

With the chaps. Anywhere with the YTs.

A bad night out

With the chaps! We have our good nights and bad nights. We all went out one night and Sam Parkin wouldn't stop going on about his Prada bag, his wash bag. He bought it for about a hundred pound! He loves it.

What would wake you from a coma?

Tiddypuds. They're like little Yorkshires that Nicho's (Paul Nicholls) mum does me when I go round there and they're quality. Sunday roast, I'm always round there.

Home life

I'm in digs with Slatts (Danny Slatter) in Isleworth. He's always on the phone to his Missus. I originally come from Barking in the East End.

Give us a Chelsea lookalike

Sam Parkin and the vicar from EastEnders, Alex. Our masseur John Kelly and Jaap Stam. Nicho (Paul Nicholls) and Screech from Saved By The Bell. Sorry Nicho.

What was the last thing you paid someone to do for you and was it worth it?

Courtney (Pitt) for cleaning my boots and he's minging. Courtney's up there for worst apprentice ever, without a shadow.

Champagne moment of the month

Steve Osborne getting a 'pro' at Reading. He got released here. I'm pleased for him and I really hope he does well, even though he's got a fat head!

. . . **He goes:** "I got it half price. Well, **not really half price**, I got it 50 per cent off though."

on the

Goal of the month

Unfortunately, last month we haven't scored a lot of goals, but I think the funniest was Mark Hughes' goal against Barnsley. The beginning of the action was quite good and then Petrescu crossed the ball in the box, Sparky had a first touch not perfect, and then the ball hit the post and came back and he headed it in the net. The goal was important for us, so it's my favourite, but it was also quite funny.

Save of the month

At Highbury, the first leg of the Coca-Cola Cup, Ed de Goey made a great save from Bergkamp, left foot, he was going on the other side and he made a great reaction. It was quite like a miracle for me. It helped us to stay in the game, so now we've ... to go through in

Newton, then Steve Clarkey came on and did his job. In that game we saw a lot of tough tackles.

Assist of the month

Petrescu when he crossed the ball when Mark Hughes put the ball in the net.

Mug of the month

The performance that we made against Arsenal in the first leg of the Coca-Cola Cup, so all of us. It's never a single mistake, it's a team mistake. And the way we played, tactically or physically or mentally, we appeared ****. We were very lucky to score when Sparky came on. Now we have a chance to go through. But the way we played we deserved to get beaten three or four-nil.

What city would be best for sightseeing in the ECWC?

I think we have to be very happy with Seville. It's one of the most beautiful cities, not just in Spain but in the whole of Europe. Of ... we're not there for

We're not there for sightseeing but to win the match.

Room mate

This season it has been Mark Nicholls mostly. He's great to room with because he doesn't snore – I do! – and he's always very helpful. When he sleeps he's like dead so I can do whatever I like. We speak a lot and he tries to teach me some new English words. I like him. But I think in the foreseeable future I'll be changing my room mate!

Who is Chelsea's Spice Boy?

I agree with all the chaps because I read this. Everyone thinks the Chelsea Spice Boys are either Berge or Robbie Di Matteo, and I think the way they wear their trousers, just to show how well endowed they are, is a disgrace.

gianluca
VIALLI

GOAL OF THE MONTH
Gustavo's against Sunderland. I had a little contribution towards it but I think it was a great goal. It will be one of the best this season.

TACKLE OF THE MONTH
Dennis Wise on me in training. We were playing one against one and he just went for it and nearly killed me! He got the ball, but not only the ball.

ASSIST OF THE MONTH
I'm not really the right person to say it but maybe my one for Gustavo's goal.

MUG OF THE MONTH
Ed de Goey because he is so lazy. He doesn't like working very much and he gets damned for that all the time.

BUSIEST PERSON AT THE CLUB
Aaron Lincoln – our kit man. He is always busy with me because he never makes sure my kit is in order. There is always something missing and Aaron says it is because he is too busy.

FUNNIEST PLAYER EVER
Faustino Asprilla was really funny because he was always joking, laughing, sometimes too much! He looked serious on the pitch but he wasn't.

LAST TIME YOU TOOK PUBLIC TRANSPORT
When we went to play in Riga, me and a few of the others took the train from Victoria to Gatwick.

BEST WIND-UP
When I was playing for Parma, someone phoned me saying that he was an inspector from the drug tests and that I was positive. He was saying I had too many things in my blood and urine and the value of these things was completely wrong. I was so confused and astonished that I could not think clearly. He was saying some of the values were pH 42 whereas dogs only have a value of 41! He wanted me to pass at least two litres of urine and bring it to Genoa. I thought he was telling the truth but he was from the local radio and he got all the information from my team-mates.

RECORD THAT GOT YOU DANCING AT THE SCHOOL DISCO
I ____ ____ a terrible dancer that

LAST EVENT YOU WALKED OUT ON
I went to see a concert which was a mixture of classical music and the kind of music they put on quietly in the background. It was killing me! After ten minutes I couldn't stand it anymore and it was due to last two hours. I was hitting my head against the wall and going crazy and after 20 minutes I walked out which wasn't good because we were there representing Parma.

IF YOU COULD DO A GOOD DEED TOMORROW
There are so many people to be helped in the world. I would help the people of Turkey because at this moment they need it a lot, and also the people of Kosovo.

WHICH OF OUR PLAYERS WOULD YOU ENTER IN AN EVENT FOR NEXT YEAR'S OLYMPICS?
Certainly Dennis Wise in the middle distance running. He can run for fun.

THE PERFECT PLAYER
Maradona's left foot, Platini's ____ foot, Gustavo Poyet's header,

Gianfranco Zola

Gianfranco Zola recalled falling for a wind-up when he spoke to the matchday programme during the 1999/2000 season, and Jimmy Floyd Hasselbaink tipped Michael Owen to impress at the upcoming 2002 World Cup.

PLAYERS AND COACHES COLOURS OF YOUR MIND

Jimmy Floyd Hasselbaink

Favourite colour
It's blue! Well, it depends. Of a car? Of clothes? Of what? (Whatever chosen, the page will be this colour). It can only go in blue, can't it!

Favourite read
I don't read much. And not newspapers! The best book I've read was The Kidnapping Of Heineken.

Favourite website
I don't go on that much. I only get e-mails off family and read that. That's it.

Favourite fashion designer
Armani and Prada. I like them.

Who cuts your hair?
A barber. A black man's barber near where I live. I go every week, once. Normally every Thursday.

Biggest indulgence
My house and in my house. In my house everything has to be perfect.

What did you listen to in the car this morning?
Capital. Capital FM. Every morning I listen to, what's his name again? Chris Tarrant. He's good. He's a young 70!

Record you have heard most times in your life
I think my first record I bought. Womak & Womak. I was 16. That was 13 or 14 years ago.

Best takeaway
None. My missus cooks everything. She is the best. Perfect.

Souvenir of Britain you would take back to your country
What's that thing called you have with gravy? Yorkshire pudding! I love Yorkshire pudding!

First person to break your heart
It was Nils Overweg who sent me away from my first pro club because I was too late. Always too late.

Two footballers to put in the boxing ring
Eidur Gudjohnsen and Robbie Savage. They like each other very much!

Star of next summer's World Cup
Michael Owen. He's doing well at this moment and he can only progress.

Worst miss
Last year ____

What have you won outside of football?
Nothing. I only played football.

Name the Chelsea team that beat Manchester City in the last game of last season when we qualified for Europe
I am going to name it for you. I am going to name it! Mario Melchiot, right-back. John Terry, Marcel Desailly, Babayaro. Winger, Graeme Le Saux. Jokanovic, Jody Morris. Dennis Wise, right-wing. Me and Gianfranco! In goal, Cudicini! (Jimmy is the first player to get a line-up right. He clicks his fingers with joy.)

Mug of the month
Billy (McCulloch, masseur). After we got back from Coventry he was sleeping in the hotel, paying for the room and not realising he had to pay for the breakfast. He went to the breakfast in the morning, and at the end of the breakfast he has to pay forty-five quid.

Goal of the month
Eidur. I didn't see the one in Levski, but I think the one at home ____

Petr Cech told us of the time he scored a ridiculous own goal in 2006/07, while Ashley Cole spoke of the enormous influence his mother had had on his career during an interview in the 2009/10 campaign.

WO
& p

Petr Cech rec
of his goal
howlers and
risked life
for a pho

profile

A Petr spectator story

It was 1997, I was watching in Prague. It was a qualifier for the World Cup in France and it was Czech Republic against Spain. I had the tickets where I could see only one-third of the pitch, because there was a barrier to separate two sectors of the stand. It was the worst experience as a supporter. Spain won 1-0 and I didn't see the goal.

How did he do that!

Mancini against Lyon this week, it was one-against-one in the box and he had really quick feet and stepped over the ball many times before scoring.

How did I do that!

When I was about 14 I played in a street soccer World Cup in Berlin. We played against Germany and conceded a late goal from a penalty. And because I almost saved it, I was so angry, when the ball came back I angrily kicked it back in. From 1-0 up we were 2-1 down because in street rules this counts as an own goal.

What was I thinking!

I did pictures for a calendar of Prague. There were famous people in it and they asked me if I'm afraid of heights. I said, no, I have no problem, so a picture was taken on the roof of the national museum at 30 or 40 metres high. I was standing with my back to the drop on a space which was about one-and-a-half metres big. Behind me there was nothing! If I took one step back, I would just drop. My wife couldn't believe it when she saw the pictures.

A Petr domestic story

In France when we bought our dog, the first time he was alone at home was for about four hours. When I got back I saw him through the window and he was chewing all the CDs, DVDs, the books in the living room by the telly. I ran inside quickly to stop the mess and as soon as I opened the door I saw that everything around was broken and chewed. It was the biggest mess I've ever seen in my life.

A dressing room moment

During my first year in Rennes we had to win the last game of the season to stay up and before the game you could feel how important it was. Everyone was nervous. It is the biggest tension I have experienced as a player.

You've got to be kidding!

I don't remember the game but recently someone scored a goal which was disallowed and they danced for three minutes behind the goal not realising, as the game went on.

Last footballer you bumped into socially

Stelios from Bolton. Greece played

Mug of the month

Easy! The Valencia-Inter fight. It was a better fight than the WWF final!

South Korea at Fulham and they stayed in the Chelsea hotel. I saw him in the reception.

Bargain signing!

(non-Chelsea)
Benni McCarthy at Blackburn.

Petr Cech at 50

I hope I'm still alive! And with a happy family, maybe working in football.

What I did last night (last Wednesday)

I watched Arsenal and Manchester United, zapping in between, and we had visitors staying from France.

Last footballer you went out with socially

Robbie, we went to a Japanese restaurant with our partners.

Goal of the month

Michael Ballack against Porto.

Assist of the month

Robben for Drogba in the Carling Cup Final.

Quote of the month

'JT is the iron man'. Three times injured in one week and he's still playing and celebrating.

International eye-catcher

Mantorras from Angola. He is now with Benfica. When we played in the World Cup Under-20s we had Angola in our group and their game was just 10 people to defend and Mantorras to do the rest. He got the ball and tried to dribble past everyone and score and it worked. But we drew 0-0.

Chelsea vs Tottenham Hotspur 29

116

GRASS ROOTS

ASHLEY COLE

OUR FLYING FULL-BACK LEARNED TO PLAY FOOTBALL IN EAST LONDON AND WAS MORE ACCUSTOMED TO LIFE AS A STRIKER BACK THEN

Why did you start playing football?
It was just what we did where I grew up in east London, we basically finished school and went to play football in the park. You only have to look at all the lads playing professional football from round my way, like Ledley King, John Terry, Bobby Zamora, Jlloyd Samuel, to realise that we all wanted it.

What was the name of the first club you ever played for?
They were called Puma FC, just a Sunday team but we played at a decent standard. Most of those lads I mentioned before were playing for Senrab, but not all in the same age group I don't think.
I was friends with Ledley because we lived in the same road and I played district football with him. So it was strange that I ended up playing against them all for Puma, but you don't really think about those things at the time.

Did you ever see someone very talented fall by the wayside as a youngster?
Yeah, I think everyone probably has. There were players who had been better than me at certain times in my life that aren't playing in the professional game at all. It's hard to explain how it happens – I think sometimes it comes down to hard work and commitment but it's also important to have that little bit of luck or be in the right place at the right time.

What position did you start playing and what other positions have you played in before settling on a chosen one?
When I was younger, I was playing up front, on the wing and a bit of everything, but mainly attacking positions. I think I was 16 when one of the youth team coaches at Arsenal, called Tom Walley, moved me to left-back and I've played there ever since.

Which person had the biggest influence on you when you were a youngster?
My mum. She brought me up and always made sure I got to football training and matches. I owe a lot to her for taking me to football and supporting me as a youngster.

Were you good at any other sports when you were younger?
Not really, I've always been a quick runner but I was only ever interested in becoming a footballer.

Who did you or your family support when you were growing up?
I played for the Arsenal youth team from a young age so I followed them. Most of the kids at my school or around Bow supported them, Spurs or West Ham.

Did you have any trials elsewhere?
No, but a few people will probably remember I went out on loan to Crystal Palace in Division One before I broke into the first team at Arsenal. I had a good spell there under Steve Coppell and it definitely helped get me ready and show the people at Arsenal I was ready to play too.

Steve Coppell managed Ash during a loan spell at Crystal Palace in early 2000

117

Team mates
with frank lampard

Frank Lampard made his 500th appearance for the Blues on Wednesday, so there's no better man to give us a insight into life behind-the-scenes at Chelsea

You've got team-mates reaching landmarks as well, with JT looking likely to make his 500th appearance soon. Also, Petr Cech made his 300th last month and Ashley Cole reached 200. We've quite a few long-term residents here...

fl That's been one of our strengths, because it has been a successful period for us. Obviously, John's been here longer than any of us and it's great that we've got that sort of captain – a lynchpin who has been here throughout. Then there's people like Big Pete, Didier and Paulo who have been here since 2004 and I think of them as having been here for ever. It's nice to keep that continuity.

music on different days and you definitely notice whose turn it is because the dance moves come out!

Who have been the unsung heroes for you during your time here?

fl I'd say all the backroom staff have had a part to play in the club's progress and some of them have been here a long time.
I actually joined the same day as Billy McCulloch (pictured left, reading a book), so I'd give him and Stu Sullivan – another masseur – a mention because both of them have been here nearly 10 years and are a real part of everything.
Bulldog and Busy Alan (players' assistants Frank Steer and Alan Barrett) as well. They really do make things tick behind the scenes and day in, day out, they are the people you rely on.
I'm sure John would say the same, as they've got the club in their blood now.

A few times this season, players from our Academy have been involved with the first-team squad. How nice is it to see new faces, who have come through the club's ranks, sat in the changing room on a matchday?

fl I think it can be tough for kids to break through when you consider the top-class players we have at the club, but it's nice to see that a few of them there, especially

k it can be tough for kids
break through, so it's nice

Does it tell you something about the club that so many people stay here for a long spell?

fl It's a good club for winning things and coming to London is a big thing for the foreign lads when they arrive, but I do think that once they are here they want to stay.
A lot of people might think that the club can be a bit posh and stuck-up, but when you come here and look behind the scenes, it's very normal and friendly.

When the supporters chant their way around the team before a game, do you see your team-mates get a lift from it?

fl Yeah, definitely. It's amazing, the best feeling you can have. Personally, I feel it because hearing your name being sung is the ultimate sign you're doing the business for the team.
When you've been at the club a while, like John and I have, you love that moment because you put everything into the game for them. And when you get something back from the fans, it's an amazing feeling. That is them saying they're with you.
You need that all the time, not just before the game and when the goals

"We make a big effort to help all new players settle in when they arrive here. That goes back to Dennis Wise's era when they embraced the [Gianluca] Vialis of this world"

are going in but also when things aren't going so well. If a shot goes flying over the bar by 20 yards and they still sing your name, that is sometimes just the lift you need, and we can only be thankful for that.

As we speak, we can see one of our newest arrivals, David Luiz, having a laugh and a joke. That shows it's an easy club to settle into, doesn't it?

fl We make a big effort to help all new players settle in when they arrive here. That goes back to a time before me, with Dennis Wise's era when they embraced the [Gianluca] Vialis of this world.
We still do it now and we're lucky to have a lot of people who speak different languages here because there is always someone to talk to for anyone who arrives. So people like David Luiz fit in easily – he's a very effervescent character.
At this point, David Luiz approaches, having heard his name, and asks Frank to say nice things to his friends in Brazil will see that Lampard is talking about him!

Have you always had the same spot in the changing room?

fl Yes, although they have altered over the years. The old one was the current away changing room.
I have the same spot in the corner with JT and Ash, but we are a big squad for mixing, we do have a good time together. Different people choose the

LET'S TALK ABOUT...

Didier Drogba on being instrumental in Chelsea reaching the knockout stages of the Champions League and heading towards 150 goals

11 DIDIER DROGBA

Interview: **Dominic Bliss**

...Valencia victory

DD It was good to qualify top of the group with a 3-0 win, the same score as in our previous game against Newcastle.

Someone has to score the goals – in that game, it was me and Rami; in other games, it will be somebody else.

The most important thing was to qualify – finishing top was a plus. It was a great night and, when the crowd is behind us like that, we are a very difficult team to beat.

...Finding form

DD As with every player, the more I play, the easier it is for me to find my habits on the pitch.

It's not easy coming back from a head injury like the one I suffered against Norwich, then coming back from an arm injury and also coming back from suspension. However, the more I play, the more chances I have to score.

...Head injury

DD That problem, after the Norwich game, affected me quite a lot and I don't talk about it too much. It was a bad experience and one of those things that rarely happens in football, but it happened

to me and now it's behind me. I feel much better now.

...Ambitions

DD You always have to write a list of things you want to achieve, especially if you come back after not playing for a while. For the first few games, you aim to adapt and feel good. Then, after a few more games, you fix different

He's done it again: Didier Drogba celebrates his second goal against Valencia

targets to improve and to score goals. So, that's what I'm doing right now and I'm quite happy with the way I'm starting to play now.

...Connecting play

DD I always connect with the players around me, that's how I try to play. This image of me as a lone striker is out there and it is a part of my game, but it's not

> I hope there is a kid watching who is saying the same things as I was when I was young, who will find the same passion for football that I discovered from these kinds of games

the best part. I feel much better and I give more to a team when I combine with another striker or the players behind me. I produce more that way and I'm more efficient.

...Big games

DD The Valencia game last Tuesday and this one tonight are both very important games. I think that's why you play football. I started to play the game because, when I was young, I was watching all these big games and thinking: "Wow, I just want to be there

playing." So, for me to be here now, I feel lucky and I want to do my best to enjoy these big occasions.

I hope there is a kid watching and saying the same things as I was when I was young, who will find the same passion for football that I discovered from these kinds of games.

...City's emergence

DD Manchester City wasn't a massive game when I first arrived in England, but now it is. They are top of the league and it is deserved – they have bought a

lot of very good players to make their team more competitive, so it's going to be difficult to play against them. It's a massive test.

...Playing Monday

DD Yeah, it's different, but, when you are on the pitch, you don't see what day it is!

I have played on a Monday night before and it's very strange when you are not playing at the weekend. However, as I said, once a game starts, you don't care what day it is.

A feature with Frank Lampard after his 500th Blues appearance in 2011, plus our interview with Didier Drogba shortly before his first Chelsea spell ended in 2012.

Landmark awaits: Drogba is in line to reach 150 goals in a Chelsea shirt

THE SEVENTIES

It was a decade of contrasting fortunes for the Blues on and off the pitch, but there is little doubt it was a boom time for the matchday programme

With new designs every season, the development of colour printing technology, increased match action imagery and more interaction with the players than ever before, the programme was very much hot property.

Remarkable sales reached a pinnacle in the 1972/73 campaign, when copies were sold to an average of 99 per cent of those attending matches at Stamford Bridge – this has been reported as a world record. The incredible demand was no doubt down to the quality of the product, but two triumphant cup campaigns at the start of the decade also had an impact.

The 1970 FA Cup final and 1971 European Cup Winners' Cup final captured the imagination of the public and, as had been common practice for some time, each programme contained a coupon which would help supporters purchase a final ticket should they collect them all.

With reported figures of up to 108 per cent of the crowd at certain matches, it's fair to say some fans were buying more than one copy – perhaps one to keep intact and one for the coupon.

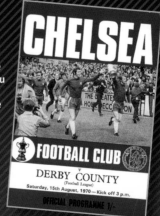

The 1970/71 season had a lot to live up to after the campaign before had brought Chelsea fans FA Cup joy for the first time. That triumph earned us a place in the Charity Shield against champions Everton. You can see extracts from that programme on page 33 and here is the programme from the opening league game a week later, against Derby County.

The cover showed Peter Osgood and Peter Houseman parading the FA Cup at Stamford Bridge before the Charity Shield and inside were action shots from that fixture.

The opposition pages featured an image of Derby's enigmatic manager Brian Clough and at the front was a round-up of the summer's transfer activity and a message from Chairman Joe Mears, who spoke of his confidence that more success could be achieved with the help of the fans. How right he would prove to be…

OUR CUP—BUT . . . .

We make this Picture No. 1 as it shows Ian Hutchinson scoring our first goal of the season at Stamford Bridge. It just happened that Everton's two was one goal too many for us.

Keith Weller, our new signing, puts in a powerful header.

THE CHARITY SHIELD GOES TO EVERTON

There are enough Everton players here to deal with this situation. David Webb watches Keith Weller's efforts.

Crash! An "Ossie" pile-driver is on its way—but it was brilliantly saved by Gordon West.

CHELSEA ????? QUIZ

1. Dave Sexton's first signing for Chelsea is no longer with the club. Who is he?

2. Flashback to last season: An opposing team, two down to Chelsea, scored the next three goals and were finally beaten. Who were they?

3. Who were Chelsea's leading League scorers in each of the past three seasons?

4. Which team did Chelsea beat three times last season?

5. Former Chelsea players now manage (a) Bristol City, (b) Swansea City, (c) Portsmouth. Names, please?

VISITORS' VIEW

DERBY FANS 'BANK' ON 1970-71 SUCCESS

four draws, a sequence that must be extended or ended today.

A year ago today Derby were stepping into the unknown, back into the First Division after 16 seasons out of it, during which they dropped into Division III from 1953-57. This time it's different, because, with method and ability in abundance, they conquered that "unknown" last season, and must start this 1970-71 campaign better equipped for the experience.

SIX WEEKS ago Derby County reported a season-ticket sellout and £130,000 banked from their sale. That was still a fortnight before the players reported back for training, and supporters cannot show much greater enthusiasm than that during a close season.

The swing in Derby's fortunes, from a once-great club struggling only three seasons ago to stay above the Third Division, to their glittering new image, is one of the success stories of modern football. It is dominated by two figures—manager Brian Clough off the field, skipper Dave Mackay on it.

If you really want to make Brian bristle, try suggesting to him that the Derby bubble might be about to burst after two great playing seasons as runaway champions of the Second Division in 1969 and a powerful fourth in the League Championship on their return to the top bracket last season.

"There's no secret about what we've achieved these last two years," says the Derby manager. "It's there for all to see. Good players putting the emphasis on skill and hard work. Tons of it. Are they the things you make bubbles with?

"Derby went up to the First Division with style. Once we'd got there, I was confident we would hold our own and that playing against the top clubs would bring out the best in our youngsters. It certainly did.

"Two years ago I signed Dave Mackay as the man we needed to lift us into the First Division. He carried on lifting us last season, and when I'm asked how much longer he is likely to go on, I just can't give an answer. "You can't put a time tag on Dave Mackay. He's ageless. Why, he's starting this season a pound lighter than he ended the last one."

With one exception Derby County's first-team "pool" comprises the same 13 players who formed the main squad a year ago. The addition is Welsh International Terry Hennessey, signed from Nottingham Forest for £100,000 in February. From the time of his arrival to the end of the season Derby were undefeated in 12 League matches—eight wins,

BRIAN CLOUGH — Derby dynamo.

But if injuries strike, isn't that pool of 13 players a wee bit small, compared with the cover at other major First Division clubs? Let Brian Clough have the last word about that: "We've been very lucky last season and the season before that with injuries. I'm not talking about them. I don't want other people talking about them, either."

Whatever Derby do on the field here today, there will be a collection of cigarette ends around the feet of Brian Clough at the end of his own afternoon's work—90 minutes of intense hunched observation from the director's box or trainer's booth. Only cigarette ends, mark you. There won't be a bubble—burst or otherwise—in sight.

LET us go back to the night of the 29th April—a night that we will always remember—when, for the first time in our history the F.A. Cup finally came to Stamford Bridge. Many congratulations to Dave Sexton and the team for giving us all an unforgettable season, not only by winning the Cup but finishing third in the League. May I thank everyone connected with the Club for helping to make it so successful.

And now we look forward to new heights, not only in our domestic Competitions but in Europe and with your support—so magnificent last season, particularly at Wembley and Old Trafford—we are confident that we can achieve further honours. On behalf of my fellow Directors I welcome you to the start of a new season. Let us hope that once again it is a season to remember. May I thank you for the wonderful support that all of you have given to our Club. I am proud to be your Chairman.

J. B. MEARS

Summer transfers: As we welcome Keith Weller to Stamford Bridge—he joined us from Millwall at the beginning of May and flew out to Venezuela to make his first Chelsea appearance on the summer tour—we also extend best wishes to those players who have left us and kick off the new season in other colours. As you know, Bobby Tambling and Alan Birchenall have moved on to Crystal Palace, where we shall follow their fortunes with close interest as two very fine players joining a club with whom we have had very friendly relations. Apart from the month he spent on loan to Palace last January, Bobby served Chelsea as man and boy for 13 seasons and, with 202 goals, stands in the record book as the highest scorer in Chelsea history. We look forward to welcoming him back later in the season to present him with an illuminated address, now being prepared, which will mark not only his record goalscoring for Chelsea but also our appreciation of his long and exemplary service to the club.

Other players who have left us for new Clubs since the end of last season include Michael Maskell (Brentford), Alan Cocks (Southport), Joe Larkin (Shamrock Rovers), Tim Haydon (Bournemouth), Roger Hawkins (Oxford United) and two juniors who have signed amateur forms for Fulham, Tommy James and Paul Corfield.

OUR JOURNEY TO EURO FINAL

Here are extracts from our 1970/71 Cup Winners' Cup campaign programmes. All the games took place over two legs apart from the final, although that did require a replay after the first match ended in a 1-1 draw

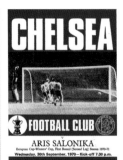

THE GOALS AGAINST ARIS THAT TOOK US THROUGH THE LAST ROUND AND ON TO SOFIA

THE NIGHT WE WON OUR LAST EUROPEAN

CUP-WINNERS' TIE AT STAMFORD BRIDGE

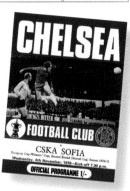

First up were Greek side Aris Salonika, who we beat 6-2 on aggregate. It wasn't totally plain sailing, though, as the first leg ended all square, and you can see the Blues celebrating Ian Hutchinson's goal in that match on the cover of the programme for the second leg, which ended in a 5-1 thrashing. Pictures from that game featured in the second round, second leg programme against CSKA Sofia. We negotiated our way past the Bulgarian side thanks to a couple of 1-0 victories. There was a gap of more than four months before our quarter-final clash, which was an absolute classic against RFC Bruges. After losing the first leg 2-0 away from home, a dramatic turnaround was required, as was demonstrated from the press reaction to our defeat in Belgium. That's exactly what happened as Peter Osgood netted a brace in a memorable 4-0 win at the Bridge to earn us a semi-final spot. There was also a rundown of UEFA rules and regulations in the Between Ourselves column.

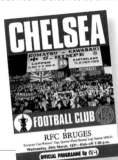

L IFE'S rules and regulations make pretty dry reading. Even in the case of those to do with football competitions, it's about as exciting as wading through the London telephone directory. But, taking the European Cup-Winners' Cup as an example, it's all got to be set down somewhere for reference, or we'd have gone on thinking this quarter-final against Bruges *could* be settled here tonight on penalty-kicks . . . which it can't (see page 3).

But extracting from the thirty-one pages of Cup-Winners' Cup regulations, principals of protocol and memorandum on disciplinary measures in U.E.F.A. competition matches throws up some interesting material. For instance, did you know that the Final on May 19 could be switched from the already announced venue of Athens to a stadium here in England? Article 6, item 4, in Regulations of the Cup-Winners' Cup makes this clear. It says: "If the two Finalists belong to the same National Association, the venue may be changed and the match played in the country of the two clubs. . . ."

Ossie makes it a night to remember!

Nine minutes to go in the second leg of the European Cup-Winners' Cup quarter-final here against Bruges . . . we were still 2-1 down on aggregate and, under the Chelsea barrage, the Belgians' defence was somehow holding out. The physical pressure was on them but, with time fast running out, the mental pressure was on us, and growing every minute. Then came this goal by Peter Osgood—playing his first match for two months—that lifted the anxiety. Having saved the tie in normal time, we won it well in the extra half-hour, with Ossie again on target for goal No. 3 and a final score of 4-0 on the night that made the aggregate Chelsea 4, Bruges 2.

We faced English opposition at the next hurdle in the form of Manchester City. For the first time in the cup run, we played at home first and established a 1-0 lead, with the scorer from that match, Derek Smethurst, featured on the cover for our league game against Burnley. The programme for the City game understandably harked back to the classic tie against Bruges in the previous round and by the time we secured another 1-0 win at Maine Road a fortnight later the Blues had secured a spot in our first European final where we would face the mighty Real Madrid. The cover for the final is pictured here.

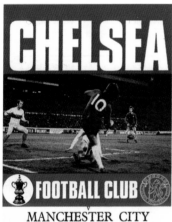

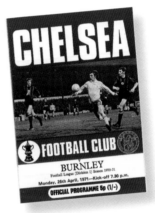

This European semi-final will, when completed at Maine Road on April 28, decide whether City again go through to the Final or whether it is Chelsea who represent England against Real Madrid or PSV Eindhoven, of Holland, in Athens on the night of Wednesday, May 19.

WAS THIS THE GREATEST GOAL AT STAMFORD BRIDGE?

After a 1-1 draw in Athens, the replay took place three days later and ended in a 2-1 Chelsea win, with John Dempsey and Osgood the goal-scoring heroes. Another point of interest from the 1970/71 campaign was a wonder strike scored by John Hollins in our 2-1 home win against Arsenal. Our next programme dedicated a page of editorial to the "Goal of the Century".

Cup hero Dempsey is our cover star, 1971/72

Our first home match of 1971/72 saw Manchester United visit the Bridge and the cover featured John Dempsey's stunning volley in the Cup Winners' Cup replay. This was explained on page five which also outlined the club's plans to redevelop Stamford Bridge, starting with the East Stand, something which would go on to dominate much of the decade. A colour poster of our heroics in Athens was also included. Turn to page 172 to read Chairman Brian Mears' thoughts after the club's two triumphant seasons.

CUP NIGHT IN ATHENS

The Talk of Stamford Bridge

WE start the new season at Stamford Bridge as we began a year ago with one of the game's prized trophies on display, this time the European Cup-Winners' Cup, and with everyone in the camp wondering whether the successful sequence of the past two seasons will become a triple triumph over the next ten months. We all know it CAN; no one can say what WILL happen.

As last year we go in search of first-team honours in four competitions, hoping that what we have achieved in all of them before can be done again in one direction—or more—in 1971-72. There is no doubt in any of our minds that the League Championship is the No. 1 target, for the important reason that it is THE No. 1 tournament, and we open the programme of home fixtures with one of the season's top attractions as we welcome Manchester United tonight.

THE NEW STAMFORD BRIDGE

LAST year we informed you of our decision to build a new Stadium costing several million pounds over the next few years. A considerable amount of work and accumulation of information has been progressing in the past months, and the Board expects to consider the Architects' initial design next month.

Assuming all necessary approvals are forthcoming, we shall commence the construction of the new East Stand—which will be the first stage of the new Stadium—in 1972.

The information resulting from the questionnaire published in last season's Programme for the match against Leeds has been processed and analysed by the computer and has provided valuable information. The main suggestions arising from the questionnaire were (1) covered terraces, (2) more low-cost bench seating.

The Club has noted your suggestions for detailed improvements to facilities which

we hope to implement in the near future.

On certain of the recommendations, such as improved toilet facilities, work has progressed. Other suggestions such as an electrical scoreboard, social facilities, etc., will form part of the new Stadium, and work has already been carried out in improving safety conditions in the Ground.

FRONT COVER SHOT

WITHOUT the first goal in our Athens replay against Real Madrid there couldn't have been the second shown on page 6. Here you see John Dempsey's great double effort that launched us to victory in the European Cup-Winners' Cup Final.

His first attempt, a header from Charlie Cooke's corner, was punched out by Borja and John met the rebound with the perfect volley. "It could have gone anywhere," he said, "but it went in for the best goal I've ever scored."

5

Having won the competition the previous season, we qualified for the Cup Winners' Cup once more and faced Luxembourg part-timers Jeunesse Hautcharage in the first round. Pictured is the cover for the first leg, which we won 8-0, while the second leg ended in 13-0 victory – both of which are club records. The match action pages pictured all eight goals from the first leg, while the letters page made interesting reading as people regaled their tales from Athens the previous season.

THE START OF OUR EIGHT-GOAL SPREE

ONE Peter Osgood starts the scoring after two minutes from John Hollins' pass in Luxembourg two weeks ago.

TWO Jeunesse goalkeeper Fusilier sends up a cloud of dust in a vain attempt to save Peter Housemann's 20-yarder (8 mins.).

9

BY winning the F.A. Cup and the European Cup-Winners' Cup in successive seasons, the modern Stamford Bridge Blues did things no other Chelsea team had done. Equally, no previous Chelsea side ever faced the sort of situation that confronts Ron Harris and his men tonight. In the 16-year history of European football, not many British clubs have started a match with an eight-goal lead. And I'm wondering what Dave Sexton will be telling the lads as a "gee-up" just before they go out. And in the other dressing-room along the corridor, what does the Jeunesse Hautcharage player-coach, Romain Schoder, tell *his* team ?

IT'S SIX BY HALF-TIME IN LUXEMBOURG — **WITH STILL TWO MORE GOALS TO COME**

THREE From Tommy Baldwin's cross, Ossie helps himself to an easy header after 20 minutes.

FIVE The 37th minute brings a John Hollins "special"—left foot from 25 yards—with the ball in the net before the 'keeper can move.

FOUR Sixty seconds later Houseman heads our fourth after Alan Hudson's free-kick.

SIX Osgood completes his hat-trick (42 mins.) with another header, this time from Charlie Cooke's centre.

10   11

THANKS to Dave Sexton and his boys, we were able to spend our first holiday abroad together. Previously, my husband was strictly a U.K. holidaymaker, but for CHELSEA alone he conquered his air-sea sickness and we spent a tremendous holiday at Loutraki, plus the thrill of seeing both matches.

My only chance of a further holiday abroad rests with CHELSEA!

Mrs. Sheila Hadley.

27 Links Avenue,
Morden, Surrey.

AND HERE ARE THE SECOND-HALF GOALS

SEVEN It might look like another Osgood, but in fact this is the 74th-minute header by Tommy Baldwin (right).

EIGHT Their No. 8 can't stop our goal No. 8—a header by the almost hidden David Webb after 81 minutes.

And full marks to photographer Richard Tonks for recording every one of our goals in Luxembourg.

12

I AM a 16-year-old Chelsea fanatic living in Edinburgh and I made the journey to Athens alone, taking two days off school. I left Edinburgh by bus at 7.30 p.m. the night before the match and arrived in London at 6.30 a.m. I then made a confusing journey by Underground to Waterloo where I joined the Chelsea party. Another hour and a half coach journey to Stansted Airport followed by a three and a half hour flight to Athens. Boy, was I glad to get there in one piece!

The return journey was similar except I took the overnight train to Edinburgh arriving at seven on Friday morning. Two hours later I was at school, exhausted, telling everybody about my journey. It was the first time I had seen Chelsea and it cost me £47. How's that for a first time? Well done Chelsea!

Adrian Webb.

23 Brighton Place,
Portobello, Edinburgh, 15

GRAND NATIONAL DRAW

THE Grand National Draw, organised by the Stamford Bridge Development Society, was made at last week's home match against Sheffield United by Eddie McCreadie and resulted as follows:

L'Escargot: Mrs. S. Gonzal, Carshalton.	Bright Willow: M. Alpine, S.W.1.
Master Vesuvius: D. Cousens, Worcester Park.	Cardinal Error: C. W. Cowen, Guildford.
Gay Trip: M. Smith, S.E.17.	Prairie Dog: J. Carey, Morden.
Black Secret: P. Hancock, W.2.	Red Sweeney: E. A. Digby, Woburn Green, Bucks.
Alotta Fort: J. Mills, Waddon.	
Specify: J. Durrant, Chelsfield, Kent.	Sagpar's Choice: P. Church, Reading.
Rigton Prince: Mrs. Brown, S.W.17.	Well-To-Do: C. B. Daglers, Bromley, Kent.
Twigairy: C. Walker, S.W.8.	Astbury: H. Leach, N.W.1.
Macronzy: Michael Rose, Aylesbury.	Black Tout: Mrs. Hannng, Burnt Oak.
Dim Wit: W. Lovell, Hounslow.	Bullock's Horn: C. Warwick, S.W.11.
Fortina's Palace: Marton, The Crown, N.W.6.	Chatham: Mrs. N. Veazey, S.W.18.
The Panther: Mrs. M. I. Lidsford, W.4.	Cloudsmere: Mrs. L. Burgess, W.13.
Pearl of Montreal: C. Hinter-bits, E.2.	Country Wedding: Mrs. F. Mason, S.W.4.
Money Boat: Mrs. D. M. Radsell, Wembley.	Dublin's Green: Mrs. R. H. Timms, S.W.6.
Swan-Shot: Mrs. Martin, High Wycombe.	Even Delight: S. Stammann, Mitcham, Beds.
Gyldenye: R. Smart, West Croydon.	Fair Vulgan: Mrs. C. A. Stanning, Edgware.
The Inventor: O. Neuse, S.W.6.	
Guy Buccaneer: B. Rainbow, S.W.6.	Just a Gamble: Mrs. V. Bissett, Beckenham.
General Symons: G. Reakcliffe, N.W.4.	Kellsboro' Wood: Mrs. G. Hoyes, S.W.20.
Limeburner: J. M. Jackson, Woking.	Lime Street: Mr. Allen, S.W.11.
Linacres: B. M. Knight, Shacklewell, Bedford.	Miss Hunter: C. R. Gerrish, S.W.16.
Nephin Beg: Mrs. D. W. Cook, S.W.18.	Nom de Guerre: J. Hogg, Enfield.
Ohre: D. Holden, Belfast.	Persrati: J. Swan, Langley, Slough.
The Pooka: D. Ashley, W.12.	Rough Silk: B. Todman, S.E.14.
Vichysoise: H. Hughes, S.W.11.	Voltore: S. C. Burt, S.W.12.
Zara's Grove: J. Ridley, Feltham, S.W.6.	

1st Prize: £100. 2nd Prize: £50. 3rd Prize: £25. 4th Prize: £12.50. Consolation Prizes: £1 to everyone drawing a horse, plus £5 for every horse finishing the race.

Injuries would eventually bring the career of Ian Hutchinson to a premature end, but a double-page spread in our programme for the League Cup game against Nottingham Forest in October showed just how much effort he put in to trying to regain fitness. Grand National Day, meanwhile, has occupied the mind of many football fans on an April matchday over the years and our programme for the game against Crystal Palace not only printed the draw for the race on the back cover, but an article revealed how our Vice Chairman Lord Viscount had a horse competing at Aintree. Sadly, Vichysoise did not finish the race.

HERE'S TO 'OUR' HORSE IN TODAY'S 'NATIONAL'

IF Vichysoise runs as well as he did in the 1971 Grand National, in which he finished seventh, Lord Chelsea will be a well-pleased onlooker at Aintree this afternoon. If he fares better, our Vice-Chairman will indeed be thrilled. And if Vichysoise should win, another name will be added to the list of horses which have triumphed in the National at very long odds.

With 20 victories between them—prize-money just short of £12,000—Lord Chelsea's string of eight horses have won more races than anyone else's this National Hunt season. His previous best total was ten winners, with nine on three other occasions.

Lord Chelsea's most successful runner this winter has been Trysting Day, with seven wins. Roman Law has won five races, Roman Holiday four, High Si two, and Knighted and Money Market one each. The two who have not reached the winner's enclosure in 1971-72 are Marndhill . . . and Vichysoise.

Looking ahead to next season and beyond, our Vice-Chairman names the five-year-old Knighted as potentially the finest horse he has owned. So far, the best has been Roman Holiday, with a career total of 14 wins over hurdles and fences, closely followed by Trysting Day (13 wins).

The target is February after **THE LONGEST TWELVE MONTHS OF HUTCH'S LIFE**

GOAL

When we won the Cup-Winners' Cup in Athens in May, Ian was there as a spectator. Then, while on holiday in Trinidad and El Salvador, this was how he spent the early summer—expecting Stamford Bridge increases to build up that right knee.

But it wasn't ALL hard work and the routine that goes with recovery. In particular, he found time while on the injured list to become Newcastle 16. 17.

On August 17, Hutch went with the Reserves to Swindon to test the knee. He scored a goal, was limping still and frustrated. By the time he plays again—February at the earliest—he will have been out of first-team football nearly a whole year. That's a large slice of any player's life. Here he goes through the agony of those weeks . . .

Now the trouble gets bigger as Trainer Harry Medhurst tells Ian: "You're going for a return to competitive football in February. As you can see, he's still got his eye on a No. 9 shirt!"

125

New-look stadium is talk of the Bridge, 1972/73

The 1972/73 campaign began with a 4-0 win over Leeds United at the Bridge and it appeared the future was bright for a young and vibrant squad. The programme also reflected reasons for optimism off the pitch. The new masthead on the cover showed imagery of how the rebuilt Stamford Bridge would look and inside was more detail on the proposed changes. The first of them had already begun with the old East Stand demolished in the summer. However, it was the lengthy and financially-draining replacement which would create many of our problems during this decade and beyond.

A SPECIAL NEW SEASON'S WELCOME FROM THE CHAIRMAN

SEASON 1972-73 opens today with Stamford Bridge looking different from what it has ever been before. In less than four months since last season's final home game the old East Stand has gone, and no doubt some among us here today will look nostalgically at that side of the ground and say that the place will never be the same again.

They are absolutely right, but everyone at Chelsea (and, I am sure, the vast majority of Supporters) is delighted that Stamford Bridge **will** "never be the same again." For a start has been made towards realising our dreams and, stage by stage, we can look forward to the time when all phases of this mammoth rebuilding programme are completed and the home of Chelsea Football Club takes its place among the very finest to be found anywhere in the game.

Inevitably, with a project of this size, there must be inconvenience to everyone while it is being carried out. For this we apologize . . . but not for the progress which it signifies. Frankly, I have never been so happy to see Stamford Bridge in such a mess, and I hope you will bear with us and be prepared to share our problems during the rebuilding period, particularly this season.

CHELSEA'S NEW LOOK—IN DETAIL

● Accommodating 60,000 spectators within optimum viewing and comfort conditions. The total spectator area is covered and, if future trends require it, all spectators can be seated.

● Improving the atmosphere and contact between spectators and players by concentrating the stands closer to the pitch and minimising the distance of the furthest spectator.

● Taking full account of the character of the surroundings and the effects of crowds and cars on the area, two major elements of the design are: (a) The possibility of reducing congestion on public roads by connecting as many as 25,000 spectators directly to Fulham Broadway Underground Station via covered approach at the North end of the stadium; (b) The inclusion of a large degree of glass on the roof and upper levels to increase the reflectiveness of the building and reduce its bulk and density within the rooftop character of the area.

BETWEEN OURSELVES

By Albert Sewell

Programme Editor

EARLIER this season a Football League representative came to Stamford Bridge to see if Chelsea would consider inserting *League Football* (previously the *Football League Review*) in the official match-day programe. No we wouldn't, we said, our various reasons including: (a) that to do so we would have to increase the programme price; (b) we believe you fans want to read in your programme of matters pertaining almost entirely to Chelsea and the visiting team and not, on and off, about all the other Football League clubs which *League Football* needs to embrace.

We have nothing against the League's own magazine. Indeed, it is very well produced, and from time to time we have quoted extracts in our programme, but we just don't see it as part of the regular Chelsea scene. The gentleman from the Football League then observed that by incorporating *League Football*, many clubs had boosted their programme sales to upwards of 50 per cent of the attendance, so couldn't it help Chelsea similarly? No chance, we said, taking out our programme sales file and showing him the figures. We thought you might like to see them, too. Updated to the last home match, this is how they read:

Opponents	Attendance	Programmes sold	%	Opponents	Attendance	Programmes sold	%
1. Leeds	51,102	44,326	87	8. Newcastle	35,273	*31,000	88
2. Liverpool	35,375	36,699	103	9. Leicester	28,456	28,220	99
3. Man. City	30,845	33,564	108	10. Notts. Co.			
4. West Ham	34,392	34,735	101	(Lge. Cup)	22,580	*23,000	102
5. Ipswich	29,647	28,434	96	11. Crystal Palace	36,608	*32,500	89
6. Derby (Lge. Cup)	26,395	27,337	103				
7. West Brom.	28,998	*28,750	99		(* = sold out)		

Which means that to crowds so far totalling 359,671 we have sold 348,565 programmes, averaging 97 per cent. It would probably have been 100 per cent but for those sell-outs at four of the last five games, but it's impossible to forecast attendances to within hundreds, even thousands sometimes. . . . League Cup-ties in particular. For example, tonight's crowd estimate is "anything between 25,000 and 35,000," so we've printed 35,000 programmes. But bad weather could reduce the attendance below 25,000 . . . and we'd have 10,000 too many programmes. It's one of the hazards of the business.

For our League Cup semi-final against Norwich City, editor Albert Sewell took the opportunity to reflect on the club's outstanding programme sales.

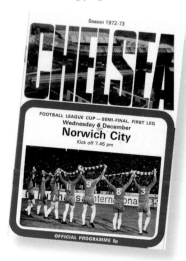

Season 1972-73

CHELSEA

FOOTBALL LEAGUE CUP — SEMI-FINAL, FIRST LEG
Wednesday 6 December
Norwich City
Kick off 7.45 pm

OFFICIAL PROGRAMME 5p

Season 1972-73

CHELSEA

FOOTBALL LEAGUE DIVISION ONE
Saturday 28 April
Manchester United
Kick off 3 pm

OFFICIAL PROGRAMME 5p

FAREWELL, BOBBY

Front cover shot

SINCE Bobby Charlton announced twelve days ago that he is retiring as a player, every game has been for him a farewell appearance—at Leeds on Wednesday of last week, the Manchester "derby" last Saturday and Easter Monday's goodbye to Old Trafford in the match against Sheffield United. Today brings the last farewell—his 604th and final League appearance (a First Division record by any one player). The first was also in London—away to Charlton Athletic on February 18, 1957; that day United won 5-1 and Bobby Charlton scored the first three of the 198 League goals that stand to his name. His grand total of first-team matches for United in all competitions today reaches 751, in which he has totalled 245 goals. He has helped his club win every major honour; he personally holds the England records for most Internationals (106) and most individual goals (49). Over 17 seasons he has graced the world's football fields with supreme skill and sportsmanship, and this afternoon Chelsea Football Club proudly adds its tribute to the most admired and respected footballer of his generation. At a ceremony on the field before the game our Chairman, Mr. Brian Mears, will present to Bobby a silver cigarette box with the inscription: "Presented to Bobby Charlton, O.B.E., by Chelsea Football Club, at the end of a wonderful playing career in League and International football, 28 April 1973." Thank you, Bobby, for the way you have enriched the game as a player and sportsman, and as you leave the field at the end of the afternoon you may be sure you are taking with you the best wishes of everyone for a successful future in Football management.

The programme for the final game of the campaign against Manchester United paid tribute to a true legend of the game as Bobby Charlton played his 758th and final match for the Red Devils. It was also time to reflect on Blues players who had shone that season, including Player of the Year Peter Osgood along with ever-presents John Hollins and Ron Harris.

THE TWO OUT OF 28 WHO'VE BEEN EVER-PRESENT

CHELSEA'S 'PLAYER OF THE YEAR' TITLE FOR SEASON 1972-73 HAS BEEN WON BY
PETER OSGOOD

Previous Winners:	
1967	PETER BONETTI
1968	CHARLIE COOKE
1969	DAVID WEBB
1970 & 1971	JOHN HOLLINS
1972	DAVID WEBB

OUR congratulations to Peter Osgood on being voted Chelsea's "Player of the Year 1972-73" in the Supporters' Club annual award. Voting has been spread over the season and when it finished last weekend, this was the result: 1 Peter Osgood, 2 Chris Garland, 3 Bill Garner.

Ossie won by a margin of 1,000 votes and, with the style and form he has maintained to the end of Chelsea's most difficult season for years, his name is worthily added to an illustrious list of previous winners.

On the right is the Joe Mears Memorial Trophy (together with the replica which the winner keeps permanently) to be presented tonight at the Player of the Year Dance at Hammersmith Town Hall.

Well done, Peter, and we also congratulate the Supporters on their choice.

One of the finest saves "The Cat" has ever made—from Keegan's penalty at Liverpool in September.

Ossie reaches his century with our second goal at home to Everton in the last home game.

600 FIRST TEAM GAMES — PETER BONETTI

AFTER saluting one Peter the Saturday before last, we offer warmest congratulations to another today—Peter Bonetti. The reason is without parallel in the Club's history, because this afternoon he is due to make his 600th first-team appearance between our posts.

If no other player here has approached this figure, it is equally certain that none has exceeded his contribution to Chelsea football. Since his first appearance, at home to Manchester City on April 2, 1960, "The Cat" has climbed to the very pinnacle of his specialist art. Strikers are measured by the goals they score, but there is no comparable statistical yardstick by which goalkeepers can be judged. If only someone had kept record over the years of all the goals Bonetti has saved!

100 FIRST DIVISION GOALS — PETER OSGOOD

JUST before Peter Osgood went on the field against Everton in our last home match he said: "I'll be glad when I get that one goal I need to complete my century in League football. The longer I stay on 99 the harder it is going to be and, goodness knows, scoring is difficult enough anyway these days."

In fact that historic goal was only 43 playing minutes away, and ten minutes from time he got another, to make victory certain at 3-1. With Sir Alf Ramsey watching, Ossie also clinched his England recall against Italy four days later—his fourth full cap and first at Wembley.

Stars sold as debt rises, 1973/74

The financial implications of the delayed new East Stand really began to reveal themselves in the 1973/74 season. The November game against Southampton reflected on two fantastic landmarks for a pair of club legends. However, it would not be long until Peter Osgood was on his way out of Stamford Bridge, along with another fans' favourite Alan Hudson – the two valuable assets sold to help finance a growing debt. By the time we played Stoke at the Victoria Ground in January, the Potters' programme featured Hudson as one of their players.

ALAN HUDSON has quietly settled into the Stoke City routine after his headline debut last week. "There are not so many pressures here," he said. "Someone was always ringing up or wanting a chat. It's been quite quiet here apart from the game, of course, which was great.

"The Stoke lads helped me to settle down. I was always able to find them with passes especially JIMMY GREENHOFF. But I was a bit sick when they pinched a goal back at the end like that. Still, there will be no problems with relegation with so many good players in the side."

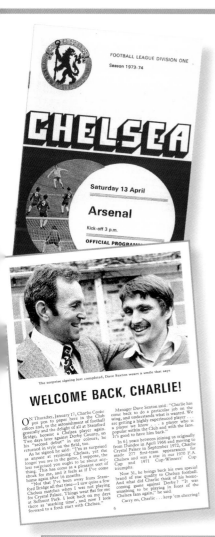

FOOTBALL LEAGUE DIVISION ONE
Season 1973-74

CHELSEA

Saturday 13 April

Arsenal

Kick-off 3 p.m.

OFFICIAL PROGRAMME

The surprise signing just completed, Dave Sexton wears a smile that says

WELCOME BACK, CHARLIE!

ON Thursday, January 17, Charlie Cooke put pen to paper here in the Club offices and, to the astonishment of football generally and the delight of all at Stamford Bridge, became a Chelsea player again. Two days later against Derby County, on his "second debut" in our colours, he returned in style on the field, too.

As he signed he said: "I'm as surprised as anyone at rejoining Chelsea, yet the longer you are in the game, I suppose, the less surprised you ought to be about anything. This has come as a pleasant sort of shock for me, and it feels as if I've come home again after 16 months.

"Not that I've been away from Stamford Bridge all that time—I saw quite a few Chelsea matches when I was not playing for Crystal Palace. Things went flat for me at Selhurst Park. I look back on my days there as 'marking time', and now I look forward to a fresh start with Chelsea."

Manager Dave Sexton said: "Charlie has come back to do a particular job on the wing, and understands what is wanted. We are getting a highly experienced player . . . a player we know . . . a player who is popular within the Club and with the fans. It's good to have him back."

In 6½ years between joining us originally from Dundee in April 1966 and moving to Crystal Palace in September 1972, Charlie made 277 first-team appearances for Chelsea and was a star in our 1970 F.A. Cup and 1971 Cup-Winners' Cup triumphs.

Now 31, he brings back his own special brand of star quality to Chelsea football. And what did Charlie think of his homecoming game against Derby? "It was smashing to be playing in front of the Chelsea fans again," he said.

Carry on, Charlie . . . keep 'em cheering!

6

The Heart that is in Chelsea Football Club

'WITH Alan Hudson and Peter Osgood leaving the Club, you are all obviously thinking: How ambitious are Chelsea? I can dispel any doubts—a club without ambition does not spend two million pounds on a new stand, and you would be right in thinking that there would be no point in rebuilding if we did not have ambitions on the field.

But for those to be achieved, an important quality is discipline and respect within a club, for without such qualities no club can achieve real distinction. I feel confident that the future will prove we are stronger for the events of the past few months.

The way our present players have responded to the Club's recent problems reflects the heart that is in Chelsea Football Club, with senior players drawing on their experience and helping young players to do extremely well during difficult times. All have been magnificent.

This is from the speech made by BRIAN MEARS, Chairman of Chelsea Football Club, at the recent dinner-dance of Chelsea Supporters' Club.

Remember, it is the Chelsea players of today and the future who matter most, grateful though we are for the efforts of all those in the past.

I reaffirm our belief and confidence in Dave Sexton as the man to bring Chelsea through this team rebuilding phase. I thank everyone connected with the Club—Players, Management, Staff—for the way they have coped and drawn together during the difficult weeks past, and I thank all our Supporters, who may not always have understood what was going on but who gave us encouragement when we needed it most.'

NEW FACES IN THE FIRST TEAM

JOHN SPARROW
Our 16-year-old left-back from Bethnal Green.

KEN SWAIN
Aged 21, comes from Liverpool—plays up front.

Come the home game against Arsenal in April, the programme printed a statement made by the Chairman at a dinner-dance in an attempt to appease disgruntled fans. It wasn't all doom and gloom, though, as the back page showed a couple of new first-team players. A couple of months beforehand, the programme discussed the return of Charlie Cooke after he had spent a couple of seasons away from the Bridge at Crystal Palace.

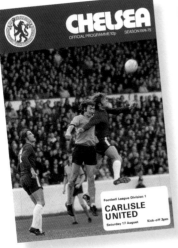

The Chairman writes . . .

FOR all of us at Stamford Bridge this is more than the start of a new season.
It is the beginning of a new era in the history of Chelsea Football Club, marked by the opening of our magnificent East Stand. Although some facilities have still to be completed in the coming weeks—such as the dressing-rooms, restaurant and guest-rooms, and floodlighting—the fact that all the seating, bars and toilets are ready is itself an excellent achievement, and I would like to pay tribute to all concerned, particularly the Ground Staff and Office Staff for their efforts, often round the clock in recent weeks, without which one of the world's finest football grandstands would not be in use this afternoon.

Inevitably with a structure of this scale, there will be a "settling down" period, and while thanking Supporters for their patience during the past two difficult seasons, I would ask you to bear with us a little longer over any snags that come to light. You may be sure we shall do our best to iron them out as quickly as possible.

We welcome new players, too. Scottish International David Hay has joined us from Britain's most successful club, Celtic, and John Sissons, signed from Norwich last week, is back in London where he began his career with West Ham. We greet them both with best wishes for a successful future with Chelsea.

We also have a larger, new-look programme, complete with colour, and although in this inflationary age we have had to increase the price we shall, as always, endeavour to make it the best in the field.

So, in various ways, we set off into 1974-75 as a "new" Chelsea. Good luck to Dave Sexton and the Players, and let us hope that all our combined efforts—including yours from the stands and terraces—will be rewarded with a successful season.

Brian Mears,

Plea to supporters as relegation looms, 1974/75

As the Blues hosted Carlisle United in August 1974, the new East Stand opened its doors for the first time and Chairman Brian Mears declared it "the beginning of a new era" in his notes, where he also discussed the revamped programme. Full-page colour photos of the players went side-by side with appeals for fans to help the club by, for example, becoming a bingo ticket seller. It was clear that our financial predicament remained delicate, a situation not helped by poor form on the field which would ultimately see us relegated.

RON HARRIS

Please send me full details of Chelsea Bingo

Name ....

Address ....

....

3 *Help Chelsea as a Bingo ticket seller*

To be a **BINGO SELLER** you must be over 18 years of age.

These *easy-to-sell* 5p tickets are issued on a sale-or-return basis.

The benefits: Sellers receive 10% commission/expenses on all tickets sold.

Fill in the coupon above and post to: Mr. G. C. Abel, Chelsea Bingo, Stamford Bridge Grounds, Fulham Road, London SW6 1HS.

No obligation is incurred.

Thank You, Agents and Members

SINCE Chelsea's Fund Raising Organisation began in August 1970, we have paid out prize-money totalling £154,000.

And the amount donated towards the redevelopment of Stamford Bridge during this period has reached £155,000.

We express sincere thanks to all Agents and Members for their part in raising such a sum—and we look forward to a new season of still more success for everyone associated with the Chelsea Pool.

JOHN HOLLINS

DO YOU WANT TO HELP YOUR CLUB?

Then here are three ways you can do so now . . .

CHELSEA 1974-75

Back row: George Anstiss (Ground Overseer), John Anstiss (Groundstaff), Bill Edwards (Electrician) Jim Bridger (Groundstaff), Dave Watkins (Groundstaff), Bert Trigg (Groundstaff), Fred Gigg (Groundstaff), John Soutar (Security), Stan Quantrill (Maintenance), Arthur Phipps (Gatekeeper), Frank Greenland (Maintenance), Ivy Walker (Cleaner), Win Thain (Cleaner), Arthur Pittman (Groundstaff).

Fourth row: Nigel Hawley (Assistant-Secretary, Finance), Arthur Meadows (Ticket Office assistant), Josie Pibworth (Cleaner), Jackie Bygraves (Office Staff), Margaret Dempsey (Office Staff), Steve Finnleston, Marvin Hinton, Ian Hutchinson, Derek Richardson, Micky Droy, Peter Bonetti, Bill Garner, Chris Garland (now Leicester), David Hay, John Dempsey, Chris Mathews (Assistant-Secretary, Administration), Ann Henderson (Receptionist), Dick Spence (Youth Trainer), Mick Mears (Ticket Office Manager), Keith Thatcher (Ticket Office Clerk), Eddie Heath (Chief Scout).

Third row: Norman Medhurst (Head Trainer), Garry Stanley, Brian Bason, John Hollins, Graham Wilkins, Gary Locke, Ron Harris, Charlie Cooke, Steve Kember, Ian Britton, John Sissons.

Second row: Lee Templeman, Francis Cowley, Jimmy Scanlon, Lee Frost, John Jacobs, Paul Hammond, Danny Godwin, Trevor Aylott, John Webberley, Reg Byatt (Combination Trainer).

Front row: Tony Green (Secretary), Ron Suart (General Manager), Les Briley, Clive Walker, Ray Lewington, Teddy Maybank, Tommy Cunningham, Mick Sorensen, David Stride, Ken Swain, Ron Armstrong (now Aston Villa), Harry Medhurst (Physiotherapist), Eddie McCreadie (Team Manager), Ken Shellito (Youth Manager).

Daily Mirror photograph by Monte Fresco

WE SALUTE LONDON'S F.A. CUP FINALISTS

In ten days' time, Fulham and West Ham United meet in only the second all-London F.A. Cup Final Wembley has seen (we were there with Tottenham for the first in 1967). So the Cup is coming back to London Town after three years in the North, and in presenting pictures of goals that took them through their semi-final replays, we offer warmest congratulations to our friends and neighbours Fulham and to West Ham, who are not quite such near neighbours but just as good friends.

Alan Taylor (behind post) heads the first of his two goals in West Ham's victory over Ipswich here two weeks ago.
(*Daily Mail* photograph).

On the same night at Maine Road, Manchester, John Mitchell (striped shirt) forces the ball into the net for Fulham's winner in the last seconds of extra time against Birmingham.

Our penultimate match of the season saw Sheffield United visit the Bridge. It came shortly after 18-year-old Ray Wilkins had been named our youngest-ever permanent captain, away to Tottenham, and the programme printed a full list of our post-war skippers. A team shot in front of the East Stand was published and, despite our own difficulties, the club showed its class by wishing London rivals Fulham and West Ham good luck in the FA Cup final.

CHELSEA'S CAPTAINS IN 29 SEASONS OF LEAGUE FOOTBALL SINCE THE WAR

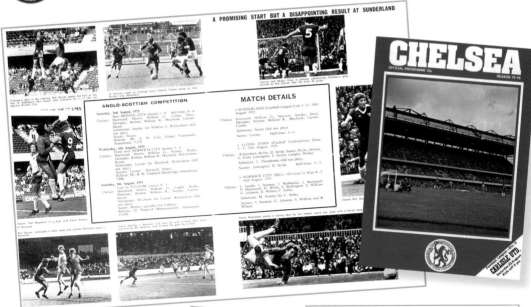

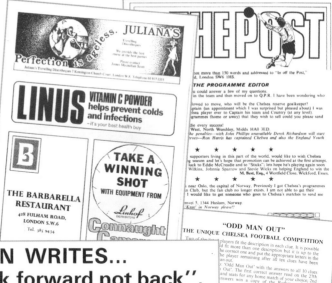

Hopes of quick return to top table, 1975/76

For the second season in succession, our opening home game in 1975/76 was against Carlisle. The Chairman discussed relegation at the end of the previous campaign and how hopes were high for a speedy return to the top flight. Also shown here are some of the other new-look additions to the programme.

THE CHAIRMAN WRITES...
''A time to look forward not back''.

The Directors welcome all our supporter at the start of a new Season.

In spite of all our efforts towards the end of last season to avoid the drop into the Second Division it was not to be and we look forward to a speedy return to the First Division.

However, if spirit is anything to go by we should have an enjoyable and successful season ahead of us. Eddie McCreadie has a good blend of youth and experience with which to work and once again we would ask for your support which last season was so vital.

We would also like to wish every success to those players who left us during the summer: John Hollins, Peter Houseman and Steve Kember and we would like to record our thanks to them for the fine service they gave to our Club.

There is no doubt that all of us at Chelsea have our sights set on a return to the top grade of English football, in our opinion our rightful place is Division One of The Football League.

We must work for success, and with the determination that exists among everyone at Stamford Bridge backed by loyal and consistent encouragement from you all, it can be achieved.

On behalf of everyone at Chelsea I wish you all a most enjoyable and successful season, and thank you for your continued support.

J. B. MEARS,
Chairman, Chelsea F.C.

MESSAGE FROM THE MANAGER

I'm enjoying this season as much as any in my career. Not many other people seem to be happy with the state of football in general, but I've never been more excited about the game in my life.

Watching our youngsters progress from game to game gives me great satisfaction, and from the way the lads play it's obvious that they are enjoying their football as well. Their spirit is infectious and I know from our supporters reactions at the Carlisle and Oxford matches, that we were producing just the sort of entertainment they wanted.

We all appreciate that our youngsters won't reach their full potential for at least a couple of years but as the season develops they will become a better, more experienced and consequently more consistent side. I would ask you to be patient with them while they experience the ups and downs of first team football. The blend of youth and experience that we are aiming at in the first team won't always be possible to achieve due to injuries. But with Gary Locke and Ian Hutchinson nearly match fit, and the competition for places very fierce, I am sure the team will steadily improve until we are in a position to put in a strong challenge for promotion at the end of the season.

I sincerely hope that you supporters get as much excitement as we do while watching the younger players develop to first team material under the excellent influence of the more senior players in the squad.

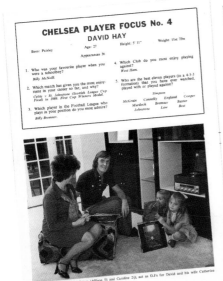

CHELSEA PLAYER FOCUS No. 4
DAVID HAY

Born: Paisley   Age: 27   Height: 5' 11"   Weight: 11st 7lbs

Appearances 36

1. Who was your favourite player when you were a schoolboy?
   Billy McNeill.

2. Which match has given you the most enjoyment in your career so far, and why?
   Celtic v St. Johnstone (Scottish League Cup Final) in 1969, First Cup Winners Medal.

3. Which player in the Football League who plays in your position do you most admire?
   Billy Bremner.

4. Which Club do you most enjoy playing against?
   West Ham.

5. Who are the best eleven players (in a 4-3-3 formation) that you have ever watched, played with or played against?

   Simpson
   McGrain   Connelly   England   Cooper
   Murdoch   Bremner   Baxter
   Johnstone   Law   Best

Two Go-Go dancers of the future (Allison 5) and Caroline 2), act as D.J's for David and his wife Catherine

It hasn't been a good year for fishing in the Hay Trout stream! It's lucky Chelsea have been finding the net a little more regularly than the fish!

David Hay in action against Nottingham Forest   15

This was Eddie McCreadie's first full season as Chelsea manager and in the programme for the September game against Bristol City, he spoke of his optimism, while David Hay was the fourth Player Focus of the campaign. A history of the programme discussed how the quality of the club's official publication from 1905 onwards had always ensured high circulation figures.

HISTORY OF THE CHELSEA PROGRAMME

"They're off"! Under the column heading "Daisy Cutters" this was the first comment in the first-ever issue of the Chelsea Official Programme (Volume 1 Number 1), on Monday, September 4th 1905, on the occasion of a "friendly" match against Liverpool.

The four pages cost just one (old) penny and were entitled "The Chelsea F.C. Chronicle", the name which continued until April 1948.

In those days when not every club produced a programme the Chelsea publication was popular from the very beginning as is shown by sales of 341,766, with gross takings of £1,424-0-6, in the 1912-13 season. At the time this was claimed to be a record "for any football club programme anywhere".

Today, in these days of inflation, receipts exceed that figure on each separate match day. In the 1970-71 season in fact the takings were £55,305.90 from 1,072,707 programmes sold.

One of the earliest features was the cartoon on the cover page. "Percy" the Chelsea pensioner was depicted displaying various emotions and sentiments which reflected the fortunes of the club at the time. At least six different artists perpetuated this character until he "retired" in May 1947.

Up to the 1914-18 war an 8-page issue was normal for a first-team game, with four pages for reserve matches. "Daisy Cutters" was retained as a permanent feature until 1939, though its brand of humour would scarcely be acceptable today. "Huddersfield's defence consisted of nearly all Bs—but not Hall".

BACK ROW:
Tommy LANGLEY
John DEMPSEY
Steve WICKS
Micky DROY
Bill GARNER
Steve FINNIESTON
Ted MAYBANK
Gary LOCKE
MIDDLE ROW:
David HAY
Ken SWAIN
Garry STANLEY
Ray WILKINS
Brian BASON
John SPARROW
Ron HARRIS
FRONT ROW:
Ian BRITTON
John PHILLIPS
Ray LEWINGTON
Peter BONETTI
Graham WILKINS

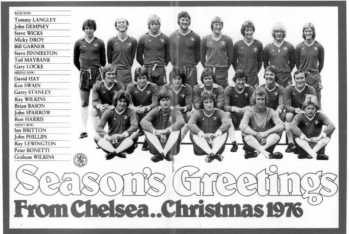

Season's Greetings From Chelsea..Christmas 1976

Chelsea ⊖ Fulham

FOOTBALL LEAGUE DIVISION TWO SEASON '76/'77 MONDAY DECEMBER 27th, 1976 KICK-OFF 3 p.m.

Neighbours arrive at the Bridge for festive fixture, 1976/77

A novel cover design saw the Chelsea crest as it appeared on the home shirt during the 1976/77 season – a campaign which put a smile back on the faces of Chelsea fans. This festive edition for the home game against Fulham on 27 December was packed with interesting content, including a page where the club answered questions from the fans, while Chelsea View set the scene at the start of the programme. Also, check out John Dempsey's delight on the back row of the "Season's greetings" team picture! We hosted Hull on the final day of the season, having secured promotion a week earlier with a win at Wolves. Match action from that game featured prominently, along with a selection of the newspapers' headlines.

CHELSEA 4 LIVERPOOL 2 WHEN WE MET HERE EIGHT WEEKS AGO

THE WAY BACK-Part 2

By MARTIN SPENCER, F.C.A. (Financial Director)

CHELSEA v LIVERPOOL

F.A. Cup – Third Round Season 1977-78 Saturday, January 7 (3 p.m.)

LIVERPOOL BEATEN—IN RHYME

"I cannot get over the occasion of the great Cup triumph for Chelsea against Liverpool. It was one of the finest in all the fifty years I have watched Chelsea (except when we won the Cup). The team was fantastic." So wrote supporter Les Ward, of 252 Carr Road, Northolt, Middlesex and then, as if to show there's no limit to the ingenuity of Chelsea fans, produced this rhyming report of our third round victory two weeks ago. Our thanks, Les, and congratulations on a poem to match the occasion.

The ground is packed at Stamford Bridge,
There's not an inch to spare,
And Chelsea's roasting Liverpool
To keep me smiling there.

It's Chelsea in the lead,
With Walker's goal beyond compare,
And Clemence so bewildered
He wished he wasn't there.

Another Walker shot rebounds from Clemence—
What a scare!
And Jones into his own net
Very nearly puts it there.

It's Charlie Cooke who's limping off,
But why should Chelsea care?
There's Finnieston, the substitute,
To take his place out there.

Bonetti, with some wonder saves,
Keeps flying through the air,
And Liverpool can't equalise
While Chelsea have him there.

We're in the second half
And Jones fouls Walker most unfair;
The free-kick isn't cleared,
There's Finnieston . . . he shoots . . . it's there!

The Shed has just erupted,
Now Neal is in despair;
He's 'fluffed' his backward pass,
Can Langley intercept? Oh, yes, it's there!

Now Liverpool attack,
A sight to see so rare,
They've scored, and it was Johnson
Who happened to be there.

There's Chelsea coming back,
Garner passes short and square,
And Walker's got another goal,
Yes, Clemence can't get there.

A corner now for Liverpool:
Can they improve their share?
Dalglish has headed past 'The Cat'
Who couldn't reach up there.

The ref. has blown, it's over,
They're cheering everywhere.
They're singing and they're chanting
And the blue and white is there.

The champs have been defeated,
The Blues had all the flair,
And when they talk about it
I'll proudly say: "I was there."

Poem helps spread the word on cup victory over Reds, 1977/78

One of the standout moments from the 1977/78 season was the stunning FA Cup fourth-round win over Liverpool, the cover for which is shown here, as well as a fan's poem inspired by the famous victory. We beat the European champions 4-2 and our league match against the Reds a couple of months later featured some brilliant action shots from the cup clash. The neatly designed opposition pages are also worth a mention. An update on the club's financial predicament showed how things were moving in the right direction, albeit with the price of match tickets increasing on a regular basis. A rather tongue-in-cheek Q&A with Peter Bonetti from the cup programme is on the back cover of this book.

PETER OSGOOD

❝ I've had two good clubs in my career—Chelsea, where I began, and Southampton, where I also had success and a crowd that were again on my side. Now I'm delighted to be back where I started, and where I shall end my playing days.

Not that I'm near finished yet. At 31 and now over my recent ankle operation, I feel I've got plenty to offer and am ready to play anywhere to prove it—sweeper, centre-half or up front. I just want to help Chelsea wherever I can.

Even after I went from here in March 1974, Stamford Bridge remained what you might call my spiritual home. I never really wanted to leave in the first place, but that was how it worked out and now I'm just thrilled to be back.

The nightmare since I was here before happened in America this past summer. In Philadelphia Fury, I joined an inexperienced side, and after only five games I suffered a bad ankle injury. I played on it when I was only half fit, and my last game over there was in late July.

Happily, the operation back here on November 8 has been a complete success. They took a flake of bone from the right ankle (that's my good one!) and now it's a matter of full-time training to get my wind back and my legs working again. My weight is no problem. At 13st. 3½lb. I have only two or three pounds to shift to be at my best on the scales.

In one way coming back to Chelsea has seemed strange. Although I've been away less than five years, there's only Ronnie Harris still in the present squad. He's one of the originals. The rest are new faces. Some of them don't yet know how to take me, but that's understandable, because to them I'm the new boy.

Everyone is asking me about Chelsea's chances of staying up now that I have returned. But it isn't just down to me to pick the club off the floor, and I'm not promising anyone anything. The situation has become desperate, and we all know we've got a mountain to climb. But I'm an optimist, so ask me again when I've got about ten games behind me.

All I know is that I can still play. I'd like to think I'll have a good influence, and am ready to give everything I have for Chelsea. ❞

PETER OSGOOD

Ossie unable to save us from drop as Blanchflower steps in, 1978/79

The 1978/79 campaign was one of our least memorable when it came to on-pitch action as we were relegated after finishing bottom of Division One with a meagre 20 points. A ray of hope for Blues fans came with club legend Peter Osgood's return in December, and he greeted fans in the Bristol City programme, having netted against Middlesbrough the week before, albeit in a 7-2 defeat. However, even the King of Stamford Bridge could not inspire a turnaround in the second half of the season and he only added a handful of appearances to his original tally. The Talk of Stamford Bridge discussed an eventful few days at the club, following the departure of Ken Shellito as manager, with Danny Blanchflower taking the role on a permanent basis, but his stint in charge would be a shortlived one.

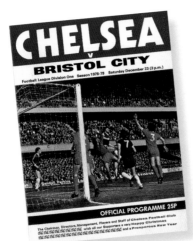

To describe four days of last week as among the most eventful in Chelsea history is to understate all that happened. On Wednesday, Ken Shellito resigned as Team Manager and Frank Upton was put in charge "until an appointment is made." On Thursday the approach was made to Danny Blanchflower to take over; at 9.30 on Friday morning Danny arrived at Stamford Bridge and within an hour we were able to announce that he had accepted. At noon Chelsea's new Manager held his first conference for Press, radio and TV, and an hour later the team left Stamford Bridge for London Airport and the flight to Middlesbrough. There, last Saturday, Peter Osgood marked his return to Chelsea with the opening goal in a match that was to go disastrously against us, and immediately afterwards came news of the task that will confront us two weeks today, away to Manchester United in the third round of the F.A. Cup.

The situation at the bottom of the First Division leaves us in no doubt as to the seriousness of our position. At the same time, we are convinced that we have appointed the best man for the job. Danny was quick to emphasise that much hard work needs to be done and that changes would have to be made in the effort to pull ourselves clear, and we welcome him to Stamford Bridge with the pledge of 100 per cent support from everyone—from Boardroom, from every member of the Chelsea staff and, we are sure, from all our supporters.

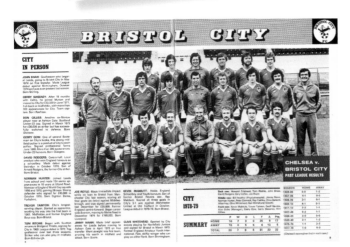

CHELSEA v DERBY COUNTY

Football League Division One   Wednesday, April 4 (7.45 p.m.)

PROGRAMME SUPPLEMENT

WITH only one point taken from the last eight matches, we have reached a position in which, while First Division survival is still mathematically possible, it must be realistically assessed that the odds against our escaping have soared towards the highly improbable. Ten games remain, six of them at home, and eight points (plus an inferior goal difference) separate us from fourth-from-bottom Wolves. So our hopes must be pinned to a future beyond this season, with the remaining fixtures of 1978-79 used towards the re-shaping of our team.

Tonight's fixture with Derby County was originally to have been played on Saturday, February 17, when adverse weather conditions caused a postponement. We apologize to spectators for the fact that we have been unable to produce a completely new programme for this re-arranged date. As we explained when, in similar circumstances, we received Coventry City in a re-arranged match in February, we would, in days before our financial difficulties,

have prepared a new edition for tonight, but in existing circumstances we could not afford to scrap the original programme.

Indeed, in this season of so many postponed fixtures, many clubs have, for economy reasons, re-issued original programmes on re-arranged dates, and we hope you will understand the position at it affects Chelsea in our particular financial state.

On Saturday we are at home again—to League Champions Nottingham Forest. We have beaten them for the past two seasons at Stamford Bridge, and after feeling the full weight of their attack in Nottingham a week ago, this is an opportunity to see what we can salvage in pride and performance against opponents who are among the best in the country.

Regarding our next two away games, the match at Bristol City on Tuesday is at 7.30 p.m., and for our visit to Arsenal on Easter Monday (April 16) the kick-off is 11.30 a.m.

As the season came to a disappointing end, there were a couple of notable editions of the programme. The Arsenal and Derby games, originally due to be played in January and February respectively but called off due to wintry conditions, were rescheduled nearer the end of the campaign. The original programmes were printed, with a supplement informing fans of the financial reasons behind the decision. The Arsenal edition also marked the final game of a true Blues legend.

FAREWELL, PETER: For a very special reason tonight's match is a poignant one in the story of Chelsea F.C. and in the life of Peter Bonetti, who, man and boy, has been part of the Stamford Bridge scene for 21 years. It marks his 600th Football League appearance – a total exceeded in the Chelsea records only by Ron Harris (614) – but celebration of this magnificent milestone is tinged with sadness in that it is the last time we shall see Peter between the posts in a first-class fixture at Stamford Bridge.

At 37, he has decided the time has come to retire from football in these parts and to take his family to begin a new life on the faraway Scottish island of Mull. Words cannot adequately express what Peter Bonetti has meant to Chelsea in all his years here: masterly goalkeeper, sportsman supreme, model clubman and a shining example to all who have been privileged to play in front of him for so long in the Chelsea team.

Thank you, Peter, for the greatness you have brought to Chelsea's football; thank you for countless magnificent displays between the posts; thank you for the honours you have helped bring to our Club; and thank you for a million memories that are shared and treasured by all who have been proud to know you, to play with you and to support you from stands and terraces.

May the future for your family and yourself be as happy and successful in Scotland as your past has been here in London. Our very best wishes go to you all as you join your family on Mull later this week, and already we look forward to seeing you back in action at Stamford Bridge just one more time—when you return for your last farewell in a Testimonial early next season.

LEAGUE APPEARANCES SEASON 1978-79			
Langley	38 (1)	Borota	11
Harris	36 (2)	Lewington	10
Wilkins (R)	35	Britton	9 (4)
Stride	32	Sitton	9 (1)
Stanley	31 (4)	Hay	8
Wilkins (G)	27	Locke	8
Wicks	23	Osgood	8
Walker	21 (7)	Iles	7
Bannon	17	Phillips	7
Bonetti	15	Fillery	6 (1)
McKenzie	15	Bumstead	5 (1)
Nutton	15	Chivers	3
Swain	15	Docherty	2 (1)
Droy	13	Frost	2 (1)
Aylott	11 (2)	Garner	1

Scorers: Langley 15, McKenzie 4, Stanley 4, Swain 4, Walker 4, Wilkins (R) 3, Osgood 2, Bannon 1, Bumstead 1, Wicks 1, Wilkins (G) 1, Opponents 2. Total 42.

Figures in brackets = Appearances as substitute.

CHELSEA | ARSENAL

COLOURS—Shirts: Royal Blue with White Collar and Cuffs. Shorts: Royal Blue with White Seam. Stockings: White.

COLOURS—Shirts: Red with White Sleeves. Shorts: White. Stockings: Red with White Band at Top.

CHELSEA	ARSENAL
1 Peter BONETTI	1 Pat JENNINGS
2 Graham WILKINS	2 Pat RICE
3 Ron HARRIS	3 Sammy NELSON
4 Eamonn BANNON	4 Brian TALBOT
5 Micky DROY	5 David O'LEARY
6 Gary CHIVERS	6 Willie YOUNG
7 Garry STANLEY	7 Liam BRADY
8 Ray WILKINS	8 Alan SUNDERLAND
9 Peter OSGOOD	9 Frank STAPLETON
10 Tommy LANGLEY	10 David PRICE
11 Clive WALKER	11 Graham RIX
Sub:	Sub:

Referee: Mr. MALCOLM SINCLAIR (Guildford)
Linesmen: Mr. J. T. Kenneth (Croydon)—Red Flag
Mr. A. G. Lisney (Tonbridge)—Orange Flag

IN AID OF THE N.S.P.C.C.
at **Stamford Bridge**
SATURDAY, JULY 14
11.00 a.m. – 1.00 p.m.
SUPER FAIR DISCO DANCING BEAUTY CONTEST CAPITAL RADIO BUS WITH DJ'S SHOPPING ARCADE CHAMPAGNE BAR BEER TENT FOOD CASINO TWO BANDS.

Don't Queue, Buy Advance Tickets
Now available from:
The Ticket Office, Chelsea F.C.
Stamford Bridge, Fulham Road, London SW6.

ADMISSION:
11.00 a.m.–6.30 pm
£2 adults
£1 children under 10
After 7.00 pm
£5 adults
£1 children under 10

ADVANCE TICKETS ARE VALID BOTH FOR DAY AND EVENING
ADMISSION - PRICE £4.

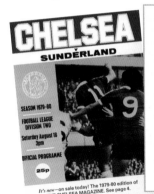

CHAIRMAN BRIAN MEARS WRITES: We were sorry to see Danny Blanchflower leave Chelsea last week, but he had been saying for some time that we should appoint a younger manager. When he joined us last December, it was not on a long-term basis, and now he has decided the time has come to depart. I would like to pay tribute to the contribution he made to the Club in the short time he was with us. He has left with the good wishes of everybody here and knowing that he will always be our welcome guest. Following Danny's departure, the Board decided to draw up a short list for the position of manager, and meanwhile Geoff Hurst continues his duties as coach and in complete charge of the playing side. An announcement of the appointment of our new manager will be made as soon as possible.

World Cup hero steps into hot seat, 1979/80

The 1979/80 season was another transitional one for the club as Danny Blanchflower was replaced by England's 1966 World Cup final hero Geoff Hurst, who had served under him as coach. We narrowly missed out on returning to Division One at the first attempt, finishing fourth, just two points adrift of table-toppers Leicester City. The campaign began with a home game against Sunderland, which featured a profile of our new Yugoslavian goalkeeper Petar Borota – a man who would go on to became a real terrace hero thanks to his eccentric behaviour on the pitch. Our September home game against Watford was the first following Blanchflower's departure, a matter discussed in The Talk of Stamford Bridge. The programme also featured a Micky Droy gallery and some novel match action shots.

NOT OUR DAY AT THE FAR-FROM-GAY MEADOW

Our first-ever visit to Shrewsbury Town's Gay Meadow ground did not turn out in the way we had hoped—but we can't pretend a 3-nil defeat didn't happen.

ABOVE: A study in concentration on our bench—left to right trainer Norman Medhurst, Geoff Hurst, in his first match in charge of the team, substitute Clive Walker and travelling team attendant Arthur Pittman.

TOP RIGHT: The nearest we came to scoring as Tommy Langley gets within striking range, but Mulhearn saved his shot.

BOTTOM RIGHT: Battling on! Ian Britton takes on two opponents in midfield.

Colour note: Why did we play in red shirts? Because Shrewsbury wear blue and gold stripes, so we could not use our normal second colours of yellow.

(Photographs by Hugh Hastings)

PRESENTATION TIME.....

Martin Spencer, our Chief Executive receives, on Chelsea's behalf, a cheque for £55,239 from Minister for Sport, Mr. Hector Monro, accompanied (left) by Mr. Clifford Barclay, Trustee of the Football Grounds Improvement Trust. The money is towards ground safety improvements that have been carried out at Stamford Bridge, and the presentation was made at the home match against Queens Park Rangers.

Ian Britton and Ron Harris hand over the Chelsea presentation mirror to Phillip Wootton, Trade Sales Manager of the ICI Trade Group, who sponsored our match against Notts County. Left is David Scott and, right, Alan Logan, Area Sales Managers for ICI.

Photographs by Hugh Hastings

24

Petar Borota is good with his hands off the field as well as on it, as his exhibition of abstract paintings shows at the local Barclays Bank at West Brompton. With him is Foss Archer, Branch Manager, left, and Brian Phillips, Assistant Manager.

Ron Harris with the illuminated address presented to him by Chairman Brian Mears at last week's Testimonial, in recognition of Ron's magnificent service to Chelsea.

DAILY **Mirror** THE BIG KICK FOR SOCCER

25

CHELSEA RON HARRIS GALLERY

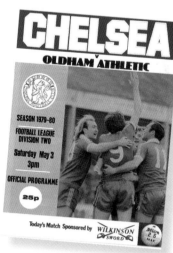

CHELSEA v OLDHAM ATHLETIC

SEASON 1979-80
FOOTBALL LEAGUE DIVISION TWO
Saturday May 3
3pm
OFFICIAL PROGRAMME
25p

Today's Match Sponsored by WILKINSON SWORD

A 3-0 win against Oldham on the final day of the season was not enough to earn promotion, which was particularly unfortunate for our all-time leading appearance-maker Ron Harris, who played his 795th and final game for the Blues that day. His gallery in the December programme against Swansea pointed out his incredible versatility – surely very few players have worn quite as many shirt numbers as "Chopper".

NUMBERS on shirts mean nothing to Ron Harris—it's the honest sweat on them at the end of a game that counts as he strides on towards his 800th competitive first-team appearance in our colours (present total 772). His is, of course, the all-time record for Chelsea appearances, and at 35 he has long been as much a part of the Stamford Bridge scene as the goalposts themselves. Last season he pulled on eight different shirts (numbers 2, 3, 4, 5, 6, 7, 9 and 12) and now, in a regular midfield role, he wears the No. 11. In his 19th. professional season, his application, dedication, commitment, loyalty and determination are as evident as they have ever been in the cause of Chelsea. Here's wishing him the success he deserves in the Testimonial he looks forward to in 1980.

THE EIGHTIES

Wembley wins, relegation, promotion and financial worries aplenty made this decade both an exciting and turbulent time to support the Blues

The Eighties began as a period of struggle for the Blues, as we nearly reached our lowest ebb with relegation to Division Three an all-too-real prospect in the 1982/83 campaign. However, there were high points soon to come, with our league form resurrected under the management of John Neal followed by two moments of Wembley glory for fans to savour. There were numerous players who would shine in our famous shirt and who very much embedded themselves in the history of the club. The ever-developing matchday programme helped fans feel closer than ever to their heroes and, as any aficionado of our official publication will know, the arrival of Ken Bates as Chairman provided a column that many would file under the "must-read" category for years to come.

● APPOINTMENTS

The new editor of the Chelsea programme is Hugh Hastings, who has joined the club as Publications and Marketing Executive. His name will be familiar as the club's photographer over the past few seasons, a duty which he will continue to perform.

On greeting the new, we wish Albert Sewell a prosperous and happy future after many years as Chelsea Programme Editor — his influence will always be apparent on this publication.

The 1980/81 season began with Wrexham our opponents at the Bridge and the entire cover was taken up with a full-colour action shot for the first time. Inside, both Chairman Brian Mears and manager Geoff Hurst expressed optimism that this would be the season we bounced back to the top flight. Coach Bobby Gould was pictured leading the players during pre-season and a feature with new club captain Petar Borota revealed why he was becoming such a fans' favourite. Chelsea Chat announced a new editor for the programme, with club photographer Hugh Hastings taking over from Albert Sewell.

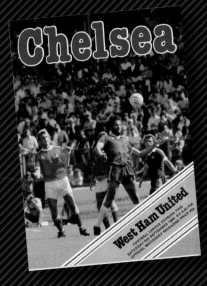

WEST HAM UNITED

Trevor Brooking

AT LAST! TWO POINTS AT HOME

Our home game against West Ham in September attracted a crowd in excess of 30,000, although the majority left unhappy following a 1-0 win to the Hammers. As you can see from the opposition pages, day-glow colours were the order of the day when it came to design.

THEY'RE BACK IN BUSINESS

Their days of pulling defences apart may have gone, but our famous ex-striking pair, Peter Osgood and Ian Hutchinson are still an active partnership — pulling pints at their public house in Old Windsor, THE UNION INN. The photograph with the two Bunny girls was taken earlier this month at the official opening and although they are not permanent features, the pub is well worth a visit, so — drop in Chelsea fans if you're down their way — Ossie and Hutch would be delighted to see you all!

Our biggest win of the season was a 6-0 thrashing of Newcastle United in which Colin Lee netted a hat-trick. Match action marked our first home win of the campaign and a man who had wowed fans with his goal-scoring exploits, Peter Osgood, was pictured with playing-turned-business partner Ian Hutchinson at their pub in Windsor.

The Chairman Writes

Once again we find ourselves without a team manager; we wish Geoff Hurst well for the future, but now it is up to all of us to pick up the pieces and endeavour to put the Club back onto an even keel once more.

Obviously, our first task is to appoint a manager as soon as possible in order that he can settle in during the summer and be well prepared to lead the operation at the commencement of the new season.

It is always our wish that you, our supporters, are the first to learn the current position at the Club but we know you will understand that this is not always possible. At times such as these it is not easy for any of us, but as I have said before, the efforts by all here will ensure that things go smoothly and on behalf of the Board I would like to thank the players, the staff, everyone here for their help and encouragement during the season. There are many occasions, I'm sure, when you must all feel that there is a lack of communication between us and this is something that I would like to try and rectify. Perhaps you would like to have the opportunity to discuss matters with certain members of the Club in order to obtain a clearer insight into the problems we face. After all, except of course for the players, you are the most important people in any club and are entitled to know what is going on. Perhaps you would let me know if this appeals to you. I'm sure that if this meets with a favourable reception, we shall be able to do something together.

May I take this opportunity to thank each and every one of you for your marvellous support, home and away, to all of us during this disappointing season. What promised so much last August has come to naught and I know that we all feel upset and frustrated. But, believe me, this is a great Club that shall soon, once again be competing in the best Division in the World.

We wish you a very happy summer and look forward to seeing you at the beginning of the new season when, once again we shall be setting out to achieve our goal of promotion. This, we must do.

Brian Mears

After a poor run of form through December 1980 into the new year, the Blues had started to steady the ship come the winter's end, although after three straight losses, our match against Bolton in March delivered a much-needed win. Mickey Fillery was featured in this edition and the strength of Hugh Hastings' match action photography was evident in every issue. Hopes may have been high for a positive finish to the campaign after three points against the Trotters, but we failed to record a single victory in our final 10 matches. The last game of 1981/82 brought Notts County to the Bridge and Brian Mears was once again discussing a managerial departure in his Chairman's notes.

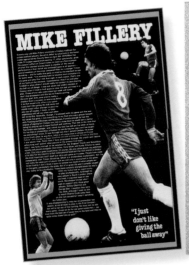

Neal appointed to steady ship, 1981/82

John Neal was the man to step into the Stamford Bridge hotseat and he was pictured alongside his assistant Ian McNeill on the front of the opening programme of the season, with Bolton our opponents. The Chairman's notes were penned by Viscount Chelsea following the resignation of Brian Mears over a summer when the club's financial problems were laid bare. At least we got the campaign off to a winning start with a 2-0 victory. As for the programme, with a full-page advert taking up the entire back page, the team line-ups moved to page three. Neal's decision to appoint Micky Droy as captain was explained in his first manager's notes, as can be seen on page 166.

FOOTBALL LEAGUE DIVISION TWO

Bolton Wanderers

SATURDAY 29th AUGUST 1981
Kick-off 3.00 pm

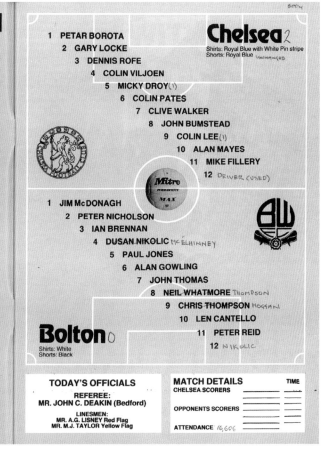

A MESSAGE FROM THE CHAIRMAN

It gives me great pleasure to welcome you all to Stamford Bridge today as the Club's Chairman. It has been a summer of considerable change and we welcome John Neal and Ian McNeill to Chelsea and wish them every success with us. Also we extend a warm welcome to the two recent additions to the Board, Norman Thomson and Stanley Reed.

Against this background one must not forget the magnificent service given to Chelsea Football Club by my predecessor, Brian Mears, who resigned his position as Chairman and Director after 20 years devoted service to the Club. It is heartening that he will still be amongst us as the Club's Vice-President. As at this time last year we find ourselves striving for the same goal in promotion to the First Division. It is essential that this great club competes once more with the elite and of course I hope this aim is achieved by next May and that our supporters receive first class entertainment 'along the way'. However, we must all be patient and realise that it does take time to build a successful side. I wish the players and management the best of fortune for this coming season and sincerely hope that our supporters are thrilled each time they take to the field.

VISCOUNT CHELSEA

GOOD AFTERNOON....

WELCOME, SUPPORTERS old and new to the beginning of a new season. Confidence and a clean copy book are the chief assets of every League club on the morning of the opening League fixtures and a fresh start is particularly welcome at Stamford Bridge this August considering our poor ending to the 1979-80 season — may better things be in store for us all this time around. Following the departures of Geoff Hurst, Bobby Gould and Brian Eastick — we wish them well in their future appointments — we have great pleasure in welcoming to Stamford Bridge Mr. John Neal, who comes to Chelsea as the first manager since Dave Sexton to have previously managed a Football League side. He brings to us a calm air of authority and confidence which will undoubtably be of help to the team, particularly the younger players. John has become one of the game's most respected managers during his 10-year stay at Wrexham and 4 years with Middlesbrough in the First Division. We warmly welcome also Mr. Ian McNeill who takes over the position of Assistant Manager from being manager at Northwich Victoria. Ian's experience was gained largely when bringing Wigan Athletic into the Football League (and subsequently knocking us out of the F.A. Cup here!). We wish them both long and very successful careers at Stamford Bridge.

Chelsea 2
Shirts: Royal Blue with White Pin stripe
Shorts: Royal Blue UNCHANGED

1 PETAR BOROTA
2 GARY LOCKE
3 DENNIS ROFE
4 COLIN VILJOEN
5 MICKY DROY (1)
6 COLIN PATES
7 CLIVE WALKER
8 JOHN BUMSTEAD
9 COLIN LEE (1)
10 ALAN MAYES
11 MIKE FILLERY
12 DRIVER (USED)

1 JIM McDONAGH
2 PETER NICHOLSON
3 IAN BRENNAN
4 DUSAN NIKOLIC McELHINNEY
5 PAUL JONES
6 ALAN GOWLING
7 JOHN THOMAS
8 NEIL WHATMORE THOMPSON
9 CHRIS THOMPSON HOGAN
10 LEN CANTELLO
11 PETER REID
12 NIKOLIC

Bolton 0
Shirts: White
Shorts: Black

TODAY'S OFFICIALS

REFEREE:
MR. JOHN C. DEAKIN (Bedford)

LINESMEN:
MR. A.G. LISNEY Red Flag
MR. M.J. TAYLOR Yellow Flag

MATCH DETAILS   TIME

CHELSEA SCORERS

OPPONENTS SCORERS

ATTENDANCE 16,606

For the League Cup encounter with Southampton in October, Around the Bridge discussed the club's inaugural fans' forum meeting, giving supporters a greater voice in operations. The match summaries page now included press reaction and Chris Hutchings featured in the regular players' Q&A, The Professionals. Elsewhere, the growing commercialisation of the game was evident from the range of Chelsea merchandise being made available. Pub-style Chelsea mirror anyone?!

TEAM POSTER 1981/82
— with full colour team photograph, autographs, fixture list and Club honours. An excellent buy at £1.50.

CLUB MIRRORS
— a new design of Chelsea pub-style mirror, with gilt frame. Just £8.99.

Reminiscent of our famous FA Cup triumph over the same team in 1978, the Blues got the better of an all-conquering Liverpool side once again in that competition, beating them 2-0 in a fifth-round tie. Next up was a home game against local rivals Tottenham and, with hooliganism blighting the game in the early Eighties, the club took the bold decision to address this with a stark warning for the trouble-makers on the front cover. The introduction and match action photos recalled our memorable win over Liverpool in round five and there were colour posters of both the Spurs and Blues captains.

GOOD AFTERNOON....

What a week! Points dropped, low gates, redundancies, all paint a sad image but the most important thing is we're still in business, and for that we must thank Mr. Kenneth Bates, who as widely-reported in the media a week ago, bought Chelsea F.C. and ensured our immediate financial future. He has a message printed elsewhere in today's programme to which no more need be added, other than to say that with gates well below the start of season break-even figure, a satisfactory solution had to be found, and found quickly, if Chelsea were to continue operating as a League club.

Mr. Bates' arrival provides the lifeline the Club so desperately needs and whilst we still face an uphill struggle to restore Chelsea to its former glory, we can view the future with a certain degree of optimism which we trust our supporters also share.

This afternoon the show goes on and we welcome to Stamford Bridge the Directors, Players, Officials and we're sure, many thousands of supporters from our friends and rivals in West London, Queens Park Rangers.

Last Saturday they made club history by winning through to their first ever F.A. Cup Final and now face Tottenham Hotspur, victors over Chelsea in the 6th round, at Wembley on May 22nd.

Rangers are hoping that by then they will once again be a First Division club. In one of the closest promotion battles in the Second Division for many years — at least for the third promotion spot — Rangers have as good a chance of any of making promotion and causing a double celebration in Shepherd's Bush in May. Regrettably, we cannot scale such heights this season ourselves and our priority during the remaining matches is to ensure our Second Division status (nothing should be taken for granted in this profession) and continue to build for next season.

We would like to wish all our supporters, in all corners of Stamford Bridge and the country, a Very Happy Easter and we look forward to seeing a large contingent of our fans down at Crystal Palace on Monday, the day after tomorrow, when the kick-off at Selhurst Park is 3 p.m. — see, and hear you then!

A historic moment off the pitch took place in April 1982, when Ken Bates bought the club for a nominal £1. Under his Chairmanship, our fortunes would change beyond all recognition and his programme column became part of Chelsea folklore until the early stages of the 21st century. You can see an early set of notes from Ken on page 172.

Chelsea MATCH MAGAZINE 50P

THIS WAS TO HAVE BEEN A COLOURFUL, COMMEMORATIVE FRONT COVER FOR TODAY'S GAME. HOWEVER, DUE TO THE PROBLEMS CAUSED BY A SMALL LUNATIC FRINGE WHO PERSIST IN CAUSING TROUBLE FOR THE CLUB, WE HAVE BEEN FORCED TO ALTER THE DESIGN IN ORDER TO MAKE THE FOLLOWING STATEMENT: IF YOU ARE HERE, MASQUERADING AS A FOOTBALL SUPPORTER, BUT YOUR SOLE PURPOSE IS TO CAUSE TROUBLE, THEN YOU ARE NOT WELCOME. YOUR BEHAVIOUR AS WITNESSED IN THE PAST, WILL NO LONGER BE TOLERATED. NOT ONLY WILL WE ENSURE THAT YOU ARE EJECTED FROM THE GROUND AND BANNED FOR LIFE FROM STAMFORD BRIDGE, BUT ALSO CHELSEA FOOTBALL CLUB WILL NOT HESITATE TO BRING A PRIVATE PROSECUTION AND CIVIL CLAIM FOR DAMAGES AGAINST YOU.

FA CUP ROUND SIX
TODAY'S MATCH SPONSORED BY BOVIS
Tottenham Hotspur
SATURDAY, 6th MARCH, 1982
KICK-OFF 3.00 p.m.

Blues in struggle for future, 1982/83

The 1982/83 season saw Chelsea's on-field fortunes reach their nadir as financial problems off the pitch heightened and threatened our future at Stamford Bridge, with property developers Marler seeking to buy the land on which our stadium stands. The programme cover had a sense of optimism about it, while the sparse back page for the October match against Oldham showed how the club were keen to make money, although there didn't appear to be many takers of the opportunities offered at this point in time. As would become common in the years to come, Ken Bates had a pop at certain sections of the written press, taking the opportunity to defend the Chelsea fanbase who had clearly been in for some criticism in certain sections of the media. A month later, the visit of Leeds saw an interesting message to the away support included on the cover – part warm welcome and part warning not to cause trouble – while an advert inside promoted a holiday to Guernsey.

Dear Supporter,
Chelsea F.C. have kindly agreed to this being my Testimonial season and to 'kick-off' the next few months activities a brand new FORD FIESTA GL provided by BREW BROTHERS is to be raffled at our next home match with Grimsby Town with tickets on sale at subsequent home fixtures. The car has all the extras and could be yours for just 25 pence — that's the price of a raffle ticket or you can buy 5 for £2 — or more if you like! The tickets will be on sale in the ground. The highlight of any Testimonial year is of course the football match against a star-studded side and this will be taking place towards the close of this season — in the meantime there will be various functions taking place such as Discos and a racing night. Details will be announced shortly. In the meantime I'd like to thank Chelsea for allowing me this Testimonial, and you the fans, for all your tremendous support of the team. Please keep it up.
All the best. Micky

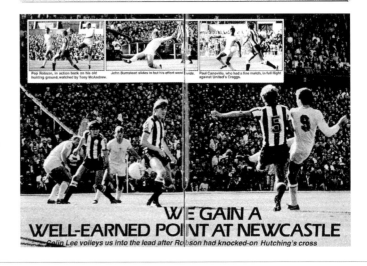

Pop Robson, in action back on his old hunting ground, watched by Tony McAndrew.

John Burnstead slides in but his effort went wide.

Paul Canoville, who had a fine match in full flight against United's Craggs.

WE GAIN A WELL-EARNED POINT AT NEWCASTLE
Colin Lee volleys us into the lead after Robson had knocked-on Hutching's cross

KEN BATES COLUMN

It was good to see Chelsea supporters playing their part in making last week's match at Newcastle the occasion it was. They cheered the team on, caused no trouble and quietly made their way home, upholding the name of Chelsea F.C. It's not easy to support your team at a ground like St. James's Park where the home supporters are so fervant and when we scored the silence was so noisy I thought the goal must have been disallowed!

Like ourselves, Newcastle United clearly have a good working relationship with their local police as the two sets of supporters were well segregated both outside and inside the stadium and if this can be achieved then the battle (football's against hooliganism) is half won. At Chelsea we welcome visiting supporters; their money at the turnstiles is as good as anyone else's and visiting fans add considerably to the big match atmosphere. Chelsea are one of the best supported clubs in the country and we boost attendance figures and gate receipts at every one of our away matches.

Derby County, for instance, (we have completely healed our past differences with them incidentally) admitted that in retrospect they may have been wrong to make no allocation of tickets available to Chelsea fans for the recent fixture at The Baseball Ground.

Our fans have been well behaved this season and I object strongly to the way in which they are being portrayed in some areas of the national press.

I cannot over-emphasise that I'm talking about a minority of the newspapers on this issue — the vast majority of the press are fair and hardworking but a small section of reporters seem to make their living by knocking the game. They desire for a cheap headline and appear to subscribe to that saying, "Never let the truth spoil a good story". I'm certain that thousands of decent Chelsea supporters feel as strongly about this as I do.

It's not my intention to wage a war with the press — that would be pointless. But it most certainly is my intention to defend Chelsea Football Club and our loyal, law-abiding followers.

In response to many requests, we are going to revive the Rail Specials to away matches and the Official Supporters' Club will be running one, in addition to coaches, to Sheffield next Saturday. We shall continue to operate coaches as they are more convenient for supporters on the outskirts of London as we offer a virtual door-to-door service. And of course they are cheaper. For people living in inner London however travelling by train is a better proposition.

I would like to welcome Gordon Dimbleby to Chelsea. His immediate task is to make the Chelsea Lottery more profitable. Please help him, and the Club, to realise this aim as the more revenue we collect from our lottery, the more we can spend on improving facilities at Stamford Bridge and if John Neal considers it necessary, the more he can strengthen the playing staff.

Enjoy the afternoon's entertainment.

KEN BATES

The end of the season was a real nail-biter for the Blues as we faced the prospect of dropping into the third tier of English football for the first time. We visited Bolton in our penultimate match, where a Clive Walker goal gave us a priceless victory. We still weren't safe heading into the final game against Middlesbrough, although it transpired that a point was enough to stay up. In his notes, John Neal praised the players and fans alike and looked forward to bright times ahead, although it might have been tough for anybody to think how much our fortunes would change over the next 12 months.

JOHN NEAL

"Going back a couple of weeks I must begin by congratulating Joey Jones, David Speedie and Colin Pates on being voted the top three players in this season's Player of the Year awards. It has been a very disappointing season but these three have done well and epitomise the spirit and application that we need at this club. That fighting, never-say-die spirit has returned in the last three matches, when we have also been supported with tremendous vigour and enthusiasm from our friends in the stands and on the terraces. I think the lads played well enough to win both our last home matches, but we had to settle for a share of the points which made last week's fixture at Bolton the most important of the season and a match we had to win. That we did I am sure is down partly to our supporters who made Burnden Park sound like our home ground and played a very important role in the victory. Had Bolton been given that level of support rather than ourselves, then I believe it most unlikely that we would have won the game. In matches of great importance such as the game at Bolton, and today's also, to hear your fans throughout the whole 90 minutes makes you walk tall and play with confidence, and it is marvellous that after a poor season our supporters are able to pull together in this way. It's a magnificent gesture which we all appreciate. The shirts the players threw into the crowd at the end of the match were a little 'thank you' to the fans for staying with us.

I didn't expect this fixture against my old club to have the bearing on the season's relegation issues that it now has, and again it is a match that we must go into with one aim; to win. There will be plenty of tension out there this afternoon as both clubs need the points, so once again our supporters are in a position to greatly influence the day's events by helping the lads with a continuation of their great support. It has been a season in which we have been made to fight for our lives, but the experience will make the players better people and professionals.

I'd like to wish our supporters a very happy summer break — they've deserved it — and thank you all for being such great supporters of Chelsea Football Club since the season began last August. I hope to strengthen our squad during the coming months and will work hard to put us in a position where we will be eager for the start of the new season, content in the knowledge that we have a team good enough to chase the honours that our supporters deserve."

THOSE ALL-IMPORTANT GOALS

Above: David Speedie rises to score against Sheffield Wednesday in his last match before suspension ruled him out of today's game and the fixture at Bolton. We look forward to more Speedie-goals like this next season, Dave.

DERBY COUNTY

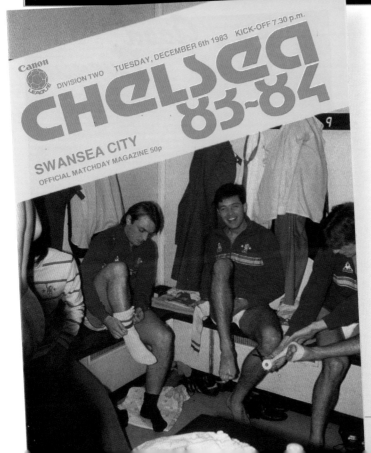

New talent brings new optimism, 1983/84

Following the disappointment of the previous campaign, Chelsea set their stall out from the first match of 1983/84, beating Derby County 5-0 at the Bridge in front of 17,000 jubilant fans. This followed a summer where the squad underwent a major overhaul as eight players left and seven came in. Among them was Kerry Dixon, who announced his arrival with a debut brace against the Rams. Fellow signing Nigel Spackman was also on target and other new faces, including Pat Nevin – who featured in the programme – and the returning John Hollins – welcomed back inside – would have a major impact on our fortunes, along with new goalkeeper Eddie Niedzwiecki. Our biggest win of the season came in December against Swansea City, who we overcame 6-1 thanks in no small part to an impressive hat-trick from Paul Canoville.

LEFT: Player/Coach John Hollins leads the first team squad in a pre-season training run at Stamford Bridge.

BLUES IN CAMERA

Left: Kerry Dixon's shot hits the post v QPR.

Middle: Our equaliser by Paul Canoville.

Right: Joey Jones heads our late winner.

LEFT: Parade of the new signings. Back: Eddie Niedzwiecki, Joe McLaughlin, Nigel Spackman, Kerry Dixon. Front: Pat Nevin and John Hollins, Alan Hudson signed the day after this picture was taken to complete our pre-season signings.

Above: New signing Nigel Spackman tussles for the ball with apprentice Terry Howard in the Blues v Yellows practice match.

Pat Nevin's free-kick beats Chris Sander for our second goal against Swansea.

We're going up!

TO ALL CHELSEA FANS THANK YOU FOR YOUR GREAT SUPPORT DURING THE PAST SEASON

News and Views of the Chelsea Blues

BLUES IN CAMERA

ON THE SPOT

Pat Nevin's been keen to take penalties all season and finally got his chance at Portsmouth last Tuesday after Nigel Spackman had missed his spot kick in our last home match. Pat's penalty was worth waiting for as he calmly sent Portsmouth 'keeper Knight (and all the photographers!) the wrong way to give us a two-goal lead. The only pity was that the kick was needed at all as Pat's overhead kick which was handled on the line would have been his goal of the season.

John Neal

Promotion back to Division One was secured in emphatic fashion with a 5-0 win over Leeds United, Dixon hitting another hat-trick in a magnificent debut season in which he netted 34 times. Here we bring you some of the other popular features from the programme during a hugely memorable campaign and extracts from the "promotion special" produced for our final home game against Barnsley. Five days after that game, a 1-0 victory over Grimsby saw us pip Sheffield Wednesday to top spot on goal difference. The Blues were back in the big time. Also featured here are John Neal's notes from the Grimsby game.

"What a marvellous last Saturday home match of the season it was and what a magnificent way to clinch promotion. It was a case of snap because our first Saturday home match of the season, which doesn't seem that long ago, was also won 5-0. The goals against Leeds were all quality goals, which I think have been the hallmark of the team during the season. They play exciting, entertaining football and I've enjoyed watching, not just the first team, but all Chelsea sides this season. It's one of the best seasons I've had in football. Every one of our sides has scored a lot of goals and played with the right spirit. At this time it's the players who deserve the plaudits. They've gone out and done a marvellous job and I thank them for giving us so much pleasure.

It's lovely to see them rewarded for these efforts with a place in the First Division. We've also had quite a few players on the fringe of regular selection and I'd like to thank them for their work during the year. Without them I don't think we could have achieved promotion. I asked for patience from the lads not selected at the beginning of the season and they've responded well. We've had some very good players watching and maybe it will be their opportunity next time.

It was a wonderful sight looking down from the directors' box after our last home match seeing the obvious pleasure everyone was getting at the success of the team. It was a memorable day. I feel very fortunate having tasted a few similar occasions, to which I am indebted to this game of football.

We've still got two important games to play and I'm hoping that we got it right at Manchester City last Friday and that if we win our two remaining matches we could yet finish in the championship position. I personally think that, having played all the teams in this division, I haven't seen one better than ourselves. As this is the final programme of 1983-84, I'd like to take the opportunity to thank everybody in the club and all our supporters for their tremendous encouragement throughout the season. I hope you have an enjoyable and restful summer and spend the time, as I will, looking forward to the day in mid-summer when the fixtures for next season are published. That will be the day when I will realise beyond doubt that we are back in the First Division.
Away The Lads!

CHELSEA PICTURE GALLERY No 14

TONY McANDREW
— AUTOGRAPH —

CHELSEA CELEBRATE IN STYLE!

Welcome back to the Canon League.

The 1984/85 season is the second season in Canon's three year Sponsorship of the Football League programme.

Canon's outstanding success in the high technology industry of cameras and business machines has enabled them to support our national game by over £3 million through the Canon League Sponsorship programme.

The Sponsorship Funds will be utilised to help football clubs keep admission prices down, encourage exciting attacking football with monthly and seasonal goalscoring awards, provide recognition to these clubs doing most to promote family attendances at Canon League matches and to reward individuals within football with Loyalty awards.

In the first Canon League 1983/84 season, the beautiful Trophies above - specially created by Garrard, the Crown Jewellers - were won by Liverpool, Chelsea, Oxford Utd., and York City. This season, all 92 League clubs will compete for these more prestigious trophies in the toughest football competition in the world - The Canon League.

Canon (UK) Ltd., Waddon House, Stafford Road, Croydon CR9 4DD.

Canon
Official Camera & Business Machines of The Football League

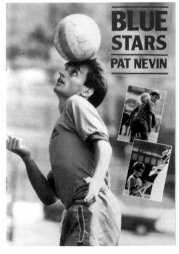

BLUE STARS
PAT NEVIN

Outlook brightens with Blues back at the top table, 1984/85

Few spells sum up the topsy-turvy nature of Chelsea's fortunes better than the two years between May 1983 and May 1985. The former saw Clive Walker's strike at Bolton salvaging our Second Division status and our first season back in Division One ended with a sixth-place finish and the outlook for the Blues was a great deal brighter. The 1984/85 campaign began with a match away to Arsenal and a huge travelling contingent saw Kerry Dixon equalise against the Gunners. There was little doubt that those present enjoyed what they saw and three days later we got our first three points of the campaign thanks to a 1-0 win over Sunderland, which saw Walker return to the Bridge as a Black Cat, having been the only player to leave the club over the summer.

Blues **In Camera**

Left: Dale Jasper in the thick of the action at Bristol City.
Above: Joey Jones and Leo Donnellan in pre-season training at the Gwydiss sand dunes in Wales.

Doug Rougvie and apprentice John Millar enjoy a brief rest during the gruelling week's training in Aberystwyth.

CHELSEA

Canon
DIVISION ONE
v SUNDERLAND
MONDAY, AUGUST 27th 1984
KICK-OFF 3 p.m.
OFFICIAL PROGRAMME 60p

TODAY'S MATCH IS SPONSORED BY THE CHELSEA F.C. VICE PRESIDENTS
RODNEY BRODY
ALAN TUCKERMAN
TERRY TURNER and
HUGH WHITTON

CHELSEA

Canon
DIVISION ONE
v EVERTON
FRIDAY, AUGUST 31st 1984
KICK-OFF 7.15 pm
OFFICIAL PROGRAMME 60p

TONIGHT'S MATCH SPONSORED BY BOVIS

John Hollins

"It has been an excellent start to the new season. At Highbury we worked as hard as the home team, if not harder, and matched them in every way. When you look at their side, which is packed with Internationals, it's quite refreshing for us to have come away with a point, disappointed that it could well have been three.

The Press, other managers, and the Arsenal players, did the talking for us after the match. They were full of praise, which was no more than the team deserved for their attitude and performance. I was more tense than usual for this game, as I returned to Highbury for the first time since my transfer. I was very eager for the team to do well — they did so.

It's a tough start to the season playing two games within 55 hours, but fortunately we didn't pick up any serious injuries at Highbury and were able to field an unchanged team for the game last Monday with Sunderland. We had a good first-half and could easily have been two, maybe three goals ahead at half-time. But Sunderland came here with their tails up after a good win over Southampton and refused to buckle. They pushed us all the way and had us at sixes-and-sevens at times but Paul Canoville was the only man to find the net during the 90 minutes and the points were ours. Having pushed forward a lot during the first 45 minutes, we were a little weary in the second-half, but our determination not to concede a goal just won us the day. So in our first two matches the lads have faced a team of Internationals and a team of new signings and honest hard-workers. Everyone thought we would struggle more in the first match than in the second but this was not the case. It just goes to prove the point if you don't or can't put the effort in, then eleven 'anybodies' will beat you. Put the effort in and make the most of the ability of your players and you should be successful.

Tonight we play Everton, who were first class against Liverpool, but then were beaten 4-1 in their first home match. There we have more contradictions. What will happen tonight? I don't make predictions, but I know that if we let our standards drop an inch then we will be punished. The team have been excellent, the support, both home and away, has been marvellous — keep this up for the next 40 games and I'm confident we will do well and get a lot of enjoyment along the way."

RARE GAZELLES SEEN ON TOTTENHAM COURT ROAD

As London's most exclusive sports store and the country's largest adidas stockists, you won't be surprised to hear that we have some rather rare examples of adidas' talents. One such example is the Green Gazelle.

Superbly styled in velour leather with rubber reinforcements and a microcellular rubber, hexagonal profile sole.

The exceptionally comfortable breed of Gazelle is also available in Red or Blue.

You'll also find blue jeans, red jeans, exclusive French and German imports.

Tracksuits and leisure clothing until now never seen in this country.

Superbly comfortable and brilliantly styled footwear and clothing for every sport. For men, women and children.

Whether you're serious about your sport or just looking for something to lounge in - make The adidas Connection, London's most exclusive sports store.

The adidas Connection

LONDON AND OXFORD'S MOST EXCLUSIVE SPORTS STORE

42 TOTTENHAM COURT ROAD, LONDON W1P 9RA. TELEPHONE 01 631 1455

CHELSEA PICTURE STORY

INTRODUCING E.R.I.C.

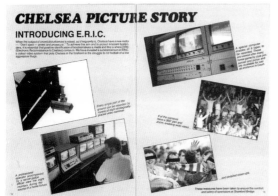

KEN'S COLUMN

FINANCIAL REPORT
As the figures on the previous page show, Chelsea moved into profit during the last financial year. The club continues to make good progress — having suffered a £662,000 loss in 1982-83, we made a £185,000 profit in 1983-84, the first returned by the Club for many years. The figures are particularly pleasing in view of the extra expenses incurred during the year and the purchase of SB shares (over £200,000) and the shops adjacent to the ground in the Fulham Road (£330,000). Commercial activities were again crucial, the figures showing a loss of £300,000 would have resulted without the contribution from this department.

Once again, the Commercial Department in effect subsidised everyone's match admission costs by 25%.

TRANSFERS
A small balance on transfer fees (before the 5% Football League transfer levy) reflects once again John Neal's shrewd activity in the transfer market. He has rebuilt the team at almost no cost.

INCOME	£
Alan Hudson	23,500
Micky Fillery	155,000
Peter Rh-Brown	60,000
Chris Hutchings	50,000
Simon Gibson	15,000
Bryan Robson	3,500
Micky Nutton	5,450
	311,450

EXPENDITURE	
Joe McLaughlin	
Duncan Shearer	20,000
Kerry Dixon	4,000
Derek Johnstone	170,000
Mickey Thomas	35,000
	77,500
	306,500

FOOTBALL AND THE GOVERNMENT
During the year clubs have been continually told how to 'put their house in order' by the Government, especially with reference to crowd behaviour. Yet they continue to take money out of football whilst giving financial aid to all manner of other leisure pursuits. Out of every pound spent, 30p has gone to the Government with nothing in return.

V.A.T.	£250,000
RATES	£41,000
POLICE	£94,000
NHS	£51,000

VERY IMPORTANT!
We understand that Marler have put in their first planning application for the development of the Bridge area and as feared it is believed to be for houses and flats with no provision for Chelsea Football Club.

This planning application can be opposed but it may be that a lot of you will want to add your objection to the many others that will be put in against this application. This you are perfectly entitled to do.

We urge you therefore to write to the Mr K Jones, Director of Planning, London Borough of Hammersmith & Fulham, Town Hall, King Street, London W.6, or phone 748-3020 ext 240, and ask for the appropriate forms to complete.

As you chanted last weekend "Chelsea Are Back" and we have certainly done well. Against Arsenal I thought we were marginally the better team and the players showed great character to recover from a goal against the run of play. Against Sunderland, although we started well and then faded, we came through our first test and we start tonight in the happy position of having four points out of two games. This has been achieved in abnormal temperatures and at the end of both matches I have been drenched in perspiration just watching them so it leaves little to the imagination how the players must have felt having to play in the 80's for an hour and a half. Hopefully with this evening's kick-off time it will give both teams a better chance to show what they can really do.

We would like to apologise to our fans (including the press) for the fact that all the ground improvements and renovations were not completed in time for the Sunderland match. You may well wonder where all the money has gone but over £175,000 has been incurred on improvements during the summer. Inevitably when working against a deadline it just isn't always possible to get everything finished in time but we do hope it will be completed for tonight's match. Finally a big THANK YOU from everybody at the Club to our fantastic supporters. Your cheering was absolutely superb at Arsenal where we outshouted the North Bank to make our lads think they were playing at home. This support has staggered everybody here and the following figures will show you why. During the summer we have processed over 6,000 Membership applications, 4,000 subscriptions for the Bridge News and we now have over 5,500 Season Ticket holders. I don't think many of you really appreciate the work that all this entails and I must give a special mention to the tremendous efforts made by the office staff who on some occasions have slept on the premises because they have been working so late.

Enjoy the game.
KEN BATES

Ken Bates' column in the Everton programme at the end of August spoke of improved finances, but also highlighted the precarious position the club was in with regards Marler's proposed purchase of the Stamford Bridge grounds and their intention to use the land for housing. Player-coach John Hollins had stepped up to lead the team and was penning the manager's notes after John Neal had suffered serious heart problems in the summer and there was a look at how the club was taking steps to control hooliganism with a new CCTV system. Also note some classic advertising from a firm we would go on to establish a long-lasting link with.

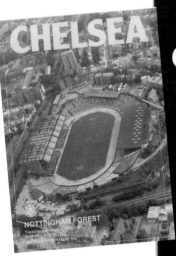

GORDON STARS IN FINE TEAM PERFORMANCE AT EVERTON

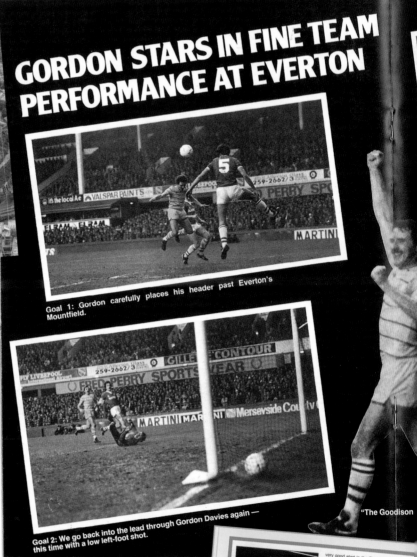

Goal 1: Gordon carefully places his header past Everton's Mountfield.

Goal 2: We go back into the lead through Gordon Davies again — this time with a low left-foot shot.

"The Goodison

By January 1985, John Neal was back on manager's notes duties and fans were wished a Happy New Year in our programme for the game against Nottingham Forest. The players were certainly sporting some classic attire, notably Paul Canoville who also featured in the Chelsea Spotlight Q&A, which you can read on page 111. Match action was from our stunning 4-3 win over champions elect Everton at Goodison, a game which perhaps symbolised more than any other how we belonged among the elite.

HAPPY NEW YEAR!
Players and supporters join in celebrating a marvellous Chelsea year at the Club Members Dinner-Dance.

A few tactical moves

The sliding tackle | The quick one-two

The substitution | The banana shot

The goal | The action replay

to help win the Milk Cup.

Milk Cup sponsored by the National Dairy Council

John Neal

"I must begin by wishing all our supporters a very happy and successful New Year. 1984 was a very interesting year for many reasons. After a terrible first few days when we lost at Middlesbrough and Blackburn we were not to lose another game until August when Everton beat us 1-0. It was a remarkable record and of course it enabled us to finish the season as Second Division Champions. It was nice to be a part of an historic season. Football is all about players and ours deserve full credit for playing so well during 1984.

I didn't get much opportunity to celebrate the season because I finished up in hospital not long after the final match but fortunately the operation went very well too, which in its own way was another 'championship success' for me personally.

As you all know, the team have made a

very good start in the First Division. It's a huge challenge facing marvellous teams every week but so far the lads have come through with honour. I thank everyone at Chelsea for working so hard during the past year enabling us to reach our present position.

We go into 1985 with lots of optimism. I know the team is capable of matching the best, so if we can improve a little on that we really would be classed as among the strongest teams in the country and that's our aim.

I hope our tremendous supporters have as much excitement and entertainment in 1985 as they had last year. Anybody who complains about the entertainment pro- now here we are aiming at the top of Divi-

All things considered I think we have made excellent progress when one remembers that only two years ago we were fighting a battle to stay out of the Third Division and now here we are aiming at the top of Division One.

Today we welcome Nottingham Forest and their manager Brian Clough to Chelsea. I've always admired and respected Brian. He's a remarkable man who has built winning teams at Derby and Nottingham during the years and it would be interesting to see what Brian could do at one of the big city clubs. He's a man who has the great strength of always speaking his mind, which hurts occasionally and has given him the reputation of being a controversial character with people who don't under- stand him.

His side will provide difficult opposition for us to overcome this afternoon. I hope we have an exciting game to start the New Year and we look forward to welcoming you again on Saturday when we begin our F.A. Cup campaign against Wigan.

Once again, from us all, HAPPY NEW YEAR!"

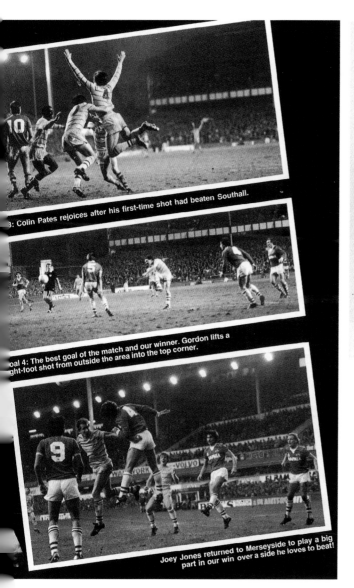

3: Colin Pates rejoices after his first-time shot had beaten Southall.

oal 4: The best goal of the match and our winner. Gordon lifts a ght-foot shot from outside the area into the top corner.

Joey Jones returned to Merseyside to play a big part in our win over a side he loves to beat!

STAMFORD BRIDGE

The recent planning sub-committee of the Hammersmith and Fulham Council met and approved the initial proposals submitted by Marler Estates for the development of the Bridge. No doubt each Chelsea supporter who lives in the area will be keen to discover which way their representative voted. This I hope to be able to tell you in Saturday's programme. Even though the vote went in favour of the plan, Chelsea supporters should not worry themselves: Marler have achieved very little so far. They still have to 1: Satisfy the council on the conditions of their proposals. 2: Obtain detailed planning consent. 3: Their plans have yet to be approved by the full council. 4: They must avoid a public inquiry which could well be called. 5: They've got to raise the finance. 6: They have to outline detailed plans, request quotes, and award the contract. 7: They then have to make proposals that are accepted by us in respect of suitable permanent alternative accommodation. 8: And give us satisfactory financial guarantees in respect of all the costs of moving and the possibility of temporary accommodation at another ground. Meanwhile there are only three years and six months to go until 19th August 1988 when we intend to exercise our option on the lease if all the steps outlined above have not been fulfilled.

Doug Rougvie and Mike Lyons challenge for a Blues' corner in extra-time.

MILK CUP 5th ROUND 2nd REPLAY
SHEFFIELD WEDNESDAY
WEDNESDAY, 6th FEBRUARY 1985
KICK-OFF 7.30 p.m.
OFFICIAL PROGRAMME 60p

CHELSEA

As well as maintaining our positive league form in the second half of the season, a standout fixture was the League Cup quarter-final against Sheffield Wednesday. After a 1-1 draw at the Bridge, an epic semi-final ended 4-4, with Canoville starring after coming off the bench to score twice in one of the all-time great Chelsea fight-backs. Extensive match action from that game featured in the programme for the second replay, which we won 2-1, with Ken Bates keeping fans updated on the stadium situation in his own inimitable fashion.

"KING" CANOVILLE'S NIGHT

8-PAGE ACTION SPECIAL

Hollins keeps success story going, 1985/86

After John Neal vacated the manager's position at Chelsea, taking on a director's position in recognition of his achievements, John Hollins seemed an obvious choice to replace him, assuming his first manager's role at the start of the 1985/86 season after an illustrious playing career. Positivity on the pitch continued with a second successive sixth-place finish and there was also silverware to relish in the form of the Full Members' Cup – a non-compulsory tournament created to fill the void of English clubs not competing in Europe due to the ban after the Heysel disaster. It may not have been the most coveted of trophies but it gave us our first Wembley triumph in what must rank as one of the greatest finals to have been played at the famous old stadium. Here are extracts from the opening programme of the season, at home to Coventry City. Colin Pates became the first Chelsea player to have the honour of a regular captain's column this season, having started penning it midway through the previous campaign.

THEY WON THEIR FIRST FULL CAPS IN THE SUMMER....

Photo of Kerry by Bob Thomas Photography

CONGRATULATIONS TO KERRY (England) AND DAVID (Scotland)

Colin's Comment

"Welcome back, one and all; I'm pleased to say that after my beginner's efforts last season I've been given a page again in the programme in which to give the players' view on Chelsea this year. I gather from letters received by Hugh Hastings the editor, that this was one of the most popular features in the programme last season which is very pleasing and I'll do my best to keep my notes short, to the point and I hope, entertaining.

Where else can I begin today's page other than hoping that you all enjoyed the summer, which, as usual, seemed to flash by. Getting married made it a special summer for me and I'm currently in the middle of trying to buy a new house, so life is nice and hectic at the moment.

The biggest change at the club since last season has of course been John Hollins taking over from John Neal as manager. It will seem odd this year not to be under John Neal's careful hand but in a way I'm pleased that he has stepped down from management; I'm sure his health suffered as a result of the excitement caused by us wining the Second Division and the man's done so much for Chelsea it's only right that he should, for want of a better phrase, be looked after properly. John, as you know, is now a Chelsea Director and I'm sure he will influence the club considerably in his new role. John Hollins we all know as a fellow-player and excellent coach so we're looking forward to working under him as manager.

As usual, we went to Aberystwyth pre-season for the dreaded week on the sand dunes. This time it was harder than ever, as new coach Ernie Walley certainly knows some strenuous training routines. Ernie's a tough character who really puts us through it. Some of his sessions were murder at the time but we will be glad we worked so hard once the season is under way and we feel the benefit of the hard work put in. The pre-season friendlies have been very satisfying and at the time of writing we are unbeaten, having kept three clean-sheets. Eddie had a big part to play in this, saving two penalties, and he looks the sharpest I've ever seen him.

Looking back to this time last season I think we are a more professional side and that the year's experience in Division One should give us more chance of winning a trophy this time around. Certainly the disappointment of losing in the semi-final of the Milk Cup to Sunderland is still in

our minds, and if we are lucky enough to get that close to winning a cup this year we'll be determined not to let the chance slip away. Last season I don't think some of us fully realised how close we were to winning something; it takes a defeat to bring home to you what you've missed out on.

By the time we meet tonight, our League programme will have started with that tough match at Hillsborough. Sheffield seems like a second home to us nowadays as we've played so many matches there in recent years. I think I've said everything I can about Sheffield Wednesday in past programmes but we reckoned it was one of the hardest games with which to start the season, particularly in view of the rivalry between our two clubs. I know they were disappointed at losing to us in the Milk Cup and finishing below us again in the League last season, so I can safely say that it must have been a hard game up there and I just hope we came back with a point or three.

Tonight we face Coventry, who took a 2-0 lead here last season before losing 2-6 in one of the most remarkable games of the season. They showed their true character at the end of last season by winning their last few games to stay up; any side that can do that should not be underestimated so we'll treat them with a lot of respect today and put that 6-2 result to the back of our minds. Let's hope we get off to a good home start! See you on Saturday for the visit of Birmingham.

Colin

WE WON THE CUP!

WE WON IT TOGETHER — WELL SUPPORTED!

Colour photos of our Wembley triumph will appear in next Saturday's programme (v Ipswich) and a special picture book is being planned.*

*Please don't call us, we'll give full details about the souvenir brochure in next week's programme, by which time price and contents will be finalised.

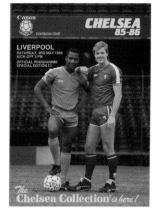

CHELSEA HIT WEMBLEY FULL FORCE

The Full Members' Cup final took place in March 1986, with extracts from the programme pictured here. There may only have been 30,000 present at Wembley, but those in attendance witnessed an absolute classic as two goals from Colin Lee and a David Speedie hat-trick earned us a 5-4 win over Manchester City. Turn to page 112 for a Q&A with the latter from an earlier game in the competition against Portsmouth. The final day of the season brought Liverpool to Stamford Bridge and the programme cover was certainly an eye-catching one as Keith Dublin and Kerry Dixon modelled the club's new range of Chelsea Collection kits for the following campaign. You just don't see shorts like that any more!

On Saturday Chelsea travel to Kenilworth Road to face Luton Town on their new plastic pitch. With this in mind and the forthcoming League meeting to discuss the spread of synthetic surfaces Colin Benson makes a personal reflection on the alternative to grass.

MUD MUD GLORIOUS MUD

ARTIFICIAL football pitches produce artificial results of that there is no doubt. I have seen matches at Loftus Road, Kenilworth Road and at Deepdale and never once have I seen a good game. The players don't like them, the managers don't like them, so why is football pursuing this suicidal course?

The artificial intrusion into League football hasn't enhanced the game as a spectator sport and certainly hasn't done anything for the players who perform on it. The magic carpet, introduced by Queens Park Rangers in September 1981, when ironically their visitors were Luton Town, simply has not carried them away to the land of championships and success.

Terry Venables — then in charge at Loftus Road — claimed that his plush new carpet would enrich the game, provide the perfect stage for skill and technique to flourish. But, although the surface is flat and true, the bounce consistent, the play does not flow and because players have difficulty in controlling the ball their football is fragmented. The maxim that an artificial surface eliminates all natural elements obstructing skill is all very well in theory, but in practice it just doesn't work that way. The very nature of the compounds used in the manufacture of the surfaces are not the same as real turf, thus the players don't get the same grip and more importantly the ball does not react the same way.

The most significant difference is the uncontrollable bounce — which I hasten to add is not as bad on Luton's pitch as it is at Rangers' although bad enough — which changes the whole concept of the game.

PIN-BALL

English football is based on hard running and balls played into space, but on artificial pitches this style is a complete non-starter. Any ball knocked in front of a player will simply skid away so the tactic has to be to knock accurate balls into feet. Even then the advantage remains with the defending players for it only needs a touch for the ball to spin away from the attacking players' boot . . . in short the synthetic field has bastardised our traditional game. As one top First Division manager remarked: "It's like playing pin ball on a football pitch."

Glasgow Rangers' former boss Jock Wallace has no reservations: He says "Football in America has died on its feet because most clubs played on artificial pitches. I toured there twice with Glasgow Rangers and told them that they wouldn't get football right until they changed to grass".

But it is not only from a spectators view that these pitches fall down. Over the past ten years in the USA they have been conducting detailed scientific investigations on the effects the surfaces have on players, and in general terms concluded that a players speed increases, due to the evenness of the field. But the statistics also showed an increase in the numbers and the severity of injuries.

GLORIOUS MUD

In addition, with well built players, the increased speed normally causes a rise of 13% in the force of impact when challenges are made.

The compact surfaces cause muscle strains because of the traction involved and consequently you get more joint trouble in ankles and knees than on grass pitches which allow the joints to slide and give a little on impact.

But for the last word I will refer to Joe Jordan who says: "The League title is not just about teams who can play on good surfaces. It is about character and guts over 42 gruelling games played in varying conditions.

"Muddy heavy pitches and other questionable surfaces all add to the flavour of the British game . . . it is what football is all about."

As for me, I will rest my case.

Padded goalkeepers and pimpled boots on QPR's Omniturf surface.

8

Injuries halt Blues' progress, 1986/87

After two successful seasons, there was plenty of reason for optimism ahead of the 1986/87 campaign. However, after a slow start which saw us win only twice in our opening 10 games, rumours of unrest in the dressing room did not take long to emerge. Our home game against Queens Park Rangers brought a third straight victory to add a positive gloss to proceedings. John Hollins bemoaned a spate of injuries which no doubt hampered our progress, something reinforced by the comments in physio Norman Medhurst's column. There was also an interesting piece on the development of Astro-turf playing surfaces as we prepared to visit the plastic pitch of Luton Town.

THE FINAL CURTAIN

FOR IAN

THE *SIMOD* SPONSORSHIP TEAM

SAVE THE BRIDGE FANS GREAT RESPONSE

The season ended with a thrilling 3-3 draw against Liverpool at the Bridge in what was the final game of Ian Rush's first spell at Anfield. The Reds legend was given a page in tribute, alongside a squad picture of the players in a kit featuring our third sponsor of the season. The names of Grange Farm, Bai Lin Tea and Simod all adorned our own Chelsea Collection strips in 1986/87 and the leisurewear was also advertised in this issue. Note the logo at the bottom of each page in the programme.

Hello. This is my first column as captain of Chelsea and I can't tell you how proud I am. It's a great honour to be asked to take on the role and that is why I couldn't refuse the invitation . . Patesy's done a great job as the skipper and hasn't done anything wrong it was just the decision of the manager to change things.

I want to make it clear that making me captain had nothing at all to do with persuading me to sign a new contract . . . The subject wasn't even mentioned in the discussions and I had already signed and was walking out of the door when the manager asked me whether I would consider being captain.

Of course I accepted, who wouldn't. I believe I have leadership qualities. I've always been quite loud on the field – the lads know that. But there is much more to being captain than just being loud. It is a matter of knowing what to say and when to say it. You also have to understand the players in your team know how to approach them. People respond to things in different ways so it is a matter of getting to know who wants to be shouted at and who needs to be coaxed with a pat on the back.

I'm quite looking forward to it. There's more to the job than just tossing the coin up.

When John offered me the job my immediate thoughts were of lifting a trophy. It would be nice to go down in history as a captain with a trophy for there have not been too many who have done that at Chelsea. Perhaps it is time to put that right.

Of course we realise that these things don't just fall off trees and that you have to work extremely hard to attain success but there is a pleasant and determined attitude in the camp now and I'm sure we have the players capable of achieving our aims . . . I felt this was happening when I sorted myself out towards the end of last season and saw the players who were coming in. New faces, different characters and senses of humour all add to the stimulus of us all . . . It's like a fresh start for everyone.

John has not given me any specific instructions. He has just asked me to keep everyone going in the game, give them plenty of encouragement and work to create the atmosphere we used to have.

CAPTAINS Corner

Joe McLaughlin

13

That sinking feeling for the final time, 1987/88

If the mid-Eighties had seemingly brought to an end the woes of the previous 10 years or more, 1987/88 saw us return to our misfiring ways on the pitch. A win against a side we shared some epic tussles with during the Eighties, Sheffield Wednesday, on the opening day gave everyone hope and after six wins in our opening 10 league matches, it seemed like a good campaign was on the cards. In the Owls programme, Joe McLaughlin took on captain's notes duties. There was also good news with the return from injury of Eddie Niedzwiecki, pictured in training with goalkeeping coach Peter Bonetti, while new signing Tony Dorigo featured in Star Portrait.

LINE Up

CHELSEA 2
Shirts: Royal Blue
Shorts: Royal Blue

EDDIE NIEDZWIECKI 1
STEVE CLARKE 2
TONY DORIGO 3
STEVE WICKS 4
JOE McLAUGHLIN (capt.) 5
JOHN BUMSTEAD WOOD 6
PAT NEVIN 7
MICKY HAZARD 8
KERRY DIXON (1) 9
GORDON DURIE (1) 10
CLIVE WILSON 11
WILSON (K) (USED) 12
MURPHY 14

SHEFFIELD WEDNESDAY
Shirts: Silver
Shorts: Aubergine

MARTIN HODGE (capt.)
MEL STERLAND
STEVE McCALL
LARRY MAY MADDEN
LAWRIE MADDEN MAY
NIGEL WORTHINGTON
BRIAN MARWOOD
GARY MEGSON
LEE CHAPMAN (1)
DAVID HIRST
MARK CHAMBERLAIN
BRADSHAW (USED)
OWEN

ATTENDANCE: 21,829

OFFICIALS
Referee: Lester Shapter (TORQUAY)
Linesmen: J.F. Hill (Red Trim) A.C. Williams (Yellow Trim)

DERBY STAR
Exclusive suppliers of match footballs to Chelsea Football Club

160

BLUES Diary

RESORTING TO ACTION

CAPS IN HAND

STEVE CLARKE FACT SHEET

BY COLIN BENSON

Chelsea FC

v MIDDLESBROUGH
Saturday, 28th May, 1988.
Kick-Off 3.00 p.m.

Official Programme £1

Commodore backs Chelsea all the way!

CAMPBELL'S CORNER

PHEW! What a week. I really haven't had time to breathe. On the very first day I took charge of the team as acting manager I received a phone call from Brighton saying that unfortunately their goalkeeper had suffered a groin strain and attempts to sign a replacement had fallen through … They had to have Perry Digweed back.

I spoke to Mr Lloyd and asked if their was any way we could keep Perry or possibly buy him. The answer was negative.

With Digweed set to return to Brighton we were left with just young Roger Freestone and with the transfer deadline only hours away I had to set things in motion.

I had seen the boy Kevin Hitchcock play and as it happens had watched him, accompanied by "The Cat", the night before and so we had first hand knowledge of his current form. I spoke to Mansfield manager Ian Greaves about the price, we came to an agreement, and the lad then travelled down to meet us at the Post House Hotel at London Airport.

Kevin was very receptive to our proposals and, as a Barking boy, was not only pleased to join a big club but was also happy at the prospect of returning to London.

He will go straight into the team today and I am sure you will like what you see. If you talk to anybody in football about goalkeepers they will mention Shilton, Woods, Beasant and Grobbelaar in the same breath, and in the next bracket will include Kevin.

I would like to take this opportunity to thank Ian Greaves, and the people at Mansfield Town Football Club, for their spontaneous co-operation in dealing with this matter.

Sadly, a terrible run of form through the winter months led to the departure of John Hollins, with Bobby Campbell taking on the manager's position in time for our March game against Southampton. His notes in the programme did not dwell on what could be achieved, more the rush he faced to sign new keeper Kevin Hitchcock – Niedzwiecki's final game for the Blues before injury ended his playing days had come at the start of November, coinciding with our downturn in form. By the time we were competing in play-off fixtures to avoid the drop at the end of the season, new sponsor Commodore was advertising its prestige computer product Amiga in our programme. Having failed to secure the win needed to ensure survival against Charlton on the final day of the regulation season, we faced play-off fixtures against Second Division sides Blackburn, who we beat 6-1 on aggregate, and Middlesbrough, who defeated us 2-1 over two legs. As part of the Football League's plan to reduce the top flight from 22 to 20 teams, we fell into Division Two. The fans didn't know it at the time, but it was not a feeling they would have to endure again.

Campbell's boys bounce back in style, 1988/89

Chelsea's start to life back in Division Two may have led fans to believe that a flirtation with the third tier could be back on the cards as no wins in our opening six games left us in a perilous position. That we finished the 1988/89 season top of the table with our highest-ever points haul of 99 is credit to the management of Bobby Campbell and the performance of his players. When we took on Swindon in February, it was midway through a club record 27 games unbeaten and off the back of thrashing Walsall 7-0 away from home, Gordon Durie scoring five of the goals. Unsurprisingly, he was the cover star of the Robins programme, which this season gave a nod to the club's earliest publication by naming its early pages Chelsea Chronicle.

CAMPBELL CALLING

JACK DUNNETT, the President of the Football League, is here this afternoon to present the Barclays League medals for the Second Division to Chelsea … the climax to a satisfying season.

I am sure that, like me, you will be happy that this season the final game at The Bridge is in May and we don't have to await the play-offs. I didn't get a holiday last year, but I am looking forward to a few days away with my family this time.

Before that, there is some business to be done. I will be carrying on for a while trying to improve things for next season.

Since the Championship was assured I have been all over the country looking at players, although not the pair I was linked with in one newspaper in the past fortnight.

I've been labelled "cautious" in the final lap of the Championship race because I would not make a song and dance until mathematics made it certain we were promoted. After a lifetime in football, I know only too well that what we have done this year will soon be forgotten.

Anyway, before we go, let me utilise my space in what I hope is the final Second Division programme I shall ever write by saying a few "thank-yous".

TO … the players. Haven't they done well? The Championship, a record number of points, a club record run of 27 games without defeat and more than 100 goals this season. I don't want to draw comparisons; they are in the record books on their own merits. A pat on the back for all 19 in the squad; all have earned their corn when they had to.

TO … our supporters. It's been a trouble-free year for them, no aggro at all, and they have given the team a lift, particularly away from home.

TO … the Chairman. He has provided wholehearted support and advice — and willingly come up with the money for new players. When I went for Dave Beasant I told him: "I've spent £725,000 of your money." His reply: "Good — I hope you've spent it well."

TO … the groundsmen. There has been a marked improvement on the pitch this season.

TO … the admin staff. They've kept me in order.

TO … the police. They've kept everything low key.

TO (last, but not least) … the Press. One of the first things I did when I took over was to get an acting unpaid Press officer to help improve the Chelsea image. I think, by and large, we have had a fair crack of the whip this season. Long may it continue.

Have a lovely summer. I hope you'll all be back come August now we are back on the First Division ladder. There's no reason, if we continue to show the same attitude, that we can't do well.

9

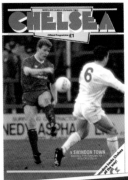

CHELSEA CHRONICLE

FRONT COVER ACTION

Action man Gordon Durie takes the limelight on the cover today-and who else? Here he is swinging into five-goal action against suffering Walsall.

KERRY GETS US OFF

TO A GREAT START!

The Blues'

AUGUST

OUR 1988, 1989 DIARY

THE season started on a disappointing note for the Blues — the Championship favourites with the bookies — when Kevin Wilson's goal was the only consolation from a 2-1 home defeat by Blackburn Rovers.

Three days later, with Graham Roberts having relieved Joe McLaughlin of the captaincy, Kevin again scored as we picked up our first League point in a 1-1 draw at Crystal Palace.

However spirits remained subdued by the news that Steve Wicks had been forced out of the game by a back injury.

SEPTEMBER

ANOTHER forgettable month for the Blues at least ended on a positive note when we registered our first League win of the season at the seventh time of asking — goals by Gordon Durie and John Bumstead bringing us victory at Leeds. Up to that point September had brought nothing but bad news.

We lost more than the match against Manchester City, where 'keeper Kevin Hitchcock made his last appearance of the season in the first team after suffering a thigh injury, lost 1-0 at Bournemouth, gave up a 1-0 lead to Oxford United and had to be content with a draw, and drew again, 1-1, at Barnsley.

But then came that first win of the season — a 2-0 victory over Leeds on September 24.

Spirits slumped, however, when Fourth Division Scunthorpe beat the Blues 6-3 on aggregate in the Littlewoods Cup second round in late September and early October.

OCTOBER

ALTHOUGH we had only picked up six points from our first seven games, we entered October with renewed spirit and it reflected in our results. The Blues opened up with a 2-1 win against Leicester — David Lee marking his debut with a goal — and were held 1-1 at Swindon before four goals cheered us at Oldham. The home game against Plymouth Argyle, saw the long-awaited return of Blues' fans to the terraces and the team registered their approval with a 5-0 win. Tony Dorigo, who had scored one of the goals in our 2-0 win against Walsall earlier in the month, was again on target, as was Graham Roberts from the penalty spot. Gordon Durie got a couple and Kerry Dixon the other.

Despite losing 0-3 at Hull (the Blues would not lose again until April 15), we completed a profitable month by beating Brighton 2-0.

Not surprisingly, Bobby Campbell won the Barclays Second Division Manager of the Month award. Notable departures from The Bridge were Colin Pates, who joined Charlton for £430,000, and John Coady, bought by Derry City for £10,000.

NOVEMBER

THE Chelsea revival continued apace when they beat League leaders Watford 2-1 at Vicarage Road to earn the Barclays Performance of the Week award from England manager Bobby Robson.

The Blues remained unbeaten throughout the month against Sunderland and today's opponents, Bradford City, and finished with a 2-0 win against Shrewsbury in the club's 3,000th Football League game.

In the Simod Cup Plymouth were hit for six and Bradford succumbed to the odd goal in five as we moved smoothly into the third round.

DECEMBER

SUCH was the confidence flowing around The Bridge that the Blues swept aside Stoke 3-0 at the Victoria Ground, despite coming down to ten men. The feeling that Chelsea were Championship material was brought home to the fans when Kerry Dixon committed himself to the club until 1993 by signing a new four-year contract. The response was magnificent with 20,000 turning up to see the

season of triumph

3-3 home draw with Portsmouth — a far cry from the 6,747 who had watched the victory over Walsall two months earlier.

A 4-1 win at Birmingham the following Friday took us to second place in the table — and we went top for the first time on Boxing Day and then stole a 1-1 draw against second-placed West Brom on New Year's Eve when Graham Roberts netted his fifth penalty of the season in the last minute.

Bobby Campbell ended the year by bringing 26-year old Australian World Cup striker Dave Mitchell to the club from Dutch club Feyenoord in a £150,000 deal.

JANUARY

THE club began 1989 by replacing one player with another. While Darren Wood bid farewell to the club and moved to Sheffield Wednesday in a £350,000 deal, Bobby spent a club record £725,000 to bring 'keeper Dave Beasant from Newcastle.

We continued to dominate the League, beating Oxford and Crystal Palace before drawing at Blackburn, but were eliminated from both Cup competitions. In the FA Cup third round we lost 4-0 at Barnsley and followed that with an equally disappointing 4-1 home defeat by Nottingham Forest in the Simod Cup third round.

FEBRUARY

THE Cup traumas were soon water under The Bridge as Gordon Durie inspired a club record away win at struggling Walsall. Gordon had a hand in all seven — netting five times himself, winning a penalty, which Graham converted, and setting up Kevin for his strike.

Two own goals helped us beat Swindon 3-2, but following a 1-0 win at Plymouth the Blues let slip a two-goal lead at home to Oldham and so were knocked off their perch by Manchester City.

However, three days later it was business as usual when goals by Kerry and Kevin brought us a 2-1 victory over Hull and returned us to pole position.

MARCH

WHILE the first team flew off to Marbella for a mid-season break, Bobby remained behind to sign Dutch Olympic defender Kenneth Monkou from

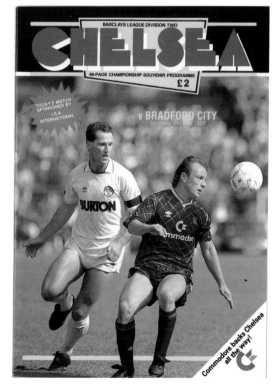

KEVIN WILSON ... after scoring the second goal in the 3-2 win over promotion rivals Manchester City at Maine Road.

Feyenoord for £100,000. The team arrived home to hear that Watford had beaten Manchester City to strengthen our hold on the top spot.

Unfortunately, the Hornets then held us to a 2-2 draw. However that precipitated an eight-game winning streak, highlighted by a crucial 3-2 win against Manchester City in front of 40,000 fans at Maine Road. Wins were also achieved against Brighton (1-0), Sunderland (2-1), Bournemouth (2-0) and Ipswich (1-0).

APRIL

THE magnificent eight results were completed with a 5-3 home win over Barnsley on April 1. Kerry, who found the net four times, was certainly no fool.

The club's record run of 27 unbeaten League games ended with the 2-0 loss at Leicester. It stretched back over six months — just one short of Liverpool's all-time record mark.

We then crowned a triumphant season by securing both promotion and the Second Division Championship with a John Bumstead strike — only his second of the season — giving us a 1-0 win at home to Leeds in front of 32,000 impeccably behaved fans, having beaten Birmingham (3-1) and West Brom (3-2) in the two preceding weeks.

But over our triumph hung the dreadful shadow of the Hillsborough disaster, which was marked by a minute's silence.

A 5-3 victory over Barnsley on April Fool's Day made promotion a formality. Including the match against the Tykes, we won 12 of our last 14 matches and the programme for our final home fixture, against Bradford, was a 48-page Championship souvenir edition. The Blues were back where we belonged and where we would stay up until the present day.

Stability ahead as cup is secured, 1989/90

Having experienced two sixth-placed finishes in the top flight in the mid-Eighties, the Blues went one better in our first season back in Division One as we ended 1989/90 in fifth spot and also lifted the Full Members' Cup again. Extracts from the programme for our first game of the campaign against QPR, as well as the Full Members' Cup final versus Middlesbrough and the Derby game soon after, are pictured. Football would change beyond all recognition in the Nineties, and Chelsea's on-pitch fortunes would soon be balanced with stability off the field, leaving us in prime position to progress. However, it's safe to say nobody could have foreseen exactly how much the club would transform over the course of the next decade and beyond...

CHELSEA 1 MIDDLESBROUGH 0

'My greatest moment

A SUPERB free-kick from England international Tony Dorigo won the Zenith Data Systems Cup for Chelsea.

The Australian full-back curled a 25th minute shot around the wall past the despairing dive of Middlesbrough goalkeeper Steve Pears to bring the trophy back to Stamford Bridge.

Middlesbrough had battled with credit, but Chelsea demonstrated that they had the quality and confidence to deal with the Division Two attack.

The match may not have had the all of the thrills and goal action of the Blues' last visit to Wembley, in the 1986 Full Members Cup Final, but it was made more tense by memories of previous encounters with Middlesbrough.

As it turned out, the Blues exacted retribution for the play-off defeat which consigned them to the Second Division two seasons ago.

The atmosphere generated inside the stadium was worthy of any FA Cup Final by the largest crowd in the country to date this season.

Although Dorigo deservedly earned his share of the headlines for the goal and Peter Nicholas collected the 'Man of the Match' award, there was no doubting the contribution elsewhere in the team.

Ken Monkou and Erland Johnsen, in particular, shone in the centre of defence. Their calm, confident approach gave Chelsea a firm footing from which to build their approach play from the back.

CURLING SHOT

Dorigo struck in the 25th minute. Simon Coleman was penalised for a foul on Kevin McAllister and as Nicholas shaped to take the free-kick, Dorigo ran in to flight a curling shot around the wall from 22 yards. Pears managed

TONY DORIGO'S WALL-BEATER GIVES CHELSEA THE ZENITH CUP AT WEMBLEY

By DES KELLY

to get one hand to the shot, but he could o help the ball into the top corner.

It was the realisation of a dream for Dori "In Australia every kid used to dream of p' ing in a Cup Final at Wembley," he said. "T was always my ambition, but to go one be and score the winner is just beyond beli

NOW I KNOW!

"I used to wonder how the guys who sco the winning goal felt. Now I know. I try 5 60 of those free-kicks in training and it's g to see that the work paid off.

"You could feel the passion of the fans there. It made the players realise just how portant the Zenith Final was. We w desperate to win it for our supporters after disappointments we have had in the other competitions.

"We never gave up. We stuck to our and we defended well when we had to. very happy. This is the best experience o career so far."

'We wanted it for the fans

PENALTIES? Y%U W%N'T GET ANY AT BARCLAYS.

20 FACTS
about QUEEN S PARK RANGERS

Tony Dorigo's free kick beats the Middlesbrough wall (above) and goalkeeper Steve Pears.

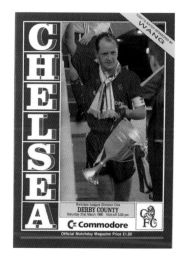

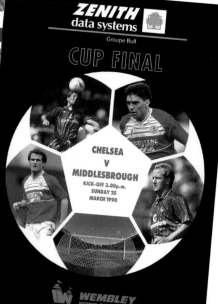

CLASSIC COLUMNS

The programme's column pages have recorded the views of our coaches, captains and owners during many important moments in our history. A selection of these can be found on the following pages, beginning with the first thoughts from some of our previous managers

HEART TO HEART

Greetings to you all!

This being a mid-week game and accordingly few Derby supporters having been able to travel, I assume that nearly everyone looking on tonight is Chelsea-minded to some degree, and I would like this our first acquaintance to be of a heart-to-heart nature.

First, in welcoming you to Stamford Bridge, I wish to express my delight at being appointed Manager of Chelsea. From my days as a player, I have had a great admiration for this Club—it was always a pleasure to play here on one of the finest pitches in the country—yet always I have felt that the Club deserved to do itself fuller justice than ever it has done in the past.

It is my job to see that this " greater standing " is forthcoming, and foremost in the making of the successful Chelsea we all want to see must be the atmosphere of one big happy family, a spirit linking Directors, Players, Administrative Staff, and You, the paying public.

In taking over my new duties, I am alive to the task ahead and, given the 100 per cent backing of everybody, I face the future with confidence. After only a few weeks here in the managerial chair, I can see the real team-spirit being fostered among those of us behind the scenes, and when it reaches you on the terraces and in the stands there can be no telling to what heights Chelsea will rise.

Here's where our Supporters come in. You folks may rightly be proud of your title " Football's Fairest Crowd," but for my part I would like to see not a little but a lot more partisanship in favour of Chelsea. All too many people come to Stamford Bridge to see a football match—instead of to cheer Chelsea.

Please prove me wrong, but it's my opinion that over the years too many bystanders have gone out of their way to grouse, jibe and grumble, to pull the Club down, rather than say a good word for Chelsea. And for years now, the players here must have been thoroughly sick of all the Music Hall publicity that has gone before. Sometimes deserved, often not. I'm not saying the spectators have been responsible for all the failures —far from it—but I hope you see the point I am trying to make.

Let's have more people " eating, sleeping, drinking Chelsea." Let's spread the Chelsea spirit across London, and let the boys really hear you when they go onto the field. Don't tell me the crowd can't make a difference! Other clubs count on the vocal support of their followers as worth a goal start—why shouldn't we? Lack of it has entitled the visiting team to think they're a goal up at Stamford Bridge. By all means be fair to our opponents, but you can also let yourselves go in support of our own lads.

We have a stiff opening programme, and a month from now ten games will be behind us— nearly a quarter of the League card—including the Champions, Manchester United, Derby (twice), Blackpool (twice), Portsmouth, Bolton and the Villa.

You will notice that there have been no sweeping changes in playing staff, with only two new faces since last season. All the players here can be sure they will be given every chance to prove their worth, as many have done already, and I am specially pleased to see some really promising youngsters among the talent I inherit. Our list of 38 professionals includes two in the Services, two part-timers, and there are others soon due for the Forces, so that we shall need to increase our numbers to cover for injuries, etc., when fielding three teams throughout the season. Additions will be made at every suitable opportunity.

My first year here promises much hard work, but feeling as I do that all London, indeed all Soccer, is with me, I am confident that Chelsea will soon attain the standing and respect so long overdue.

And lastly, don't forget those cheers. I'll be listening!

Yours in all sincerity,

Ted Drake

Ted Drake urged Chelsea fans to get behind the team in his first notes in 1952, while John Neal wrote about his choice of captain after taking over in 1981. Also featured on the opposite page are the first columns from Glenn Hoddle, who took charge in 1993, and Ruud Gullit, who became our player-manager in 1996.

After watching the players for the last three weeks one of the first jobs I had to do was to appoint a Club Captain and as most people will have learnt by now my choice was Micky Droy. I think he possesses all the requirements for a good captain. He's an excellent professional who has given good service to Chelsea Football Club and wants success both for himself and the Club. With this in mind I think that he's going to be an excellent ambassador for us on and off the field. It's an important job as the players are out of my hands once they're on the field and Micky's got to make the decisions for me. I'm sure that he will do well.

In every club I've been to, I've always made sure that the senior professionals are very good, because without good senior pros. you can't have good kids. You can't bring on youngsters if the seniors have got bad habits but if they are good players, with the right habits and the correct attitude like Micky Droy has, then you've got chances, and that's very important for us as we are quite a young squad.

GLENN · HODDLE

FIRST of all, I want to thank everyone at Chelsea for giving me such a generous welcome and making me feel at home straight away.

I am very happy with the way things have gone since I arrived. The pre-season training has gone well and although there are things that need ironing out, there have been many positive signs.

I was a little concerned that the supporters would be suspicious of me, having seen me in a Spurs shirt for 13 years.

Hopefully, the Makita Tournament and the 4-0 win over Spurs have killed such thoughts. I was delighted with the way we performed and I saw signs of the players performing as I want them to in the new system.

Chelsea are a big club and I am determined to bring them some success. Even in my short time here as manager, I have been aware of the fantastic support at the club. The thing that hit me is the passion shown by the fans. It's as great as anything I have seen in my career.

I can feel a sense of expectancy at Stamford Bridge and I like that. I am much happier when there are positive vibes around the training ground and on the terraces.

There is no point in me being half-hearted. This is a high-pressure and high-profile job but I will give it everything I can.

I have had pressure ever since I broke into the Spurs side when I was 17. Being a manager is just an extension of that pressure.

Most Chelsea fans thought very highly of David Webb and rightly so, and one of the things I have to concentrate on is getting the support from everyone at the club.

One thing I have noticed is the size of the job. There are so many people to delegate to and deal with and there are 34 professional players here at Chelsea.

One of the most difficult things to do at a football club is to achieve the right spirit, especially among the players. After all, I can only make 11 of those 34 happy each week.

I expect my players to be disappointed and work hard if they are omitted, but never to be bitter. I believe in team spirit and my door will always be open for anyone at the club, be they YTS or first team players.

There has been much said of the system but I should say that it doesn't matter how you play. It is quality footballers that bring you success.

I would like to take this opportunity to welcome Peter Shreeves to the club. He was the youth manager when I was in the youth team at Spurs and I have worked with him in various capacities ever since.

Now I am in the hot seat but I am sure Peter's experience as first team coach is going to help me. It is important to me that I have a No 2 with the same ideas on the game and I know that I can go on the field and play and have every confidence in the

man on the bench.

I am not sure how much I will be seen on the pitch. I'm just taking things day by day. Every so often my knee becomes sore because of the hard grounds.

It is essential that I am sensible. If I am not playing well or not fully fit, I won't play and I have yet to see whether the pace of the game in the Premiership is too much for me and I am sure that will become apparent very quickly.

My aim is to be as successful as I possibly can. The club has not had much success recently and I will be trying to help us win some silverware.

But it is important how we get success. I wouldn't want to get it by playing dreadful football. The principle of winning by playing good, attractive football means a great deal to me.

All the best for the new season.

Glenn Hoddle [signature]

GLENN HODDLE, Dennis Wise and Steve Clarke with the Makita Trophy after their superb 4-0 victory at White Hart Lane.

EMERGENCY EVACUATION

If an emergency evacuation of the ground is necessary, the following message will follow an alarm signal over the public address system: *"LADIES AND GENTLEMEN, DUE TO UNFORESEEN CIRCUMSTANCES IT IS NOT POSSIBLE TO CONTINUE WITH THIS EVENT. PLEASE LEAVE THE GROUND AS QUICKLY AND QUIETLY AS POSSIBLE USING THE EXITS INDICATED TO YOU BY THE STAFF".* The alarm signal will be tested 30 minutes before the scheduled kick off time of every match.

Ruud Gullit

WELCOME EVERYONE to our first game at Stamford Bridge.

Everyone here is very excited about playing for the crowd in our first home game.

At Southampton on Sunday we should have

Honours

European Cup Winners' Cup
Winners: 1970/71.

Football League Champions: 1954/55.

FA Cup
Winners: 1969/70.
Runners-up: 1914/15, 1966/67, 1993/94.

Football League Cup
Winners: 1964/65.
Runners-up: 1971/72.

Full Members Cup
Winners: 1985/86, 1989/90.

won. We *could* have won. Sometimes you have games where you create chances and don't take them.

The good thing was that everyone was disappointed by the result. This was a good sign. There was disappointment on everyone's faces in the dressing room because they knew we can perform better.

Tonight will be totally different. We are playing against a team who want to have better results than last year.

I think slowly Chelsea will play better and better. We have three new players and a new way of approach with training and everything. It will take time to settle.

The only thing I ask from my players is that always they do their best. Nothing else. Not even that they play well. So long as they give 100 per cent I'll be happy.

I'm very happy with our pre-season.

The organisation has been as it should be. We have some new staff and new positions. Everyone has their space, their job and it has worked very well. You can see people improving.

The only difficulty is that we now have no stand behind the goal. We shall miss the crowd there.

I hope the new stand rises quickly, as quickly as possible, but thankfully this is not my concern. That's for our president — or chairman, as you say here — Mr Ken Bates.

Last year you all understood very well our purpose in games. We hope to play more for better results. We were 17 times up in games that we didn't win. This has to change quickly, but all things take time.

At home I want to play

with 12 men, not 11. That 12th man is all of you. Away teams must come here and say, going to

Stamford Bridge is hell.

Once again, thanks for last season. Now let's all do even better this season.

gianluca VIALLI

gianluca VIALLI

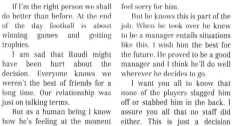

I understand that this has been one of the most amazing weeks in Chelsea's history.

But you supporters have to understand that whatever the board does is always for the best interests of our club.

Some of you might feel a little bit sad because of Ruudi's departure. Some might worry that now we are achieving something we shouldn't make such radical changes. Some might think that I'm the wrong man for the job.

But the real Chelsea supporter will never ever forget that whenever these decisions are taken they are for the sake of the club, to ensure the future in the best way.

honours

FA Cup

If I'm the right person we shall do better than before. At the end of the day football is about winning games and getting trophies.

I am sad that Ruudi might have been hurt about the decision. Everyone knows we weren't the best of friends for a long time. Our relationship was just on talking terms.

But as a human being I know how he's feeling at the moment and it's not a great feeling. I truly feel sorry for him.

But he knows this is part of the job. When he took over he knew to be a manager entails situations like this. I wish him the best for the future. He proved to be a good manager and I think he'll do well wherever he decides to go.

I want you all to know that none of the players slagged him off or stabbed him in the back. I assure you all that no staff did either. This is just a decision taken by the board because they had to analyse the situation and act for the best of the club.

For me, this came out of the blue. I chatted with Colin about what I wanted to do in the future and player-managing was something that interested me, but not so soon.

When he asked if I was ready to take over now it took me 24 hours to evaluate. The job brings great pressure and my responsibilities will increase enormously.

my best. I will professionalism, enthusiasm into beginner, so of mistakes. But I'll absorbing things learning, then and I will make 's me whose

relationship know I will No-one likes sitting in the

m and told rstand that team like g up with ot like. For we need

together. I them, I'll e, and I'll ve on and k with all ve great

ourselves ant. We l is only

with a

get off s very asm of

the team and the supporters. It will improve our spirit.

But if you want to be great, and be great for years, you have to go through nice moments and bad times. And you must treat wins and defeats in the same way. You have to get on with defeats the same as you do with wins. Your attitude must stay the same. Maybe if you lose you have to work even harder.

In life I believe you always get what you deserve. If you have done everything right, what you deserve will come.

You Chelsea supporters have been unbelievable to me so far. I can't ask you for anything more now that I am player-manager.

I am not worried about you. I know that you will always be behind all of us. I don't have to ask you for any more encouragement, your support has always been outstanding.

We are going to be working altogether for the best of the club, to make you happy, to make you supporters of a winning team, playing nice football that you all enjoy.

Ciao,

[signature]

Gianluca Vialli reflected on the steep learning curve that awaited him after taking over as player-manager in 1998, while his successor, Claudio Ranieri, introduced himself to Blues supporters after being appointed manager in 2000. On the opposite page are José Mourinho's first notes from both his spells in charge, in 2004 and 2013, and Roberto Di Matteo's column from 2012.

FIRST PERSON CLAUDIO RANIERI

I know Chelsea are a good club in Europe with great fans

Hello, Chelsea supporters. You may not have heard of me before I came to you last month, but I had heard of you.

I knew that Chelsea are a good team in Europe and that the fans are great. You fans helped a lot last Saturday at Manchester United.

I understand that it was a trauma for you with the change of manager, and with matches coming so fast it was very difficult.

But the life of football is like this, and Chelsea must continue to move ahead. I hope that as with your last three managers, Hoddle, Gullit and Vialli, I can do something to be held in great affection.

I thank you with all my heart for the help you gave us last Saturday in my first match.

The thing I heard which really hit me hard was the Chelsea fans

chanting our name in the silence of Manchester when their fans said nothing after we had scored our first goal.

It's so very important, the rapport between the fans and the team.

At home, our stadium has to be a stadium of fire with you behind the team. It is with your help that the team can do a lot of the things to which they aspire.

As a man, I don't like to promise anything or give any predictions of what we will do. But I know that Chelsea wants to win a Championship. I want to win a Championship also.

Who knows, it may be possible to realise this project that we both want.

We have three years to get to know each other. This is my first contact with you fans, and you must know I will give my all with

N BUYING TICKETS MAKE SU

all my heart and all my love to achieve something for Chelsea.

I wish to put on record my thanks to the previous and existing staff for all the work that's been done because the players are a great group of highly tuned athletes.

It is vital that the players fight for the club and fight for you fans, and they played well and showed great spirit in that Manchester game. We knew that Manchester would start the first 20 minutes very strong, and the thing I liked a lot was the way the team set about adjusting to gain the result.

I'm very pleased with the goals of Flo and the very good game that both Morris and Le Saux played.

It is a shame losing Roberto Di Matteo because he's a very important player. I hope he will

be back with us as soon as possible.

We started off quite well at St Gallen, but as they showed in the first leg they are very good on the counter-attack.

In fact, their two goals on Thursday came from mistakes by us when we were attacking. We knew we had to play well after winning only 1-0 in the first leg

And I think we deserved a goal for the way we played in the second-half.

But now Europe is finished and we must think to the future and the rebirth of the Blues.

determination and heart.

You fans, also, must stay close to the team. It is important that they have the chance to grow in your affection.

I played against Gérard Houllier and Liverpool when I was at Valencia. They went through on away goals. It was zero-zero at Anfield and 2-2 in Valencia. So I look forward to a better result today.

With all our hearts, let's go forward.

A NEW DAWN

In the first of his programme messages, manager José Mourinho outlines what we can expect from him, and how each of us can help Chelsea achieve greatness

MANAGER'S NOTES
MOURINHO

CHELSEA: 2004/05 squad

Hello.

It's been one-and-a-half months since I came to Chelsea, and during that time one thing has become clear: My decision to come to the club and to England was the best I could have made. I have never enjoyed work as much as I am enjoying it now.

I try to influence the players to think about football in my way, but at the same time I'm hoping to retain their culture. So far, this relationship and balance has been fantastic.

I cannot promise to you, the supporters, the Championship. But I understand what is expected – the Premiership, every match, every opposition; it is all top level.

What I can promise is this: that I am here working with a fantastic group of professionals. The squad is not only good on the playing side, but they are also fine human beings. We are a strong group, ready to fight together for our dreams.

But happiness and success depend not only on us, but on the relationship we build with our supporters – you, our foundation. And that is crucial to the club.

The pre-season was really difficult because of the European Championships. Many players arrived very, very late. They then had to start with a new manager and new players. It can be hard to build a team in such a short time. Because of this we need the best from you supporters today. We can build on the strong understanding between us as a team.

Nobody wins or loses a Championship in the first match. Today's match is just three points, no more. It is not crucial for the rest of the season, but it is obviously nice to start well and with happiness.

And our desire is to bring success and happiness, today and everyday, to everybody. There can be nothing better than to start fighting against a big opposition to do that.

Let's have some fun.

  roberto di matteo
INTERIM FIRST-TEAM COACH

Everyone is committed to the cause of getting results

These are my first programme notes as interim first-team coach and my message is that we face a big challenge between now and the end of the season, but it is one we are looking forward to together.

In this time, I want to see a team that is committed to the cause of this club, players that help each other on the pitch, who are united to combat

any opposition we come up against. I would like to ask the supporters to be right behind the players and show them their support to help give us the confidence to win our games.

I was very pleased to go through to the sixth round of the FA Cup with the win at Birmingham on Tuesday night. We showed we have fighting spirit here – and that will

be important again today against a strong Stoke side.

I would like to welcome their manager Tony Pulis and Stoke City to Stamford Bridge today for what will be a competitive game.

Between now and next Sunday, we have three home fixtures here in three different competitions, showing how much this team has to play for. We are now at the stage of the season where you play for everything and, with that in mind, we are happy to have a full squad available.

This means I have had to leave some players out today, but – because of the number of fixtures we have coming up – we will need everybody at our disposal in what is a crucial time of the year.

We are fortunate to have great depth of quality in our squad, with top-class options available to us across every position on the pitch.

We are going to be playing many games over the next two months and, so, utilisation of the squad will be a vital requirement.

All we can guarantee is that we will give 100 per cent effort and commitment – you can be sure of that from us. If we do that, then a team of this quality will always have an excellent chance of winning our matches, whoever the opposition may be.

Thank you for your support and enjoy the game.

> We are fortunate to have great depth of quality in our squad, with top-class options available to us in every position

Spirit: Beating Birmingham in the FA Cup fifth-round replay

R. di Matteo

JOSE MOURINHO
FIRST-TEAM MANAGER

I am excited to be back home and we need your support

It is great to write again to my Blues brothers, and I start with a question: How would you feel if Mr Abramovich asked you to manage and coach our first team? How would you feel as a Chelsea supporter? Proud? Excited? Motivated? Ready?

That is exactly what I felt.

That is why I introduced myself as the Happy One, that is exactly what I feel every day when I drive to

Cobham or to Stamford Bridge. I am at home again; I am where I want to be again; I am, once again, in a club that is much more than my club – it is also a passion. A passion that I share with every one of you.

This summer, the boss celebrates 10 years of amazing work at his club. I celebrate my return, but this match is not a testimonial! This match is Premier League: Day One, against

a team full of confidence because they have just gained automatic promotion; a team led by my friend Steve Bruce and supported by a few thousand fans in the away end, all of them with the mentality they created last season – play to win; play to get a result.

I congratulate them all and I wish them a great season in the Premier League, and I tell every one of you that this match will be a hard one – this match demands from us all that we can give. That is why I ask, in a humble way, for your support to our team. We need you. We need your support.

We welcome to the club our new players – Andre Schurrle, Marco van Ginkel, Kevin De Bruyne and Mark Schwarzer. Mark is an experienced goalkeeper and the other boys are young – they need our support as they settle down. We will support them technically and you can support them emotionally to feel that they belong at Chelsea.

We need to feel that Stamford Bridge is together, creating a great football atmosphere, an atmosphere that everyone enjoys, but where our opponents feel they are not playing against 11 – they are playing against 40,000.

> I AM, ONCE AGAIN, IN A CLUB THAT IS MUCH MORE THAN MY CLUB – IT IS ALSO A PASSION. A PASSION THAT I SHARE WITH EVERY ONE OF YOU

CAPTAINS OF OUR SHIP

WISE WORDS

IT'S NICE TO start afresh having got last season's injury and court case out of the way. Thank you all for your support throughout that difficult time.

I must admit I was really surprised by our two summer signings. Obviously, I'm delighted that they've come to Chelsea because it's made a buzz around the ground and amongst the players as well. Whilst everyone's been splashing out loot, six, seven million, we have bought Ruud Gullit and Mark Hughes.

We were beaten by the odd goal at Feyenoord last weekend. It may sound strange but that probably did us a favour to lose a game before the big start. Unfortunately I had to sit that one out. I'd picked up a slight knock on the shin so it wasn't worth taking the chance. But the lads played well and created a few chances but never managed to put the ball away. They finally broke us down with a good goal in the last 15 minutes.

I know you're going to find this hard to believe but there's been a change in Gavin Peacock. He gambles now. We had a £5 bet going last season on who'd score the most goals. Naturally I beat him by one. And don't forget I only played half the season. We've kept the bet going this year. So I'll be a fiver richer this time next year. Cheers Gav!

And hasn't the ground changed? It's really taking shape now and it's going to look absolutely magnificent when it's finished. More important for us on the playing side is that the pitch has been widened. It will benefit us the way we are going to play.

But on to today and our clash with the FA Cup winners Everton. They'll be up for it after last weekend's Charity Shield win over Blackburn. It'll be a hard game and I'm looking forward to it. We need to get off to a good start. With you behind us it's almost worth a goal start. Let's hear you . . . !

Alright!
Dennis Wise

A couple of Dennis Wise's columns, from the Everton game in 1995/96 and ahead of our 1999 Champions League tie with AC Milan, with Gianfranco Zola and Gus Poyet stepping in for Wisey in February 2000.

Wise Words

Bigger than the Final

This is a fantastic moment for Chelsea. What a start in the Champions League, to get a game we'd never dreamed of.

If you're gonna play a team to start your Champions League life, make it AC Milan One of the best in Europe.

We're looking forward to this. Now we can find out how far we've progressed.

It's new to us in European terms. We don't know the situation, how many points you need to qualify and so on. We just have to go out and play and if you don't win, then draw, but get some points.

I think Juventus went through last year drawing all their games and winning one.

A lot of our players know what Milan are about, having played against them or for them and that's a bonus for us. Milan are hugely talented. So this is going to be good for players who haven't been involved in anything like this before.

We didn't mind who we got when the draw was made. We knew whoever it was we'd get one great side and that all of them would be top quality.

We'd get full houses and great games.

I think we're ready for this kind of competition. We've got a strong squad, players who have won things. We're looking forward to all the games.

We played at the San Siro a few years ago in a friendly and they beat us 2-0, but that didn't count. We put out one team first-half and another in the second.

We've played and won the Cup Winners' Cup Final. But this is new. This is a lot bigger.

It's something we want to do extremely well in and we're

capable of doing so.

We haven't talked about it much. We've got so many games, we've got to be up for every one, whether it's Watford away on Saturday or AC Milan at home tonight. If we want to do well we have to keep our unbeaten record going. We want to keep it going as long as we did last year.

We're second in the League with two games in hand on Manchester United and we've got to win both those games. The League's opening up early. They've started like a house on fire and have their points in the bag.

It's nice to have points in the bag. But we've had to play Champions League and are second having played two games less than the majority of teams. We couldn't have asked for a better start. It's a lot better than last year.

It's already looking into the League what it's going to be like for the season. Saturday's game wasn't fantastic, but it was all about getting three points. Teams are coming here making it hard for us.

Milan will make it hard. But we're defending well too, we're competing going forward, so we'll make it tough for them.

I think it'll be a wonderful game. Two quality sides competing against each other. Alright!

Dennis for England but not for Chelsea

In Italy we used to do things this way. If the team wins and wins playing well, nothing has to be changed for the next game.

I am writing this in the canteen at the training ground on Thursday and Dennis has just walked away at that!

Apart from all this, it was really good to be captain here. It means a lot to me. It's a big responsibility and I tried to do my best.

The game against Gillingham wasn't the best, but we scored a lot of goals. It was not an excellent performance by us, but it was good. I think you crowd enjoyed watching many goals. Now we go to Wembley to play the semi-final. We have another big game coming up.

It's good for Dennis to be back in the England team. He has played very, very well for so long and in my opinion with Emile Heskey was the best on the pitch.

I am not surprised. I have said many times Dennis deserved to be in the England team. He deserved to be playing in it a long time ago.

It is bad news for us all that Sir Stanley Matthews isn't with us anymore. I know he was a great player and a great man who everyone will miss.

I was aware of him when I was in Italy, of course. I met him for the first time when I was invested as Footballer of the Year. He gave me the award and I was really impressed. He was charismatic,

close to him, it was very special. It was a special day for me anyway, of course, but I remember him and I think his giving me the award made it even more special.

So, back to now. We are into the FA Cup semi-final, we have done well to get there and we have to finish the job.

Before that, we have a lot of games to play starting with Watford today. We want to keep this momentum going as long as possible. We want to keep pressurising the four teams above us.

It is important to switch on immediately for this game and be focused.

You all have to back us all the time, to be our 12th player. Sometimes we have difficult moments and especially then you have to support us.

Be noisy all the time. The support, the noise, gives us energies, we get drive from it. We need it. We really do need it.

So please, shout, shout and shout. Be noisy. It's very important for the team.

Ciao.

We try not to be very borrr-ing!

Okay, okay. I'm here again because obviously the rest of the captains are suspended.

So I want to say to everybody, welcome to this quarter-final of the FA Cup. I think everybody believes this is a really important competition.

We want to win to get to the semi-final at Wembley.

I've only played at Wembley once, in the Charity Shield, and I lost on penalties and didn't get to

take one – I was on the fifth! – so I want to go back and win!

You know we all need your support, but especially I want you to understand sometimes our performances. It can be difficult.

Like against Wimbledon, we didn't play well for 70 minutes. But you have to look not only at what Chelsea are doing, but also at the opposition.

Wimbledon defended very deep. Sometimes they don't care about the spectacle. The only thing they want is to defend and let the time go away.

So if we don't start well, everybody gets a little bit nervous. Normally then part of the support starts booing, booing at some player even, and that is the worst thing to do because after that it gets even more difficult.

If you see after my goal against Wimbledon, the reaction of the supporters was magnificent. The team could feel that reaction, and then altogether we play one of the best last 15 minutes of the season, scoring goals, creating chances.

So – be patient! Pa-sahh-ient! Help us as much as you can. Because let me tell you, I need to play a friend at Wembley. That would be

a very important game for me and everybody at Chelsea. This is a great opportunity to play the last FA Cup Final at the old Wembley. To play it and win!

Altogether, we can do it.

We enjoyed three good goals against Wimbledon last Saturday. That is football. Sometimes we play for 70, 75 minutes so boring – borrr-ing! – and after we play very well because of the quality. They were three very different goals.

Individual action, team action, but all with the same finish.

I think my goal was more difficult than the Sunderland one because of the ball to me. The Sunderland one was coming from the side, not too high. This one was so high. You have to make a quick decision and it was perfect. I didn't believe it myself, like none of you I think, but it was lovely.

So then we get confident, everybody wanted to go forward, be available for the ball. We had two on the right, normally that is a difficult position, but Jody and Gianfranco got one decent movement, played the one-two very well, Jody crossed and George Weah headed in.

I think with the third goal that everybody thought Jody would put it to the left of the goalkeeper and he changed at the last moment and put the ball the other side. It was fantastic. Not just me, but the Wimbledon goalkeeper expected the ball there.

Three-one was a good score. But today, any win will be a good score. Come on, EVERYBODY! Come on!

◢ I'M SO PROUD TO CAPTAIN THIS CLUB. I'VE BEEN HERE SINCE I WAS 14 ▽

CAPTAIN'S TEAM TALK JOHN TERRY

Captain John Terry gives us an insight into the team morale, and the singing talents of the new management!

Welcome back for the new season, all you Chelsea fans.

When you have come through the ranks like I have, your initial aim is to make the first team. Then, after becoming a regular, your next ambition is to become captain.

I was captain many times last year, learning so much from Marcel. Before that, I had Wisey teaching me not just about stuff on the pitch, but also how to lead in the dressing room. All this experience soon adds up, creating the role of being captain.

I'm so proud to captain this club. I've been here since I was 14 and I still love playing here. Captaining this team just fills me with pride.

But the big thing is the club, not me, John Terry. It is about what *we* want to achieve. We're targeting the Premiership, the Cups, the Champions League. And pre-season has seen a step-up in the players and in training, so we can only get better.

What is also clear is that the lads all get on so well off the park. I think the trip to America did us the world of good in that way. We were away for so long, spending every hour of everyday together. At Harlington, you just go home.

The banter within the team is great. The foreign lads want to mingle and there's good balance between everyone.

We've got plenty of new players, so lets all welcome Big Pete, Paulo, Ric, T, Alexei, Robbie, Didi and Kez.

On the trip, every new face had to give us a song. Big Pete had the worst one out of the new players pre-season. His was a love song, and he couldn't stop laughing only managed getting a few lines out. Then he got a few things thrown at him!

Bill Blood was up announcing everyone, telling the same old jokes. Then the new management all got up together and gave us a Portuguese song. It wasn't too bad to be fair. We held back on the throwing because we weren't too sure of ourselves. Hurling things at new management can be risky. But they didn't deserve it anyway.

New management, new players, same traditions!

Now I'm looking forward to hearing you supporters sing. Hopefully at the end of the season you'll be singing along to some silverware. That's how we have to improve on last year.

Finally, a special 'hello' and thanks to Kasia who has sponsored my kit since I started.

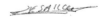

John Terry was given the armband full-time at the start of 2004/05. Below, Marcel Desailly's first notes as full-time captain in the 2001/02 campaign.

Chelsea Rock

We are taking a new road now

DESAILLY

To have both the manager and the fans wanting me to lead the team makes me feel very proud.

Welcome to everyone for our first game of the season and for my first as full-time Chelsea team captain.

I understand while I was away with France this week, some newspapers back here in England were suggesting that I was reluctant to be taking on this big job. Nothing could be further from the truth.

All I had said was that I believed being the captain of the national team is different from being the captain of Chelsea, and that maybe I would have to learn more new things to do the job here than to do the job with France.

I am very happy to be captain of Chelsea. It will help me to lift my level because I know I will have to be there at my best all the time, and I know I will have to carry people sometimes when they are in difficulty on the pitch.

I am also happy to know that

Before we look at the season starting today, I think first we must thank the players who have left Chelsea in the summer for all they have done for the club over the last few years – years that were some of Chelsea's best ever.

It looks like the club are taking a road for a new beginning now and you can feel that because when Dennis Wise decided to leave the club, it had to be the start of something new.

But I believe that this new can be something great.

So we must welcome the players who have joined us. They have been picked specially because we needed their quality.

They now have to understand what Chelsea need from them and they

and they are going to lift us.

This first game is the most important one because it will give power to ourselves for the rest of the season if we win well, and power to the fans who are looking for a winning Chelsea from the start.

Also we have a completed stadium to push us on a bit more. I have been training in it and it looks magnificent – a top stadium that will drive the team on to top performances.

Now we just need the crowd to help us like you have in the past. For sure we will have difficult moments but everybody, the team and the fans, must be as one.

I have been saying to Chelsea fans all these years to be patient. Now I am saying support us. Support us because we are going to win something.

MESSAGES FROM THE TOP

The Chairman writes . . .

OUR SUCCESSES of the past two winters have brought a new image to Chelsea F.C. As a result, I doubt if any Club looks forward to the 1971-72 season with keener anticipation than we do now, and I know this goes for our Supporters, too.

May 21, 1971 goes down as a date to remember—the day when Dave Sexton and our Team, so superbly led by Ron Harris, defeated the old masters of European football, Real Madrid, in Athens and brought the Cup-Winners' Cup back to Stamford Bridge.

Just a year ago we saw the F.A. Cup paraded here for the first time. Tonight you have the opportunity to salute the Team on another wonderful achievement as they display a European trophy here also for the first time, and my fellow Directors and I heartily congratulate them on this magnificent addition to our growing list of honours.

I would also like to thank everybody connected with the Club for their valued contribution to that success, and in this I include, of course, Chelsea Supporters for the splendid part they played.

Support such as we had again last season gives the Team tremendous encouragement, and we look forward to hearing you in just as good voice in 1971-72. On behalf of us all at Stamford Bridge, I welcome you at the start of another season, and I know you will join me in wishing Dave Sexton and the Team the best of luck in their efforts to make it as successful as the last two have been.

Brian Mears.

KEN'S COLUMN

In welcoming my old friend Jim Gregory's successful Q.P.R. to the Bridge this afternoon I am sure I am speaking for everybody when I offer my hearty congratulations on reaching the F.A. Cup Final for the first time in their history. It's really different from when I used to stand on the terraces held up by old railway sleepers and they were an average kick-and-rush Third Division team. Their position in the football world today is a tribute to the undying energy and enthusiasm of their Chairman, Directors, Manager and Staff, and certainly I for one think they deserve all the success that their hard work and enterprise has brought them.

I remember too when Spurs were relegated from the First Division not so many years ago and the Board responded by giving their Manager Keith Burkinshaw a new contract who then unobtrusively built up Spurs to where they are today.

If I have gone on at some length about these two clubs it is to demonstrate how I believe you build success. You do it slowly and patiently on good foundations to ensure that the success enures. I hope that the events of the last seven days prove to be the first steps on the long road to success which will enable Chelsea to regain its rightful place in the Football League — a permanent member of Division One.

To do this I believe that not only must the players give their all but Supporters must be made to feel part of the Chelsea they love. This means communication between the Board and the Fans. Consequently I am looking forward to meeting all members of the Executive Club, the Box Holders and members of the Official Supporters Club next week. I have already met a large number of the Official Supporters Club at the Player of the Year Dinner and I must say I was overwhelmed by the spirit, enthusiasm and devotion shown by the many fans I met there. Certainly if your enthusiasm and loyalty is anything to go by we should have won the Grand National let alone the Second Division this year!

I hope between now and the end of the season to meet as many of you as possible but with the best will in the world I obviously cannot meet everybody. However, I would love to hear from you and how you think the Club can be improved. What is more important what if anything can you do to help to improve Chelsea? No comments on the team please, that is the province of the Manager who must stand and fall on his own efforts without outside influence but any other topic, i.e. accommodation, the social side, away travel, anything at all — I would be delighted to hear from you if you write to me care of the Club. It may take some time to answer the letters if I receive the large number I am hoping to get but I promise each one will be answered personally.

Chelsea belongs to you the fans — without you there would be no Chelsea and it's about time your opinions were considered when formulating future policy.

Enjoy the match and shout for them, and here's a thought — if Rangers play a bit of good football give them the applause they deserve too.

Yours sincerely,
KEN BATES

Above, Brian Mears reflects on our first European triumph at the start of the 1971/72 season, and an early column by Ken Bates after he took control of the club in April 1982. Below, Bates discusses the historic moment when uncertainty over the future of Stamford Bridge came to an end in the 1992/93 season and, right, his final column of the 2002/03 campaign as we faced Liverpool in a match where we would clinch Champions League qualification.

The Chairman Ken Bates

IT'S NOW OR NEVER

... the real Cup Final, not ...k at the Millennium

...h Liverpool and Chelsea ...w par last Saturday, the ... for the Mother of all ..., winner takes all. ...over the last ten months ...ght, it all rests on the ...es with both teams up ..., we have home ... you 38,000 fans who ...nd your team. Let ... your support from ...n Sandwiches' are

...e been there ...y special guest ...tteo which proves ...welcome at

... the season, we ...intments but we ...gress. Last ...th getting in ...lt. This year ... and in

...adness. ...tion means ...familiar ...ey have ... them luck ... on their ...ou for

...at there ...player ...mmer. ..., an

...tion of ...ayers

careful with their money will be comfortable for life.

Off the field also, Chelsea has made solid progress this season. Remember the doom and gloom merchants last summer. The club was in dire straits, would have to sell the best players, etc etc. The reality was somewhat different. We have sold no players or other assets. We have met our liabilities on the agreed dates and we are slowly but steadily reducing the mountain of debts outstanding on players.

The suggestion in the media was that Chelsea Village was dragging down Chelsea FC. In fact the reverse was the case. The club's finances were ring-fenced to avoid such a thing happening.

Trevor Birch inherited a squad which had too many over-valued, over-paid, injury-prone, fringe players and although there will be a substantial reduction in players' cost for next season, the real saving will come in 2004 with players coming to the end of their contract and whose departure will not affect the quality of the squad.

The other positive note is the fantastic support you fans have given this year. Our average League gate this season has been 39,725 the gate receipts for the game today is probably a Premiership record at £2.25m, with next season's ticket sales already exceeding £15,75m. Your support has been – and is – fantastic. I can promise you one thing, your money will not be wasted as some of it has in the past. Trevor Birch is instigating a review of all costs and overheads, cutting out all expenditure that is not absolutely vital to the team's effective operational ...

The facts need explaining to you on the groundsharing publicity. Fulham cannot play at Loftus Road after next season in the Premiership. The FAPL Board has decreed that it is simply not up to standard and approached Chelsea to help out, at least on a temporary basis. We had private talks last December only to read about it in the press the following week. In March we were approached again and so-called 'confidential' discussions resumed once more only to read about it in the media.

That is not the way Chelsea do business and therefore we have decided that Fulham isn't the kind of club we would like as a partner. We wish our neighbours well and look forward to welcoming them to Stamford Bridge, but only once a year (Cup-ties, excepted).

Tomorrow Chelsea – a so-called racist club which does not care for the community – is hosting the Asian Tiger Cup Final here at Stamford Bridge. Asian football is an unknown phenomena and growing apace. I have the honour of presenting the Cup and medals. I have invited Charles Clarke the Education Secretary to attend as my guest, after all, if he can do an away day to Lancashire he must have the time to pop down the road from Westminster. But he has refused.

The 'Cracked' Mirror is a newspaper in serous decline. Circulation is down 100,000 since Harry Harris left them for the Express and Star whose circulation has increased 140,000. To help stem the decline, I have invited Des Kelly who branded me as a racist to attend, report on the match and give Asian football some much needed publicity. Let's see if he turns up!

A big thank you to all the staff behind the scenes. They work terribly hard and without them we would not have ...

KEN BATES

It was 7.03 pm last Tuesday when my car 'phone rang. Yvonne, our finance director, was on the line: "The documents are just coming out of escrow, we have the ground."

The eight year battle was over. Stamford Bridge had returned to Chelsea Football Club.

My day had started early. Unable to get back to sleep after waking at 4.45 am, I watched early TV, had the dogs down the farm just after six, and was on the road at 7.30 am to arrive at the lawyer's office at 10 am. Legal complexities never cease to amaze. We had been planning for over three months, and come the big day there were still documents missing, points to be agreed, compromises to make. The Cabra liquidator, the SB Receiver, SB's directors, their respective lawyers, the Bank's lawyers, the Bankers themselves, all had to have their say. There were just three of us and our lone solicitor; 79 documents to sign in duplicate; last minute bargaining as each side tried to nick another point; arguments over costs; brinkmanship; pedantic behaviour; bluff and counter-bluff. It all went on with Colin Hutchinson, our chain-smoking Managing Director, wilting before my eyes suffering withdrawal symptoms in a smoke-free zone for eight hours.

contributions to The Save the Bridge Fund, the Labour group on the Hammersmith & Fulham Council, David Mellor, and of course the Royal Bank of Scotland who, in the final analysis, decided that Chelsea would not be thrown out of Stamford Bridge, stepped in and bought the ground and then leased it direct to us.

... mention must be made of ...

Of our victory, the Mirror managed about eight lines in an inside page, with no byline — in keeping with the mean spirit displayed towards both Chelsea and me personally over the years.

However, what exactly is the deal and where do we go from here?

The deal is a very good one, both for the Royal Bank of Scotland and Chelsea. The Bank gets a secure income on an otherwise dead asset; Chelsea have security of the ground.

We will pay a fixed rent, with no reviews for 20 years. At the end of that time we can buy all the land for a fixed price of £16.5m. However, we have another nice option. The ground has been split into six separate leases and we can buy all or any of them at any time for a predetermined price so that, for example, when the housing market recovers we can buy out the residential lease, sell it at a profit and use the money to reduce or further purchase another lease.

Thus, the importance of the BSkyB deal. Our share of the money more than covers the rent for the next few years.

What now? Well, with the uncertainty of the ground's future ... tackle the ...

ROMAN **ABRAMOVICH**

ROMAN enjoys the title win last week with elated Chelsea staff and players

CHELSEA VS LEICESTER CITY SATURDAY 23rd AUGUST 2003

The Owner
Roman Abramovich

Dear Supporters,

You have all been so warm since I arrived at Chelsea, and I want to thank everyone for making me, my family, and my colleagues so welcome.

I especially want to thank the shareholders who enthusiastically took up the offer to sell your shares so that we could move quickly in helping Chelsea Football Club become one of the élite clubs in Europe.

It was only earlier this year that I decided to become involved in the Premiership, and when my team looked into clubs with the best possible fundamentals and prospects, Chelsea really did come first. The ground, the location, the Champions League qualification, the staff and players and the fan support were, and remain, a wonderful foundation.

I don't want to change what works. I just want to help take what we have at Stamford Bridge to the next level. And I want us all to work hard and have a lot of fun doing it.

The atmosphere and the electricity when we beat Liverpool last week was amazing. I believe the English Premier League offers the best atmosphere and level of competition in the world, with Chelsea clearly among the top clubs in the league. I look forward to a long and fruitful partnership, and to sharing the excitement, future successes, and fun of Chelsea Football Club with fans old and new.

I wish you all a thoroughly enjoyable season.

Roman Abramovich

BRUCE BUCK
CHAIRMAN

Today we will celebrate what has been a momentous season

Today we will receive the Premier League trophy, ending in style what has been a phenomenal season for the Blues.

This afternoon will be one of celebration for the club, and rightly so, considering how dominant we have been. We will set a new club record for fewest losses in a season, surpassing the mark set in José's first year with the club, and we are also setting a new mark for the Barclays Premier League: no side has topped the table for as many days as we have in a single campaign.

The first-team squad, along with the manager and his backroom staff, deserve a huge amount of credit for their efforts throughout a season which also saw us win the Capital One Cup after beating Tottenham Hotspur in the final at Wembley Stadium. I

know how much you all enjoyed that day.

Our superiority was reflected at the PFA awards ceremony, where Eden Hazard was selected as Players' Player of the Year and he was joined by five of his team-mates in the Premier League Team of the Year. Eden's wonderful contribution was also recognised by the Football Writers' Association, who voted him as their Footballer of the Year.

On top of that, he was named Barclays Player of the Season and José deservedly received their managerial honour.

The club's success hasn't been limited to the first team. Congratulations are also in order for the Academy, who won the FA Youth Cup for the fourth time in six years shortly after winning the UEFA Youth League for the first time. The Ladies are also doing us proud,

sitting at the top of the FA Women's Super League 1 table ahead of the mid-season break and looking forward to a trip to Wembley for the FA Women's Cup final in August thanks to a goal from PFA Women's Players' Player of the Year Ji So-Yun. And that's before Emma Hayes' side even think about their inaugural Champions League campaign – good luck to them with all that lies ahead.

I would also like to take this opportunity to thank Samsung, who have been our official club sponsor for the past 10 trophy-filled years, and Right To Play, who we have enjoyed eight wonderful years with as our global charity partner. We have done so much fantastic work with both organisations.

Finally, I would like to thank all our fans for your support this season. We could not have achieved any of this success without you and, after the final whistle, we can all celebrate in style as we regain a thoroughly deserved piece of silverware.

I hope many of you will be coming along to the victory parade tomorrow and I also wish you a very pleasant summer as we look forward to making more history next season and beyond. Keep the Blue flag flying high.

Thank you

A message from Roman Abramovich

It is with great pleasure that I offer my heartfelt congratulations to the Chelsea Football Club board of directors, chief executive Peter Kenyon, manager José Mourinho, captain John Terry, the staff, and especially the players on bringing the Premiership title to Stamford Bridge!

Winning the League this year is especially moving as it comes on the 50th anniversary of Chelsea's last title and at the beginning of the club's Centenary year celebrations.

I would especially like to congratulate the fans – you have waited patiently and this victory has only been possible thanks to your support. I am very honoured to share in your joy.

My heart also goes out to those

long-term supporters who did not live to see Chelsea reach the pinnacle of English football once again, and I would like to dedicate this trophy to them. Fifty years is much too long to wait, and I am confident that we will not have to wait that long again.

I view this championship as just the beginning of a new era for Chelsea and would like to reiterate my long-term commitment to the club.

Much has been said about the financial outlay over the past two years. However, this must be seen in the context of placing Chelsea on a level playing field with the other top clubs in England and Europe for a sustained period.

We have made solid investments

on the field in players, management, training facilities and an academy that will nurture the next generation of home grown talent. Off the field, a team of executives and senior managers has been put together to grow the business and capitalise on the playing success.

All of this is a long-term, deliberate strategy with the aim of building the most successful football club in the world in the next ten years and beyond. Under chairman Bruce Buck, Peter Kenyon and José Mourinho, we have a strong leadership team that shares my vision.

Many challenges lie ahead and I look forward to sharing many more moments with all of Chelsea's fans around the world.

Roman Abramovich thanked the fans for their warm reception at the start of 2003/04 campaign after he purchased the club, and expressed his joy at the end of our triumphant 2004/05 season. Chairman Bruce Buck also wrote of his delight after we won the title in 2015.

GLORY DAYS AT THE BRIDGE

These are my Champions!

John Terry, Frank Lampard, Wayne Bridge, Ricardo Carvalho, Petr Cech, Joe Cole, Carlo Cudicini, Didier Drogba, Damien Duff, Paulo Ferreira, Mikael Forssell, William Gallas, Geremi, Eidur Gudjohnsen, Robert Huth, Jiri Jarosik, Glen Johnson, Mateja Kezman, Claude Makelele, Nuno Morais, Scott Parker, Lenny Pidgeley, Arjen Robben, Alexey Smertin, Tiago, Baltemar Brito, Steve Clarke, Rui Faria, Silvino Louro, Andre Villas, Mick McGiven, Gary Staker, James Melbourne, Dr Bryan English, Mike Banks, Andy Rolls, Mauro Doimi, Billy McCulloch, Stuart Sullivan, Alberto Andorlini, Ade Mafe, Rob Brinded, George Price, Debbie Dawling, Sophie Rutherford, Gwyn Williams, Stewart Bannister, Mick Roberts, Malcolm Sheldon, Julie Say, Nick Perruccio, Dave Ward, Andrea Cavenaghi, Suzanne Foederer, Frank Steer, Alan Barrett, Derek Bradley, Claire Lait, Jane Wilkins, Anthony Grant, Danny Hollands, Yves Makabu-Ma Kalambay, Filipe Morais, Filipe Oliveira, Adrian Pettigrew, Dean Smith, Jimmy Smith, Joe Tillen, Sam Tillen, Steven Watt, Danny Woodards, Neil Bath, Brendan Rodgers, Mark Beeney, Glen Driscoll, Gerry Harvey, Damian Matthew, Lee Congleton, Jimmy Fraser, Bob Orsborn, Hayley Prior, Dean Furman, Ed Brand, Michele Gallaccio, Ben Hudell, Michael Mancienne, James Russell, James Simmonds, Jack Watkins, James Younghusband, Phil Younghusband, Jason Griffin, Jonathan Eves, Daniel Kirton, Kevin Fowler, Scott Tingley, Chris Baker, Alan Clark, Karyn Clark, Michael Kebede, Haruna Danjuma, Gavin Piddington.

CAPTAIN'S TEAM TALK — JOHN TERRY

"TODAY I'LL BE LIFTING THAT TROPHY WE'VE ALL DREAMED ABOUT"

Today is a special day for everyone involved at the club – let the Premiership party begin!

What a mixed week, winning the Premiership at Bolton and having a great day, to a few days later feeling the worst I've ever felt after a football match.

Today, I think we'll get Tuesday at Liverpool out of our system.

We've won the Championship. Today I'll be lifting that trophy we've dreamed about. Everyone is going to enjoy themselves big-time today. I want to hear you like I've never heard you before.

WE'VE WON THE LEAGUE! In fact, we've run away with it in the end. The gaffer called it early in the season, that we'd do it at Bolton, and that's exactly what we did. It's all been done through sheer hard work.

The gaffer's been brilliant all season. And now today we party. It's going to be a really special moment everyone will look back on for years to come.

You have got to be unbelievable today. You've got to be louder than ever.

WE ARE THE CHAMPIONS.

And then we've all got to come back and do better next season. We've got to do better in the Uefa Champions League. We were a better team than Liverpool over the two legs but they beat us, so good luck to them. I hope they win it.

But what's important is that we've got the team to win it and I believe we will claim the Champions League title in the future.

As we lift the trophy I want to say

thank you to the gaffer and all the staff. They've been brilliant and key to the Chelsea Football Club success.

A big thank you to Roman and everybody behind the scenes at Chelsea, all the girls in the office, Peter Kenyon, everybody who does so much work for Chelsea Football Club.

A big, big thank you to you also. It was such a great atmosphere at Bolton. You must have waited for an hour afterwards, and when we came back out it was unbelievable.

I had the camcorder out on the bus, singing with Coley and Eidur on the top. It was special.

We've always enjoyed great support, but even you can try and be more intimidating next season. We all have to improve, you, us, everyone. I want to give a personal thank you to my team-mates, every single one of you. I love you all.

And to the medical staff, and to everyone at the training ground. Jase the groundsman has been around since I was a boy at the club, and the

training ground pitches are spot-on, much better than we've had. Thanks to him and his staff.

The masseurs who stay up late before games getting us prepared are always available. Thanks to Bill and all of them.

Thank you as well to the players' partners, kids and families. We're away a lot of the time and it can be difficult. Their fantastic support makes it easier for us.

I want to say hello to TB who's coming over from Madrid and sitting with Aaron upstairs. They both used to work for the club, they're mad Chelsea fans, TB has a tattoo on his arm of Chelsea winning the FA Cup in 1997, and is here especially to see us lift the Premiership.

Finally, on behalf of all the lads, thank you gaffer from all of us. You've been special every day.

Come on the Champion Chels!

Champion Chels!

Chelsea Football Club is an Official Supporter of the 2012 London Olympic bid

LONDON 2012 CANDIDATE CITY

TED DRAKE CALLING . . .

On the occasion of our last home match of the season it is my duty and privilege to thank the players and staff for making this Jubilee Year what we hope will now prove to be the greatest in the history of Chelsea Football Club.

Their efforts have taken us to the top, not only of the Football League, but of other spheres in which we compete—Football Combination, Metropolitan League and Juniors—and in the games that remain to be played I know they will do everything possible to see that this wonderful record is maintained.

Just as sincerely I would like to express my thanks to you, the Supporters, for all that you have contributed to these achievements. When I came to Stamford Bridge three years ago I sought your co-operation from the terraces and the stands towards the building of a "new" Chelsea, and the response you have given has inspired every one of us within the Club. Your vocal encouragement has been magnificent, and because of it we can hold our heads high. It would indeed be a fitting reward if all our dreams were to be realised today in the Stamford Bridge setting.

This looks like being the decisive afternoon for ourselves and the clubs bidding with us for the title of Champions. Yet even in this hour of hope and expectation we spare a parting thought for our opponents, Sheffield Wednesday. With their great tradition and one of the finest grounds in the country, they are out of place in anything but the First Division, and we wish them the speediest possible return.

3

Ted Drake thanks the fans on the cusp of our first league title in 1955, and José Mourinho and John Terry after our first Premier League triumph in 2005.

MANAGER'S NOTES

WE HAVE TO BE AT OUR BEST TO ACHIEVE OUR AIMS IN LEAGUE AND CUP

So it is the last game of the season and we know exactly what we need to do to win the league – win against Wigan. If we do this, we don't need to look at anybody else's result and this has been our philosophy for some weeks now, win our own games and stay at the top.

We cannot affect the Manchester United result today so we will not worry about it, we are focused only on our game, on our aim.

It has come to the last game with two very good teams still trying to win the league and we know that if we win, we will maintain our place at the top until the end.

Last weekend we got a very important win at Liverpool, where we played with passion, spirit and heart. The result was good and the performance was fantastic – our players showed confidence and we played as a team.

So there is only one more game, yes, but it is exactly this, one more game. We cannot think of this match today as anything other than one we have to win and only after we achieve that aim can we celebrate anything. Our

'We cannot think of this match as anything other than one we have to win and only after we achieve that can we celebrate anything'

attitude today is to go out and beat Wigan because we need three points here to win our first league title for four years.

So there are two more games left in this season and two trophies still to be won. At this moment we have won nothing, it is an incredible situation to be in at the end of an incredible season for us.

We hope and we believe that we

can end it with a Double but we know that to achieve this we have to work hard, have the right mentality and give our best performance against Wigan today, then for the next week in training and also against

Portsmouth in the FA Cup Final. There is still work to be done.

Congratulations to the youth team, who won the FA Youth Cup this week, a fantastic achievement for them and for the club.

And thank you all for your support at Liverpool and for all the season, home and away, in victory and disappointment.

I have a lot of respect for the supporters in this country after my first season as a manager here and especially for the Chelsea fans.

You have helped us with your songs and your spirit and we are now close to achieving our aims in the league and the FA Cup – I hope we can repay you with the right result today and I will see many of you at Wembley next Saturday.

We played with passion and spirit at Anfield

JOHN TERRY
CAPTAIN'S NOTES

Rounding off a remarkable season with all of you is brilliant

What a season it has been! Top of the league from August until May, champions of the best league in the world again and Capital One Cup winners.

Lifting the trophy today in front of our supporters will be the perfect way to end the season. It is the first time in five years and it will feel special to share the moment with you guys here today and again at the bus parade tomorrow.

On behalf of all the players, I want to say a massive thank you to our supporters. You have been superb, home, away, and in Europe, all season long. We want you to know that we appreciate everything, so – from me personally and also from every member of the team – thank you.

Huge thanks also go to all the staff at Stamford Bridge and Cobham who work so hard day in, day out for

this club. Our fantastic medical team deserve praise for the work they do and the support they give the team, and also the grounds staff, who do a great job.

Congratulations to Ruben Loftus-Cheek on his first Premier League start against Liverpool, to Izzy Brown on his Chelsea debut against West Brom and to all the other young players who have trained and travelled with us this season.

Enjoy your summer and we will see you back here in August, when we begin our title defence. We got a taste of how difficult it is going to be next season when we went away to West Brom on Monday. Once you've won it, everyone wants to beat the champions and we know we have to come back ready to go again. We won't rest on our laurels – this is a new group and we have won our first two trophies together this season. Let's make sure we come back ready to contend for more next year, but first let's enjoy the day – these moments are special.

Come on the Chels!

Rueben Loftus-Cheek made his first start in the game against Liverpool

Carlo Ancelotti discusses the prospect of our first domestic Double in 2010, and José and JT's notes at the end of our triumphant 2014/15 campaign.

JOSE MOURINHO
FIRST-TEAM MANAGER

We have worked hard to be champions and we want to finish with a win

Our players were made to win. Every day, in every training session and in every match they worked at a high level of intensity. They worked with great concentration, commitment and ambition.

Every week, we played one more match and every time we put one more point on the table it meant one less point to be champions and one less match to play.

Then, when we clinched the title, the warriors were empty, dry, and then it is difficult to be ready to compete. But we will try again for our last match. We will try to recover the qualities to win this

match before our big moment – the cup in our hands.

I have to mention also the fans at West Brom on Monday night. At the end of the match, it was a great feeling to go over to them, with one finger up to show that we are number one and we are champions.

I would also like to wish our senior opposition scout Mick McGiven and his wife a happy 40th wedding anniversary.

THE NINETIES

These were the years when football changed beyond all recognition, and there was no better place to witness that transformation than at Stamford Bridge

How many fans who were following the club at the start of the 1990s could honestly hold their hands up and say they foresaw the revolution which would take place at their football club over the course of the next decade and beyond? If your hand is in the air while reading this, we certainly hope you put your money where your mouth is and placed a few shrewd wagers on the Blues.

Either way, there have been some incredible memories for fans to savour in recent times, and the Nineties was very much where this transition picked up pace, thanks in no small part to the arrival of Glenn Hoddle as player-manager.

The matchday programme captured everything – indeed, this was the last decade when the publication remained the main public voice of the club before the internet revolution really kicked in.

With the birth of the Premier League, football as a whole in this country was transformed and no club encapsulated the array of foreign talent which would flood into the English game more than Chelsea – the arrival of a certain Dutchman as player and manager heralded a new style of football, and in the programme fans could hear from the many footballers who would arrive at

the Bridge from across the globe and assume iconic status.

Of course, let's not forget the British talents who also shone – after all, a certain Dennis Wise penned the skipper's notes for a decent chunk of these years and allied to his undoubted talent as a footballer, it's probably fair to say that Wisey takes the prize of being the man behind our most amusing captain's notes of all time. If those who arrived from far-flung lands weren't prepared for the onslaught of banter, they soon would be.

BLUES STAR
KEN MONKOU

Our first matchday programme of 1990/91 was for the season opener against Derby County, a game Chelsea won 2-1. Bobby Campbell welcomed two new signings who would impress in the Blues midfield – the aforementioned Dennis Wise as well as Andy Townsend. Also in this edition was a new feature entitled Personality Spot in which Chancellor of the Exchequer and soon-to-be Prime Minister John Major appeared. Other well-known Blues fans to appear in the piece over the course of the season included snooker player Jimmy White and celebrity astrologer Russell Grant.

As you can see from the December programme against Coventry City, a colourful spread of opposition info gave the lowdown on our visitors each week, and the history between the two clubs was discussed in Down the Years. Fans got to hear more from the players in Blues Star, on this occasion featuring Ken Monkou. The player poster was another regular feature just being introduced, Kevin Wilson took the honours against Sunderland, and the most recent club events were chronicled in the News and Views pages. Meanwhile, a bygone page from the programme, Kit Sponsors, featured a very youthful-looking Graeme Le Saux and the facing page showed our players undergoing some rigorous exercise alongside TV-am's fitness guru of the time "Mad" Lizzie Webb.

Porterfield takes charge, 1991/92

After a mid-table finish the previous season, Bobby Campbell's reign as manager came to an end in the summer of 1991, with his former assistant Ian Porterfield taking the helm. Here you can see his first notes as Chelsea gaffer, for the opening game of the season against Wimbledon which ended in a 2-2 draw. Ken Bates discussed ground renovations in his column before paying tribute to Campbell and welcoming Porterfield, while new signing Tommy Boyd featured on the cover. The player who would go on to have the greatest impact of the new faces at the Blues was Paul Elliott who starred in the new-look player interview Star View, which was accompanied by the Star Points Q&A.

A MAN FOR HIS TIME

MORE about the ground and Cabra et al in the next programme, but meanwhile, turning to the playing side, I must first pay tribute to Bobby Campbell. He came to The Bridge when Chelsea was disorganised and demoralised.

Under his leadership we won the Second Division Championship by a record margin, achieved our highest First Division position for 20 years and won the Zenith Cup.

His legacy is the largest number of promising youngsters for two decades. He was a man for his time.

His successor, Ian Porterfield, is a popular choice among both players and supporters and he has wasted no time in reorganising his backroom staff. Perhaps we can now put to rest the bogey of the little clubs and have a really successful season.

Again, welcome back.

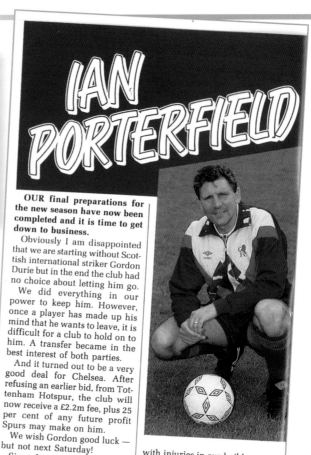

OUR final preparations for the new season have now been completed and it is time to get down to business.

Obviously I am disappointed that we are starting without Scottish international striker Gordon Durie but in the end the club had no choice about letting him go.

We did everything in our power to keep him. However, once a player has made up his mind that he wants to leave, it is difficult for a club to hold on to him. A transfer became in the best interest of both parties.

And it turned out to be a very good deal for Chelsea. After refusing an earlier bid, from Tottenham Hotspur, the club will now receive a £2.2m fee, plus 25 per cent of any future profit Spurs may make on him.

We wish Gordon good luck — but not next Saturday!

Since I arrived back at The Bridge, I have found the spirit in the club is excellent.

During an extremely productive summer, we have worked hard towards finding a better understanding between the players off the pitch, but primarily on it.

Pre-season events have gone pretty much as I expected, as we have tried to build a winning formula. I want to make it clear our No. 1 intention is to win matches! No. 2 is to achieve that playing good football.

I believe that once we start getting into winning habits you will see the confidence come through in the team's play.

We have been unfortunate with injuries in our build-up, as key players such as Ken Monkou, Jason Cundy and Graham Stuart have all missed training and matches at times.

I AM very happy with the two major signings that we have made this summer.

Paul Elliott has settled in very quickly since he joined us from Celtic. He knows this part of the world, coming from London, and, I am sure, will prove a great asset to the club.

As many fans will be aware, Chelsea have wanted to sign Paul for some time. At one stage it seemed as if he would be a difficult man to get but Celtic's new manager, Liam Brady, was prepared to let him go and I was

PAUL ELLIOTT

Full Name: Paul Elliott
Born: London
Date of Birth: 18-3-64
Status: Single
Hobbies: Reading and soft soul music

Two strikers were signed mid-season in 1991/92, with Clive Allen and Tony Cascarino bolstering our ranks. The latter made a goal-scoring debut in a 1-1 draw with Crystal Palace in February, a game which came off the back of our first league win at Anfield in nearly 60 years. Ken Bates did not hide his joy at our win over Liverpool and here you can see the detailed rundown on opposition sides the programme went into. There was also a feature with homegrown product Jason Cundy, accompanied by a poster and statistics, alongside which was Albert Sewell's What Happened To piece.

In his interview, Cundy spoke of his desire to reach the FA Cup final, although our run came to an end at the quarter-final stage with a replay defeat to Sunderland. The programme for the first encounter at the Bridge rounded up the men who had been banging in the goals for us in the competition that season, and another recruit who had been brought in that season to add some steel to our midfield, Vinnie Jones. Fans also heard from Sky commentator Martin Tyler and youth-team graduate Andy Myers.

LEAVING IT TO VINNIE

ROUND Three and it was the old Wimbledon double act that saw us to a 2-0 win at Hull.

The poisoned pens were poised to write the Blues off in another Cup upset but VINNIE JONES (top left) set the ball rolling six minutes before the break, with Dennis Wise soon to follow after half time.

An FA Cup winner with Wimbledon, Vinnie knows what it takes to get to Wembley and he set The Blues off on the Cup trail with a far post header, after Paul Elliott had flicked on Dennis' corner.

"I'd already scored a few Cup goals this season and all week in training I was telling the rest of the players 'Just leave it to me lads.' Now they will think I was serious."

MEET THE NEW MEN ON THE BLOCK

WHAT'S the difference between our new strikers Mick Harford and John Spencer?

About a foot. Big Mick, who signed for £300,000 from Luton on Tuesday, is one of the best and most experienced targetmen/goalscorers in the business. He stands at an imposing 6ft 2ins, but looks bigger.

Wee John, signed for £450,000 from Glasgow Rangers, also on Tuesday, is a Scotland under-21 international and sees himself as a natural goalscorer. He stands at 5ft 6ins, but looks smaller.

Both met up for the first time at Chelsea's Harlington training ground on the day they signed, still shaking off the effects of their first Don Howe training session and a whirlwind 24 hours of transfer talks.

John takes up the story:

"Everything happened so quickly. One minute I was at home in Glasgow, the next I was on a flight to London.

"I see this as my big chance and the move could not have come at a better time for me. My chances were limited at Rangers by the likes of Ally McCoist and Mark Hateley, but I know I will have to battle for my place at Chelsea. I've always scored goals and I hope to continue that in London," he said.

John, who claims to be taller than Dennis Wise, "in high heels", is a Glasgow man through and through. But he also enjoyed a spell in Hong Kong, during the 1989-90 season, when he struck 25 goals in 28 games.

"I averaged about 35 goals-a-season in the Rangers reserve side and I hope to add to that in the Chelsea first team," he said.

John's first task, however, is to find a home for himself and fiancée Amanda. They are to marry next summer.

No such problems for Mick, already settled in Luton, where he lives with 5-year-old son William.

"That was obviously a consideration when I signed for Chelsea," he said, "but ultimately it is the football that matters to me the most.

"I could have joined Everton, but Chelsea impressed me from the first moment I met manager Ian Porterfield. I'm an old friend of Kerry Dixon and I hope I can carry on where he left off and score lots of goals."

Chelsea are Mick's eighth professional club and he is already familiar with a few of the Stamford Bridge faces. Paul Elliott was a youngster with a broken leg during Mick's first spell at Luton, a club where he also met youth coach Peter Nicholas.

Chelsea now have four recognised forwards battling for a place in the front line. Dennis Wise will make five, after he has three-match suspension, carried over from last season. John, said: "I don't care who I'm playing with, as long as I'm playing. I've seen a lot of the top English clubs on television and I'm confident I can strong players are ... but I know I can score goals."

John follows on in a long line of Scots who have pulled on the famous blue shirt and we wish him and Mick all the luck for the season.

A NEW SEASON, A NEW LEAGUE AND NEW RULES

Hands off is the goalie's golden rule

NICK CALLOW
ON THE FINER POINTS OF FOOTBALL

IN attempt to put an end to one of the most wasting aspects of time wasting, the International Board have approved FIFA's proposal which effectively outlaws the backpass.

A goalkeeper shall no longer be able to handle the ball when a player deliberately kicks it back to him. If he does, an indirect free-kick will be awarded where the ball was handled.

If the keeper handles the ball to the goal area, the free-kick will be taken from the nearest goal line.

The only allowance in the new rule is that keepers will be allowed to pick up the ball which is headed or chested back to them.

So what does this mean to what we will be seeing on the field of play? Time will tell. No doubt, coaches and strikers will be looking for loop holes and FIFA have already had to outlaw players getting down on their knees to pass the ball back to the goalkeeper.

Another rule change, also aimed at speeding up the game, is that a goal kick or free-kick awarded to the defending side can be played once, be taken from other side of the box.

The International Board, which consisted of four members on FIFA and one from each of the four Home Football Associations, also ruled that players without shinpads or boots will be ordered

Clive Allen finds himself in the referee's book.

off the field of play and not allowed to return without them.

Furthermore, when a player is sent off for a second bookable offence, the referee will show both the yellow and red cards to make it clear that he has been dismissed for the double booking.

And it has been agreed that teams can have even goalkeeper on the substitute's bench, who can only be brought on in the event of an injury to the No.1.

The most colourful change for the new season will bring the end to one traditional tension chant. In Premier League and Football League matches, referees will wear green, purple or yellow shirts. Short and socks will remain black and the traditional all-black strip be used if there is a clash with team colours.

Dave Bennett and Kevin Hitchcock (right) need to be on their guard.

THE OFFICIAL STORY OF THE 1991/92 SEASON

THE BEST OF THE SEASON ON VIDEO

£12.99

• A permanent record of a highly eventful season
• 90 minutes of wall-to-wall action, goals, drama and excitement
• Don't miss out – it's a must for all Chelsea fans

Available at the club shop and all good video stockists.

TELSTAR

37

Whole new ball game as we secure our future at the Bridge, 1992/93

The Premier League was launched to much fanfare in the summer of 1992, heralded as "a whole new ball game" and the 1992/93 season was one which brought good news for the Blues as our future at Stamford Bridge was finally secured in December. However, progress on the pitch was far from rapid, leading to the return of a familiar face for a brief stint as manager at the end of the campaign. Our first programme for the rebranded top flight came for a game against Oldham Athletic. Graeme Le Saux was given the biggest billing on the cover alongside a picture of Ian Porterfield with new signing Robert Fleck, who was profiled inside with fellow forwards Mick Harford and John Spencer who had also joined in the summer. It was Harford who grabbed a debut goal in a 1-1 draw with the Latics – a result which was perhaps an anti-climax for skipper Andy Townsend who ended his first column of the season with the clear message of intent: "It's time to achieve." The programme also discussed the introduction of the new backpass rule.

FOUR SIGNINGS IN A WEEK — NICK CALLOW lays out the welcome mat

ROBERT FLECK became Chelsea's record signing on Wednesday when he signed a five-year contract in a £2.1m deal. Mal Donaghy became the fourth signing of the week when he joined from Manchester United for £150,000.

Mal, a Northern Ireland International defender, has also had a spell at Luton.

Record signing Robert Fleck starts work today with Chelsea's other new signings John Spencer, Mick Harford and Mal Donaghy

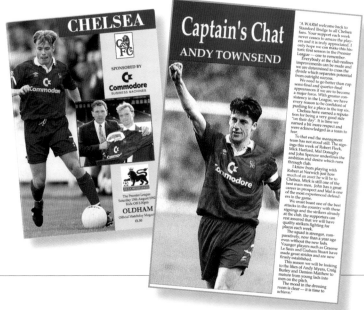

CHELSEA

SPONSORED BY

Commodore
BUSINESS MACHINES

The Premier League
Saturday 15th August 1992
Kick-Off 3.00pm

OLDHAM

Official Matchday Magazine
£1.50

Captain's Chat
ANDY TOWNSEND

'A WARM welcome back to Stamford Bridge to all Chelsea fans. Your support each week never ceases to amaze the players and it is truly appreciated. I can only hope we can make this historic first season in the Premier League – one to remember.

Everybody at the club realises improvements can be made and we are determined to cross the divide which separates potential from outright success.

We need to go better than cup semi-final and quarter-final appearances if we are to become a major force. With greater consistency in the League, we have every reason to be confident of pushing for a place in the top six.

Chelsea have earned a reputation for being a very good side "on their day". It is time we earned a bit more respect and were acknowledged as a team to fear.

To that end the management team has not stood still. The signings this week of Robert Fleck, Mick Harford, Mal Donaghy and John Spencer underlines the ambition and desire which runs through club.

I know from playing with Robert at Norwich just how much of an asset he will be to Chelsea. Mick is still one of the best ever men. John has a great career in prospect and Mal is one of the most experienced defenders in the game.

We must boast one of the best attacks in the country with these signings and the strikers already at the club, the supporters can rest assured that we will have quality strikers fighting for a place each week.

The squad is stronger, comparatively, now than a year ago even without the new lads. Younger players such as Graeme Le Saux and Graham Stuart have made great strides and are now firmly established.

This season we will be looking to the likes of Andy Myers, Craig Burley and Damien Matthew to mature from young lads into men on the pitch.

The mood in the dressing room is clear — it is time to achieve.'

KICKING OUT THE KICK-IN

THIS year marks the 110th anniversary of the throw-in. There are people who want to make sure the 111th anniversary is the last.

Within FIFA's International Board, those who dictate the laws of the game believe it is time to banish the throw-in.

Kick-ins are being proposed as the replacement. They will be experimented with during August's under-17 world championships in Japan. If the experiment is successful, kick-ins will replace throw-ins after the 1994 World Cup in America.

"We're returning to the basics," FIFA secretary Sepp Blatter said. "In the beginning there was a kick-in. The throw-in came in as a penalty for the team unable to keep the ball between the lines. Soccer has developed enormously over the past 20 years, so we have to react to that."

What is he talking about? The two-handed throw-in was introduced for a good reason in 1883 and this proposed rule change could ruin the game.

Picture the scene. When a side are awarded a kick-in they are going to hoof the

ANOTHER rule change is in the pipeline... but is it just a change for change's sake?

ball down the pitch as far as they can. The proposed kick-in would seem little different

VINNIE JONES — the throw-in is one of his attacking ploys

to a free-kick.

Midfielders might as well hang up their boots, because they are not going to see much of the ball. Already we see goalkeepers coming out of their areas to take free-kicks from anywhere in their own half.

Today's balls are so light that any professional player can kick from one penalty area to another and the finesse of the game will be lost as players pump the ball into the opponent's box from everywhere and hope it runs kindly for a striker.

Pity the poor old defenders. Most teams send their big centre backs into attack to win the ball in the air from free-kicks. With this new rule, they will be tired out after ten minutes of running up and down the pitch for kick-ins.

Not only that but surely the flow of play will be ruined. Already we have too many delays while lumbering giants plod up the field to take their positions in

Graeme's slipped disc

KEEP OFF THE PITCH

By Nick Callow

IN THE SPOTLIGHT ... CRAIG BURLEY

Dutch experience is Craig's inspiration

In the Liverpool programme later in the season, the possibility of kick-ins replacing throw-ins was also discussed, although that proved to be an idea with no legs. The fans' thirst for interviews with the first-team squad was being quenched with a wealth of articles in each issue. Supporters heard from Mick Harford, Graeme Le Saux and Craig Burley in this issue, and there was also a catch-up with former terrace hero John Dempsey.

JOHN FINDS THERE IS LIFE AFTER CHELSEA

THE medals he proudly owns are a lasting reminder that John Dempsey was a member of Chelsea's FA Cup-winning team against Leeds in 1970, and that he played and scored when they beat Real Madrid to take the Cup-Winners' Cup in Athens a year later.

Then the 6ft. 1in. centre-half completed a personal hat-trick of Final appearances in the League Cup against Stoke at Wembley. He was capped 19 times by the Republic of Ireland for whom, though born at Hampstead, he qualified through Irish parentage.

CHELSEA WELCOME MANCHESTER UNITED

THREE KEY MEN FOR UNITED ... PAUL INCE

The making of a midfield general

14 SOUTHAMPTON BOXING DAY —

... RYAN GIGGS

Youngster who stays in control

KICK OFF 12.00 NOON   15

... PETER SCHMEICHEL

Safe hands at a bargain price

16 KEEP OFF THE PITCH

Credit has to be given for the development of some truly original ideas in the 1992/93 campaign. In the Manchester United programme, the content of former Red Devil Mal Donaghy's fridge was the topic of discussion, alongside a Q&A with David Lee. And with the superstar status of footballers on the rise, the opposition pages were increasingly detailed, providing readers with more information on our visitors. There was also some fantastic news in Ken Bates' column which revealed how the eight-year battle with property developers over the future of Stamford Bridge was over. Turn to page 172 to see his words.

Passing talents earn David's admiration

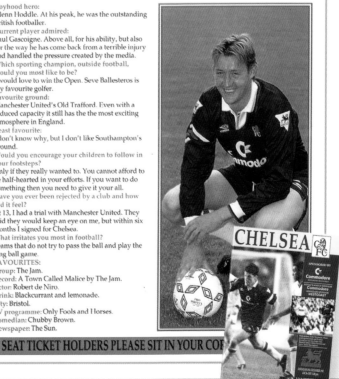

Boyhood hero:
Glenn Hoddle. At his peak, he was the outstanding British footballer.
Current player admired:
Paul Gascoigne. Above all, for his ability, but also for the way he has come back from a terrible injury and handled the pressure created by the media.
Which sporting champion, outside football, would you most like to be?
I would love to win the Open. Seve Ballesteros is my favourite golfer.
Favourite ground:
Manchester United's Old Trafford. Even with a reduced capacity it still has the the most exciting atmosphere in England.
Least favourite:
I don't know why, but I don't like Southampton's ground.
Would you encourage your children to follow in your footsteps?
Only if they really wanted to. You cannot afford to be half-hearted in your efforts. If you want to do something then you need to give it your all.
Have you ever been rejected by a club and how did it feel?
At 13, I had a trial with Manchester United. They said they would keep an eye on me, but within six months I signed for Chelsea.
What irritates you most in football?
Teams that do not try to pass the ball and play the long ball game.
FAVOURITES:
Group: The Jam.
Record: A Town Called Malice by The Jam.
Actor: Robert de Niro.
Drink: Blackcurrant and lemonade.
City: Bristol.
TV programme: Only Fools and Horses.
Comedian: Chubby Brown.
Newspaper: The Sun.

SEAT TICKET HOLDERS PLEASE SIT IN YOUR CO...

Open the fridge ...

NICK CALLOW takes a look inside Mal Donaghy's (below) fridge to discover the secrets of a footballer's eating habits.

... and grab a snack

30 KEEP OFF THE PITCH

WEBB IS TOTALLY SOLD ON CHELSEA

THREE Sundays ago, when the phone rang late-night at David Webb's Southend home, he hoped it might be a customer for the 20-ton crane he was trying to sell. Instead, it was Ken Bates selling *him* something.

And when Webby put the phone down, he was Chelsea's new manager. In the previous day's programme for the match with Aston Villa, it had been mentioned on this page that he was "between jobs". Now he is back home.

He is playing for his long-term future as Chelsea's manager. He is playing for Chelsea's future, which has become overcast these past two months through the sequence of 13 matches without a win. And, between now and May, players are playing for their futures here, too.

For in terms of Chelsea football, it will be no use Ken Bates having won the battle to Save the Bridge, no point drawing up multi-million pound plans to make this London's most spectacular stadium, if there isn't the team to go places as well.

Of his at-present temporary return to Stamford Bridge, David says: "If the chairman had offered it for only a week, I'd have said 'yes'. To me, this is the best job in football, and this is a big, big club."

• • • • • • • • • • • • • •

ALBERT SEWELL says 'Welcome Home' to one of Chelsea's favourite sons

• • • • • • • • • • • • • •

YES, it's wonderful to be back. It is almost 19 years since I left Chelsea as a player, but there's no time for taking stock and looking back.

I face an extremely difficult job but I hope I can justify the confidence people have shown by bringing me back to the club.

There is a lot of work to be done.

I know what Chelsea fans want to see, but please be patient. I am not a magician. I am, however, prepared for hard graft.

I am only interested in people who want to work for Chelsea Football Club and play their heart out for it. The club's supporters deserve that and are entitled to demand that.

To say that our defeat at Blackburn Rovers last Sunday was disappointing would be putting it mildly. That was not the sort of performance I expect from a Chelsea side whether it's me as manager or anyone else.

We were second best at Blackburn and conceded a soft second goal. We must

DAVID WEBB

be more professional and work harder to get ourselves out of this run.

I know Chelsea and know what people respond to at this club. There will be no excuses from me if we do not live up to expectations.

Every decision I make will be for the good of Chelsea and I will live or die by my actions. Time will tell if I make the right ones.

Kevin Lock, the former West Ham and Fulham player, has joined us on the coaching staff. Kevin and I worked together at Southend and I felt it was important, from the start, to have someone around who knows how I work. He will be a great asset to the club.

Tonight, for my first home game back at Chelsea, we face Arsenal. Some people may want to describe it as a big match, but every team presents just as big a task as any other.

So many teams have been inconsistent this season. When we come up against a team not playing to their best, we must take advantage of that and nab the three points.

I have received heart-warming letters from supporters welcoming me back to the club and I know by reading them how much you all want the same success for Chelsea as I do.

Your letters of support encourage all of us and I will be doing everything to repay your faith in me. I want to turn things around for this club.

Let's get Chelsea back on track.

Captain's Chat

ANDY TOWNSEND

'TODAY it is Monday, last week it was Sunday and it has even been on a Friday evening. Television has changed the old tradition of football matches being played on a Saturday afternoon and then followed by a mid-week game.

We have not fared badly with the arrangements though Queens Park Rangers had a hard time at the beginning of the season when they started on a Monday night and then less than 48 hours later were back in action.

That did not really seem right and as far as I can see has not been repeated.

At Chelsea we have fared quite well and the change in the tradition that stems back years and years is something all players have got to live with. Players have got to come to terms with the shifting timetable.

That said our supporters have been absolutely magnificent through our bad run and all I can say is please, please, keep it up.

You have no idea how much we appreciate this fantastic support when things have not been going according to plan.

It has been a funny old season and I honestly believe that far more teams are evenly matched this time around than ever before. Those around fifth in the table could so easily swap places with three or four of the bottom sides.

If we won the last ten of our 12 games we could so easily end up in the top five. That is how close it has been.'

Off-pitch success was not replicated on the field and in February Ian Porterfield's spell as manager came to an end, with 1970 FA Cup hero David Webb arriving as temporary boss. He penned his first notes in the Arsenal programme, talking of the big job ahead to bring the good times back to Stamford Bridge. A 1-0 win over the Gunners was the start of a seven-match unbeaten run, although there was clearly more ambition at the club than in years gone by and the summer of 1993 saw the arrival of a new gaffer who would instigate a bright new dawn for the Blues.

Hoddle in the hot seat as Wise gears up for new role, 1993/94

Glenn Hoddle arrived as Chelsea player-manager ahead of the 1993/94 season and the programme for our opening game of the campaign against Blackburn understandably had a great deal of coverage about our new gaffer, including an in-depth interview. You can see his first programme notes on page 167. Paul Elliott penned the captain's notes and, on the facing page, Dennis Wise discussed his new motor. It wouldn't be long until Wisey would be pulling on the skipper's armband and ribbing his team-mates in his own column. The tenacious midfielder was among those publicly listed as a Chelsea Pitch Owners shareholder, as the scheme to protect Stamford Bridge from any future threat from developers was explained to readers. There was also a feature with one of Chelsea's well-known fans from another sport as cricketer Graham Thorpe discussed his love of the Blues.

KING OF THE BRIDGE

Glenn Hoddle, the new Chelsea manager, has already cleared one barrier — here he tell CHRIS DIGHTON of his hopes for the season

EVEN a man who, it seems, has tasted nothing but success in his career has fears about the future — and in that respect, Glenn Hoddle, the new Chelsea boss is no different.

There are good footballers and then there are the men like Glenn Hoddle, true stars of the game who draw a crowd on the strength of their ability alone.

The initial worry for Hoddle at Chelsea was winning across the board acceptance from the crowd, after all, so much of his brilliant career has been at north London rivals Tottenham.

Emphatic victory in the Makita Cup, including that 4-0 thrashing of Spurs in the final, should assuage the doubts of all but the most cynical.

Talk to the man and you find a manager totally dedicated to the Chelsea cause.

"There have been a lot of positive letters from the Chelsea fans and their response has been good ever since I walked through the door," he says.

"But of course there was a little bit of suspicion, and rightly so. I came in for David Webb, a hero at the club who some thought should have got the job.

"And then Chelsea fans will have known me as the man playing against their side — so beating Spurs has broken the ice and was important for me, the players and the supporters.

"Believe me the passion in that match was there and nobody was holding back. Having said that it would be foolish to read too much into the result although it was nice to win."

That two-day tournament at White Hart Lane was Glenn's first chance to parade a team before the fans and he discovered an asset at the club

GLENN HODDLE — on his reserve debut for Chelsea.

that he had not fully appreciated before.

"The noise they make is fantastic — it really is worth a goal. I'd heard about the travelling supporters but not realised just how forceful they can be," he says.

"There is a craving for success at the club and if that support can be channelled in the right direction I'm sure we will have some more exciting times."

Glenn, who played for Spurs, Monaco, Swindon and for England, is very much his own man and knows exactly what he wants to do with the footballing side of the business.

"You can't detach yourself from outside pressure but it won't deter me from picking the players I want, even when things are not going well," he adds.

"I've lived with that sort of pressure for years."

So what will the Chelsea fans see this afternoon? Glenn is determined to

22 ARE YOU PLAYING TEAM SELECTOR? ENTRY FORMS

The driving ambition of Dennis Wise

CLUB CAPTAIN

Steve Frankham Assoc
SURVEYORS & CONSULTA

Batting for England, cheering the Blues

DENNIS WISE IS A CPO

KEEP OFF THE PITCH

49

THROWING OF ANY OBJECT IS AGAINST THE LAW

A GOOD PITCH FOR A GREAT CHELSEA DEAL

By NICK GREEN

SHAREHOLDER, ARE YOU? 071-610 2235

45

CHELSEA

Master of The Bridge — Glenn Hoddle arrives at Chelsea.

When we took to the field for our final home game of the season against Sheffield United, there was no need to play down our FA Cup hopes, with the final against Manchester United a week away. Mark Stein was pictured prominently in the season review, having netted nine goals in seven consecutive games earlier that term – a club record in the Premier League era which still stood at the time this book went to print. The player feature was with Gavin Peacock who had enjoyed a fine first season for the Blues. Having scored the winning goal in both our 1-0 wins over the Red Devils in the league, it was hoped he could emulate his form at Wembley. Sadly, it wasn't to be – if only Peacock's first-half effort which cracked the crossbar had been inches lower – and the wait for major silverware would go on a little longer…

send out attractive footballing sides and cites the success last season of Aston Villa, Manchester United, Norwich and even QPR, as a return to what is best in football. The long-ball game, it seems, has been found out.

"I've come here knowing the way I want to play and my first job has been to mould the players into that way of thinking," says Glenn.

"This is where the rest of the staff like Peter Shreeves, Graham Rix, Eddie Niedzwecki and Gwyn Williams come in and from pre-season training I've been pleased with the way it has gone.

"However, we must keep things in perspective and for certain there will be times when we have to dig deep, play tight, and battle hard. As much as you want to turn on the style there are outside forces that have some influence.

"To set targets would be foolish but I know in my own mind what I want although it will take some time before I can judge our progress constructively."

But what about Glenn Hoddle the player? He has joined Chelsea as player-manager and

CONTINUED ON PAGE 25

The Management — Peter Shreeves, Glenn Hoddle and Graham Rix.

23

22

SKY TURNS TO BLUE FOR RISING CHELSEA

PAUL MORGAN LOOKS BACK ON A SEASON WHERE MISERY HAS TURNED TO DELIGHT

THE BLUES, are on the verge of completing a remarkable season today with their last game in the FA Carling Premiership at home to Dave Bassett's Sheffield United.

They have gone from being in the relegation frame to emerging with a comfortable mid-table position and an FA Cup Final appearance against Manchester United to come in seven days time.

The Final against United was no more than a distant dream back on December 27 when we lost 3-1 at Southampton, completing a run of 11 games without a win.

It was in that match a 3.1 million strike Mark Stein broke his duck for the team — and the title soon turned.

In the middle of the disastrous run, former players and football experts were crying out for manager Glenn Hoddle to ditch the passing style he had brought to Stamford Bridge.

...

INFLUENTIAL ... John Spencer and right, Dennis Wise

...

twice against Manchester United and his double in the FA Cup semi-final, have rightly grabbed the headlines. But it was Stein's goal-poaching instinct that pulled us out of relegation trouble.

Mark, made a big-money move to Stamford Bridge in October and after an impressive record in the lower leagues was cast as the Chelsea saviour.

...

PEACOCK UNRUFFLED BY THE TOP FLIGHT

It is hard to believe but this season was Gavin Peacock's first at the highest grade

GAVIN PEACOCK has, in his first full season in the top flight, surpassed the expectations of most — but not his own.

...

...

Peacock's most noticeable career asset this season was his consistency.

...

The second half of Hoddle's first season at the helm was dominated by our run to a first major cup final in 22 years. By the time of our February game with Tottenham, Dennis Wise was on captain's notes duty and there was little room for emotion from Glenn Hoddle. The former Spurs man was wary of getting hopes too high of a Wembley visit and after welcoming his old team-mates Ossie Ardiles and Steve Perryman to the Bridge, declared: "After we have beaten them, I will be happy to wish them the very best for the rest of the season." Those words followed by a 4-3 win in a classic tie was a great way to eradicate any lingering doubts amongst any Chelsea supporters who questioned Hoddle's ties with our rivals.

OUR success so far in the FA Cup has been fantastic for everyone in the club and for the supporters but we are back to rolling up our sleeves today and getting on with the real job of chalking up vital FA Carling Premiership points.

Our priority is to stay in the FA Carling Premiership and it is important that we focus on the task in hand.

It is a point I have made to the players in training during the last week and it is also something that the fans must take on board.

Oxford was a great result in the FA Cup and it was good to get a quarter final home draw but we must not be distracted by thoughts of Wembley — relying on the Cup for glory is risky because so much can happen in a football match in the space of a minute and you could so easily be shot down.

TEAM CAPTAIN'S CORNER

"We came back from Portugal on Wednesday after flying out there for a three day training break to prepare us for the run in to the season.

The idea was basically for the 20-man squad to relax, train and play some golf — but most importantly concentrate the mind on the job ahead.

Today, we have a big game, Tottenham always is a key clash but even more so given the FA Carling Premiership position of both clubs.

If we could win today that would peg Tottenham into the scrap at the bottom of the table and with two games in hand over them our situation would be that much better.

When there are a lot of teams battling it out and separated by just a few points a win one or two can really help to lift you up the table — and that is why we would benefit from beating them today.

I know Spurs have suffered a bad run and I also know that all have suffered and — just hope that theirs doesn't end today. They need to get a result — but then we need one as much as them and I have never lost to them since being at Chelsea.

Those ingredients should make it some game and after all the excitement of the Cup — which has been sensational this season and provided some incredible results — this is back to the grafting work.

All the players know they need to liven up, get some results and our minds should be well concentrated after Portugal.

DENNIS WISE

Having signed a contract to the year 2000, Dennis Wise gave us the lead against Ipswich. Neil Shipperley shares the celebrations.

CHELSEA FC 1994/95

COMING NEXT THE NORTH STAND

Our next home game is against Everton on Saturday, November 26. The North Stand will be open for you to watch from. It is the first permanent stand to be built here since the East Stand opened on August 17, 1974, a year behind schedule.

THERE WILL BE no 'behind schedule' on the North Stand.

Ken Bates has stringent penalty clauses in the contract with the builders to ensure things happen on time.

Work will continue behind the scenes after the Everton game, and the stand will not be fully finished until mid-December.

Against Everton you will be able to enjoy the following:

1. Both tiers will be open for you to sit in with the Upper Tier available to Members only.
2. Chelsea Broadway, the lower concourse, will be open. Here you will find two of the four North Stand bars, Strikers and Keepers, and the two fast food outlets, the Whistle Stop Bars. They will serve regular

fast food products, but look out for specialities. Talk of an Everton Pie for the first game is already in the air (no jokes about it having lots of holes at the back, please!). Channel Chelsea, the in-house TV system, will be up and working.

The Upper Concourse facilities, those for members only, will become available on the Liverpool game on the weekend of Saturday, December 17.

Here there will be two more bars, Back Four and Midfielders, two more Whistle Stop Bars, and access to the two suites, Tambling's and Dixon's.

Similarly, Drake's, the main supporters' room, and on match days the Chelsea Pitch Owners shareholders' room, will open against

All the lads were very disappointed with the result in the Cup Final but we were knocked out by how many of you turned up to cheer us on the Sunday morning. What's it going to be like when we do win something?

Getting into Europe just for reaching the Final is a great consolation. Pre-season we've played a lot of games abroad as a taster for our European challenge. The gaffer's taken us to Copenhagen and to Valencia to play some foreign sides in their own backyards, to see how they play and what we might have to cope with. The first couple of games were hard but we're gradually getting used to the European games.

In the Makita Tournament, although we didn't win the Cup again this year, we gained valuable experience against Napoli and Atletico Madrid. We had a lot of chances against Napoli and maybe we should have beaten them but that's the way it goes. Two sloppy goals on the break. But we'll learn from that. We didn't really know how they played. But in the Cup Winners Cup, we'll have the opposition watched so the gaffer will choose the team and system to suit.

We've already got quite a few foreign players but now even the Scots are real foreigners! Seriously, I think it's disgraceful that Craig Burley who's been at Chelsea all his career is not even assimilated.

It's great that Batesy's put the money back into the club from the Cup Final bringing in three new class players. I'd never seen Paul or Scotty play before but from what I've seen pre-season, they seem to be two quality players and I'm sure they'll do well for us. Paul looks very sharp. Unfortunately Scotty picked up an injury and he's only managed a couple of games. We all know David Rocastle.

what he's capable of. I'm really looking forward to playing alongside them.

As for the new guidelines for refs, it's better for the forwards now that they've brought in this rule about tackling from behind. It gives them a chance to get the ball up to feet and to turn without being whacked in the first minute. It puts your mind a little bit at rest too knowing that someone isn't going to go through you in the first minute. I just hope things don't get silly and out of hand by people being sent off for minor fouls.

But there's obviously got to be some common sense by referees regarding treatment on the pitch. What happens if a player swallows his tongue? We won't know what to do. You can't drag him to the side of the pitch. And if a player gets a head injury, they should call the physio on straight away.

But for now, we're concentrating on our first League game and looking for three points from Norwich. Alright!

Last year Ellie — Paul Elliott — was part of the team which started the campaign Let's Kick Racism Out Of Football. All the lads are delighted that William Younger's are bringing Ellie back to all our home games and that he remains a part of Chelsea. Racism has virtually been kicked out of Chelsea, so let's all keep up the progress this season. Let's stay on top of it. Otherwise we'll set Frankie on to you!

Dennis

Dennis Wise — Team Captain

Back in Europe with a new stand, 1994/95

The upshot of our FA Cup final appearance was that the Blues were back in European competition in the 1994/95 season, which began with a home tie against Norwich City. Summer signings Scott Minto, David Rocastle and Paul Furlong appeared on the cover and Dennis Wise talked about our forthcoming European Cup Winners' Cup campaign, as well as highlighting the club's good work to combat racism. In our Coventry programme in November, there were two bits of good news, with the announcement that Wise had signed a new long-term deal and that our revamped North Stand would be open for the next home match.

FANTALK

Being back in Europe is of special significance to one Blues' fan. PETER OSGOOD enjoyed some of his greatest nights in European competition. But it is the current team which has got his adrenalin pumping

WHAT'S HAPPENING at this club is something all of us former Chelsea players always wanted to see: a return to the style and the glory of the '60s and '70s.

Of course we've always been Chelsea supporters, we're Chelsea players through and through, but there were times you have to admit when it's been hard to love the old club. Not now, though.

They're playing some of the best football for decades and it's lovely to see them doing so well. Fantastic results for us at the start of the season, and the whole place is buzzing — Chelsea are back among the big boys.

But what I'm especially pleased about is that Glenn and the squad's hard work has been properly rewarded — with a place on the European stage.

Obviously going back into Europe is a special thing and brings back a lot of happy memories. Of course, I was a member of the team that last won the Cup Winners Cup for the Blues in 1971, and scored eight goals in one tie for the side that went out only on the 'away goals' rule the following season. We've waited 22 years to see the next lot have a go at bringing the trophy back to SW6. That's a long time, too long. And it's lovely to see the club back in the ring.

I've got a feeling they're going to do very

well. They're a settled side now, a nice footballing side. Good at the back, that's the main thing. Dave Sexton — bless him, no matter how many rows I had with him . . . and I did! — the thing he always emphasised was that we had a good back five: the back four and the goalkeeper. And you build on that foundation. Now Glenn's arrived and done a superb

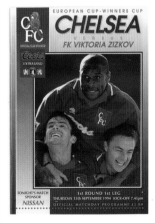

Our first competitive European encounter since the 1971/72 season saw Czech side Viktoria Zizkov visit the Bridge. Hoddle spoke of how exciting these nights could be and this match was no let-down as we won 4-2. The Into Europe feature focused on ties against overseas sides from yesteryear and Peter Osgood starred in Fan Talk to discuss our return to continental action.

GLENN'S VIEW

WE'VE HAD A reasonably good start domestically. Now we can concentrate on our European quest tonight. There's a good buzz and expectations around the place.

I can't help but think back to my Monaco and Tottenham days in Europe, and they were always special. I expect the feeling to be the same at The Bridge tonight and, hopefully, for the rounds to come.

It's a great experience for the players, the management and supporters. For managers we can pit our skills against some of the top European coaches. Players can go out and produce performances of the highest level against different European opposition.

And it's also going to be an education for you fans because there's no doubt about it, the European scene is completely different to the Premiership. You'll perhaps have to see the value of us being patient, as we will

have to practice it on the pitch.

For sure, Viktoria Zizkov will get lots of men behind the ball, they'll have a

EMERGENCY EVACUATION

sweeper playing deep. Patience will be the key.

However, we must have a go at them in the first 20 minutes. You crowd must help us test them.

One thing we should never lose sight of, as I know from my games in Europe, foreign teams fear coming to England and facing opposition with the closeness of our support, the atmosphere of our surroundings. They find it very hard to overcome at times.

Let's not let our visitors down tonight!

We'll be looking for a good lead to take over to the

Czech Republic. But whatever the score is after 90 minutes, we're only at half-time. We've got to play responsibly.

If we get it right, this can be a magical competition for us. It may be Chelsea's first European game for 23 years, but we are not here to make up the numbers. We are here to progress.

Last time we played at The Bridge we enjoyed a tremendous 3-0 victory over Manchester City. Many aspects of our game were very exciting. Creatively we were getting closer to what I want to achieve. There were

spells of good passing with chances created near goal.

It was wonderful to hear 'Ten Men Went To Mow' in unison on three sides of the ground, including the Upper Tier. Even the lads in the dressing room afterwards mentioned it.

City manager Brian Horton mentioned it too, and said the atmosphere was completely different. He said it was at times electric.

I've said all along that you being close to the pitch can help.

You only had to look at St James' Park last Saturday to see how a crowd can help the team on the pitch. I know that kind of support is achievable here.

I'll look more into that game against Blackburn. In the meantime, let's show Europe that we have supporters deserving of a place in Europe. Be loud, be happy, and be sensible. Let's make sure Chelsea is a club Europe can love and respect. Lots of noise, but no problems.

Welcome to Viktoria Zizkov. Welcome to exciting times at The Bridge.

INTO EUROPE

SPECIAL - SPECIAL - SPECIAL
Cup Winners Cup
First Round ties to date

AN entirely new generation of Chelsea fans draws for this season's European competitions were a special experience. Viktoria Zizkov. Tickets? Travel arrangements? Visas required? Even in the club, too, from dressing-room boys the scenes were of excited anticipation.

Back in September 1970 that Chelsea

mounted our first, and successful, bid for the European Cup Winners' Cup. Then it was off to Greece and the coastal resort of Salonika to face the little known Aris club. A two-day coach trip was £14, with a £2 supplement for a four or five star hotel. Match seat 30 shillings (£1.50). For the wealthier a special air charter flight from Luton Airport was on offer.

Ian Hutchinson puts Chelsea two up against Aris Salonika in 1970.

PLEASE REMAIN SEATED

The second round of the Cup Winners' Cup pitched us against Austria Memphis, with John Spencer's stunning solo goal in the away leg featuring on the cover of our Everton programme, as well as inside. We faced a familiar opponent at the quarter-final stage in the form of Club Brugge, a side we had beaten in a classic tie on the way to winning the trophy in 1970/71. The match winner back then was Peter Osgood so he was an obvious choice for the European Hero feature. Mark Stein spoke of his desire to net more goals just over a year on from his hot scoring streak and he was on target in a 2-0 win to earn us a semi-final spot.

A CLOSE ENCOUNTER WITH... MARK STEIN

IT HAS BEEN nothing if not incident-packed since Mark Stein moved to the club. Firstly he had to justify the large amount of money that the club had spent on him.

"I think there is no doubt that you feel you need to prove something to a club and the fans when you arrive. I don't think that the size of the transfer fee is something that really affects you directly, but you are only a human being and you can't just forget it. I went a few games at the start without scoring and in reality that was the main pressure that I felt. I suppose it combines with other factors and that includes the size of the fee that the club has bought you for."

Mark's arrival wasn't exactly perfectly timed. Wisey had been missing for several games and the performances and position in the League were entering

> "I want to get back to my best form and score goals... and right now I'd like to play in Europe, that is something I've never done"

the critical zone. Ironically Mark scored his first Chelsea goal at possibly our worst performance of the season, losing 3-1 at Southampton. But things were about to turn.

"For me personally things got better straight away. When we beat Newcastle at Stamford Bridge the day after the Southampton game it really made me feel good. Not only did I score the goal in a 1-0 win but it was our first victory for a while and it was a goal at home. I hadn't scored at home yet and I didn't like the idea that the fans hadn't seen me do anything. I had been scoring week in week out when I was at Stoke and I was bought to score. I think that goal against Newcastle was the turning point for me." From then on Mark began to hit the target with unnerving regularity. In 24 appearances to the end of

the season he smashed 14 goals and there is little doubt that without those strikes we would have been in serious trouble at the foot of the division. Then came the injury.

"Just as things were starting to go well I got injured at Manchester United. From then on I was struggling to get fit to play in the Cup Final. But the real blow came before the start of this season. We had qualified for Europe and the club was looking to go places, and to get injured again just before the start of the season in a friendly was a real disappointment. I think with hindsight that I wasn't ready to play in that game at Southend. I actually slipped off the edge of the pitch trying to keep a ball in play, and that did the same tear in my ankle ligament as before. At the time of course I felt fine though, the second injury was a shock there's no doubt."

Something else of which there is no doubt is that nothing is worse than a player getting injured, especially for the people who have to put up with a brooding, unfulfilled footballer at home.

"My family were brilliant at the time. I was upset because I had never really been injured much before, it had simply never happened to me. I find it very frustrating when I'm just coming in to get treatment and having to stand there and watch the lads train or play matches. That isn't what I was bought for, so that can get to you too. So, for it to happen twice so close together was a blow, but everyone who is close to me was a real help. I owe them I think."

Since returning from injury Mark has had to contend with the fact that during the summer Glenn has imported Paul Furlong.

"It has given the manager options. Last season we didn't really have that sort of option to use which meant that a lot of time myself and John Spencer were playing up front together. I think

you realise as a professional that any manager at any club wants to be able to change his team yet to keep it as strong as possible, so that is why he bought Paul to give him that extra alternative. When you are at a big club you have to expect competition for places."

In the future of course there is only one thing, or maybe two, that Mark wants to do.

"I want to get back to my best form and do what I'm paid to do which is score goals... and right now I'd like to play in Europe, that is something I've never done."

Let's hope he can do both tonight.

GLENN'S VIEW

WHAT A GREAT Easter holiday on the points front.

It's been an anxious time here in the League for you, and for the players, staff and directors. But now we've got the break on the psychological barrier. We've found the edge we've been missing.

There was a lot of pressure on the players for the Villa game, and they responded magnificently. It was a battling performance. All round the pitch we won our one-on-one battles. We wanted the win more on the day.

Paul and Mark linked up nicely for the goal, and it was a great finish by Mark Stein. He had one good chance in the game and he took it. A superb strike.

I was hugely encouraged by you supporters. After the poor result and team performance against Southampton you all performed magnificently, particularly in the North Stand. It was tremendous the way everyone was behind the team kicking the same way. It's easy to sing when we're on our way to Wembley or in European quarter- and semi-finals, but at Chelsea you showed form when we needed it most.

Forty-eight hours later we played our fourth game in eight days at Old Trafford where Manchester United still had their championship hopes alive. That was always going to be tough, but after so many games extra effort was needed.

The boys never cease to amaze me. When the chips are down they have responded. The more this season has gone on the more we have seemed to get results when no-one expects it.

Gareth Hall, David Lee and Kevin Hitchcock have come in and given magnificent performances. The whole team felt we could get something at Manchester, and at the end Mark could have nicked it.

I said at half-time that if we lost we won't be relegated. But if they don't win their championship hopes are gone. And I reminded everyone we lost 4-0 in the Cup Final. We had to go out and weather the storm, but we did and got a great result.

We're still not out of the woods in the Premiership. But the light is a bit brighter every game. One good win could secure our place now. But it's still very tight and we can't show complacency.

And so to tonight. I feel that with your great support, if we can get an early goal we can put Real Zaragoza under tremendous pressure and win the game. We need to take our chances.

I'm sure if we score you supporters will help us go on and get a second and third. We can worry about a fourth after that.

But we must balance our need to get at Zaragoza with care because an away goal could kill us. We must divide ourselves between all out attack and defending very securely. If we do it, it will be a magnificent achievement.

It has been a magnificent achievement to get to the semi-finals. Not many people thought we would. Now we must score three without conceding. We will attack. Zaragoza hadn't lost at home for 18 months when we played them, but they have lost something like their last eight away games. It will be interesting if we can get a couple of goals before half-time as against Bruges.

Congratulations to Graham Rix and the youth team on reaching the League Cup Final. The first leg is at Upton Park on Monday night. The youth team has played exciting football this year, and it would be lovely for Graham and all of them to finish on a high with a trophy.

They're not out of it in the League yet. It's been a relatively successful season for them so far, and it would be splendid to top it off by winning something. I hope many of you can go and support them.

Against Bruges you were tops.

Now let's see if you can lift the roof off the stands to help us on our way tonight.

Glenn Hoddle

EMERGENCY EVACUATION

If an emergency evacuation of the ground is necessary, the following message will follow an alarm signal over the public address system: *"LADIES AND GENTLEMEN, DUE TO UNFORESEEN CIRCUMSTANCES IT IS NOT POSSIBLE TO CONTINUE WITH THIS EVENT. PLEASE LEAVE THE GROUND AS QUICKLY AND QUIETLY AS POSSIBLE USING THE EXITS INDICATED TO YOU BY THE STAFF".* The alarm signal will be tested 30 minutes before the scheduled kick off time of every match.

Steve Clarke celebrates Old Trafford point.

I'VE SEEN IT all now. Gav missed training after Manchester United with a little cut elbow.

He had a little plaster put on it. What an excuse! You wouldn't get away with that at school.

The boys were all pleased that day though. We did Blackburn a favour at Man United, but then they went and cocked it up in the evening.

We're Man United's bogey side at Old Trafford. It was good to get another draw there.

And it was good to see Big Nose go home sulking last Saturday. Nah, I'm joking. I spoke to Andy after we beat Villa and he was fine, an old mate. But they're in trouble at the moment, aren't they.

Anyone's in trouble right now if they're not winning. We still need another three points to be safe. People are looking for 49 or 50.

Palace still have to play West Ham, Villa have to play Norwich. It's tense.

But tonight . . . this'll be tense. We're ready for a hard battle. I think if we get an early goal, you fans and the players can get at Zaragoza and make them uneasy. You lot can help us to a couple more goals with your support. An early goal and they should be twitching. We can win. It may take extra time, but we can win.

I'm still out unfortunately. Nightmare '95, eh? But Eddie's getting close. Thank God. His talk, his intelligence level, is so low I've given up talking to him . . . And this week I've had Dimmi in the treatment room, Andy Myers and Mints. They're all so laid back I've just been going off and doing my weights.

Maybe them being there will get me fit quicker though!

Well done Spenny, back in the Scotland squad. I almost miss you from here!

So get at 'em lads. Do the hard work. Get us to the final. I should be fit by then.

Dennis Wise

EUROPEAN HERO No. 4 RON HARRIS

CHELSEA v REAL ZARAGOZA

DENNIS WISE IS A CPO SHAREHOLDER — ARE YOU?

Real Zaragoza were the side standing between us and the club's second European final and, following a 3-0 defeat in Spain, we had it all to do in the return leg. Sadly, we just missed out as the tie at the Bridge ended in a 3-1 victory. Gavin Peacock was the victim of Dennis Wise's mickey-taking in the skipper's notes and Glenn Hoddle was full of praise for his players after a positive run of results domestically.

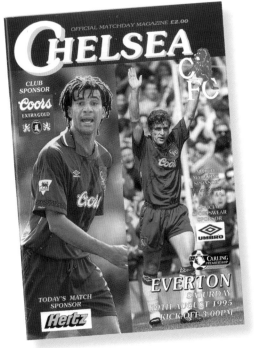

New era dawns as Gullit and Hughes join the Blues, 1995/96

Chelsea's rising stock in English football was demonstrated perfectly by the two summer signings who appeared on the cover of our opening programme of the 1995/96 season and Blues Diary featured pictures of when Ruud Gullit and Mark Hughes signed for the club. There was also a feature with Gullit and you can see Dennis Wise's On The Ball Q&A from this programme on page 112. The September game against Southampton marked the club's 90th birthday with a special anniversary programme produced for the occasion. Programme editor Neil Barnett was providing yet more access to the squad through his Spy in the Camp column and the growing interest in the statistical side of the game was reflected in the Statman page.

BLUES DIARY

First day in a new shirt

Above: Press conference in Drake's. The questions ranged from Ruud's musical perferences to where he was going to live, and football as well. Colin Hutchinson and Glenn Hoddle enjoyed this explanation of life the Gullit way.

Right: The newspapers need the photographs. A new team, an old pose. Just look that way please. Mark Hughes looks left to a massive building site. Still, he seems happy to have come to the home of the club he supported as a boy.

ONE ON ONE

Eddie Newton ON Andy Impey

I'VE KNOWN ANDY Impey for years, man. We used to play against each other when we were youngsters.

He was with Tops, a youth team associated with Yeading. I was at Harrow Club. He's always been called Chalkie, it was always his nickname.

The first time I ever played against him I scored a hat-trick. Header, right foot, left foot. The perfect hat-trick. And it wasn't enough. They beat us 5-3. I played centre-forward and he was central midfield. He always played there then.

We used to play loads of five-a-sides against each other. I was a White City boy, he was Yeading. He was at Chelsea for a while, even before I got here. I don't know what happened, but he moved on. Gwyn would be the one to tell you all about that.

I've been out with him a few times after games, and we have a good laugh. I've been to a few concerts with him too. Intro at the Palais, R Kelly at Wembley Arena, a few at Hammersmith Odeon. He's more into the reggae then me, well into it.

Queens Park Rangers snapped him up from Yeading for a small fee and he hasn't looked back. He was their Player of the Year last season.

He's strong, gets up an down well, he's got good skill. And he's got lots of pace. I can't believe it, man. I didn't know he had pace when we were younger. He never showed it. Suddenly he's using it up and down the wing.

I still think he can do well in midfield, so I don't know where he'll finish up. He works really hard for Rangers, covers a lot of ground. He covers the right-back, covers the midfield tucking in, gets forward and attacks behind the defence to get crosses in.

And now he's been training with England. He got called up last season when he was playing really well. He fully deserves it. He's improved a lot since Yeading and he deserves everything he gets. If he keeps going he's got a chance at the top.

But it's not easy for him at the moment. He's in a

team fighting for their lives. You're not going to shine there. It's got to be a team effort to get out of trouble.

I remember a game a few years ago at Rangers when he and Andy Myers had a great battle. I tell you man, sometimes I was laughing there in the midfield. They were at each others' throats all the way through the game. And they're the best of mates. Both played really well. And I wouldn't have given either the edge on the day. Great battle. They nullified each other.

So he'll do well, Chalkie. Stylish player, gets the ball down, passes it and can get behind you.

I hope Rangers stay up. I used to support them when I was younger. Chalkie can shine next year.

I'd like to thank everyone out there who has sent me cards and letters. I've had loads.

I'm doing fine now. I'm at home doing nothing except keeping my upper body strong. It's a waiting process. It's boring but it's got to be done. I just occupy myself round the house. I'm hoping that in the middle of April I can get the cast off my leg and start working again.

So all your good wishes cheered me up when I was down. You're great. See you soon.

Eddie Newton

Chelsea won Programme of the Year in the 1995/96 campaign and some of the interesting features are shown in the edition produced for the QPR game in March. The opposition pages included Eddie Newton discussing a good friend of his from the opposition, Andy Impey, and younger fans were now getting a page dedicated to them. Front Line showed action from our FA Cup quarter-final win over Wimbledon, but we lost at the next stage against Manchester United. The Red Devils had thwarted our hopes in the competition twice in three years, but the wait to get our hands back on the famous trophy was nearly over…

FRONT LINE

UP FOR THE SEMIS

EMERGENCY EVACUATION EXERCISE

...RIL, KICK-OFF 3.00PM, CATEGORY 'B'   3

FROM TRAGEDY TO TRIUMPH

There was sad news early in the 1996/97 season with the death of the club's vice-Chairman Matthew Harding. You can see the tributes to him from our Tottenham programme on page 206.

The best way of honouring the ardent Chelsea fan came later in the season when the Blues secured our first FA Cup victory in 27 years. On the next four pages you can see the programmes from every game in the run,

which began with a 3-0 win over West Brom. Liverpool were beaten 4-2 in a classic fourth-round tie and we overcame Leicester 1-0 in a replay in round five.

Fratton Park was the venue for the quarter-final against Portsmouth and we secured a semi-final berth with a 4-1 win before overcoming Wimbledon 3-0 to reach the final. The trophy was secured with a 2-0 win over Middlesbrough at Wembley.

FA Cup Fantalk

WELL, WHATEVER other matches happen in the course of the 1996-97 season, none comes any bigger than this one: certainly not in Skinner and Baddiel Mansions.

It's caused all sorts of tenancy problems: for example, the terms of the lease do not *allow* him to paint his room blue and white striped.

I've even gone so far as to buy him some extra blue paint so he can paint in the white bits, but all he does is complain that he doesn't *see* why his room should have to

Peschisolido threat

DAVID BADDIEL on FRANK SKINNER

look like the rest of the flat.

Also, I've begun to suspect that that bird's nest on top of the chimney did not always have an enormous plastic throstle in it. Although I've managed to turn this to my advantage by claiming that that's who's constantly singing 'Chirpy Chirpy Cheep Cheep' (rather than a loop-tape of the Chelsea 1970 team doing their FA Cup song).

What really worries me, however, is that often, over the last four years, I've heard my flat-mate's bedsprings creak; since last Monday

though, I'm sure they've actually been going *Boing-Boing.*

It's ridiculous. I feel like I'm in one of those quirky *Football Focus* features on domestic football rivalry, where the husband supports, say, Stoke, and the wife, Port Vale.

Well, we've got through writing and performing three TV series together; we've got through hiding in a specially constructed bunker from Jason Lee; we've even got through a long and drawn out custody argument over Statto (neither of us wanted him

obviously). So we'll get through this.

Although obviously, should West Brom win — (should, for example, Sparky fall over in his own third and let Paul Peschisolido in for a soft goal) — he's out on his arse.

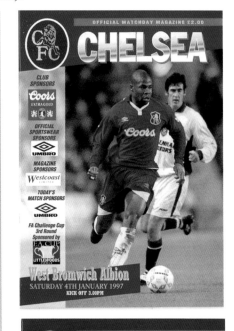

OFFICIAL MATCHDAY MAGAZINE £2.40

CHELSEA

CLUB SPONSORS
Coors

OFFICIAL SPORTSWEAR SPONSORS
Umbro

MAGAZINE SPONSORS
Westcoast

TONIGHT'S MATCH SPONSORS
Heinz

FA Challenge
Cup 5th Round
Replay
Sponsored by Littlewoods

Leicester City
WEDNESDAY 26th FEBRUARY 1997
KICK OFF 7.45PM

DAN PETRESCU

Ruud Gullit

THERE IS A GOOD SPIRIT IN our Chelsea.

It takes time for everybody to be aware of what we are doing. Now I see players sticking together as one all through the camp. They understand the squad thing.

If one is not playing and the team wins, then he knows we all win.

Someone is always going to be disappointed at not playing. That is good. As long as he is aware that when the team wins we all win.

So I want to say this: Vialli is doing very well. He is showing good spirit in his training. The other players are supporting him. His attitude is very good in a difficult time.

The papers say one thing, but every day at training is something else. He is ready, always tuned in, he's been a great example to our youngsters.

What Dennis did for him last week when he scored was so great for our team. I was so happy with that gesture.

There were people running from midfield, people jumping in front of me as we'd scored, so I didn't see Dennis running towards us. It was so funny when he was suddenly there.

The loss of Doobs is so bad. He was doing well for us and for himself.

But this is the lesson of life. One day you are up, next day you are out. He will learn and come back stronger.

You realise you can't waste your time. Every day you must be happy with what you are doing.

Doobs will come back very healthy. In the meantime, we must do anything we can for him.

Frank Sinclair replaced him and did well. Here we had it again — it was important the replacement was tuned in. Frank was, and he did what was asked.

Paul Hughes' debut was outstanding. You can only dream of that. His dream came true.

What I need is experienced players to show young players what it means to be on top, how your life forms during the week, what you do at training, slowly working through everything. It's good for young players to play with good players. It's also easier playing in a team that is playing well.

Neil Clement, Jody, Nicho, Paul Hughes, and there are others also. These people get a chance at Chelsea. Not just the big guys.

I say it again and again; it is important everyone is tuned in. You must take your chance when it comes.

Today is the easiest kind of game for me. I don't have to get the player's tuned in. They already are.

We can't win the Championship by beating the top teams only. We can only win it by beating the so called lower teams. It is the same for everyone.

But today is a one-off and we have to beat a big team. We are tuned in.

Honours

European Cup Winners' Cup
Winners: 1970/71.

Football League
Champions: 1954/55.

Front Line

ROBERTO LAUGHS OFF MILAN TALK

Roberto Di Matteo went straight on *Clubcall* after returning from our friendly in Milan last week and rejected headlines linking him with the Italian club.

Following Gianluca Vialli pledging himself to Chelsea in *Matchday Magazine* on Saturday, Roberto said: "I don't know who keeps saying this because I've settled down very well in London thanks to my team-mates and the club. I'm very happy here.

"I feel good. I feel my team-mates and the club expect something special from me. I try to do my best, and it's a good time for me. I feel very good and the team is playing well. It makes everything much easier for me.

"I don't want to leave, and that's for sure."

Contents

WEDNESDAY 5TH MARCH — KICK-OFF 7.45PM

3

FA CUP TRIVIA
The Blues and The Beatles

To honour our guests from Liverpool today, our squad offers up their favourite all-time Beatles song.

Craig Burley
I don't know any. Name me some . . . Nah, I don't like The Beatles. I wasn't born then.

Steve Clarke
I don't like The Beatles. They're not my taste. Anything except The Beatles is my taste.

Neil Clement
Beatles? Aagh! Let me think while I get a can of Lucozade. (After the can is opened) I don't know any. Name some. Later ones . . . 'Let It Be'. I like than one.

Nick Colgan
You want to ask my Missus, she's older than me! I don't know! 'Yellow Submarine'?

Roberto Di Matteo
I don't remember the . . .

Frode Grodås
'Let It Be'. Beautiful song. I like some Beatles songs, not all. But they've done a lot of great songs.

Ruud Gullit
(Sings) "Ob-bla-di, Ob-bla-da, Life goes on — ra! La la la la life goes on." Yeah!

Kevin Hitchcock
The Beatles? . . . The Beatles! . . . 'Yesterday'. That's the first one I can think of.

Mark Hughes
Not many to choose from is there! 'Yesterday'. I suppose. I'm a big softy really.

Paul Hughes
I don't know one. (Sings) "You love me, yeah, yeah, yeah." What's the title of that?

"All You Need is Love"

They've completely passed me by.

Erland Johnsen
'Hey Jude' is the best. My sister used to listen to Abba and The Beatles. I've got to admit I've got the 'Gold' album even now. But she used to listen to Baccara as well. Oh, do you remember them? A girl duo. They were just terrible.

Dmitri Kharine
No, I don't like The Beatles. We hear them in Russia, but you won't have heard of my music. It's Russian.

Frank Leboeuf
(Sings) "Yesterday, all my troubles seemed so far away."

David Lee
I'm too young for that. I haven't really got one. I know a lot of them I suppose. I know — 'Daytripper'. I heard that the other day and that's a really good song.

193

WEMBLEY HERE WE COME

Franco celebrates after scoring another brilliant goal (below) to put us 2-0 up at Highbury

Wise Words

GREAT!

I've been here seven years and now I can say I'm fortunate to have reached two Cup Finals with Chelsea. This will be my third overall and Hughesy's fifth. We've done okay in the FA Cup.

I remember speaking to Stan Bowles a few years ago. The main ambition in his life had been to play in an FA Cup Final, and he played for 15 years and never got near it.

It's a wonderful week leading up to the final, and the day itself is a wonderful day. You

really enjoy it. And it's even better if you win.

I thought we showed a lot of people last week that when it comes to the big event we're up for it. We showed a lot of class. I think we shocked people outside Chelsea, the way we played.

It was great for you lot. You were magnificent as usual. You enjoyed it all, didn't ya! Be sure, there's more to come!

We've still got to concentrate on the League of course. If we win the next four games we could still just qualify

for Europe. It would be great to finish with a strong League run to take into the Cup Final.

I've got a slight dead leg following the Wimbledon game, so I didn't go to Newcastle. I think I did it with all the celebrating.

Clarkey didn't go up either, so I'll hand over to Sparky. He'd been skipper twice before Newcastle and was looking for third time lucky. A draw at Man United and a defeat at Nottingham Forest. We're waiting for him to break his duck.

Alright!

WE WERE ALL DISAP-pointed at Newcastle, especially with the first-half.

Individual mistakes led to the goals, but that wasn't the simple reason why we lost.

We came more onto our game in the second-half after we'd been told a few home truths and we gave a far better performance. A Premiership performance.

I felt sorry for the supporters who had come all that way to see us play like that in the first-half. We've got to make sure it doesn't happen again because you can't turn on and turn off form as you want.

It wasn't good enough and we know it.

Mark Hughes

THE F.A. CUP SPONSORED BY LITTLEWOODS

F.A. CUP
LITTLEWOODS

OFFICIAL MATCHDAY PROGRAMME £3.00

SEMI-FINAL
Sunday 13th April 1997
ARSENAL STADIUM
HIGHBURY
Kick-off: 12 noon

WIMBLEDON
v CHELSEA

LEGENDS

AMERICA'S PREMIUM BEER

F.A. CUP
SPONSOR LITTLEWOODS

Wimbledon v Chelsea

Wimbledon	Chelsea
1 NEIL SULLIVAN (GK)	1 DMITRI KHARINE (GK)
2 KENNY CUNNINGHAM (D)	2 DAN PETRESCU (D)
3 ALAN KIMBLE (D)	3 RUUD GULLIT (M)
4 VINNIE JONES (D)	4 FRANCK LEBOEUF (D)
5 DEAN BLACKWELL (D)	5 STEVE CLARKE (D)
6 BEN THATCHER (D)	6 ANDY MYERS (D)
7 OYVIND LEONHARDSEN (M)	7 GIANLUCA VIALLI (F)
8 ROBBIE EARLE (M)	8 MARK HUGHES (F)
9 DEAN HOLDSWORTH (F)	9 DENNIS WISE (M)
10 MARCUS GAYLE (F)	10 MICHAEL DUBERRY (D)
11 CHRIS PERRY (D)	11 KEVIN HITCHCOCK (GK)
12 JON GOODMAN (F)	12 CRAIG BURLEY (M)
13 PAUL HEALD (GK)	13 DAVID LEE (M)
14 BRIAN McALLISTER (D)	14 ROBERTO DI MATTEO (M)
15 NEAL ARDLEY (M)	15 SCOTT MINTO (D)
16 MICK HARFORD (F)	16 ERLAND JOHNSEN (D)
17 DUNCAN JUPP (D)	17 PAUL PARKER (D)
18 ANDY CLARKE (F)	18 FRANK SINCLAIR (D)
19 JASON EUELL (M)	19 JODY MORRIS (M)
20 PETER FEAR (D)	20 MARK NICHOLLS (F)
	21 NICK COLGAN (GK)
	22 EDDIE NEWTON (M)
	23 GIANFRANCO ZOLA (F)
	24 NEIL CLEMENT (D)
	25 PAUL HUGHES (M)
	26 DANNY GRANVILLE (D)
	27 FRODE GRODAS (GK)
	28 CRAIG FORREST (GK)

MANAGER : JOE KINNEAR

MANAGER : RUUD GULLIT

Today's Officials

Referee:
G. R. Ashby

Assistant Referees:
S.S. Babski

M. Warren

Fourth Official:
G. Poll

IN THE EVENT OF A DRAW

CHELSEA ARE BACK

Our second FA Cup Final in three years was celebrated by **Mark Hughes** (opposite) after he had scored our third goal. **Gianfranco Zola** gave Blackwell warning (left) of the twists and turns to come with this first-half dummy. In the second-half we scored following another. **Mark Hughes** second goal in the last minute (below) thundered past Sullivan. **Dennis Wise** who had a terrific game set the tone by outbattling Perry and Kimble (bottom).

Ruud Gullit

NOW THAT EVERYBODY has this FA Cup the passed behind them, we can focus ourselves again on the competition that is Premier League games.

Premier League games are very important. I as a coach am so pleased that the FA Cup

Honours

Europea Cup Winners' Cup
Winners: 1970/71.

Football League
Champions: 1954/55.

FA Cup
Winners: 1969/70.
Runners-up: 1914/15, 1966/67, 1993/94.

Football League Cup
Winners: 1964/65.
Runners-up 1971/72.

Full Members Cup
Winners: 1985/86, 1989/90.

FA Charity Shield
Winners: 1955/56.
Runners-up: 1970/71.

Univers International Tournament
Winners: 1996.

Division Two
Champions: 1983/84, 1988/89.
Runners-up: 1906/07, 1911/12, 1929/30, 1962/63, 1976/77.

FA Youth Cup
Winners: 1959/60, 1960/61.
Runners-up 1957/58.

match is behind us now. We can really go for these last four games in the Premiership.

Last Sunday was a great day for the players and for you supporters. I really want to thank you for your support. It was just so pleasing all round.

But it came after defeats against Middlesbrough, Arsenal and Coventry.

Arsenal was a bad game, we didn't produce football as we can. The good thing was that everyone was disappointed. The players' reaction afterwards, at least, pleased me.

Coventry was the same. The players were thinking about the FA Cup game. I, of course, demand of my players more. Sometimes I do ask myself if I ask the players too much.

But we must concentrate on every game as it arrives. I as a coach have to make my players ready for that.

It is not that I think the League is more important than the Cup. But it is as important I have no preferences. I just want us to be a part of everything.

If you can, then you must do it.

For the Premier League I want more. We lost again at Newcastle on Wednesday. I think players were emotionally and physically tired after the semi-final, and maybe they were still tuned into that. But I want more in the League.

I wasn't frustrated or angry after the game, I still have great confidence in them. But on the evening we played more against ourselves than Newcastle. We gave goals too easily. We put them in the driving seat.

But I just must say again how pleased I am that last Sunday was great for you. It was a great atmosphere and you gave great support.

Thanks for that again.

The players did the rest. Now they must carry on. Every week.

Congratulations to Leicester on qualifying for Europe next season after their determined Coca-Cola Cup campaign. Well done.

CHANNEL CHELSEA

our in-house TV station broadcasts throughout the Matthew Harding Stand and in the East Stand executive areas as well as on the big screen. The show is presented today by Graham Done.

Today's highlights

Chelsea v Wimbledon semi-final highlights	Blues goals this season
Graham Done interviews Ben Bates and Colin Hutchinson	Team News
Leicester v Chelsea October '96 highlights	Match highlights
Graham Done 'In The Dug-Out'	End of match player interviews

THE F.A. CUP FINAL

SPONSORED BY
LITTLEWOODS

CHELSEA
v
MIDDLESBROUGH

F.A. CUP
LITTLEWOODS

SATURDAY 17TH MAY 1997
KICK-OFF 3.00PM
OFFICIAL MATCHDAY PROGRAMME £6.00

Wembley

DOUBLE THE FUN ON OUR CUP RUNS

Success continued in 1997/98 with two trophy triumphs as the Blues won both the League Cup and the Cup Winners' Cup. We start by looking at programmes from the European run, which saw us overcome Slovan Bratislava, Tromso, Real Betis and Vicenza before beating Stuttgart 1-0 in the final in Stockholm

SLOVANISTA

Pohár víťazov pohárov   Ročník 1997/98

ŠK SLOVAN BRATISLAVA
* * *
CHELSEA FC LONDÝN

Štvrtok 2. októbra 1997 o 20.35 hod.
Štadión na Tehelnom poli

HLAVNÝ ROZHODCA: Alan Harrer (Luxembursko)
ASISTENTI: Raymond Wekker (Luxembursko)
Claude Birenbaum (Luxembursko)
REZERVNÝ ROZHODCA: Franco Maraglino (Luxembursko)
DELEGÁT UEFA: Pentti Aisja (Fínsko)
POZOROVATEĽ UEFA: Alexander Suchanek (Poľsko)

VELKOMMEN TIL
2. runde Europacup

TROMSØ I.L. - CHELSEA FC

Alfheim Stadion, 23. oktober 1997 - kl. 21.05

blues DIARY

Cup Final 1997

F ulham Road was packed as Chelsea brought the FA Cup home on May 18. Frank Sinclair, Eddie Newton and Paul Hughes (*above*) found so much to smile about. Dan and Daniela Petrescu (*top right*) found so much to see. Ruud Gullit and Estelle Cruyff (*right*) enjoyed the trophy as Betty Leboeuf, Roberto Di Matteo, Graham Rix and Bernie Dixson enjoyed the crowd.

2.2 THE MONTHLY GLOSSY CHELSEA MAGAZINE IS AVAILABLE FROM THE CHELSEA MEGASTORE — £2.95

blues DIARY

how we celebrated

looking ahead

Saturday September 20
Coventry Youth v Chelsea Youth, Premier Youth League, The Sky Blue Lodge, Lemington Rd, Ryton-on-Dunsmore, 11am.

Sunday September 21
Chelsea v Arsenal, Carling Premiership, Stamford Bridge, 2pm.
Chelsea Accidentate launched.
Dulwich Hamlet WFC v Chelsea Ladies, Pioners Close FC, Dulwich Common, 2pm.

Monday September 22
Chelsea Reserves v Arsenal Reserves, Avon Insurance Combination League, Kingstonian, 7pm.

Wednesday September 24
Manchester United v Chelsea, Carling Premiership, Old Trafford, 8pm.

Saturday September 27
Chelsea v Newcastle, Carling Premiership, Stamford Bridge, 3pm.
Chelsea Youth v Derby Youth, Premier Youth League, Harlington, 10.45am.

Sunday September 28
Car boot sale, 9am-2pm, 20p. (Cars £6, vans £10, access from 7am).

Collier Row v Chelsea Ladies, CIS WFA Cup 1st Round, Hornchurch FC, Hornchurch Stadium, Bridge Ave, Hornchurch, Essex, 2pm.

Monday September 29
Southampton Reserves v Chelsea Reserves, Avon Insurance Combination League, Staplewood, Long Lane, Marchwood, Southampton, 7.30pm.

Wednesday October 1
Team flies out to Slovakia.

Thursday October 2
Slovan Bratislava v Chelsea, European Cup Winners Cup 1st Round 2nd Leg, Slovan Stadium, kick-off 20.35.

Chelsea Village Antiques Market, Stamford Bridge, 9am-2pm. Admission free to buyers.

Sunday October 4
Middlesbrough Youth v Chelsea Youth, Premier Youth League, Rockliffe, Trollesby Rd, Middlesbrough, 11am.

Sunday October 5
Liverpool v Chelsea, Carling Premiership, Anfield, 4pm.
Car boot sale, 9am-2pm, 20p. (Cars £6, vans £10, access from 7am).

Chelmsford LFC v Chelsea Ladies, Rittle College Sports Field, Lordship Rd, Rittle, Chelmsford, 2pm.

Tuesday October 7
October ONSIDE published. Postal copies will be sent out later in the week.

T hree years ago we'd paraded pride. This year we paraded achievement. Dennis Wise with Geraldine Lennon (*left*) shows the trophy to the crowd, and the crowd shares the glory. Now for the follow-on. Let's drive on with the European Cup Winners Cup.

---

wise WORDS

Tonight's game is bigger than the Coca-Cola Cup Final. Really!

T onight's game is the biggest of the season so far. We've won the Coca-Cola one and this is the trophy we all really want to win.

The biggest!

We want you punters to be noisy just like theirs were. Their supporters were magnificent, everything they did was brilliant.

But you're the champions when it comes to support, so the boys are looking for a champion performance from you tonight.

We'll be going out there and really going for it. I believe better side than them with better players.

They're well organised and have good discipline, so we have to match them to that, but if we do we'll be alright.

They won in Vienna but they didn't get a lot of chances. Their goal was quite spawny (or 'came to being unlucky) if it a bit.

We'd just come off the...

> I so desperately want to win this Cup. It makes for a good CV, doesn't it!

We played well in the last round against a great team in Real Betis and now we can do it alright.

It's very important to me to for us to get in a European final. I so desperately want to win this Cup. It makes for a good CV, doesn't it! Cup Winners Cup winners, Coca-Cola Cup winners, third or fourth in the League is tremendous. Not a bad season.

But right now third or fourth in the League is tremendous. We're not going to win that. This is the trophy for Chelsea.

We're Britain's only team in Europe and we've got to go all the way.

Our home European form since I've been here has been terrific. I hope we can keep it going tonight.

Alright!

But now we've played them we know and I think we can beat them.

So everybody get behind us and come healthy mayhem. Frighten the life out of everyone.

"The weather's alright, we're happy tonight, working in a Winter Wonderland"

---

freeze FRAME

real betis

half way there - but only half!

Tore Andre Flo celebrates his first good goal with Roberto Di Matteo (*left*) who supplied the pass for him to turn and sprint away from the grounded Olías (*opposite top left*).

Chelsea felt we were denied two more good goals: Dan Petrescu's effort (*opposite top right*) was cancelled out for offside and Gianfranco Zola's bat (*opposite bottom*) was judged not a penalty but a dive and worthy of a yellow card by referee Duzounov. Defender Vidakovic had to go off injured, however.

Real Betis 1 Chelsea 2

freeze FRAME

vicenza

edge ahead

Vicenza bring a one goal lead to Stamford Bridge, but it could have been different. Frank Leboeuf sped off with Zauli in chase (*left*) late in the search of the equaliser. Gianfranco Zola (*opposite top*) cut in from the right and sent a cross against the near post. Dennis Wise got away from a Zola free-kick and crossed (*opposite centre*) into an unprepared penalty area. Gianluca Vialli, going forward, felt the strength of Vialari (*opposite bottom left*). Vialari also had pride with Tore Andre Flo (*opposite bottom right*) when he came on.

Vicenza 1 Chelsea 0

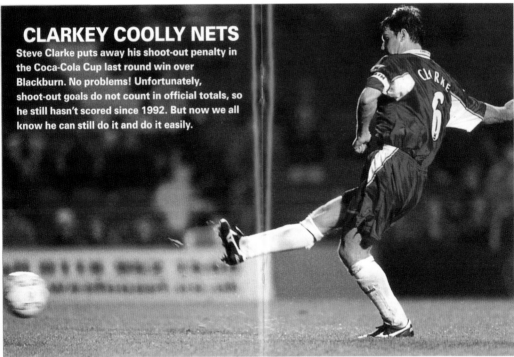

CLARKEY COOLLY NETS

Steve Clarke puts away his shoot-out penalty in the Coca-Cola Cup last round win over Blackburn. No problems! Unfortunately, shoot-out goals do not count in official totals, so he still hasn't scored since 1992. But now we all know he can still do it and do it easily.

Here we bring you programmes from the victorious League Cup run, which began with a penalty shoot-out win against Blackburn. Southampton were beaten in round four before another win on penalties over Ipswich in the quarters. We beat Arsenal in the semi-final, which contained Gianluca Vialli's first notes as player-manager (see page 168), overturning a 2-1 deficit to beat them 4-3 on aggregate before we overcame Middlesbrough 2-0 in the final.

front LINE

LUCA BECOMES OUR MANAGER

When Gianluca Vialli got 'Bould' over at Highbury ten days ago he had no idea he would be Chelsea manager for this Coca-Cola Cup second leg. The reasons behind the surprise leaving of Ruud Gullit and the installing of Gianluca are explained in *Ken Bates*, Page 8, and a special three page *Colin Hutchinson* beginning on Page 13. See also *Spy in The Camp*, Page 58 and read Luca's special *On The Ball*, Pages 46-49.

**FAREWELL RUUD
THANKS AND GOOD LUCK**

GOOD LUCK LUCA

wise WORDS

he club's made its decision and everyone has to stick by it. Ruud started off exactly the same way as Luca is. He became player-manager and we won the Cup in his first season.

It will be great for you to give Luca all the support you did with Ruud. He's a lovely man and he'll do the best for our club.

1969/70

eople frequently forget that the season Chelsea won the FA Cup by beating mighty Leeds in the Final, we also knocked them out of the League Cup.

After Ian Hutchinson's goal had dismissed Coventry at Highfield Road, the swinging Blues were drawn against the powerful Leeds at Elland Road.

Bonetti was in outstanding form and the best the home side could manage was a 1-1 draw. Alan Birchenall scored for Chelsea.

The replay at Stamford Bridge was won by an early Charlie Cooke goal and a later Birchenall strike in front of 38,485, our biggest League Cup crowd ever at the time.

FREEZE frame

REAL MADRID 0 CHELSEA 1 Chelsea won the UEFA Super Cup with Gustavo Poyet's 83rd minute goal (below). Earlier efforts by Celestine Babayaro (opposite top left) past Sanchis and Panucci went wide and by Frank Leboeuf past the diving illgner (opposite top right) hit the post. Gus' first effort to find the surging Gianfranco Zola (centre right) in the build-up to the goal was blocked by Sanchis, but he and Franco finally broke through. Dennis Wise celebrated the score with Gus (opposite bottom left) in front of Chelsea's fans and Gus joined Frank with the Cup (opposite bottom right).

CHELSEA V real madrid

CHELSEA'S SUPERSTARS

Super start to new season as we beat Real, 1998/99

The 1998/99 season began with more silverware as we beat Real Madrid 1-0 in the European Super Cup in Monaco. Our next match was against Arsenal and the programme paid tribute to Steve Clarke, whose Blues playing days had reached an end after an impressive 421 appearances.

GIANLUCA vialli

It is our fourth trophy in less than 16 months. That's not bad, is it!

But, again for the thousandth time, I would like to underline that this is just the starting point of the future of this club. We have to keep improving. There are still so many things to reach.

We must keep our feet firmly on the ground and play like we haven't won anything. That is the secret, I think, after winning something.

When you play in the Premier League or in Europe you play against strong teams. On paper they might be as strong as you. The only way to beat them is to be mentally more focused. You must have more desire.

BRIDGE news

Award winners at the Player of the Year Dinner/Dance were Dennis Wise, your Player of the Year for 1998, Gustavo Poyet who won the Chairman's Award and John Terry who took the Young Player of the Year Award.

After eight years at Stamford Bridge Dennis Wise was voted Player of the Year in Chelsea's most successful season since 1955 when we won the League. Ken Bates presented him with his trophy (far right) and he thanked all the voters and his team-mates whom

he then called up on stage and led them in a round of 'Singing In The Rain'.

Considering he won the Wimbledon Player of the Year award the season they won the FA Cup, his top form has become synonymous with the greatest achievements of his clubs.

Steve Clarke has left us after 421 games, four winners' medals, nearly 12 years, a lot of heartache, bundles of glory and a bucketful of invested loyalty.

He sat in his Newcastle hotel bedroom last week, just before leaving for his first morning of training, and admitted: "I'm gonna miss all my friends. I'm gonna miss the supporters. I think that I'd been there so long and I'd seen the low spots, the relegations and the times out of the team, that it allowed me to appreciate all the more the last four years."

It was hardly a surprise when Ruud Gullit came in for him and it is an enormous opportunity, going from being reserve right-back and player-assistant-coach at Chelsea to assistant manager at Newcastle.

While his playing registration has moved up there, he has not been given a contract as a player and cannot appear for their first team, but just their reserves. So effectively, a day or two after his 35th birthday, he has retired from playing.

Steve signed for Chelsea in January 1987 for £422,000

"I happen to do well every time the team wins something," he laughs. "In the two finals last season I set up the first goal in the Coca-Cola and the winner in the Cup Winners Cup.

"I set up the goal in '88 as well. Maybe it's fate, you're meant to do well.

Two awards ten years apart! He laughs again. "I've got a long wait for the next one, don't I!"

The Chairman's Award went not so much to an unsung hero as a special case. The chairman praised Gustavo Poyet (left) for the way he remained optimistic and continued to mix in with his new team-mates after his injury and came back so quickly from it.

Gus was taking stick at the training ground next day. "Now I have a new name, Ken Bates' son." He laughs as readily as Dennis. "Every player call me his son! I was surprised. I knew I don't win Player of the Year, I don't have to speak, I can stay quiet with my friend Albert. And then Ken Bates say: 'Say something!' I think: 'No! No!' But it was really great."

The professionals vote for Young Player of the Year and central defender John Terry (above) was selected in just his first year.

"I was very surprised," he admitted. "I thought Jon Harley would get it because he had a good season. It means a lot, I'm still shocked now. I was shaking when they called out my name and I didn't know what to say."

All the same, he delivered his first public speech, albeit one sentence, and learned a little of what life is like to be a professional footballer.

Maybe in ten years time he'll be crooning 'Singing In The Rain'.

Kerry Dixon to become our fourth highest appearance maker ever. He famously scored his tenth goal at home to Liverpool in his 417th game.

Graham Rix said: "I'll miss him off the pitch as a mate, a golf partner, cards partner – he was good company."

Last January he was awarded with a special cut glass bowl to acknowledge his 600th game for us. Over the last few years he has carved out a special place in the hearts of all Chelsea fans which will surely stay forever.

"I really wish Chelsea good luck in the Premiership this season," he said. All Chelsea wish him luck too. A great servant has moved on and will be hugely missed.

GUS HEADS US INTO THE CHAMPIONS' LEAGUE

Gustavo Poyet heads the only goal of the game against Leeds from Graeme Le Saux's cross to ensure we finish third

Unfortunately, our run in the Cup Winners' Cup ended with defeat to Real Mallorca at the semi-final stage, although there was a jubilant end to the season as Gus Poyet's header in a 1-0 win against Leeds secured third place and qualification for the Champions League for the first time. You can read an early Q&A with John Terry from the Real Mallorca programme – which also featured an interview with Ray Wilkins, who had returned to the club as coach – on page 114.

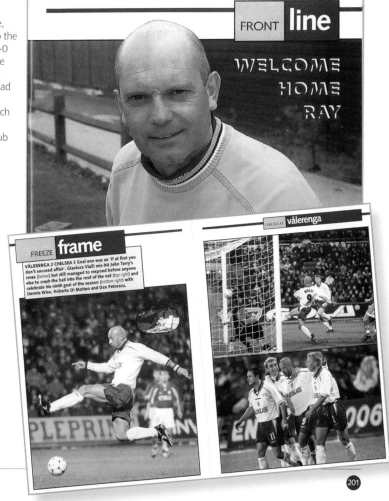

FRONT **line**

WELCOME HOME RAY

CHELSEA AT **vålerenga**

FREEZE **frame**

VÅLERENGA 2 CHELSEA 3 Goal one was an 'If at first you don't succeed affair'. Gianluca Vialli mis-hit John Terry's cross (below) but still managed to respond before anyone else to crash the ball into the roof of the net (top right) and celebrate his ninth goal of the season (bottom right) with Dennis Wise, Roberto Di Matteo and Dan Petrescu.

WISE **words**

Yet we're a little bit disappointed not to have been at the top.

The results in the last few matches have gone quite well but we've drawn too many games. So we've still got to qualify for the actual Champions' League.

All the same, it's the first time Chelsea have finished third since, I don't know . . . 1970?

Now we have to set our sights higher again next year and if we keep doing that you know what will happen.

This is the best Chelsea team I've played in. If we improve next year like we have in each of the last few years, we'll be up with Manchester United and Arsenal again and hopefully above them.

Bruno N'Gotty	Pierluigi Orlandini	Sebastiano Rossi	Mirco Sadotti
Date and place of birth 30th June 1971, Lyon Height and weight m.1.84 - kg. 86 Position Defender Serie appearances and goals 25/1 European Cups appearances and goals 25/2 Caps and goals to summer 6/0	Date and place of birth 9th October 1972, Bergamo Height and weight m.1.82 - kg. 77 Position Midfielder Serie appearances and goals 125/15 European Cups appearances and goals 9/0	Date and place of birth 20th July 1964, Cesena Height and weight m.1.97 - kg. 94 Position Goalkeeper Serie appearances and goals 315 European Cups appearances and goals 35	Date and place of birth 18th May 1975, Arezzo Height and weight m.1.88 - kg. 86 Position Defender

Ray saw young Paolo and Demetrio emerge

Money. Power. Relegation. Big teams can get relegated.

Like it happened to Manchester United and Tottenham in the 1970s – and weren't Manchester City once a big team? – so it happened to AC Milan at the turn of that decade.

They got relegated for match fixing – before the present owners took control – and ...

"Now he carries 15 years of experience, he works his socks off and he's really a very classy footballer.

"Albertini was a young man when I was there and he always looked like he was going to be a special player.

"Now it's good to look at Demis ...

... of the problems they'll pose us.

1966. In the Inter-Cities Fairs Cup Blues record-scorer Bobby Tambling forced a diving save from Milan goalkeeper Balzarini while keeper Peter Bonetti dominates his penalty area in front of an empty net.

They've played for Chelsea and AC Milan

Jimmy Greaves (top left)
Marcel Desailly (above)
Ray Wilkins (top right)
Carlo Cudicini (bottom left)
Ruud Gullit (bottom right)

Chelsea Gold – your chance to win £1,000 weekly   49

... ing of any object is against the law

Chelsea 3 Skonto Riga 0

It is a criminal offence to trespass on the pitch other than in an emergency

We face Euro elite on Champions League debut, 1999/2000

The 1999/2000 campaign was another hugely memorable one for the Blues as our inaugural season in the Champions League saw us take on some European heavyweights as we reached the quarter-final. There was also success domestically when we won the last FA Cup final at the old Wembley, thanks to a 1-0 over Aston Villa. On these pages, you can see extracts from some of our first Champions League programmes, from Skonto Riga in qualifying, to classic group-stage ties against the likes of AC Milan (for a Gianfranco Zola Q&A from this programme turn to page 115) and Galatasaray and a night to remember at the Bridge against Barcelona in the quarters.

Ken Bates

Welcome to the European Champions League to, AC Milan and the officials, delegates and sponsors of UEFA. It is a great honour to participate in the most prestigious club competition in the world and starting with tonight the six games will be a true taste of how far we have progressed in the last decade. It seems light years away from the days when we were playing – and getting beaten by – the likes of Tranmere, Reading, Swindon, Scarborough and Barnsley.

Pinch yourselves, because no you are not dreaming – it really is happening. Chelsea are now part of the big time and we intend to stay in such exalted surroundings.

It is perhaps appropriate to recognise and thank all those fans who were there in the rainy days at Shrewsbury, Gillingham, Brighton and other exotic places. I hope that this long journey which started against Oldham in 1982 (with a gate of just 14,000) has been worthwhile. Whenever you have been asked to contribute to the Club you have never been found wanting and your spirit is epitomised by the fan I met at the weekend. He is a social worker in Cambridge and lives in rented accommodation. He worked out that in the 30 years he has supported Chelsea he has spent somewhere near £95,000 following the Blues. Enough for him to have been able to buy his own house.

Rock solid

Gully is floored, Deschamps is sharp and the Rock is out in front as he helps secure another clean sheet

Was Chelsea – Milan the best football ever at the Bridge?

There may have been only Dennis Wise who was English on the pitch at kick-off time, but Chelsea v AC Milan was played at English Premiership pace with Italian technique.

"I think it's up there with the best games of the Bridge since I've been here," considers our captain.

"It was so quick, and with the tempo and the quality of the opposition it has to be one of the best."

The game was not a surprise to

him. "I expected them to be like that, but it was interesting for me because I wasn't sure how I'd cope with it, nor how the team would. Obviously we had knowledge of all their players, but you're not sure how it will go, how the level of play will be.

"Now we know we can compete with them and better. It shows how far we've come in a few years."

Didier Deschamps is used to playing at that level if not in that

Desailly dominated Bierhoff

mix of pace and technique, and he found the game special in quality.

"I thought Chelsea played a very good game," says the double Champions League winner in quickly improving English. "Now all the players are sure Chelsea are a competitive team against all the teams, Milan AC, showed we can beat every team.

"Maybe we were not lucky. It was possible we could win against the big Milan with all their European experience."

There were so many great performances from Chelsea players, and none more so than from Gianfranco Zola.

"It was a really good performance," says the Italian. "We didn't concede anything to Milan, especially with the quality in football."

He thinks back to other games when two great teams have gone for the points through the 90 minutes, like at home to Manchester United last season –

Zola leaves the Rossoneri in his wake

Terry's Chelsea pain and Barcelona triumph

Terry Venables played his last ever game for Chelsea in the Nou Camp against the club he was later to manage.

The occasion was the first leg of the 1966 Inter-Cities Fairs Cup semi-final.

"It was a very glamorous tie even then," he recalls. "They were a very big club, but nothing like the colossus they have become.

"For them, and Real Madrid, they didn't really care about the Fairs or UEFA Cup, or the Cup Winners' Cup until the later stages.

Then they hit the stadiums.

"The League Championship and Champions League is much more important to them. What makes tonight's game much bigger?

Although the failure in Barcelona was only the first leg, Terry was already sure that his days at Stamford Bridge were numbered.

"I remember Tommy Docherty coming into the dressing room before the first game and introducing a new signing, Charlie Cooke. I guessed then that he was my replacement. The transfer by Spurs had very nearly been sorted out by then.

"I was in New York with my new team-mates by the time of the third game against Barcelona. Although, to be fair, Charlie did a very good job for Chelsea over a number of years.

"We were well beaten in that game in Spain although a lot of that was to do with the fact that we had played a lot of games in a very short period of time.

Of course, at that stage in his career Terry had little idea that he would one day return to Barcelona as first team coach. The more made him appreciate just what a phenomenon the Nou Camp club is.

"They are machine. There is no other club like them. They don't represent Spain in European

competition, they represent Catalonia. That is a great honour but also a great burden.

"We would get off the coach at the Bernabeu to play Real Madrid and people would be shouting 'Welcome to Spain!'

"It all went back to the Civil War. General Franco wouldn't let the people speak Catalan in public so they would come to the stadium just to speak their language. The club then became the focus of national identity.

"Manchester United are quite rightly regarded as a massive club but I think they have explored all the ways they can go. Barça haven't started yet.

"They might decide to stay in private hands but if they were public they would be huge. They haven't even got shirt sponsorship because they don't want it."

Terry Venables had a very successful spell as coach of Barcelona. In his first season in charge he won the Spanish League, their first such triumph for eleven years, and only their second in a quarter of a century.

Then the following season he led Barça to the Champions Cup Final where they were unfortunate to lose on penalties to Steaua Bucharest.

He wasn't the only member of that Chelsea class of 1966 to graduate to management. George Graham is perhaps the best known apart from Terry but there were others as well.

"John Hollins is doing well for himself. Ken Shellito and Eddie McCreadie both had time in charge of Chelsea. Allan Harris was my assistant at Barcelona. Peter Bonetti is a very good goalkeeping coach, John Mortimore and Frank Upton have been around the game for a long time and I believe Barry Bridges and Frank Blunstone both had spells as managers.

Terry of course, is not directly involved in football now but he is present at Stamford Bridge tonight in his role as a television summariser.

"I'll be at the first leg and then in the studio for the highlights programme in two weeks time. It's a game I'm really looking forward to, Barcelona are quite rightly the favourites for the whole tournament but Chelsea are in the last eight on merit and if they are brave and have a go at their defence, then they have a chance." (PR)

1996 Quarter-Finals
Borussia Dortmund 0 Ajax 3
Legia Warsaw 0 Panathinaikos 3
Nantes 4 Spartak Moscow 2
Real Madrid 1 Juventus 2
(Scores are aggregate)

1997 Quarter-Finals
Ajax 1 Atlético Madrid 3
Borussia Dortmund 4 Auxerre 1
Man Utd 4 Porto 0
Rosenborg 1 Juventus 3
(Scores are aggregate)

Terry Venables

Is this the world's greatest Stadium?

FUTBOL: UN ESTADI DE 120.000 ESPECTADORS

Cha-pi! Cha-pi!

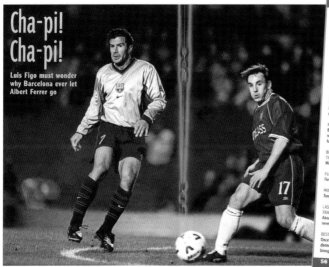

Luis Figo must wonder why Barcelona ever let Albert Ferrer go

Brain Of France

GOAL OF THE MONTH
The George Weah goal, the one where he flicked it with his head against Gillingham.

SAVE OF THE MONTH
Ed has had many. The one at Tottenham with his feet, that was important.

TACKLE OF THE MONTH
Any one of Dennis or Frank, they do so many.

ASSIST OF THE MONTH
The Jon Harley goal, the pass by Didier, the cross by Dan – a magnificent goal.

MUG OF THE MONTH
Bernard Lambourde. I can't say why, just he is always doing funny things.

BUSIEST PERSON AT THE CLUB
Mr Gwyn – always Mr Gwyn.

FUNNIEST PLAYER EVER
For me it is Tore Andre Flo.

MOST SERIOUS PLAYER EVER
Tore Andre Flo.

LAST TIME YOU TOOK PUBLIC TRANSPORT
About five years ago in Paris. I never took the Metro in Milan.

BEST WIND-UP
Once in Milan, Maldini stole a donkey – a real live donkey and brought it to training.

RECORD THAT GOT YOU DANCING AT THE SCHOOL DISCO
Kool and the Gang - 'Get Down On It'. With my white tie and dark shirt.

WHEN DID YOU LAST DOUBT YOUR SANITY?
Last week, losing to Marseille.

WHO WOULD YOU LIKE AS A FRIEND?
Ken Bates. Then he can give me a three year contract.

LAST EVENT YOU WALKED OUT ON
A Mariah Carey concert, it is not my sort of music.

IF YOU COULD DO A GOOD DEED TOMORROW
Something for Mozambique, or for children, they are the most important.

WHICH OF OUR PLAYERS WOULD YOU ENTER IN AN EVENT FOR NEXT YEAR'S OLYMPICS?
Gus Poyet for speed talking.

THE PERFECT PLAYER
Marco van Basten.

THE WORST PLAYER
Vialli! Is this going in the programme?

CHAMPAGNE MOMENT OF THE MONTH
Jes Hogh and George Weah for their new babies.

"The Jon Harley goal, the pass by Didier, the cross by Dan – a magnificent goal.

Our third FA Cup triumph came following wins over Hull, Nottingham Forest, Leicester, Gillingham and Newcastle, with extracts from some of the programmes featured here, as well as the edition produced for our league game against Derby.

Magic **Moments**

The quickest goal but the longest celebrations ever

66 I enjoyed the whole day. In fact I enjoyed it from the night before. We stayed in a nice hotel near Wembley, we had stayed there for the semi-final, and then the whole day was just perfect, wasn't it. Like a dream, a nice dream. 99

66 It was the best celebration at the end I've ever been in, and I think it will be the best ever because it was Chelsea's first trophy for so long. Maybe if we win the League it will be like this. 99

66 I don't know how the chant to our fans started. I don't know who said something, we just did it. And then after that we did it for every Cup. 99

66 The next day we went down Fulham Road with the Cup and that was great on the bus. It was a fantastic turn out from the fans. Then we went to Thailand and it was a great trip, on the plane and the whole week it was one long celebration. So when I think back, I think back not just to my goal or anything else, but to the whole week. 99

Roberto Di Matteo

SHOT IN HEAD ON DUTY

As promised in the Wimbledon programme last week, here is action from the team's paintballing expedition. John Terry (top left) shows off his mask and where he was shot in the head. Gustavo Poyet (left) reveals where Dennis Wise shot him under his mask and cut his cheek. Ray Wilkins and Gus Lebeuf (left) practise on a foot-baller... the Swede who got away.

Brain Of France

GOAL OF THE MONTH
George Weah against Tottenham because he gave us the three points in his first game. It was important for him and for us. I would like to say that the Worst Player At Cards is Chris Sutton. He's a disaster. I have to play with him, but it's very, very difficult. He's my partner. But he's been with me all season so he's getting better now he's quite good now.

SAVE OF THE MONTH
Ed de Goey, which game was it? It was against Coventry I think. It was a cross and a striker got on the far post, and he turned it over with his hand.

TACKLE OF THE MONTH
I think some of Keane against Arsenal on Monday. Unbelievable! Against Vieira. He's very good on the pressing, but he tackles very hard, very, very hard, and I think two or three of them were not good ones.

ASSIST OF THE MONTH
Franco for the Dennis Wise header against Leicester. The free-kick. It's important to give a good ball on the free-kick.

MUG OF THE MONTH
Maybe Marcel, I did not see him for three weeks. He doesn't train, he is just injured.

BUSIEST PERSON AT THE CLUB
Aaron (Lincoln) because every morning something is missing, no? That is normal.

FUNNIEST PLAYER EVER
I think Di Livio from Juventus. He is joking every time. He's a good man.

MOST SERIOUS PLAYER EVER
After me, I don't know: Gianfranco Zola, because everyday he's thinking about soccer all the time. He's a good professional about his life, off the pitch and on the pitch.

LAST TIME YOU TOOK PUBLIC TRANSPORT
With Chelsea, when we go to the airport.

RECORD THAT GOT YOU DANCING AT THE SCHOOL DISCO
No, I don't know dancing. I'm a disaster, really. I have no rhythm, you know? It's too difficult for me!

WHEN DID YOU LAST DOUBT YOUR SANITY?
When I have an injury on my achilles. I need an intervention, and about three, four months after I was afraid I would not recuperate, all my qualities. It was December 1994, and I stopped for four months and a half, I think, and I was very afraid. It was very difficult.

WHO WOULD YOU LIKE AS A FRIEND
De Pardieu. He's a very famous French actor. I think he's the best French actor. Maybe he looks a bit like me because he has not a good face. But he's playing very well.

LAST EVENT YOU WALKED OUT ON
I was at the cinema in Paris with my wife, it was a French film and it was rubbish. "La Bouche" PFF! Disaster. It's a new one, one month ago it's going out. Oh, I was sleeping inside.

IF YOU COULD DO A GOOD DEED TOMORROW
I think the most important, now we are 2000, everybody can eat.

WHICH OF OUR PLAYERS WOULD YOU ENTER IN AN EVENT FOR NEXT YEAR'S OLYMPICS?
Marcel on the bicycle. I've never seen Marcel on a bike.

THE PERFECT PLAYER
You can take some of everybody, but I think Zidane for the moment is the best player. He has all the quality. I think it's enough. Zidane like he's playing now, the best.

THE WORST PLAYER
I think all the players who didn't play the ball. The most important is the mentality, and the most important is going to play the ball. And sometimes I saw players who didn't play the ball.

CHAMPAGNE MOMENT OF THE MONTH
Every morning when I see my son, he's going to wake up me, and he wants to play. I think it's a great moment.

Didier Deschamps

"Maybe he **looks a bit like** me because he has **not a good face**"

The Chelsea 2000 FA Cup Final song

("Will there ever be a Blue Tomorrow?...")

Dennis Wise: "Believe it... alright!"

No matter how long we've had to wait
It's all been worth it,
Counting out our dreams from celophane
Now we all deserve it.

It's hard to believe that only yesterday we were
Worried about Stamford Bridge and the future,
But he believed that things could change...
Oh, oh, oh.

How the Blue Tomorrow gets closer each day,
We will follow the Chelsea till our dying day,
Just look over your shoulder,
See the army dressed in blue,
We'll go where you go (Oi!)
And fight every fight (Oi!)
with you.

Chelsea, Chelsea!
Chelsea, Chelsea!

So many years with so much stress
But we didn't mind it
Now we live on the edge of great success
And we quite like it.

You've gotta believe that we are proud of
what you've done
And no matter what (What!), we're gonna be
the Champions!

And we'll be there, as we are now...
Oh, oh, oh.

Cos the Blue Tomorrow gets closer each day,
We will follow the Chelsea till our dying day,
Just look over your shoulder,
See the army dressed in blue,
We'll go where you go (Oi!)
And fight every fight (Oi!)
with you.

Chelsea, Chelsea!
Chelsea, Chelsea!

There'll be blue streets and bars
When there's football life on Mars,
We're gonna rule the universe,
Cos we're Chelsea, Chelsea, Chelsea,
CHELSEA!

Let's sing Blue It The Colour
And give Wembley it's last Blue Day...
Cos Chelsea, Chelsea, Chelsea is the way

CHELSEA, CHELSEA, CHELSEA is the way
CHELSEA, CHELSEA, CHELSEA is the way
CHELSEA, CHELSEA, CHELSEA is the way
CHELSEA, CHELSEA, CHELSEA is the way
CHELSEA, CHELSEA, CHELSEA is the way

Chelsea, Chelsea!
CHELSEA

SUNDAY·PICTORIAL

WEMBLEY STADIUM STORMED BY EXCITED CUP FINAL CROWD

Aston Villa
v
Chelsea

THE F.A. CUP SPONSORED BY AXA-FINAL T

It's open-top bus time again

1997

1994

Blue Tomorrow
The boys recorded the song and video at the Angel Studios, Islington, 11 days ago as Cup Final fever started to take grip

CFC Wise Words

The biggest incentive ever to win the Cup!

Thank you to all the fans for this season.

You've been fantastic. It's been a super show from you, especially with trips abroad and so many games at home to come to.

We're all sorry that we haven't qualified for Europe. We feel we've under-achieved a bit because of that – at the moment!

We need to get into Europe through the FA Cup next week. That's what the club is focusing on right now.

But you fans have been behind us all the way and everyone here appreciates it a lot.

We really have played an awful lot of games. It's taken its toll on us.

This is the first time we've experienced life in the European Champions League and still in the Premiership too, and at times we've looked and felt jaded.

You've helped us come through a lot of the games, but it hasn't always been easy.

It takes time to get into the swing of a demanding schedule like that. Some of us might not be so young, but we're only just learning.

If we can win the FA Cup next week, and if we play at our best we know we can, then I think we'll all look back on this season with a lot of affection. Last eight in Europe, a whole list of big, big games with unbelievable atmospheres where we've performed as well as we ever have, top five in the

League and a piece of silverware. More games than the club has ever played before because of our success. That would be some season.

But we have to win.

There's so many incentives. And after the year we've had, one of the best is our summer!

We don't want to play in the Intertoto Cup. If we have to play in that we start training on June 26th. If we don't we start on July 17th. That is the biggest incentive EVER!

In the meantime, a lot of our players won't get a quiet summer anyway because they're going to Euro 2000. Good luck to everyone who goes. Don't get injured.

I'm gonna be a proud man next week. I hope to be captaining Chelsea in my 403rd game for the third time in an FA Cup Final at Wembley.

Give your all, all you punters. Enjoy it like it should be, get dressed and painted up, sing loud with 'Blue Tomorrow', outsing Villa and have a party.

There's nothing so good as a Wembley celebration, and our summer depends on it.

Let's have a long summer. Alright!

TRIBUTES

The matchday programme has, over the years, honoured the lives of numerous club legends after they have passed away

Ray Deane and Matthew Harding at a Chelsea Pitch Owners lunch.

It's seven o'clock on Thursday morning as I sit here at the farm gathering my thoughts, trying to put pen to paper. Lots of little things come to you as I've watched the sunrise, one that Matthew will not see, at least not from this angle. Perhaps I should just tell it like it was . . .

1993-1996

I first met Matthew Harding on 2nd September, 1993. About a week earlier I got a call from Janet Rainbow. "Chairman, I've just had a guy in buying five CPO shares. Said if you don't raise money for the North Stand phone him. He's a lot richer than you are. Strange looking guy, wearing an old T-shirt and jeans." A few checks tracked him down and he came to the Bridge this time in a suit when I told him of our plans and we went to lunch. The Kings Road was blocked so I dumped the car and we walked to The Imperial Arms, later to become one of his favourite watering holes.

I think we were fascinated with each other, so alike and yet so different, with one thing in common — Chelsea. About a week later he came back, said he'd put up £5m. Work on the North Stand started a month later.

In conversation last summer he suggested we celebrate our three years together with lunch at the Savoy Grill, where we celebrated signing the original deal. Unfortunately it was shut, so we went to the Dorchester instead.

Over another three hour lunch (Matthew liked his food spread over a long period) we talked widely and at great length, our differences behind us with the July agreement when he became vice-chairman. We talked enthusiastically of the future. Two semi-finals and a final in three years was at least a start on the field, the final corner of the North Stand had just opened and the Southern Complex was rising before our eyes. Lengthening the pitch cost us 4,000 seats in the proposed South Stand so we had agreed to try and scrap the flats and build not only a bigger West Stand but the finest stand that had ever been built with top class facilities for all tastes and pockets. (Ironically we are having a final presentation from the architects this afternoon. When I spoke to Ruth, his brave wife last night, despite her grief she was determined that the ground should be completed as soon as possible — "Matt would have wanted that".)

We talked enthusiastically about the team, how it had been transformed in quality at all levels and felt that the best was yet to come. After losing at Bolton, he was characteristically chirpy. "Oh well, I suppose we're stuck with

the FA Cup again".

Matthew Harding came from a privileged background and became one of the lads. He was a genius who discovered a gap in the insurance market and cleverly exploited it. His success generated huge wealth and cash which he spent lavishly, giving kindly to a huge range of good causes often behind the scenes and without any fuss.

He wanted to be loved by everyone, had many acquaintances but had few close friends. A workaholic he had just started to build what could have been one of the biggest international groups in the world of insurance and his dominant presence will be sorely missed by his colleagues at The Benfield Group.

Matthew died still a mystery, an enigma, because behind the veneer of bonhomie he was a loner, a deep thinker. Very good company, a star in the cut-and-thrust of friendly repartee but given to monosyllabic replies if you probed deeper. Equally at home drinking Chateau Lafite Rothschild with the nobs as he was pulling pints with the lads, particularly his beloved Guinness.

Recently somebody said to me "Live every day as if it is your last — because one day you'll get it right."

Matthew Harding did just that and I shall miss him.

Ken Bates.

Floral tributes laid in the main entrance to vice-chairman **Matthew Harding** who died on Tuesday night along with four others as they flew back from Bolton v Chelsea. Today there will be a minute's silence before the game in memory of those who died.

Goodbye Ian

Ian Hutchinson, who died at 9.30am on September 19th, the day we played Viking, joined Chelsea for £5,000 in July 1968 from Cambridge United, then in non-League football.

He went on to play 144 games, seven as substitute, scored 58 goals, and famously won the FA Cup before retiring through injury in 1976.

Hutch was the bravest, strongest, unluckiest player imaginable. He allowed Peter Osgood, previously the target man because of his size, to play off him, and they were arguably the best front partnership we have ever had. Certainly they were one of the best.

If the long throw, arms whirling at the end of a determined run, transformed football, his ability to score goals, withstand challenges and go past defenders, should never be forgotten.

This week, his manager Dave Sexton remembered him.

"He was like a breath of fresh air," said our former boss. "We had a lot of sophisticated players, but we needed someone to have a go. We could score classic goals but we needed to get bread and butter goals.

"He was great with his head, but for a big bloke he was quick on his feet, he was underestimated on that, but he brought us that edge. He led the line heroically, and we won the Cup.

"It was difficult for him because he had to pick things up as he went along."

Hutch's heroics led to successive injuries and operations. The supporters loved him because he never gave up.

Following retirement he had a year as our commercial manager with an office in an East Stand executive box, and he remained in close friendship with many of the Cup winning team.

He had been ill for a long time with liver problems and died aged 54.

He was a Chelsea 'great'.

Peter Sillett 1933-1998 – a champion

Peter Sillett, our right-back in our only Championship season, died last Friday evening aged 65.

He was, unarguably, a Chelsea great.

Signed from Southampton for £12,000 in 1953, he gave wonderful service for nine years, playing 288 games and scoring 34 goals. He also won three England caps.

One of those goals was probably the most important in Chelsea's history. His fiercely struck penalty during Easter against Championship contenders Wolves sealed a 1-0 victory and from thereon the title was always going to be ours.

A year after he joined us, his brother John came too. John later managed Coventry to FA Cup success, but as a player he wasn't of the same ability.

He said this week: "Peter remembered so many good times at Chelsea. They were his years of enjoyment in football.

"The moment of his life in the game was that penalty against Wolves. Chelsea had missed five in a row that season, Roy Bentley and Johnny Harris, and the job had fallen to Peter. It was such a vital match. Whoever won it was going to win the Championship. In front of 75,000 too, I don't think he felt too confident.

"I was in the stand. It ripped the back right out of the goal. He was a tremendous striker of the ball.

"I'm bald because of him. He made me pull my hair out. It was the hardest thing having to follow him. All my life I've been John Sillett, brother of Peter.

"Somewhere he was called the Rolls-Royce of full-backs. Under pressure he never panicked. He had a good touch, unbelievable skill for a big fella. He could always wriggle himself out of trouble.

"Stanley Matthews said he was the best full-back he ever played against. That's the highest acclaim!

"I remember a free-kick against Blackburn. Ronnie Clayton was their captain. It was about five yards in the Blackburn half and Ronnie shouted for a wall. Fred Else was in goal and he shouted: 'When I want a wall at that distance I'm packing in.' Peter hit it and it flew in the top corner. Ronnie ran to Else screaming: 'I warned you. I'm telling the manager when we get off.'

"I remember in a London Combination Cup tie at the Den against Millwall, Davies in goal shouted for a wall, he wanted five and no-one would go in it. I think Peter scored a hat-trick of free-kicks that day.

"Then we played against Luton. I was at right-back and Peter was left. He was splaying against a player he hated to play against. Billy Bingham. Peter was a gentleman compared to me.

"I said, why don't you give him a whack? He said, if you want to change over, you do it. So we did, and I kicked him and got sent off. I remember him doubled up as I walked off and Ted Drake said: 'That's a clever thing to do.'

"In the dressing room, Ted Drake said to Peter: 'You want your bumps read, winding him up to change over.'

"He broke his leg at Villa. Derek Dougan fell on it and at the end of that season he looked at me and said: 'That's it. I can't go through that again.'

"He had chances to sign for loads of First Division clubs but he signed for Albert Tennant, an old Chelsea coach, at Guildford. He played there for years."

Peter's Championship captain Roy Bentley adds: "He didn't have an athlete's physique. He was big. But he wasn't slow. He was as good a striker of a ball as I've ever played with.

"He didn't like training but he never let you down with his fitness.

"He was an amusing bloke. Easy going. People liked to be in his company. Once a friend always a friend.

"We both played for Great Britain in Ireland against the Rest of Europe. Peter only had one cap at the time, but he'd done so well he'd gone straight in. He was a good player. Terrific tackler.

"We all had dinner at the House of Commons last year and you'd think he'd never had a care in the world."

On leaving Guildford Peter managed in non-League, spending many years in Ashford where he also ran a pub. He was a heavy smoker which is what everyone believes led to his cancer.

Tony Banks laid on that House of Commons dinner.

"I loved him," says the MP. "He was one of my heroes. He was very underrated. Very versatile. He could switch from right to left.

"He was so cool on that screaming penalty against Wolves. So unflappable. I was right behind the goal. It never went more than three inches off the ground. Thud! If the goalkeeper had got in the way it would have taken him in with it.

"I asked John if I could go and see him last week, but he said I shouldn't. He had lost seven stone. I want to remember him as he was. He was probably the hardest hitter of a dead ball I've ever seen in a Chelsea shirt."

Peter leaves behind wife Connie, children Carol-Anne, David, Stuart and Jonathon and seven grandchildren.

He also leaves an immovable pile of memories, legends and facts. He was a Champion and will always be remembered as one.

Programme tributes to Matthew Harding, Peter Sillett, David Rocastle, Ian Hutchinson and Keith Weller.

Goodbye to a nice guy David Rocastle

For many fans, David Rocastle may only appeared to have been at Chelsea one season. He made 39 of his 40 appearances in 1994/5.

But for everyone within the club he was here for four years. He didn't leave until late in the 1997/8 season.

The stories in the media of his popularity as a man, told and retold since his death on March 31st, couldn't be truer.

There was a huge Chelsea turn out at his funeral the day before we played Derby.

Colin Hutchinson and Claudio Ranieri were joined by Dennis Wise, Kevin Hitchcock and his wife, Gianfranco Zola, Graeme Le Saux, Gustavo Poyet, Ed de Goey, Jody Morris and John Terry.

From the backroom staff went Gwyn Williams, Steve Clarke, Mike Banks, Mick McGiven, Terry Byrne, John Kelly, Ade Mafe, Ted Dale and Gary Staker.

Four office staff travelled down from Stamford Bridge, plus myself.

And Chelsea old boys were represented by Nigel Spackman and his wife, Graham Rix, Eddie Niedzwiecki, Mark Stein, Paul Furlong and Nick Colgan who flew down from Scotland.

Also there were Anne Hoddle, former wife of Glenn, with the former head of the training ground canteen service.

Spackman and Rix were two managers who missed the last day of training before a game to attend.

Earlier in the week Nigel Spackman spoke of his friend.

"I saw Rocky three weeks ago. I came down and saw him and Jan. Little Monique who's four was there, but Ryan and Melissa were at school.

"Rocky came downstairs to see me and we sat and talked for quite a long time.

"The way he looked wasn't the Rocky we remember and were all so fond of.

"I don't think anybody has got a word against him. He was a gentleman, such a lovely lovely man.

"When I got the phone call last Saturday I was devastated. It will take people close to him a long time to get over it."

Nigel knew a little too much about Rocky before he got to know him at Chelsea.

"Obviously, I played against him in the famous Liverpool-Arsenal game when they won the League. I respected him so much as a player but most of all as a person.

"When he moved to Chelsea he moved in round the corner from me in Windsor and we got on so well. He's got a lovely family and our families got on very well.

"We've got to try and remember him now as a great footballer and a healthy young guy."

Rocky's room mate at Chelsea was Paul Furlong.

"He was very helpful to me," says Paul. "He was the guy you'd go to for advice and talk to in confidence. And he was always up for a laugh.

"His knowhow was important to Chelsea for a while, especially when we played in Europe. He was very helpful to me in Europe."

David Rocastle was signed from Manchester City for £1.25m in 1994 by Glenn Hoddle.

Two of his finest moments in that first season were in Europe: his 35 yard lobbed goal in the pouring rain at home to Viktoria Zizkov, and his marauding left-wing performance at home to Bruges in the Cup Winners' Cup quarter-final second leg.

But injury spoilt his following season: he made just one first team appearance although he was available for more.

And then he spent two years in the reserves, often captaining them, as he failed to win a squad number under Ruud Gullit.

A knee operation had restricted his running. In 1998 he was released and moved to Sabah in Malaysia.

Gwyn Williams knew him for a lot longer than his Chelsea spell.

"I've known him since he was 13 and played for South London Schools. He came here a couple of times to train with us, but eventually signed for Arsenal."

At Arsenal, of course he won the Championship twice and the League Cup, but that knee injury kicked in. He moved to Leeds and Manchester City before joining us.

His first season was successful, but not after. On top of the 40 first team games in all he played 56 in the reserves, many as captain.

Gwyn recalls: "He was so good. He didn't mean once, he was so enthusiastic, and as Gianfranco said when he came, even though Rocky was in the reserves, he made him feel welcome."

Terry Byrne was the physio at a lot of the reserve games.

Terry recalls: "He and Dave Lee were the only two senior players in regular reserve games, and Rocky took it upon himself to help guide the young players coming through, and to act as their minder. He became very popular with the young players."

Jody Morris confirms this. "I was going through a sticky patch and we were playing regularly together, and he took me on one side and said if I ever needed to talk to anyone he was always there.

"We played some good football together. He was helpful to all the young lads on and off the pitch. We all loved him. I was devastated by the news."

Gwyn says that when Rocky was injured, he tried to persuade him to take up coaching with our schoolboys as a way into the management process, but Rocky wanted to concentrate on getting fit.

When he died six weeks short of his 34th birthday he had been ill for over a year, but was still optimistic right up to the last few days of his life when his final deterioration was very quick.

Chelsea Football Club is so grateful for his services as a player and a man, and commiserates with Jan, the children, his mother and two brothers and two sisters. (NB)

Club mourns loss of KEITH WELLER

On Friday November 12, one of Chelsea's 1971 European Cup Winners' Cup heroes, Keith Weller, died following a battle against leiomyosarcoma, a cancer of soft muscle tissue. He was 58.

Though a little late on the scene, Weller epitomised the glamour of Chelsea's King's Road swingers. As an Islingtonian he was at home with the glittering lifestyle of a squad he joined in the summer of 1970 from Millwall for £100,000.

His arrival was a surprise – so much so that his glue-in sticker for that season's *Soccer Stars* annual featured a hastily retouched shirt!

Some felt that the purchase was aimed at keeping his prodigious talent from others, and it's true he had to fit in where he could in a settled side: right of a front three, or in right midfield.

But elegant Weller top-scored with 13 League goals in his only full season for the Blues. His dynamism is underappreciated now at Chelsea.

He could ping a decisive pass or shot and was very effective on set-pieces.

It was his indirect free-kick against Manchester City in the Cup Winners' Cup semi-final that City keeper Ron Healey pushed into his own net to settle the tie. He played in the final and replay of that competition against Real Madrid to earn the only medal of his career.

It's a measure of his impact that David Webb cites seeing Jimmy Bloomfield at the Bridge, negotiating Weller's sale to Leicester City, as the beginning of the end for Dave Sexton's team.

Weller moved on the day after the 13-0 European demolition of Jeunesse Hautcharage for the same fee as he arrived. The Blues bowed out tamely in the next round.

He eventually settled in Seattle, USA, where he was later diagnosed with cancer.

Another ex-Blue, Alan Birchenall, worked tirelessly to raise money for his treatment.

The thoughts of Chelsea's staff and players are extended to his friends and family at this sad time.

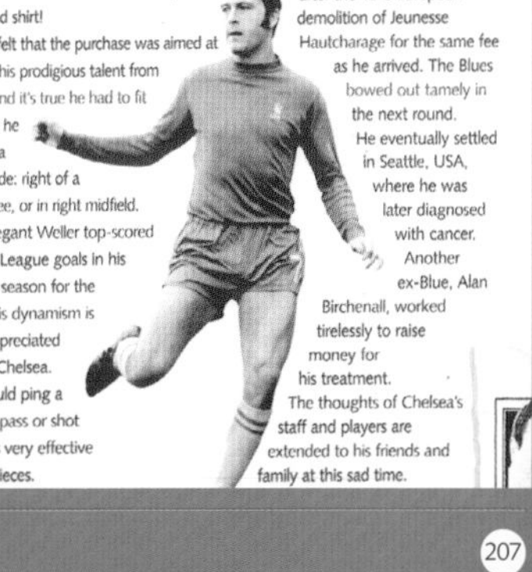

CHELSEAFC
OFFICIAL CENTENARY SEASON MATCHDAY MAGAZINE 05/06

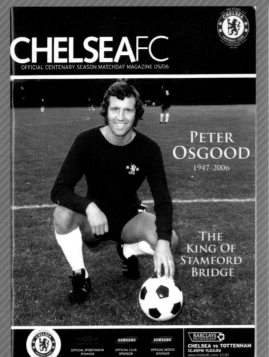

PETER OSGOOD
1947-2006

THE KING OF STAMFORD BRIDGE

OFFICIAL SPORTSWEAR SPONSOR · OFFICIAL CLUB SPONSOR · OFFICIAL MATCH SPONSOR

CHELSEA vs TOTTENHAM
12.45PM 11.03.06
www.chelseafc.com £3.00

Peter Osgood, the King of Stamford Bridge, featured heavily in the matchday programme following his death in 2006. Also included here are tributes to Ian Porterfield, Dave Sexton, Lord Attenborough and John Neal.

OSSIE OBITUARY

The King who reigned supreme

From bricklayer to master marksman, Peter Osgood is assured of his place in folklore at Stamford Bridge
By Neil Barnett

Peter Osgood, rejected by football's scouting network as a schoolboy, made his Chelsea debut aged 17 and went on to become this club's greatest centre-forward.

He was part of the side that won our first FA Cup and our first European trophy.

Born on February 20, 1947 in Windsor, he was rejected after trials at Arsenal and Reading and in 1962 left school to become a bricklayer.

When he was 16 his uncle wrote to Chelsea requesting a trial. It went so well that, with scouts from several other clubs watching, at half-time he was withdrawn and immediately offered a contract.

Before he established himself in the first team, he played in the youth team's Junior Floodlit Cup Final at West Ham and the reserve team's London County Cup Final at Brentford and scored in both. He scored more than a goal a game for the reserves.

In November 1964 manager Tommy Docherty took him to a League Cup fifth-round tie at Third Division Workington where, before substitutes, he sat with the manager and watched an embarrassing 2-2 draw.

Docherty threw him in for the replay on December 16, replacing England centre-forward Barry Bridges who had scored both goals in the original match.

With 10 minutes to go and the score still 0-0, he ghosted on to a Terry Venables pass and slipped a left-footed shot past the goalkeeper. Before the end he converted in a scramble. Chelsea won 2-0. A star was born.

He didn't play again that season. But the following campaign Docherty chose him to face Roma in the Inter-Cities Fairs Cup, the predecessor to the Uefa Cup, and then in the 13th league game of the campaign put him in the team and told him to relax. He played for the next 10 matches and Bridges was moved to the right wing.

Immediately the 6ft 2in No 9 was a success. He glided across the ground, he tricked and manoeuvred his way past opponents, he scored and set up goals. He had grace and unique technique.

In the Inter-Cities Fairs Cup his star shone brightest. Against Austria Vienna he dived to head the aggregate winner. Against AC Milan he struck a venomous left-footed half-volley from outside the area to draw the aggregate. Against Munich 1860 he scored another winner. His goals were at Stamford Bridge. The country was talking about him and demands for an England place were already being made. A King was born.

At this stage he was not leading the line. Playing next to George Graham who did that, he was the second striker. But when Graham was swapped for Tommy Baldwin at the start of the following

10   Chelsea vs Tottenham Hotspur

Ossie shows his skill and grace at Stamford Bridge in 1972

A minute's appreciation for Ossie

Today is the opportunity for Stamford Bridge to celebrate the life and career of the King, Peter Osgood.

Last week's minute's silence against West Bromwich Albion, to mark the passing of Ossie, was impeccably observed by both sets of fans.

This week is a celebration of his career. There will be a minute's appreciation just before kick-off, signalled by referee Graham Poll. In the centre circle will also

be a wreath which will say, 'Ossie, King of Stamford Bridge'.

Chelsea players will be wearing black armbands and both teams will be joined at the centre of the pitch by some of Ossie's former team-mates and colleagues.

At the time of going to press the following were due to be attending: Ron Harris, Tommy Baldwin, Alan Birchenall, Peter Bonetti, John Boyle, Barry Bridges,

Charlie Cooke, who has flown in from the USA, John Dempsey, George Graham, John Hollins, Steve Kember, Paddy Mulligan, who has flown in from Ireland, Bert Murray, Terry Venables, David Webb and our former club secretary Chris Matthews.

Also in the crowd today as special guests of Chelsea will be Lynn, Peter's widow, his sons Anthony, Mark, who has flown in from Cyprus and Darren, Elaine

Hutchinson, widow of Ian and Ossie's close friend Andy McLoughlin.

Highlights of Ossie's glittering career will be played regularly on the big screens so please come onto the ground early to enjoy those great moments.

This matchday programme is dedicated to him with the special commemorative cover and features tributes from his former team-mates.
• For Peter Osgood memorial news and how you can pay your respects see page 17.

OSSIE HUMOUR

Ossie sharing his vocal chords with Alan Hudson (centre) and Eddie McCreadie

When Peter Osgood was around you could always be sure that he would greet you with a big smile and have gag-a-plenty lined up to provide the laughs.

An entertainer on and off the pitch

Raise a smile with some of Peter Osgood's favourite tales

OSSIE TRIBUTES

'The King has died. Long live the King'

Chelsea FC chairman Bruce Buck pays a club tribute to the late Peter Osgood, The King of Stamford Bridge...

Ossie saluting the fans at Stamford Bridge just four weeks ago as his half-time walk...

OSSIE TRIBUTES

'To buy him today you'd have to recoup the money the Tonbridge depot robbers stole!'

Several people can't be here in person today to pay their respects to Peter Osgood, so they have sent these tributes, starting with The Doc...

Tommy Docherty
Ossie's manager - 1963-67

Ron Sheilto
Ossie cleaned his boots as a trainee - 1963-65

Marvin Hinton
Team-mate, room-mate - 1964-74

Dave Sexton
Ossie's manager - 1967-74

Eddie McCreadie
Team-mate - 1964-74

Bobby Tambling
Team-mate - 1959-70

Alan Hudson
Team-mate - 1966-74

OSSIE OBITUARY

season, his role changed. It made no difference to his progress.

On October 1, 1966 he scored another virtuoso goal in a 4-1 win at Manchester City which put Chelsea top of the league. But in the very next game, a League Cup tie at Blackpool, his leg was broken in a tackle by Emlyn Hughes and he missed the rest of the campaign, including the 1967 FA Cup Final defeat.

When he returned he was bigger, stronger, less mobile, less pacy, just as skilful – a similar yet different player. In 1967/68 he didn't miss a game, playing in 48 matches and scoring 16 goals.

But he was struggling to reproduce the heights of before his injury and in 1968/69 spent over half the season in midfield where his skills flourished.

He was still there for the first game of the 1969/70 season which Chelsea lost 4-1 at Liverpool. Various configurations were tried over the next few weeks before, on November 8, a pattern was established. Charlie Cooke on the right-wing, 18-year-old Alan Hudson in midfield with John Hollins and Peter Houseman on the left, and Ossie up front with Ian Hutchinson. Ossie scored once, Hutch two, in a 3-1 win over Sheffield Wednesday and Chelsea shot up the table and went on to win the FA Cup for the first time in 1970. In fact, he scored in every Cup Final he participated in for Chelsea.

Hutchinson played the barnstorming centre-forward role, again allowing Ossie to become the free spirit. Not only was he one of ▶

Osgood (far right) holds the FA Cup aloft with John Dempsey in the bath at Old Trafford

DAVE SEXTON
1930-2012

Ian Porterfield

OBITUARY
'HE WAS ONE OF FOOTBALL'S NICE PEOPLE'

That was Paul Elliott's tribute to former Chelsea manager Ian Porterfield, who died this week. It was one of many from the friends he made during his time at Stamford Bridge

Club mourns the loss of a legend

JOHN NEAL
1932-2014

"HE WAS A FABULOUS READER OF CHARACTERS. MOST OF US KNOW HOW MUCH WE OWE HIM; AND I CERTAINLY WAS ALWAYS AWARE OF THAT FACT"

A LEGEND REMEMBERED

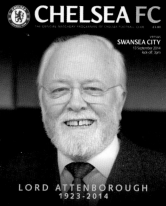

CHELSEA FC
THE OFFICIAL MATCHDAY PROGRAMME OF CHELSEA FOOTBALL CLUB £3.00

versus
SWANSEA CITY
13 September 2014
kick off: 3pm

LORD ATTENBOROUGH
1923-2014

21ST CENTURY

A new millennium brought unprecedented success for the Blues as domestic dominance engineered our elevation to the European summit. Driven by a change in ownership, these were exciting times, especially as the trophies kept on coming

At the start of the 21st century, Chelsea's fortunes had already begun to transform in such a way that fans were fully accustomed to seeing us win major silverware again. We had experienced success in three separate cup competitions at the tail-end of the last millennium, as well as qualifying for the Champions League for the first time, and the club had certainly come a long way from the one that had tasted life in Division Two just over a decade beforehand.

The goal now was to move to the next level. There was no argument that we possessed a squad packed with talented players who were clearly capable of beating anybody on their day, but in order to compete with the best sides in England and across Europe for the very biggest honours, something else was required.

Of course, the arrival of Roman Abramovich in the summer of 2003 was the catalyst for the most successful period in the club's history as a grand total of 13 pieces of major silverware were won from the day the Russian bought the club until the end of the 2014/15 season.

The matchday programme has captured this era perfectly, with fascinating features from some of the best players in the world, to insightful manager's and captain's columns, not to mention an array of celebratory material to accompany our numerous successes. Much of the material in this chapter may be fresh in the memory banks of many readers, but it doesn't make it any less enjoyable.

New season – new men

Welcome to Chelsea Jimmy Floyd Hasselbaink (*top left*) – interviewed Page 24; welcome Mario Stanic (*top right*) – interviewed Page 26; welcome Christian Panucci (*bottom left*) – interviewed Page 44; welcome Eidur Gudjohnsen (*bottom right*) – interviewed Page 52.

Hasselbaink here to win some medals

To all those Premiership defenders who hated the sight of Jimmy Floyd Hasselbaink when you saw him last – we have some bad news for you!

Jimmy reckons he's now even more dangerous.

"I learned a lot in my time in Spain," he warns. "And I've played with a lot of good players at Atletico Madrid.

"I have definitely become a more mature player than I was at Leeds. There's no one thing special I have added to my game but I had quite a hard time over there and that makes you stronger."

Jimmy's certainly done his best to preview his progress in pre-season. From scoring within minutes of pulling on a blue shirt for the first time at Kingstonian, through to striking a blow against big rivals at Wembley, it has all been going rather to plan.

"It's always a relief to score and it is always a relief to win," he says, contemplating his Charity Shield goal last Sunday. "Of course it was a special feeling. It is always important for your self-esteem and morale to hit the net and I was very happy and very pleased."

The 2000/01 season began in jubilant fashion for the Blues. Having beaten Manchester United 2-0 in the Charity Shield, we saw off London rivals West Ham 4-2 in an entertaining Premier League opener at the Bridge. The programme looked back at the previous season's FA Cup triumph and welcomed an array of new talent including Jimmy Floyd Hasselbaink, who had scored his first goal for the club in our Wembley victory over the Red Devils.

Charity Shield won again at last

Chelsea nearly took the lead through Mario Stanic's far post header (below) from Gianfranco Zola's cross, and through Jimmy Floyd Hasselbaink's shot (bottom) after he'd forced his way past Silvestre, but both efforts were wide. Still, after 21 minutes Jimmy hit the target (opposite top) for the first time as a Chelsea player when he powered his drive through Stam. One-nil to us. Frank Leboeuf dealt with goal (centre right). Near the end Ed de Goey made sure of another clean sheet (bottom) when he beat out Beckham's free-kick.

Gianluca Vialli made way for new boss Claudio Ranieri, who was introduced to fans in the programme for our October fixture with Liverpool. His first notes are on page 168. Meanwhile, Frank Leboeuf reflected on our thrilling 2-2 draw against Arsenal – a match which the Frenchman said highlighted the growing pace of the game. Although the season was something of an anti-climax, as we finished without silverware and sixth in the league, there was good news in the final programme, against Everton, with the announcement of a new deal for Gianfranco Zola and the opening of the revamped West Stand.

Continental teams, English pace

Was there a faster game this season than Chelsea v Arsenal? Frank Leboeuf went bombing through Grimandi and Kanu – all overseas players – with the match being played at a fraught, English pace. Will it be the same today with the overseas players of Chelsea and Liverpool?

" I think everybody tries to play the English football and not the other way round. You come to England because you want to play English football "

" You have to adapt and bring your experience. You don't try to slow it down, you just try to keep your identity up. "

" Since more overseas players have come here, the Premiership has not changed at all. I think it's as quick now as when I first came. It's probably stronger technically and tactically, but it's as physical. "

" You have no time to rest in English football. You just have to find time to rest a little bit. But you still have the same rules, you can still tackle more from behind in English football, so you can still give 150 per cent when you stand off in another country. Or if you didn't stand off there, you'd get sent off. Here, you just go fast and give everything of yourself "

FRANK LEBŒUF

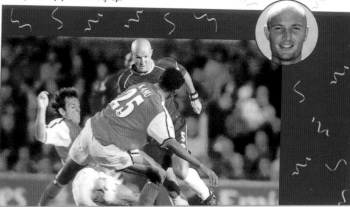

Franco forever! Four year deal

Having agreed his new contract which will keep him at Chelsea for another four years, Gianfranco Zola talked reflectively about this season.

"Sometimes you have to slow down to accelerate again.

"Hopefully this is the age, and we can learn from our mistakes and try harder next year."

His new contract keeps him as a player next year and the following one, and after that for another two years in a capacity yet to be agreed.

He hasn't got coaching qualifications at the moment and intends to focus on playing for now, so what that capacity will be deliberately remains an open

question.

Colin Hutchinson sealed the deal and then declared: "It was always my hope that Franco would finish his career here, and in the many discussions we have had over the years he has stressed how important it is to him that he goes out at the top.

"He's not a player to slip down the divisions. With his pride and professionalism, I'm sure that it will happen the way he wants."

On the extra two years after playing, Colin added: "He's so loved by the supporters, he'll be a wonderful ambassador for the club. We haven't discussed in depth what he'll do. It could be anything."

There was no concern at Franco's age in giving him two more years as a player.

Because of the way he approaches his football, aged 35 at the beginning of next season, it is still felt he has something to give.

"I'm going to give it my best shot," he said. "I believe I can still give something on the pitch. Obviously I am not like I was five years ago, I can't play 60 games a season. But I believe I have something to give."

Today he is giving something for that UEFA Cup qualification place.

The man who many believe to be the finest player in the history of Chelsea plays on.

Future legend ready to make his mark, 2001/02

The 2001/02 campaign began with a home match against Newcastle United. Frank Lampard did not make his Chelsea debut until the following week, away to Southampton, but he was introduced to the fans in the Magpies programme following his summer switch from West Ham. Perhaps the most telling comment of his opening programme piece was "I see myself as a goalscoring midfielder". Over the next 13 years, we would watch Lamps set previously unseen tallies for the Blues. This programme contained Marcel Desailly's first programme notes as full-time skipper (see page 171) and a look into the mindset of a future leader of the club in John Terry's Self Portrait. There was also a plug for Chelsea TV, which had recently launched as a subscription channel.

NEWS & ISSUES NEW SIGNINGS

When East End boy becomes West End boy – welcome Frank Lampard

When £11m Frank Lampard signed for Chelsea from West Ham, he said that one of his ambitions was to reclaim his place in the England squad.

He has achieved that even before making his Chelsea debut. Last week he was Sven-Göran Eriksson's West London boy as England took on Holland (who had four West London boys – three Chelsea, one Fulham).

And he had a new haircut to go with it. The razor blade's come out.

AI

"It's a thing I've wanted to do for a while," he laughed while in Italy with Chelsea last weekend, "but I didn't have the courage.

"My sister says I've got a head like a football. It's a big head physically. I feared it was too round. It probably is!

"But with a change of colours, I thought I'd have a change of image.

"Obviously I'm very happy with the England call-up. It's always such a great experience, I want to be there, and to begin my Chelsea career being an England man is very good."

This is the second season running Frank Lampard is playing his first game of the campaign at Stamford Bridge. A year ago it was for West Ham in their 4-2 defeat. That was a difficult time for him.

The previous year he had started the season early in the Intertoto Cup and finished it late captaining England Under 21s in the European Championships. That season demanded its toll.

"I got a little injury pre-season and took it into the game against Chelsea," he admitted. "And then I had an injury at the end of last season.

"This season I feel as fit as ever, if not more so. I'm refreshed mentally.

"It's been such a massive change, and I've really been looking forward to playing, to being involved in a new set-up.

"The training's been different. The Italian preparations are different from the basically English set-up I had at West Ham. That taught me so many good things, but now it's different ideas which can add to those.

"It's very much more scheduled here. There's a big pre-season plan. We're running to specific times, doing more leg weights than I've ever done before. So you're getting quicker and fitter as pre-season proceeds.

"Obviously, it's all to the same end product in both ways. Here we spend more time with the fitness coach than at West Ham. And with the double sessions almost every day, and the second one being late, you're getting home at seven or eight o'clock at night. That's longer than what I'm used to."

Around the training ground and training camp he's generally laid-back, quiet and relaxed.

But that didn't stop him giving his all when he had to participate in the traditional 'new boys' performance at the training camp.

"I sang 'Maybe It's Because I'm A Londoner'," he laughed. "It's the only song I know the words to," he added pointedly.

This, of course, is untrue. There is a certain song about 'Bubbles' that he's grown up with. But he is definitely Chelsea now.

And his Chelsea credentials were further established when

Frank's games pre-season

"It's often said that I'm quite calm off the pitch yet fiery on it.

Being on a football pitch is a totally different atmosphere to normal life. You have to be really pumped up. How many people in their life go through the emotions you go through on a football pitch?

Not many. I think it's very difficult to judge people's characters when they're in such a heated environment.

I don't think I'm explosive away from it. It's all down to frustration. Players in general tend to do reckless things if they get frustrated over a period of time.

I'm quite a determined person though and I think I'd be competitive whatever I did. I hope I'm as driven as I was when I was younger. It is important you remain that way throughout your career."

Graeme Le Saux

First Person | Chelsea v Everton | News and Issues | The Fans | Happy Anniversary | Behind The Scenes | Statistics

Chelsea Rock

Personality chairman needs personality team

First of all today, I want to say hello and happy anniversary to Mr. Bates. Wonderful, wonderful!

When he came so many years ago, he started everything, slowly, slowly, and he must be proud of what he has done.

DESAILLY

By personality, I mean we must play with more confidence and play the ball, the ball!

Now all Europe knows of Chelsea and the club has been winning quite a lot. I can only say congratulations and that I have a lot of respect for him.

In our last game at Stamford Bridge against Derby, the team didn't play well. After Liverpool we were not quite right – maybe it was tiredness, I don't know.

At half-time, the manager was really, really, really upset and we were a little bit lucky to win but we have no regrets about this. The three points were important for us. Also there was nothing special with Ravanelli this time! Everybody has been professional.

After that game, we arrived in Ipswich not so confident as we have been recently. We did not know how we were going to react and understand why we didn't play really well...

By personality, I mean we must play with more confidence and play the ball, play the ball! Sometimes it is more like we are afraid or we are expecting something to happen.

Today we face Everton and I am sorry that we will not find Gascoigne with them. I was looking forward to playing against him again as I did when I was at Lazio.

But still Everton have other players I know a lot about. There are Ginola and Campbell, although they may not play today, but even then, they will still have a good team.

They do not need many points to be safe this season so they will come here believing they can get them today, making it difficult for us.

The result will depend on the spirit of Chelsea. The weather is going to be good, the pitch is going to be good so we have to straight away from the start show there is nothing for them in this game.

We are happy because we still have two possibilities to do well this season - in the Premiership by reaching the Champions League and in the FA Cup by reaching the Final. We are intelligent enough to realise both are important.

I can promise you we will not be thinking about the semi-final until after we have played Blackburn on Wednesday. Today is the Premiership so we will give our best for this. Today is also a day for Chelsea to show everyone that we have personality.

First of all today, I want to say hello and happy anniversary to Mr. Bates. Wonderful, wonderful!

DESAILL...

When he came so many years ago, the team started everything, slowly, slowly, and he must be proud of what he has done.

Now all Europe knows of Chelsea and the club has ...n winning quite a lot. I can...

By personal... mean we mus... with more confic... play the ball, ball!

When the Blues took on Everton in April 2002, it was a landmark for Chairman Ken Bates who was marking his 20th anniversary at the club. Among those to praise him was skipper Marcel Desailly. A few weeks later, our Manchester United programme contained interesting articles with John Terry and Graeme Le Saux. You can read a Q&A with Jimmy Floyd Hasselbaink on page 115.

PLAYERS AND COACHES JOHN TERRY

Considering the question of nerves, and when he has suffered most from them, softly spoken John Terry comes up with an admission.

"I do get a bit nervous before every game. I think that's good. You can't take anything for granted.

"I think it was the Fulham game when I was most nervous. It was my biggest for Chelsea. We went up two days before and had more time to think about it.

"We had a few hours in the afternoon on the Sunday to sleep, and I couldn't. Then before the game I felt a little bit more nervous than I usually do."

What then did he feel about his full debut back in January 1999, a freezing afternoon in Oldham when he played right-back in the FA Cup?

"Obviously, I felt nervous then. I got told the afternoon before. Luca pulled me in training, and I didn't really have time to take it in. So I was nervous but not as much as I expected to be."

The first time he played centre-back from the start he doesn't remember (Bradford away, 2000) so it can't have been difficult on that occasion. But his England Under 21s debut was definitely a case in point.

"Away to Finland, and it was the same again. I don't think I was down to play, but Howard Wilkinson went off to take the full team, and there were injuries to centre-halves and he took, I think, Wes Brown with him the afternoon before the game.

"So a few hours before

Sammy Lee took me to one side and said he was going to play me. So again, I had no time."

JT!

FA Cup semi-final winner John Terry may appear to know no fear, but he suffers from butterflies

What about after his appearances in the non-sports pages of the newspapers recently? Have those made him nervous come the next match?

He is hammer-sure about this. "I don't think the papers put extra pressure on me. They might with some, but with me it's in one ear and out the other.

"I concentrate on my game and they've not affected me at all."

If not the watching papers, what about the watching Sven-Göran Eriksson, a regular Chelsea viewer?

"No! He could be at any game and I don't know about

Twelve stitches in the forehead and a bloody post. John Terry with the upright he crashed into after the 3-0 win over Everton

Manchester City   Saturday 22nd March 2003, Kick-off 3.00pm

Tottenham Hotspur   Saturday 1st February 2003, Kick-off 3.00pm

Blackburn Rovers   Saturday 22nd February 2003, Kick-off 3.00pm

CHELSEA vs MANCHESTER CITY

300 CLUB: GIANFRANCO ZOLA

Signed at 30, and now he's played 300

Gianfranco Zola made his 300th Chelsea appearance in our last home match.

He is Chelsea's record goalscorer in the Premiership; no-one has won more trophies with the club and he is the only Chelsea player ever to have been made Footballer of the Year.

And just for good measure Chelsea supporters have voted him the greatest player in our club's history.

That's not a bad record for someone who, according to some at the time, only came here to boost his pension fund.

"A lot of people were thinking that it was the last stage of my career and there was not much time left for me to give something to football," says Franco.

"I am pleased to have proved them wrong because my motivation was always football not money."

Sometimes it is hard to remember that the club Franco joined, while still ambitious, was not the one it has become. It had been 25 years since we had won a trophy and had appeared in European competition just once in that time. Chelsea may have seemed a strange choice for Franco.

"I was highly motivated to come to Chelsea. I was having a bad time and needed to move. It was a new challenge and a new country.

"Also, I just had my 30th birthday so it was the right time in my life for the change in culture as well as the change in club.

"When I came here Robbie Di Matteo and Vialli were here and I spoke to them. They said some very positive things about the club and its ambitions. I knew that it was a good club and it was going up. I knew that

> I am so proud to play for Chelsea and the supporters here, and it gives me so much pleasure that people think I can contribute

it was the right move."

Of course, that long wait for a trophy ended in Franco's first season. He rates winning the FA Cup that first time as the greatest moment in his career and the significant stage in the development of the team.

"It was an unbelievable experience and a fantastic atmosphere. It gave me the most satisfaction. There was a momentum about the whole tournament.

"I will always remember the game against Liverpool when we were two down and came back to win. The atmosphere was sizzling and we could feel it in the air.

"That is the FA Cup. It is such a fantastic competition because it is so uncertain. Every team always fights against the big clubs so anything can happen and whoever wins deserves to."

And without the FA Cup win there would have been no Cup Winners' Cup, and another special Franco moment would not have existed.

"That was a great moment for the club because we wanted to prove ourselves in Europe. I was injured before the final and nearly missed it.

"I went back to Italy for treatment and it was quite miraculous the recovery. I didn't play before the final and was substitute but came on to score immediately. It was a dream after the problems I had to play."

IPS

Zola signs off in style but there's no fairytale finish as trophy hunt continues, 2002/03

For a club that had really got a taste for winning things again in the latter years of the 20th century, a third season in succession without silverware may have been a tough one for fans to stomach on the surface, but a finish inside the top four in 2002/03 led to historic changes, and nothing would ever quite be the same again for Chelsea FC. Here we bring you extracts from several programmes during the second half of that campaign, including a feature with Gianfranco Zola who enjoyed an inspired final season with the club, achieving his best goals haul of 16 and passing the 300-appearance landmark. We also have the programme from our final fixture against Liverpool, which ended in a 2-1 win as we secured that all-important Champions League spot.

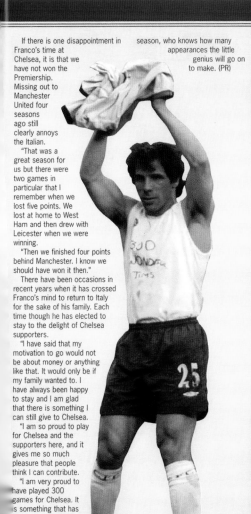

If there is one disappointment in Franco's time at Chelsea, it is that we have not won the Premiership. Missing out to Manchester United four seasons ago still clearly annoys the Italian.

"That was a great season for us but there were two games in particular that I remember when we lost five points. We lost at home to West Ham and then drew with Leicester when we were winning.

"Then we finished four points behind Manchester. I know we should have won it then."

There have been occasions in recent years when it has crossed Franco's mind to return to Italy for the sake of his family. Each time though he has elected to stay to the delight of Chelsea supporters.

"I have said that my motivation to go would not be about money or anything like that. It would only be if my family wanted to. I have always been happy to stay and I am glad that there is something I can still give to Chelsea.

"I am so proud to play for Chelsea and the supporters here, and it gives me so much pleasure that people think I can contribute.

"I am very proud to have played 300 games for Chelsea. It is something that has made me very happy."

With Franco in such outstanding form this season, who knows how many appearances the little genius will go on to make. (PR)

The Franco connection

"I have said it many times that I have a fantastic relationship with the Chelsea fans.

"I never tire of saying it. I have the best reception that any footballer can expect from his supporters.

"I have never had the connection with supporters like the one I have now at Chelsea and I am not just making that up to flatter them because I know that it is true.

"All through my career I have wanted to have this connection and I am so proud that it has happened here.

"I am very lucky because I have also earned respect from opposition supporters and also the press in England. I have never asked for anything other than that.

"And what can I say about the supporters voting me as the best Chelsea player ever. It is very humbling for me. Let's talk about something else because this is beginning to embarrass me."

IPS

The Captain
Marcel Desailly

CONCENTRATE ON DOING NORMAL JOB

COLOURS OF BOUDEWIJN ZENDEN'S MIND

Thanks fans

Russian revolution brings us silverware solution, 2003/04

The date of 1 July 2003 brought an historic moment for Chelsea FC, as Roman Abramovich purchased the club and changed our fortunes beyond all comprehension. Leicester City were the visitors for our first home game of the season, with the programme containing an exclusive column with Mr Abramovich (see page 173). We soon faced Zilina in a Champions League qualifier, winning 5-0 on aggregate to go through to the group stages.

August 13, 2003
Back in the UEFA Champions League

Top John Terry, Carlo Cudicini, Mikael Forssell, Eidur Gudjohnsen, Marcel Desailly, Frank Lampard. **Bottom** Glen Johnson, Gérémi, Wayne Bridge, Damien Duff, Juan Sebastián Verón.

MSK Zilina 0
Chelsea 2

MSK ŽILINA VS CHELSEA
Wednesday August 13th 2003

CHELSEA VS LIVERPOOL
Sunday May 11th 2003

CHELSER vs ARSENAL WEDNESDAY 24th MARCH 2004

UEFA CHAMPIONS LEAGUE: The Story So Far

2003/4

Qualifiers
August
1. Marcel Desailly led the team out in Zilina.

Group Stage
September
2. Chelsea supporters enjoyed Prague. 3. The team arrived to win in Prague.

October
4. Adrian Mutu hit the winner at home to Lazio and we went top of the Group.

November
5. Lazio 0 Chelsea 4. Europe sat up, and Hernán Crespo stood up after scoring the first.

December
6. The bench sheltered from missiles under umbrellas in Gelsenkirchen after going one up against Besiktas.

Round One
February
7. Germany again. It was just another away game as the kit and supplies were unloaded in Stuttgart.

March
8. Damien Duff couldn't find a way past Hildebrand at home but we were the qualifiers over Stuttgart which is why we're here today.

BLUE PRINTS

CHELSER vs AS MONACO WEDNESDAY 5th MAY 2004

ARSENAL vs CHELSEA
Tuesday April 6th 2004

Arsenal 1
Reyes 45

Chelsea 2
Lampard 50
Bridge 86

Arsenal
Lehmann; Lauren, Touré, Campbell, Cole; Ljungberg, Vieira, Edu, Pires; Reyes, Henry (Bergkamp 81).

Chelsea
Ambrosio; Melchiot, Gallas, Terry, Bridge; Parker (Gronkjaer 45), Lampard, Makelele, Duff (Cole 82); Gudjohnsen, Hasselbaink (Crespo 82).

Attendance
35,486

Referee
Markus Merk

Blue Prints
1. Damien Duff, pressured by Edu, shot just wide after a great run had taken him past Touré. 2. Just five minutes of football passed between Reyes giving Arsenal the lead, and Frank Lampard equalising after Lehmann failed to hold Claude Makelele's shot. 3. Eidur Gudjohnsen's drive from Joe Cole's cross looked to have won the tie, but Ashley Cole cleared off the line. 4. So instead, two minutes later, Wayne Bridge won the tie with his third Chelsea goal, Eidur having supplied the

There were plenty of European matches to savour during this season, as we reached the semi-finals of the Champions League for the first time. The quarter-final against Arsenal was a classic nail-biter as we won 3-2 on aggregate, and action from that match appeared in the programme for the encounter with Monaco in the last four, where our run in the competition sadly came to an end.

It was not only in Europe where we fared well in 2003/04, but also in the Premier League, recording a second-place finish – our best since we were crowned champions in 1955. The programme for our April game against Everton contained an interesting piece with Peter Osgood, who named his all-time favourite Chelsea XI. The final game of the campaign was against Leeds and the programme reviewed a whirlwind period for the club. The fans may well have sensed that something special was coming, but perhaps not so soon…

PETER OSGOOD'S GREATEST XI

Passions for the club matters most of all

Peter Osgood admitted a problem in picking his Greatest Chelsea XI.

He'd be biased too much to the players of his day. But when he went away to select his team, putting it in 4-3-3 formation, he found room for a few from the modern era too.

Peter Bonetti

"He was absolute class. He was second best in the world to Banksy. Cudicini's a great goalkeeper, but Catty did it for 20 years."

Steve Clarke

"He was just so consistent. Mr Reliable. And he had passion for the club. He looked after himself so he played to a good age. Not only was he a good player, I think he was underrated."

Ron Harris

"Chopper! He was the Guv'nor. Don't worry about Paul Ince and all his talk. Paul Ince wouldn't last two minutes with Chopper – or Buller as we called him."

John Terry

"Again, a passionate lad, passionate for the club. That's so important. Plays with passion. And he does it against the best. Another leader. He'll be the England captain one day."

Eddie McCreadie

"Different class. He was quick, he had flair, he was fast into the tackle and got in hard – another hard player and another really good player."

Charlie Cooke

"He could do absolutely anything except score goals. He was quick, he was strong and of course he was a great dribbler. And he was a great passer as his pass for me in the Cup Final Replay proved. Apart form scoring goals he had everything."

Alan Hudson

"What a class act! Probably the best player I actually played with at Chelsea. He could get the game by the scruff of its neck and take complete control of it. Great passing, great dribbling, great engine."

Dennis Wise

"You can see it at Millwall now with him and the way his side is playing.

Wisey had and still has passion. He was full of life at Chelsea, he was a good footballer who influenced games and he was a good leader."

Gianfranco Zola

"Not quite the King of Stamford Bridge, that will always be me, but what a special man, what a great player for club and country. Love him."

Mark Hughes

"Every club he's gone to he receives a great reception when he returns. Manchester United and us, obviously, but Southampton, Blackburn, everyone. He's always given 100 per cent and he gets in just in front of my big mate Hutch, Ian Hutchinson."

Jimmy Floyd Hasselbaink

"I was a goalscorer and I know goalscorers. He's consistent and he's second to none. He scores great goals and wins games, and he does it regularly. He's nearly as good as I was! That's why I like him!"

Peter Osgood played 380 games and scored 150 goals for Chelsea, won the FA And European Cup Winners' Cups, scoring in the Finals, and scored in the League Cup Final as well. He is the King. He is doing corporate work at the club again.

Hasselbaink	Hughes	Zola	
Wise	Hudson	Cooke	
McCreadie	Terry	Harris	Clarke
	Bonetti		

Chelsea Village Restaurants: Fishnets – 020 7565 1430; K

CHELSEA vs LEEDS UNITED SATURDAY 15th MAY 2004

Congratulations on our best position for 49 years

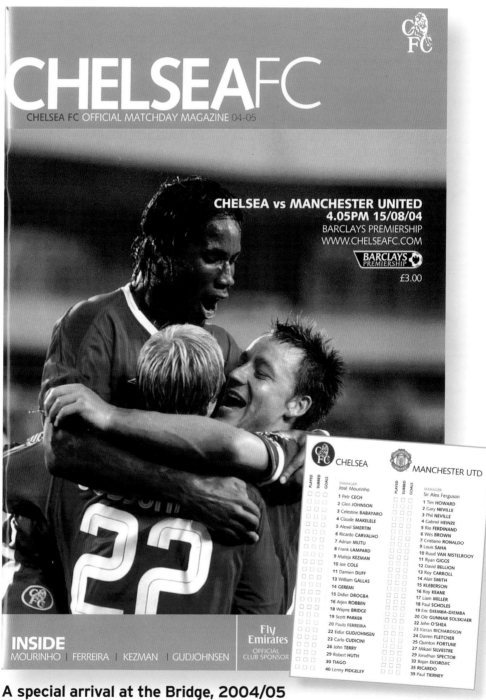

A special arrival at the Bridge, 2004/05

The programme took on a distinctive new look at the start of the 2004/05 campaign, with silver featuring prominently on the cover, although following the arrival of José Mourinho as manager, the only thing the club would be going for this season was gold. You can read Mourinho's first notes as Blues gaffer on page 169. These appeared in the programme for our opening game, versus Manchester United, who we set our stall out against with a 1-0 victory.

A couple of programmes of note during the opening stages of this incredible season came against Porto and Bolton. We faced the Portuguese side in Champions League Group H, after they had won the competition the previous campaign under Mourinho. He spoke of the importance of the fans in his notes, while the news pages highlighted the development of the club's new state-of-the-art training centre in Cobham. Bolton would become famous opponents for other reasons later in the season, but the programme for our home game against the Trotters contained a story on the unveiling of a new club badge as part of our centenary celebrations.

COBHAM: A solid foundation for the club to build on

Unveiled: the badge for the
NEXT 100 YEARS...

New designs to begin Centenary celebrations

Chelsea last week launched a new badge that will represent the club for the next 100 years.

The new design was unveiled at a packed Stamford Bridge press conference by Chelsea's life vice president Lord Attenborough, the club's chief executive Peter Kenyon, manager and first team coach José Mourinho, and business affairs director Paul Smith.

It replaces the previous badge which has been in place since 1986. Prior to that there have been only three official club badges during Chelsea's history.

Fans have been keen for many years for a return to the badge first used by the club in 1953 which was also the official badge when the League Championship was won, marking Chelsea's 50th anniversary in 1955.

There have been many campaigns run in fanzines requesting the club badge return to a more traditional style, and even a petition with several hundred signatures calling for change. As a result, the club took on board the overwhelming view of its supporters resulting in the new badge which is based significantly on the 1950's original.

The badge will be effective from May 2005, in time for the club's Centenary Season and a special

100 years of Chelsea: next season's special Centenary badge (left) and (above) the new regular badge of the club

Centenary version of the badge will be used during that year. The Centenary badge will feature on a special Centenary home kit during the 2005/06 season.

Kenyon opened the proceedings with an introductory speech during which he also revealed that the name Chelsea Village is to be phased out. From now on only one brand, Chelsea Football Club, will exist. The chief executive explained: 'We are incredibly proud of

Chelsea's heritage. The design of this new badge is based on the one from the 1950's and it was a conscious decision to do this.

'As we approach our Centenary Year, and the club embarks on a new and very exciting era, it is appropriate that we have a new identity that reflects our tradition and can represent us for the next 100 years.'

Lord Attenborough, a Chelsea fan for six decades, then regaled the audience with tales of his history with the club, including how he first got involved with Chelsea. It transpired

that when Lord Attenborough filmed the classic movie Brighton Rock in 1947, (the story of Pinkie Brown played by Richard Attenborough, a small town hoodlum whose gang run a protection racket based at Brighton race course), Richard trained with Tommy Lawton and John Harris for the part.

After his talk, Lord Attenborough played a short video of Chelsea's greatest moments, which will also be seen during today's matchday build-up, and then unveiled the new badge to a round of applause.

Lord Attenborough said: 'It is an emblem that personifies not only our past but also our excitement, dedication, ambition and aspirations for the future. I think it is terrific. It is beautifully designed and we couldn't ask for more artistically, because it says something.'

Smith followed Lord Attenborough to explain the idea behind the new badge, saying: 'The catalyst for this change was the Centenary, and we thought it would be a fitting moment to pay tribute to the club's longevity.

'A new era for Chelsea deserves and demands a new badge. In the past 100 years, Chelsea has been content with being the most popular club in west London. But the new Chelsea vision sees us challenging the idea that we can be the most popular club in the western hemisphere, and we add the eastern hemisphere to that challenge.

'Chelsea is a commercial enterprise, but first and foremost it is a sporting organisation and you can see from the design there is a balance between Chelsea and Football Club.

'Some people see this as a retro design, but for us that is a positive comment. We have taken the most famous and popular crest in Chelsea's history as the framework.'

The final word was left to José who summed the whole event up during a question and answer session.

'When I look to this lion, it looks arrogant, it is aggressive, it is powerful. He is proud of being a Chelsea lion,' said Mourinho.

'The last thing we do every game before we run onto the pitch from the dressing room is ask each other 'who are you', and everyone shouts from the heart, 'we are Chelsea!' and with this new identity, we may have some extra help.

'For me, for my players, and for the people working with me who feel the responsibility of winning, I think this badge will make us even more aware of our ambition.'

MANAGER'S NOTES
JOSÉ MOURINHO

After an excellent performance in the Premiership José calls on a big response from the fans in tonight's clash with his former club, the European champions

Good evening. Before tonight's match you think this must be a beautiful football night.

On one side is the European champions, on the other is a top team like Chelsea with big ambition in this competition. When you think about it you must believe this will be a great football match.

Before this match it was originally planned that I would receive an award from Uefa for being last season's winning coach in the Champions League.

It should have been presented in Monaco at the Uefa gala the night before the Supercup, but I couldn't be there because of our Southampton match. I had too many tasks here.

SO GLAD WE MADE IT
Mateja and Eidur celebrate a fantastic win at the Bridge

A major factor in the success Chelsea enjoyed under Mourinho is often cited as the fact we won the first piece of major silverware available under his stewardship. Here is the cover of the programme for our Champions League last-16 tie against Barcelona – our first home match after beating Liverpool in the League Cup final in Cardiff. JT's notes for the visit of Barca makes interesting reading. After losing the first leg 2-1 in Camp Nou, he dismissed claims the Blues were not up to the challenge, a point perfectly proved with a stunning 4-2 win on one of the most memorable European nights the Bridge has ever seen. Action from that game is shown in our West Brom programme, which also discussed the club's 100th birthday party held at The Butcher's Hook pub opposite the ground – the site of our formation in 1905 when it was known as The Rising Sun.

Birth of **the Blues**

MATCH REPORT

The Blues sealed our first title in 50 years with three games to spare thanks to a 2-0 win at Bolton on 30 April 2005. Our final Premier League game, at home to Charlton, was one of celebration as we lifted the trophy for the first time.

Champagne moment

 BOLTON 0 CHELSEA 2

Frank Lampard did his trademark badge-kissing celebration after scoring the two goals that confirmed Chelsea's first League championship triumph in 50 years, then the bubbly was popped

In 1983 Chelsea won a crucial end of season game in Bolton to ensure their survival in the old Second Division; how times change. Twenty-two years on and Bolton was again the venue as the Blues ended a 50-year wait to be crowned the greatest team in the land.

This performance was not perfect. John Terry revealed after the game that José Mourinho had offered to wear the players' shirts for them at half-time, such was his frustration. Shots from Frank Lampard and Jiri Jarosik were all the Blues had to show for their first-half efforts and they were a little fortunate to emerge with the score still goalless.

The manager would have been even more disappointed had Petr Cech not denied Stelios in the opening minutes and then Kevin Davies twice.

But Mourinho's words had the desired effect and after the break Chelsea played like champions, not by overwhelming Bolton – those kinds of performances came earlier in the season against Blackburn, Norwich and Newcastle at the Bridge, and against Fulham and Charlton away – but by resolutely grinding out a win against a team who are determined to reach

PAT NEVIN

It has been a real team effort under an outstanding manager. Chelsea have proved themselves over the whole season and deserve to be champions.

Chelsea 4 Blackburn 0

Saturday October 23

When Chelsea were being accused of being boring at the start of the season, José Mourinho warned that someone would be on the end of a thrashing, and it was lowly Blackburn. Eidur Gudjohnsen scored his first Chelsea hat-trick, one from the penalty spot, and Damien Duff made it four.

ARJEN ROBBEN clearly came prepared for the celebrations

LINE-UPS

Chelsea

Cech

Geremi Carvalho Terry Gallas

Makelele
(Smertin 90)
Lampard   Jarosik

Tiago
                    Gudjohnsen
          Drogba (Huth 65)   (Cole 85)

Diouf   Davies
                    Giannakopoulos
                    (Pedersen 63)

Speed   Okocha
          Hierro   (Nolan 63)

Gardner N'Gotty Ben Haim Candela
                    (Jaïdi 77)
          Jaaskelainen

Bolton

Unused subs
Chelsea: Kezman, Cudicini
Bolton: Poole, Fadiga

MATCH STATS

Saturday April 30, 2005

Goals: Lampard 60, 76 (Chelsea)
Booked: Candela, Diouf, Jaaskelainen, Nolan (Bolton); Makelele (Chelsea)
Sent-off: None
Referee: Steve Dunn (Gloucestershire)
Attendance: 27,653
Venue: Reebok Stadium

their own goal of European qualification. The spirit of the side was personified by John Terry, who played on despite a black eye which restricted his vision.

The breakthrough came, inevitably, from Lampard, who is now Chelsea's top scorer this season. On the hour mark he calmly stepped inside two defenders before firing home, and then 15 minutes later he again demonstrated his cool by latching onto Claude Makelele's breakaway pass and going round the keeper to score.

After that, the result – and the title – were in the bag, although it had taken another world class save from Cech – this time when his own player, Geremi, headed goalwards – to stop Bolton getting level in between Lampard's goals.

After the game, Chelsea's new championship-winning captain said: 'This is best feeling ever. We've worked so hard for this all season.

'We always seem to struggle up here. Kevin Davies was causing problems up front and to be truthful we got a bit of a telling off from the gaffer at half-time. He wanted each of us to liven up.'

Of goalscoring hero Lampard, Terry said: 'He was only saying last night

how great it would be to score the goal that won Chelsea the Premiership. I'm made up for him. I've run out of words for how good he is.'

The on-pitch celebrations in front of the Chelsea fans at the final whistle, which included the spraying of champagne, throwing of shirts and much collective running and diving, continued into the dressing rooms – where the players were joined by Roman Abramovich – and even onto the team bus when several players jumped onto the roof.

For the Chelsea faithful, they will go on much, much longer.

Lampard's first goal

Petr Cech's clearance was flicked on by Eidur Gudjohnsen before finding its way via Didier Drogba to Frank Lampard inside the box. The England midfielder then demonstrated why he is Chelsea's top scorer this season by showing a striker's instinct to ghost past two players and fire home. That was his 17th of the season, and number 18 followed soon after.

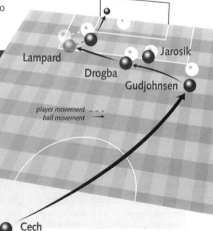

Lampard   Jarosik

Drogba
                    Gudjohnsen

player movement ----
ball movement ——→

Cech

West Brom 1   Chelsea 4

Saturday October 30

A poor first-half ended with William Gallas giving Chelsea the lead and the Blues never looked back after the break with Eidur Gudjohnsen and Damien Duff scoring either side of Zoltan Gera's consolation before Frank Lampard rounded off a wonderful display with a superb solo goal.

WRIGHT MAN FOR THE JOB

He's the big summer signing the fans wanted and he could make his home debut today. Shaun Wright-Phillips has arrived and couldn't feel more at home with life at Stamford Bridge...

By Neil Barnett

Shaun Wright-Phillips is enthusiastic, full of banter, he's confident – he's fitted into the first team squad straight away.

At 23, he was ready to join a big club and fight for the right to be selected rather than know he was an automatic choice each week. What he didn't know was how much the fans at Chelsea wanted him.

All through the January transfer window on the *Chelsea TV* phone-in and on various website chat pages, his was the number one name of discussion. The use of two wingers in an attack-minded formation had convinced many of the Chelsea faithful that this was the shape to build on, and that meant the squad needed another top man.

'I wasn't aware of that feeling at first,' Shaun declares, 'but since I've been here I've come to realise, and it's a great feeling.

'At the training ground when I meet fans I can tell by the way they come up to me.'

His settling into the camp was made easy by the England international players already in our ranks. Within hours of arriving he was telling everyone that he would beat computer football champion Glen Johnson no trouble.

And when he was challenged to put up or be scorned he retorted: 'I don't just talk, I deliver!'

For him, of course, coming to London is coming home. He grew up in south-east London, but left home at 16 to join Nottingham Forest.

He has two young children, son D'margio, three years old, and daughter D'neay, two. The joke at Chelsea is that he now has a third.

'That's what everyone says,' he laughs. 'They all say it.'

The third is Carlton Cole who he is close friends with. They know each other well from their England Under-21 days.

On the US tour Shaun was constantly knocking on Carlton's door and ensuring he wasn't late for any meetings or training sessions.

'I try to help out,' he laughs, with a big shrug. 'I hate being late. I'd rather get in early and just sit in the car.

'Carlton's alright at home, it's just in hotels. He sleeps in. But sometimes he goes down early and will knock on my door!'

Shaun is delighted with how Carlton has returned to the Bridge and been added to the squad. 'He deserves it,' he says. 'He's a great player and a great person in general. We get on well.'

It's been an eventful start for Shaun. He's won his first medal in his first game, the Community Shield, and came on at half-time at Wigan to play on the wing for 15 minutes and then drop back to wing-back as Chelsea switched to three defenders.

Now he'll be looking for a starting place in the line-up.

He has a big smile on his face. 'It's something all players want to do, win things, and to come and play one game and have the chance to walk away with a trophy, I can't be unhappy. The medal's in the flat until I get a cabinet in my house. I hope I'll need a big one.'

And that will not be in central London. 'I'm gonna be a suburb guy,' he exclaims. 'When I come away from training I like peace and quiet, to be

Chelsea vs Arsenal | 17

Centenary season celebrated with title defence, 2005/06

Having been crowned champions in May, the Blues beat Arsenal in the Community Shield before embarking on a 15-game unbeaten run in all competitions. We also faced the Gunners in our first home league fixture and the silver from last year's programme had now turned to gold, marking our centenary celebrations, as well as the previous campaign's triumphs. Among those featured was new arrival Shaun Wright-Phillips.

> Chelsea started a major industry in football in 1948 with the launch of the magazine-style programme

Proud Albert in the tunnel at Stamford Bridge with his MBE

The breakneck pace at which the Blues started the 2005/06 campaign blew many of our opponents away. Our long unbeaten sequence contained nine straight Premier League victories. The last of those was against Bolton in October, who we beat 5-1. The programme announced a new-look museum at Stamford Bridge and a feature with one of the main catalysts of our success, Claude Makelele. In our December programme against Fulham, there was a blast from the past as the club produced an in-depth feature on former editor Albert Sewell shortly after he received an MBE.

Museum opens its doors

Take a walk through our history as Lord Attenborough welcomes you to a century of Chelsea...

Anyone who's seen the film *Jurassic Park* will no doubt remember the moment that the extraordinary theme park is unveiled to the audience by Lord Attenborough's character John Hammond with the dramatic line, 'Welcome... to Jurassic Park', as the camera simultaneously pans across his spectacular creation.

Standing on a replica terrace at the start of the new Chelsea Centenary Museum, you can't help but be reminded of that moment, especially as Lord Attenborough is on hand to reprise the line to set the scene ahead of the new tour.

It's another sterling performance from Attenborough, who won an Oscar for directing *Ghandi*. He is, of course, a lifelong Blues fan and now the club's Life Vice President, and after he's guided you through a video presentation of some of Chelsea's greatest moments, you're then free to wander through the artefacts that perfectly document a century of highs and lows for the club, from its humble origins in 1905 to José Mourinho's all-conquering champions of 2005.

Designed by the company Weird and Wonderful, construction of the museum – located in the former Galleria in the Shed End – began at the end of last season. After months of meticulous planning and

gathering of artefacts, it is now finally open.

The museum is separated into ten sections, one for each decade of the club's existence. In each of these sections you can trace the team's progress through league tables and timelines while reliving the iconic moments of that particular era through video footage on plasma screens.

On the wall (the wall of balls) there is a celebration of all 627 players to play for Chelsea, with details of appearances and goals. Many of those famous names, including all of the current squad, as well as the likes of Ron Harris, Peter Osgood and Alan Hudson, have added their signatures to the wall. Look out for John Terry's, which says champions!

Further on in the tour and JT is brought to life in a lifesize waxwork mannequin, as is Frank Lampard and there is also a lifesize model of Roy Bentley, which is displayed in a cabinet with the original copy of his contract.

Much of the material was generously

donated by supporters, perhaps most notably by one lifelong fan who paid £22,000 for José Mourinho's famous grey coat (the proceeds of which went to the club's official charity CLIC Sargent) and he then kindly lent it to the museum for display.

Like all good stories, this journey through 100 years of Chelsea history has a happy ending. At the end of the Centenary Hall lies the 'crown jewels' in the trophy cabinet, where as well as artefacts from FA Cup triumphs and the two European Cup Winners' Cup glories, you can see the League Cup and the Community Shield and some of the more obscure honours the Blues have won over the years.

The climax, though, is the holy grail – the Premiership trophy. Entry to the Centenary Museum costs £5 for adults and £3 for concessions. If you want to take a Centenary Stadium Tour as well it's £13 for adults and £7 for concessions. For more information call 0870 603 0005.

The first visitors to Chelsea's new Centenary Museum after being greeted by Lord by Attenborough (below left)

Holding back the years

By March, and with the Blues hurtling towards a second consecutive title, José was hailing the heroics of our players, and assistant manager Steve Clarke discussed how the club was enjoying a history-making period. This was also a time of mourning for everybody connected with Chelsea as we lost one of our all-time greats, Peter Osgood. You can see the tributes to the King of Stamford Bridge on page 208.

HISTORY IN THE MAKING

Assistant coach Steve Clarke sees a bright future for Chelsea and he knows that if things carry on the way they are then no one will be able to accuse Chelsea of having no history

By Neil Barnett

The hero is the team

This group of players have given you three trophies and now we have an FA Cup semi-final to look forward to as well

Good afternoon. We are in the semi-finals of the FA Cup, but today we must think about the five victories we need to celebrate winning the Premiership title for the second year running, and we must go for it.

I understand the critics of those who don't want to see this club grow up. I also understand the great respect that you all show this group, a group that gave you a Premiership, a League Cup and a Community Shield. Now it's giving you a great lead in the current Premiership and a great semi-final to play in one month's time.

Today we have a game against a difficult side, a side that last season got a draw here, a side that beat us in Manchester, and a side that again gave us a difficult match when in December we beat them 1-0.

A team is a team, and teams win matches. There's a saying at the moment, 'The hero is the team', and I agree with that.

But to be honest, I feel that it is very unfair when match after match, week after week, I see Makelele go home without the Man of the Match award. This 'old' man is incredible week in, week out, and the other players are happy to have him here among them.

The players all appreciate the respect you show them

RECOR...

CHELSEA FC

SAMSUNG mobile

A comprehensive 3-0 win over Manchester United sealed our second Premier League crown in emphatic fashion and you can see extracts from the final home programme of a record-breaking campaign here.

There's no place like home...

Chelsea can equal the all-time top-flight home record by winning today. Set in 1905/6 by Newcastle, it is **Won 18, Drew 1** of 19 league games. At present we have **Won 17 and Drawn 1**. Our own all-time record, set in the old Second Division in that same season, is **Won 18, Lost 1**. So we can beat that today.

If we win our remaining three league games we will total **97** points, which would break the record-setting **95** points we totalled last season. Not surprisingly, we have established a number of other club and league records this season...

MANAGER'S NOTES
JOSÉ MOURINHO

One point from a great achievement

'It means so much to me'

John Terry after being voted our 2006 Player of the Year

CHAIRMAN'S MESSAGE

SAMSUNG mobile

The fans have to be the 12th man to spur on JT and co today

We have had an excellent Centenary year

high & mighty

All the 'superstar' talk in the media about Michael Ballack is way off the mark. As the gifted midfielder has shown throughout his career and already here at Chelsea, he's a team player with a genuine height threat

By Neil Barnett

New arrivals help lead Blues to cup double, 2006/07

Michael Ballack and Andriy Shevchenko were among the summer signings ahead of the 2006/07 campaign. The Ukrainian striker starred on the cover of the programme for our first league game, against Manchester City, alongside another new face, Salomon Kalou, while Ballack was the main feature inside. Our October Champions League tie against Barcelona came just four days after Petr Cech had suffered a horrific head injury against Reading, and the Barca programme reflected on the unfortunate events.

We all wish Petr a speedy recovery after surgery

We visited Pete and wished him a speedy recovery on behalf of everyone

Seeing a mate in a hospital bed puts football in perspective

Skipper JT keeps you updated on Cech's condition in Oxford

A large crowd of us went to see big Pete in hospital on Monday.

We basically went in in twos. José and Silvino went first, then I went in with Didier.

Brito, Robbie, Joe Cole, Shaun, Geremi, Kalou and Hilario all came too.

When Didi and I were there, he shuffled back to sit up a bit more and took his oxygen mask off and he was quite relaxed. But he was tired after the operation.

He didn't remember anything about the incident, but he was okay. He was really pleased to see the lads and the message to you is he's doing well.

Martina, his wife, is with him 24/7, she's really looking after him. She's been great.

This puts football and results all in perspective.

On behalf of everyone I've wished big Pete a speedy recovery. Our thoughts are with him, his wife and family.

After his injury on Saturday, we still won the game.

We're up there with the best teams in the world when we want to play football, but we can also mix it when we have to. Over the last two or three years we've shown we've got what it takes if teams try it on with us.

We needed that against Blackburn a couple of years ago and last season there were several games when we went down to 10 men.

Now we've done it again.

Boula was brilliant on his first game

CAPTAIN'S TEAM TALK
JOHN TERRY

in central defence. And it was welcome back Coley at last.

He's been a nuisance in the treatment room. He's been desperate to train and play and it was great to see him back.

Now it's welcome back to Eidur. It'll be great to see him again. Obviously we've been speaking to him on the phone.

He's enjoying life over there and enjoying playing. I know he'll get a warm welcome from the fans, he's

been a great servant to Chelsea over six years.

We love him here, the players all love him and miss him and we all saw at the last home game of last season what Chelsea Football Club meant to him.

These nights like tonight are great. The Champions League at a full Stamford Bridge is always electric. A win tonight will put us in a great position in the group.

Come on the Chels!

Our goalkeeper was back in action by January, in time to appear in the League Cup semi-final against Wycombe. In our Champions League programme against Porto, Cech was pictured celebrating with his team-mates after we beat Arsenal 2-1 in the Carling Cup final.

access all areas

Hilario shows a safe pair of hands at 25,000 feet

Left: Chelsea TV's Alison Bender gets a soaking from Drogba and Maka

JT leaves the dressing room with cup in hand ready to return to London

Sheva welcomes ...ck after he was ...rged from hospital

Petar Borota

The 2006/07 campaign was a season of success on two fronts in the domestic cups, with the Blues creating a unique piece of history by beating Manchester United 1-0 to become the first club to win the first FA Cup final at the new Wembley, having been the last to do so at the old stadium. Our run in the competition featured home ties against Macclesfield, Nottingham Forest, Norwich and Tottenham. You can read Petr Cech's Q&A from the Spurs programme on page 116.

Eye for figures

Who among our current players is our top scorer in the FA Cup? **John Terry!** Our defender lists well in the all-time top scorers too.

Chelsea FA Cup appearances
Cudicini 28, Terry 23+5, Lampard 20+4, J Cole 8+4, Makelele 6, Geremi 5+1, Bridge 5, Drogba 4+1, Carvalho 4, Wright-Phillips 3+1, Robben 2+4, Ferreira 2+2, Essien 2+1, Diarra 2, Morais 1.

Chelsea FA Cup goals
Terry 9, Lampard 5, J Cole 2, Drogba 1, Ferreira 1, Robben 1.

Top FA Cup appearances
R Harris 64, Bonetti 57, Hollins 51, Bentley 42, McCreadie 41, Armstrong 39, J Harris 38, Wise 38, Tambling 36, Clarke 34+2, Osgood 34, Cooke 32+2, Barber 32, Bettridge 31, Hinton 30+3, Harrow 29, Molyneux 29, Zola 28+3, Cudicini 28, McNeil 28, Ford 26, Gray 26, Law 26, Miller 26, Le Saux 25+3, Campbell 25, Houseman 25, Spence 25, Boyle 24+1.

Top FA Cup scorers
Tambling 25, Bentley 21, Osgood 19, Zola 11, Gudjohnsen 10, Houseman 10, Bridges 9, Gallacher 9, Hilsdon 9, M Hughes 9, Peacock 9, Terry 9, Whittingham 9, Wise 9, Dixon 8, Hasselbaink 7, McNichol 7, Mills 7, Poyet 7, R Smith 7, R Turnbull 7, Cock 6, Hutchinson 6, Thain 6, R Thomson 6, Vialli 6, Webb 6.

JT has bagged nine FA Cup goals for the Blues - the most in the current squad - including this one against Newcastle last season

Golden Boot
Goals scored for the first, reserve and youth teams this season
Drogba 20, Lampard 9, Stoch 9, Sahar 6, Sinclair 6, Shevchenko 6, Kalou 5, Ballack 4, og 4, Essien 3, Tejera 3, Woods 3, Carvalho 2, Saarelma 2, Smith 2, Younghusband 2, J Cole 1, Cummings 1, Elmer 1, Fernandes 1, F Ferreria 1, Geremi 1, Hutchinson 1, Makelele 1, Robben 1, Terry 1, Worley 1, Wright-Phillips 1.

International appearances this season at Full and Under-21s levels while with Chelsea
Lampard 6, Terry 6, Ballack 5, Carvalho 5, A Cole 5, Diarra 5, Cech 4, Essien 4, Makelele 4, Robben 4, Younghusband 4, Boulahrouz 3+1, Drogba 3, Ferreira 2, Geremi 2, Shevchenko 2, Sahar 1+1, J Cole 1, Gallas 1, Wright-Phillips 0+3, Bridge 0+1, Mikel 0+1.

International goals this season at Full and Under-21s levels while with Chelsea
Younghusband 6, Ballack 4, Carvalho 2, Shevchenko 2, Drogba 1, Essien 1, Gallas 1, Geremi 1, Lampard 1, Robben 1, Sahar 1, Terry 1.

International appearances this season at Under-19s, 18s and 17s levels while with Chelsea
Elmer 7, Mancienne 5, Bertrand 4+2, Woods 4, Ofori-Twumasi 3+1, Fernandes 1+1, F Ferreira 1+1, Cork 1, Sinclair 1, Taylor 1.

International goals this season at Under-19s, 18s and 17s levels while with Chelsea
Woods 3, Ofori-Twumasi 2 (1 pen).

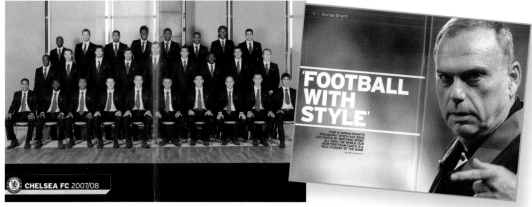

CHELSEA FC 2007/08

'FOOTBALL WITH STYLE'

THAT IS AVRAM GRANT'S PHILOSOPHY WHICH HAS BEEN CULTIVATED BY WATCHING SPORT ALL OVER THE WORLD. OUR NEW FIRST-TEAM COACH IS A TRUE STUDENT OF THE GAME

Season starts with José farewell and ends in European heartache, 2007/08

The players were looking extremely smart in a squad photo with a difference in our first programme of the 2007/08 season, for the game against Birmingham City. By the time of our match against Fulham at the end of September, it was time to say farewell to José Mourinho after his first spell as manager had come to an end. The programme paid tribute to a man who had brought unparalleled success to Stamford Bridge and featured new boss Avram Grant. Wayne Bridge was pictured enjoying one of the many state-of-the-art facilities at our Cobham training ground which had opened in the summer, as well as talking about his love for Star Wars!

'A NEVER-ENDING LOVE STORY'

José Mourinho reflects on three great years at Chelsea

'My time here was a beautiful and rich period of my career'

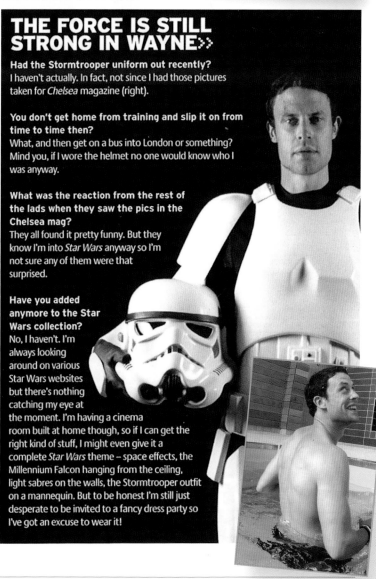

THE FORCE IS STILL STRONG IN WAYNE>>

Had the Stormtrooper uniform out recently?
I haven't actually. In fact, not since I had those pictures taken for *Chelsea* magazine (right).

You don't get home from training and slip it on from time to time then?
What, and then get on a bus into London or something? Mind you, if I wore the helmet no one would know who I was anyway.

What was the reaction from the rest of the lads when they saw the pics in the Chelsea mag?
They all found it pretty funny. But they know I'm into *Star Wars* anyway so I'm not sure any of them were that surprised.

Have you added anymore to the Star Wars collection?
No, I haven't. I'm always looking around on various Star Wars websites but there's nothing catching my eye at the moment. I'm having a cinema room built at home though, so if I can get the right kind of stuff, I might even give it a complete *Star Wars* theme – space effects, the Millennium Falcon hanging from the ceiling, light sabres on the walls, the Stormtrooper outfit on a mannequin. But to be honest I'm still just desperate to be invited to a fancy dress party so I've got an excuse to wear it!

Carlo Cudicini is very proud of his Chelsea appearances milestone

MAKE MINE A DOUBLE HUNDRED

ON 1 DECEMBER 2007 CARLO CUDICINI MADE HIS 200TH APPEARANCE FOR THE CLUB AGAINST WEST HAM AT STAMFORD BRIDGE. WE SAT DOWN WITH THE ITALIAN KEEPER TO REFLECT ON NINE YEARS WITH THE BLUES

WORDS: GARRY HAYES

It is an honour to have played so many games for this fantastic club," was Carlo Cudicini's response when asked how it felt to have joined the Lou genuine ranks of everyone players that have made over 200 appearances for Chelsea.

"I never thought when I joined that I would ever reach this number, but now I have I feel honoured. It's not a bad record to have. Chelsea is a massive club and I am proud to be a part of its history.

Cudicini may be modest in his assessment of his nine-year spell at Stamford Bridge, but since his arrival as a free signing in 1999 from Castel di Sangro – a small club from Italy's Serie C – he has been nothing short of a revelation, few looking at his background, it's not hard to see why he has achieved so much in England.

A two-AC Milan and Lazio goalkeeper, Cudicini comes from a family with such football

A season of unrest saw the players respond in fantastic style as we reached our first Champions League final. In the last-16 we faced Olympiacos, with Carlo Cudicini celebrating his 200th Blues appearance in that programme. We faced a familiar foe at the semi-final stage in the form of Liverpool, who had knocked us out in two of the previous three seasons. This time, the Blues prevailed with a 4-3 aggregate win and our final programme of the campaign, for the game against Bolton, looked ahead to the final in Moscow, which sadly ended in penalty shoot-out heartache for the Blues. Our wait for the continent's biggest prize would go on…

All roads lead to Moscow

THE FORTHCOMING CHAMPIONS LEAGUE FINAL IS THE MOST HIGHLY ANTICIPATED GAME IN CHELSEA'S HISTORY AND EVERYBODY ASSOCIATED WITH THE BLUES IS LOOKING FORWARD TO A MEMORABLE NIGHT

WORDS: GARRY HAYES

Didier Drogba runs off to celebrate after Chelsea grab a potentially vital away goal

Liverpool 1
Kuyt 42

Chelsea 1
Riise o.g. 90

Chelsea put themselves in the driving seat of this Uefa Champions League semi-final after a dramatic draw at Anfield.

Liverpool upped the tempo in the last 15 minutes of the first half and could have taken the lead when Torres was put through on goal after half and hour, only for him to miscontrol a Gerrard pass and hit a shot tamely at Cech.

However the Reds did take the lead five minutes before half-time with a

midfield and Florent Malouda and Didier Drogba playing up front with Joe Cole ahead of Salomon Kalou and Nicolas Anelka.

from Dirk Kuyt and the stoper then made an easy save from a scuffed Steven Gerrard shot.

shooting chance after 64 minutes, then Florent Malouda got tackled just as he was about to shoot from eight yards out.

Then with eight minutes left a flurry of chances came to both teams. First John Terry was harshly penalised as his hooked shot was cleared off the line by Jamie Carragher, then Liverpool had two chances in as many minutes – a Gerrard ball-volley was brilliantly

had come on for Joe Cole – flashed a low cross across the six-yard box. With Anelka lurking at the back post, ready to tap the ball in, John Arne Riise opted to clear with his head, sending the ball into his own goal, levelling the scores and completely changing the complexion of the tie.

'A score of 1-1 away from home is always an advantage but it will another tough game at Stamford Bridge,' said Avram Grant. 'I hope at

Frank Lampard and Peter Kenyon are delighted after signing the deal

Blues back on the trophy trail with new men at the helm, 2008/09

Luiz Felipe Scolari took on the manager's job at the start of the 2008/09 season, which opened with a 4-0 win over Portsmouth. The programme discussed Frank Lampard penning a new deal, while 2007/08 Chelsea Player of the Year Joe Cole expressed his urge to get going again.

Lampard signs new Blues deal

Frank Lampard signed a new five-year contract with Chelsea on Wednesday, keeping him at the club until 2014.

With Lampard putting pen to paper, he becomes the latest player to commit his long-term future to the club following Wayne Bridge, Petr Cech and Michael Essien, who all signed contract extensions over the summer.

'I want to finish my career at Chelsea,' said the 30-year-old midfielder. 'It is something I've said many times and after signing this contract I am very happy and positive I will finish as a player here.'

Arriving from West Ham United for £11 million in 2001, Lampard has gone on to to make 369 appearances for the Blues and is the club's seventh highest goalscorer with 110 goals.

Last season he scored 20 goals for the fourth successive season, including a vital penalty against Liverpool at Stamford Bridge in the Champions League semi-final that all but secured the club's first ever European Cup Final appearance.

New Chelsea boss Luiz Felipe Scoalri said he was delighted to maintain the services of Lampard for another five years.

'He is a key player for me and vital to Chelsea's future successes,' the Brazilian explained. 'Frank is one of the best professionals I have ever worked with.

'Every day he tries to learn something new and bring different elements to his game.'

• Turn to page 16 for an exclusive interview with Frank.

'I'M ITCHING TO GET BACK'

ENGLAND'S ABSENCE FROM EURO 2008 MEANT THAT JOE COLE HAD THE SUMMER OFF - AND THE TALENTED PLAYMAKER CAN'T WAIT TO RETURN TO ACTION

WORDS»PATRICK MASCALL

BLUES APPOINT HIDDINK

GUUS HIDDINK

I'M EXCITED BY TONIGHT'S GAME AND THE CHALLENGE AHEAD

My first week at Chelsea went very well, in training and then on Saturday, when I had my first game in charge of the team. It's always exciting to begin a new challenge and even better when you win, especially when you score a very good goal like we did.

It was not easy for us for the whole game but we were the best team for long spells and defended with strength when we had to.

Now we have a good performance to build on and some positive ideas to take forward with us into our next games. I was pleased to have that week to work with the squad so I could get across my way of working in training and also see how this team works. We now know each other better and I'm looking forward to the rest of this season.

Tonight is my first home game and in a competition I know very well. First of all let me say I hope to enjoy a fantastic atmosphere on my first night in Stamford Bridge.

The Champions League is a special competition and I know how important it is to this club. When two big teams like Chelsea and Juventus meet it is always an exciting occasion for everyone and I'm sure everyone here will welcome Claudio Ranieri. But it's also important we use this home game to put ourselves in a strong position for the second leg in Turin in two weeks.

The next step for us is against Wigan here on Saturday and, after beating Aston Villa last weekend, it's very important we make sure we continue to play in the same way, with everyone using the ball well and defending with commitment. Most of all, we want to get as many points as possible before the end of this season to put pressure on the teams above us in the table.

But we will start thinking about that challenge after tonight's game. First we are concentrating on what we have to do against Juventus. With your support, we can hope for a great atmosphere and an excellent game on the pitch as well.

We were the best team against Aston Villa and can build on that win

Scolari's stint as Chelsea boss was a shortlived one, and by the February Champions League encounter against Juventus, Guus Hiddink was the man penning the managerial column, having stepped in until the end of the season. A 1-0 win over the Italian side was followed by a thrilling 7-5 aggregate win over Liverpool before more semi-final heartache, this time controversially at the hands of Barcelona.

When Chelsea won the FA Cup in 2000, Ray Wilkins was part of the coaching staff. He's hoping for a return up Wembley Way this year.

Thank you, Wembley!

IT'S A SHOUT NORMALLY HEARD FROM STADIUM ROCK SINGERS BUT RAY WILKINS HAS AS GOOD A REASON TO SAY IT AS ANYONE, HAVING ENJOYED SOME GREAT MOMENTS THERE, INCLUDING A TRIUMPH WITH CHELSEA IN THE LAST FA CUP FINAL AT THE ORIGINAL WEMBLEY

INTERVIEW»DOMINIC BLISS

As a player Ray Wilkins played in some pretty memorable games and for a series of top clubs, but despite his successes elsewhere, his time at Chelsea did not coincide with the best period in the club's history.

Our famous FA Cup triumph of 1970 preceded Wilkins' progression to the first team by some years and it was not until he had moved on to pastures new with the likes of Manchester United, AC Milan, Rangers and QPR, that the Blues returned to the hallowed turf of Wembley again, albeit for the Full Members Cup Final in 1986.

However, it was the FA Cup that finally brought Wilkins to Wembley with Chelsea for the first time in 2000 – a chance he thought had passed when his playing days came to an end.

'It was a great chance to go to Wembley on such a wonderful occasion as part of a Chelsea squad,' says Wilkins, reflecting on his days as Gianluca Vialli's assistant manager and that triumph in the

'Some of the foreign players tend to get a real buzz from the big occasion and playing at Wembley'

There was more success in the FA Cup this season, which began with victory over Southend. The programme heard from a man who knows all about winning at Wembley, Ray Wilkins, who oversaw our fifth-round away win over Watford as caretaker manager.

LAST LINE OF DEFENCE

Former Blues shot-stopper Dave Beasant discusses his forced transfer to Stamford Bridge from cash-strapped Newcastle and his debut, when he managed to keep a certain Ian Wright quiet

14 JANUARY 1989

CHELSEA 1-0 CRYSTAL PALACE

DORIGO

STAMFORD BRIDGE

Above-right: Beasant is unveiled as the Blues' new keeper in 1989 with manager Bobby Campbell. Below: Surveying young starlets on a visit to Cobham with the Glenn Hoddle Academy

After spending 10 years at Wimbledon, I had signed for Newcastle in a five-year deal, but early on in the season a 'shares issue' blew up and the authorities demanded they sell their most saleable assets, which included me. So after only six months in the North-East I was on my way back down south to London. And no, I didn't leave because it was too cold up there!

I don't think the transfer would have happened if I'd moved directly from the Dons because Stamford Bridge was so close to Plough Lane, but I was more than happy to sign for the Blues.

Chelsea were in the Second Division when I joined them, but looking at the squad I knew we had enough quality to achieve something.

Crystal Palace were a decent side in those days with Steve Coppell in charge. Their big stars were Ian Wright and Mark Bright, who had justified reputations as prolific goalscorers.

We ended up winning the game through a Tony Dorigo goal. Wrighty came up to me and said: "How is it I never score against you?" That's the sort of compliment you want from a top striker.

After the Crystal Palace win we had a great run, going 23 games unbeaten, finishing the season on 99 points. Our unbeaten record went in April against Leicester, on the same day as the Hillsborough disaster. As a team we were pretty deflated but then news started filtering down that the FA Cup semi-final was abandoned. When we found out why, it put things in perspective. It was a sad day for football.

In a funny sort of way, winning the Second Division at the end of the season and then going on to win the Zenith Data Systems Cup the following season, it felt like Chelsea were on the up again. It sounds Mickey Mouse compared to what we're achieving now but we hadn't won a trophy since 1971, so it meant a lot to us.

LIKE FATHER, LIKE SONS

I'm currently working at the Glenn Hoddle Academy out in southern Spain. There's a big Chelsea connection out here and I'm with Nigel Spackman, Graham Rix and, of course, Glenn. We're helping players who have been released from club's books.

I'm lucky enough to have a few family members working out here. My sons Nick and Sam are at the Academy along with my nephew James. The upside is that I can spend a bit of time with them, but being a senior coach I have to treat them the same as I treat everyone else which isn't always easy. Overall I'm really enjoying it.

Chelsea: Dave Beasant, Steve Clarke, Tony Dorigo, Graham Roberts (Gareth Hall), Joe McLaughlin, Darren Wood, Kevin Wilson, David Mitchell, Kerry Dixon, David Lee, Clive Wilson

Ancelotti rises to challenge to secure Double, 2009/10

The 2009/10 Premier League season began with a home fixture against Hull City and the programme featured Carlo Ancelotti's first column as Blues gaffer. Updates to the publication included a piece on Chelsea debuts over the years. The new year gave a sign of the free-scoring ways to come as we beat Watford 5-0 in the third round of the FA Cup before a 7-2 win over Sunderland in the Premier League. Didier Drogba featured in the programme for our fifth-round tie against Cardiff City, which the Blues won 4-1 as we closed in on another final appearance.

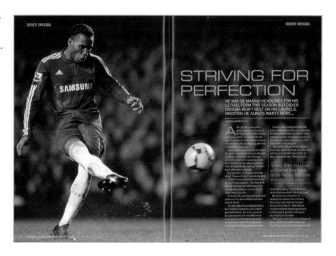

STRIVING FOR PERFECTION

HE MAY BE MAKING HEADLINES FOR HIS LETHAL FORM THIS SEASON BUT DIDIER DROGBA WON'T REST ON HIS LAURELS, INSISTING HE ALWAYS WANTS MORE...

THE CHALLENGE AHEAD EXCITES ME

Now it begins! This is my first game at Stamford Bridge and my first as a Premier League manager and, honestly, I am very excited about this.

My first month here has been very good, we had a fantastic tour of America and some great results there. Then we returned to England and I have enjoyed working at Cobham very much as well – even the weather is good for football because we have a little sun but also rain, which is good for the pitches. I hope also that my English is improving well because it is very important for me to communicate everything I want to say in English.

Now I have had time to get to know my squad and I have seen them playing in the system we want to use. I have options, with so many great players to choose from. We have not had to spend lots and bring in many new players because we are happy with our squad and the new players we have brought in are high quality in the positions we wanted.

The work we have done together means we are in good condition for the start of the season and I think we showed this against Manchester United in the Community Shield. It was a good first competitive

game for me as manager. I could not relax in this kind of match, but we showed our strength, mentally and technically, to win with penalties.

Okay, I understand not every game will be at Wembley but last week I saw the passion of English supporters, players, coaches – everyone. The atmosphere was something special and I hope for more here, but I hope today there will be a Chelsea atmosphere.

This match is something totally new for me – I have had games

against Manchester United before but with Hull, nothing. They are a new challenge, a new team and this is what I will enjoy about my first season in English football.

I wanted these challenges when I moved from Italy and I hope there will be happy memories from my first game here.

'I have had time to get to know my squad and I have so many great players to choose from'

Our form in pre-season was very promising, with four wins out of four on the tour of America and a victory at Wembley Stadium against Manchester United in the Community Shield

Our third Premier League crown was wrapped up in emphatic style as we beat Wigan Athletic by a record 8-0 scoreline at the Bridge and the following week we went on to win our first domestic Double, beating Portsmouth 1-0 in the FA Cup final. Didier Drogba top scored with a remarkable 37 goals in all competitions and the news pages discussed him winning Player of the Year. Ancelotti's notes from the Latics programme are on page 175.

Drake's modern team

It's in our DNA. Who they were makes us who we are today. Every programme, CSI examines rare photos and discovers the stories behind them

At the start of this season, for the first time, a Chelsea manager has had to name a basic squad of 25 players to contest the Premier League title.

Fifty-five years ago Ted Drake lined up with his own team, hoping that the new ideas and footballers he had begun to introduce in 1952 would make the club's 50th jubilee year a special one.

The picture (above) looks like a straightforward enough scene, a team photo just like any start to the season. But who were some of the key characters involved and what was going on at the time?

① TED DRAKE
Succeeded Billy Birrell in the hot seat at Chelsea in 1952 and was the club's first tracksuit boss, dropping the 'secretary' part of the title secretary-manager preferred by all his predecessors. In August he officially announced that his team should no longer be referred to as 'The Pensioners' but 'The Blues,' and demanded more partisan support from the long-suffering souls of Stamford Bridge. His modern ways paid dividends.

HOTSHOT DROGBA CROWNED PLAYER OF THE YEAR

Didier Drogba on why surprising defences is the best form of attack.

DIVIDE & CONQUER

CSI CHELSEA SCENE INVESTIGATION

Words: **Rick Glanvill**

Bright start to the campaign but there's no silver lining, 2010/11

We picked up in the 2010/11 campaign where we had left off the previous season, hitting West Brom for six in our opening Premier League game. Former fans' favourites Roberto Di Matteo and Eddie Newton were in charge of the Baggies at the time and were interviewed in the programme – little did any of us know they would be back at the Blues in the not-too-distant future, guiding us to arguably our greatest triumph of all time. New-look history feature CSI examined rare photos and told the story behind them. In our September programme against Blackpool, Didier Drogba was the player feature, discussing his aims for the season after an incredible 2009/10.

② SEAMUS O'CONNELL
An amateur forward who was allowed to play for Chelsea through an agreement with Bishop Auckland FC, he was the son of a Cumbrian cattle dealer. His debut in October 1954 was an astonishing affair. Hitting a hat-trick on your Chelsea bow was one thing, but still seeing your side lose 5-6 to Manchester United was quite another. Despite being unavailable for parts of the season, the farmer's boy reaped a vital harvest when he played.

③ JACK OXBERRY
Ted Drake first met his reliable right-hand man and first-team trainer while playing for Reading. He was an uncompromising taskmaster and Drake's conduit into the players' heads. Note that he is wearing a smart new blazer. It might not have been as stylish as Dolce&Gabbana, but it did bear the smart new 'lion rampant' badge – another innovation of the Drake era, replacing the monogrammed 'CFC' style that had been used from the club's foundation in 1905.

④ PETER SILLETT
Defender whose goalscoring record at free-kicks and penalties – all thumped with ferocity – were a considerable boon to the Chelsea armoury.

⑤ ROY BENTLEY
Captain, leader, legend, as the modern homage to a later player, John Terry, has it. The Bristolian, an England International, was the dominant force of Ted Drake's Blues.

Brazil midfielder Ramires signs in

Florent the Machine

IT'S BEEN FLORENT MALOUDA'S BEST SEASON YET IN A CHELSEA SHIRT AS HE HAS CHURNED OUT THE GOALS AND ASSISTS – AND HE IS HOPING HIS FANTASTIC OUTPUT HELPS TO BRING SOME SILVERWARE TO THE BRIDGE

WORDS: RICHARD GODDEN

Florent Malouda is in a relaxed mood as we meet at Cobham ahead of one of the last training sessions of a thrilling Premier League season.

As cool and calm a customer as you are likely to find, the 29-year-old certainly won't have lost any sleep ahead of today's match against Wigan which will decide the destination of the title. But don't mistake that for overconfidence from the French winger – he knows there's still a job to be done.

Flo, what has the mood in the camp been like after last weekend's fantastic win at Anfield?
We were happy with the result but it was the same time, we are still focused and aware that we have to come through against Wigan. When you look at the atmosphere around us, maybe people could be celebrating but we don't want to celebrate yet. We know it's going to be difficult and we have to finish the job.

So it's just a case of worrying about us beating Wigan today and not even thinking about what's going on in Manchester United's game against Stoke City?
Of course. You concentrate on today, the Liverpool game that's past. We owe them a better game than we did against them and after that match yesterday, Liverpool gave up the game, but they never gave us credit for what we achieved. So we don't have the right to be too relaxed and underestimate, we have to finish it well.

The win over the Reds meant that not only did we do the double over them this season, but also Man United and Arsenal. However, you look at it, that's a fantastic achievement.
Yeah, and it's strange that we always have to remind people of that. If we are at the top of the table with one game left, that means we deserve it. Sometimes we're so modest because we never celebrate the opposition. So that's why I don't want to because what people say, now I'm just ready to play the game at my best level. That's the focus and the main edge that every player has.

'If we are at the top of the table with one game left, it means we deserve it'

Team mates with alex

The Brazilian defender on the importance of having good neighbours and why Salomon Kalou's attempts at speaking Portuguese have him in hysterics

Who would you say is your best mate here at Chelsea?

a It's hard to tell who's the "best" friend. Everyone here at the club is friends and we all get on really well with each other – there's always a nice atmosphere. But with Ramires being here, and as my neighbour, I guess I spend more time with him.

As the theme tune to the soap told us, "Everybody needs good Neighbours"... Does your fellow Brazilian fall into that category? And do you really live next door to each other?!

a He is a neighbour to me in the changing room, as well as living next

chelseafc MARSEILLE

The 2010/11 season introduced a new style of programme for European match nights which proved popular with fans, with a matt white cover complemented by perfect binding to give these editions an extra-special feel. The first-team player Q&A was called Team-mates and Alex took the honours in the programme for our first home Champions League game of the campaign against Marseille. Sadly, our run in the competition came to an end at the quarter-final stage against Manchester United – a game in which Frank Lampard made his 500th appearance for the Blues. He was the player feature and you can read a piece with him talking about the landmark on page 118.

Roller-coaster ride of emotions for European champions, 2011/12

As seasons in the history of Chelsea Football Club go, the 2011/12 campaign will take some beating for surprises, tension, drama and, come the end, sheer jubilation. West Brom were the visitors to Stamford Bridge for our first home game, with André Villas-Boas penning his opening notes after replacing Carlo Ancelotti as manager in the summer. Our first Champions League game of the campaign was against Bayer Leverkusen and the programme caught up with Michael Ballack, who played for the German club before and after representing the Blues.

Michael Ballack
Ex-Chelsea midfielder

It's good to see you Ballack at the Bridge

Interview: **David Antill**

During four years with the Blues, Michael Ballack played a key role in many of the club's recent trophy successes, culminating in Premier League and FA Cup glory in his final season. He rejoined his former side Bayer Leverkusen last summer and explains how tonight's return to the Bridge is a dream come true.

How did you feel when the Champions League draw paired Bayer Leverkusen in the same group as Chelsea?

I was very happy when I saw the draw, it was one of my wishes that we would play Chelsea in the Champions League because I played there for four years and it is a fantastic draw for me personally. So, when it came true, I was really happy.

I was at Stamford Bridge a few months ago at the Champions League quarter-final against Manchester United working for German television. It was a good experience and it's a little bit more relaxed than when you're playing, of course. I also visited Chelsea a few times after I left, watching from the stands.

I had a good four years with the club and the last year, especially, was a successful one with the Double.

Expert insight: Michael Ballack working at the Bridge for German television in April

andre *villas-boas*
MANAGER'S NOTES

Togetherness will be crucial in quest for major honours

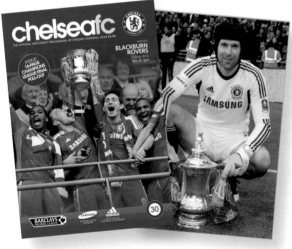

roberto di matteo
INTERIM FIRST-TEAM COACH

FA Cup success can be
stepping stone to Munich glory

john terry
CAPTAIN'S NOTES

Players are ready for the
ultimate final challenge

The effect of Roberto Di Matteo taking on first-team managerial duties was an instant one. In mid-March we faced Napoli at the Bridge in the Champions League last 16 and, trailing 3-1 from the first leg, we turned it around with a 4-1 win after extra-time. The programme for our game against QPR portrayed the scenes of jubilation after the final whistle at Camp Nou, where a 2-2 draw with Barcelona was enough to take us through to our second Champions League final. Our final programme of 2011/12, for a home game against Blackburn, was one of celebration following our 2-1 win over Liverpool in the FA Cup final, and also one of hope as a 16-page pull-out looked ahead to the Champions League final against Bayern Munich. Here you can see some ecstatic scenes from the final which appeared in a special one-off publication the club produced after we had beaten Bayern on penalties in their own backyard.

actionreplay

Match Stats		
Possession %	72	28
Shots on target	5	3
Shots off target	12	4
Corners	10	1
Offsides	1	1
Fouls	8	10
Yellow cards	2	6
Red cards	0	1

Tremendous: Chelsea players show their joy at the final whistle

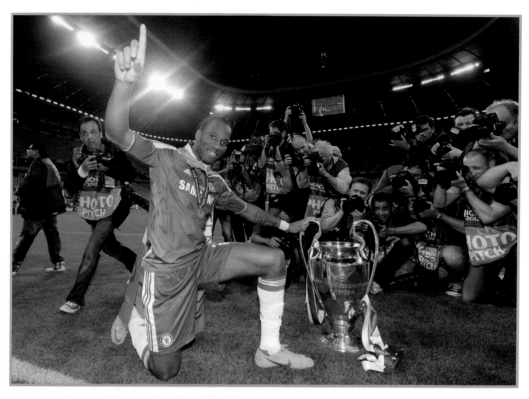

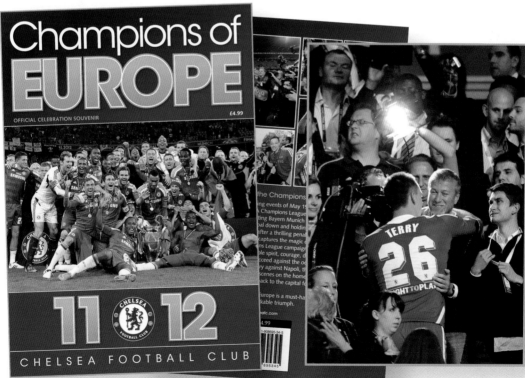

CHELSEA FOOTBALL CLUB
THE INSIDER SW6

1. FRIENDS REUNITED
Didier Drogba catches up with former Blues team-mate Michael Ballack after beating the German player's current side, Bayer Leverkusen, 2-0 at Stamford Bridge.

2 AND 3. WELCOME, JUAN
Juan Mata is mobbed by Spanish fans on his return to Valencia and receives a warm reception from a young fan at the Mestalla.

4. HORSING AROUND
Petr Cech and David Luiz enjoy the country life in the peaceful surroundings of the team's hotel near Genk.

5. SNAPPED IN NAPLES
The players line up for an impromptu team photo while taking in the sights around Naples.

6. ANDRIY MAKES NIGHT EXTRA SPECIAL
Former Chelsea striker Andriy Shevchenko congratulates his friend Branislav Ivanovic on scoring the Blues' extra-time winner at home to Napoli.

7. RAMIRES TAKES A WALK DOWN MEMORY LANE
Ramires appreciates the imagery around the Stadio da Luz, showing that his and David Luiz's achievements at Benfica haven't been forgotten.

8. DIDIER HITS THE HIGH NOTES
After securing a place in the Final by seeing off Barcelona at Camp Nou, Didier Drogba serenades his team-mates with a sing-along.

CHAMPIONS LEAGUE SPECIAL

More European glory as new man takes over the reins, 2012/13

The 2012/13 season was another intriguing campaign in SW6. Our opening home game was against Reading and The Insider took fans behind the scenes on our pre-season trip to America. The new Connect Four feature looked for quirky links between the Blues and our opponents each week.

We go inside the Chelsea camp for exclusive behind-the-scenes photographs of the boys in blue

How do professional athletes take in a foreign culture? By trying their hand at the native sports, of course. The Chelsea squad had a great chance to do just that during the summer tour of the United States, starting at the Virginia Mason Athletic Centre, home of the Seattle Seahawks.

Branislav Ivanovic seemed to get particularly enthusiastic about American football (1) after he, Petr Cech, Frank Lampard, Romelu Lukaku and Kevin De Bruyne swapped sports with local NFL stars KJ Wright, Malcolm Smith, Mike Morgan, Cameron Morrah and Winston Guy.

There was more to come in Miami too. While getting ready for a training session at the Sun Life Stadium, David Luiz, John Mikel Obi and Yossi Benayoun were among a group of players who started their own basketball match (2). The rules may have veered away from the traditional slightly, not least with a kit hamper taking the place of the basket, but there were definitely signs that some of the Chelsea squad could have done just as well as sportsmen across the pond.

There was a touch of glamour when the team were visited at their Seattle hotel by Hollywood comedians Will Ferrell and Zach Galifianakis (3), who had their photo taken with our FA Cup and Champions League trophies before receiving personalised Chelsea shirts.

Sticking with the movie theme, John Terry, Sam Hutchinson and Gary Cahill gained some inspiration for the rigours of pre-season fitness training by recreating a famous scene from Seventies blockbuster Rocky in Philadelphia, running up the steps outside the city's Museum of Art (4).

From the football fraternity, AC Milan legend Paolo Maldini (5) caught up with his former international team-mate Roberto Di Matteo and his players in Miami. More impromptu was the appearance of ex-Colombia midfielder Carlos Valderrama, who turned up at a signing session with his family, all decked out in Chelsea shirts. Needless to say he caused quite a stir, especially when David Luiz spotted his hero and insisted on a photo (6) with the man he names as one of only three footballers possessing better hair than his own. The others? Raul Meireles and Ruud Gullit!

Kerry Dixon scored goals for fun during a three-year spell with Reading before joining Chelsea, for whom he bagged 193 goals – second only to Bobby Tambling in the club's all-time scoring list...

Tambling was the Blues' goalscorer in the 1967 FA Cup Final, which we lost 2-1 against a Tottenham Hotspur side containing Jimmy Greaves...

CONNECT FOUR

Exploring quirky Chelsea links in the world of football

Ancelotti was a member of the Italy squad at the 1986 World Cup in Mexico, a tournament at which Kerry Dixon was part of the England set-up that reached the quarter-finals.

Prior to joining Spurs, Greaves had a brief spell with AC Milan, the Italian giants who Carlo Ancelotti led to Champions League glory on two occasions as a manager...

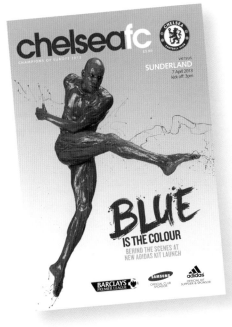

By the time of our home game against Manchester City at the end of November, Rafa Benitez had been named as interim first-team coach. Although the decision may not have been universally popular with Blues fans, the former Liverpool manager did bring more major silverware to the Bridge. After dropping out of the Champions League following the group stage, we entered the Europa League for the first time and won the final in Amsterdam thanks to a 2-1 win over Benfica. You can also see the jubilant scenes following that match taken from the last programme of the season against Everton, an edition which honoured Frank Lampard after he became the club's leading scorer of all time. One of our most innovative kit launches was unveiled towards the end of 2012/13, as you can see from the Sunderland programme cover and Insider.

We go inside the Chelsea camp for an exclusive behind-the-scenes look at the boys in blue

The striking artwork from the adidas It's Blue, What Else Matters? campaign to launch the 2013/14 Chelsea home kit will no doubt have caught many people's eyes around Stamford Bridge today, and our players certainly appeared to have a lot of fun when it came to making those images.

We're sure you'll agree that the finished products look spectacular and the members of the Chelsea squad involved maintained their high spirits while the adidas film crew slopped, squelched, splashed, poured, sprayed and submerged them in paint from head to toe.

Demba Ba was one of the stars bringing the set to life by showing flawless technique despite the off-putting situation (1).

Credit has to go to the people at adidas, who seemed to come up with a never-ending list of creative ways to cover the Chelsea players in paint, such as having Gary Cahill walk through a blue waterfall (2) in one shot that reminded The Insider of contestants being gunged in a Nineties game show!

"I went through a sheet of paint that was falling from the sky and I sort of appeared through the paint," explained the defender. "They used some crazy effects, but I have never done anything like that before."

Fellow centre-back John Terry showed his nerves of steel when allowing himself to fall backwards into a large pool of the paint (3) to create one of the messier sections of the photo shoot. However, it has to be said that, large as the splash zone was, much of the mess (4) was made by Terry himself when making his way back to the edge of the pool.

Juan Mata certainly seemed to be enjoying the unusual afternoon's work and was having so much fun that he didn't want it to end (5). Luckily the adidas crew were on hand to give him another round with their buckets of paint (6) and provide an excellent example of just what the players put themselves through to create the stunning imagery to accompany the new kit's launch.

You can pre-order the new Chelsea FC home kit at **www.chelseafc.com/allin** and view a behind-the-scenes video of the photo shoot on adidas' YouTube channel.

José returns for second spell as we mark special milestones, 2013/14

The hot topic in football at the start of 2013/14 was the return of José Mourinho to Stamford Bridge. He featured on the front cover of the programme for the opening game of the season against Hull, but there was the added bonus of a special wrap, featuring a message to fans, marking 10 years of success since Roman Abramovich bought the club. The programme also recognised the 30th anniversary of our promotion back to Division One with a regular piece in each issue. You can see Mourinho's first notes of his second spell as gaffer on page 169. Didier Drogba returned to Stamford Bridge when we took on Galatasaray in the Champions League round of 16 and the Ivorian told the programme of his emotions at the prospect of turning out against us. We eventually bowed out at the semi-final stage to Atletico Madrid, when Damon Albarn discussed his love of the Blues in The Last Word.

GUEST APPEARANCE

Didier Drogba acknowledges fans in the first leg of this tie against Galatasaray

Interview | David Antill

DROGBA GETS READY FOR HIS RETURN

A season-ticket holder at Stamford Bridge for more than 20 years, Damon Albarn has a feeling that a repeat of our 2012 heroics could be on the cards…

I really enjoyed the first leg of this semi-final last week. Considering what happened, with the change of goalkeeper so early in the game, everybody worked their socks off to keep Atletico at bay and that has given us a great opportunity to go through to the final.

Having to switch keepers following Petr Cech's injury was quite a profound change and I thought Mark Schwarzer did brilliantly.

Unfortunately, I'm doing a gig tonight, so I won't be able to be at the Bridge, but I will find time to watch it before I go on stage. Hopefully, we will get the result we're all looking for so I can go out there a happy man.

Although I'm sad about not being here this evening, I will make going to Lisbon a priority if we get through – I wouldn't want to miss it for the world. I've been to two other European finals – Stockholm in 1998 and Munich in 2012 – and, having witnessed two victories, I would love to make it a hat-trick.

I've been going to the football with my daughter for the last six or seven years and being in Munich with her was an amazing experience. It was a beautiful day, I felt the fans were treated superbly and what high drama we had as well.

I get the feeling we're gearing up for a repeat of that Champions League triumph, having overturned a 3-1 deficit against PSG in the quarter-finals and then put in a brilliant defensive display in Madrid last week.

Nobody thought we could make it to the final or win it two years ago and a lot of people have been saying the same sort of thing about us this time. There are certain things mirroring what happened back then – we've got our fair share of suspensions and injuries this evening but, at these key moments, Chelsea seem to be able to create miracles.

If I cast my mind back to our last Champions League semi-final, I'm not sure I could handle the drama of that second leg in Camp Nou tonight, but as Fernando Torres is my daughter's favourite player, it would be perfect if he could score the goal that clinches our spot in the final again.

Good luck tonight, boys. I'm sorry I can't be there, but I'll be cheering you on from afar.

NOBODY THOUGHT WE COULD WIN IT TWO YEARS AGO AND A LOT OF PEOPLE HAVE BEEN SAYING THE SAME SORT OF THING THIS TIME

Celebrating the 2012 Champions League triumph

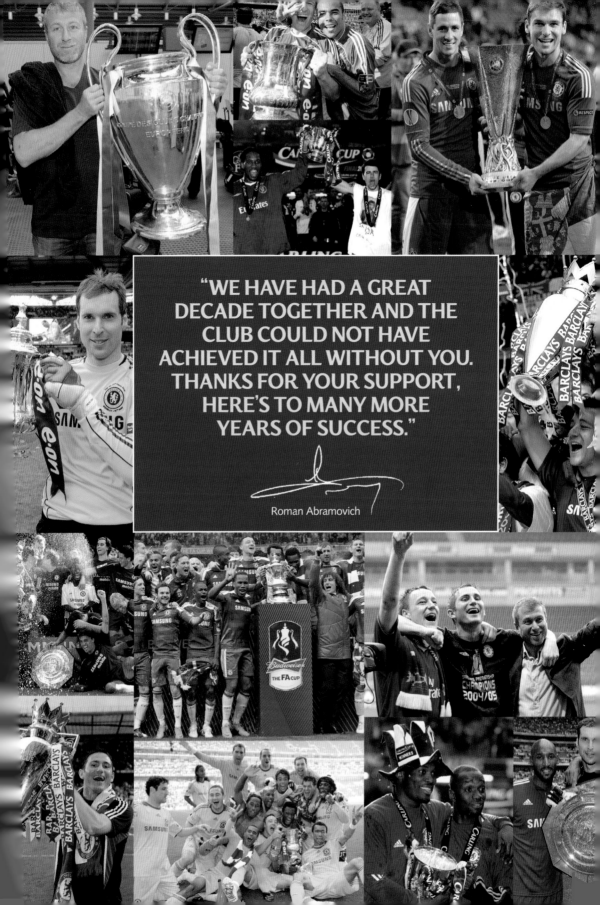

"WE HAVE HAD A GREAT DECADE TOGETHER AND THE CLUB COULD NOT HAVE ACHIEVED IT ALL WITHOUT YOU. THANKS FOR YOUR SUPPORT, HERE'S TO MANY MORE YEARS OF SUCCESS."

Roman Abramovich

CHELSEA REMEMBERS

Compiled by | **David Antill**

Honouring the brave Blues

On the cover of today's matchday programme is Vivian Woodward, a star for both Chelsea and England in the early part of the 20th century who fought for the British Army during World War One.

Woodward is pictured in a team line-up from a footballers' battalion, the first of which was launched in December 1914 at Chelsea Town Hall following heated debate about the continuation of professional football after the outbreak of war four months earlier.

Chelsea's hierarchy supported the initiative; not only did several current and former players sign up, but club secretary Bert Palmer became Honorary Recruiting Officer, prompting the attestations of 60 to 70 soldiers, some of the first being Chelsea players Teddy Foord and William Krug.

Hundreds of professional players would go on to enlist from around 50 football clubs, including Chelsea, with a second Football Battalion formed in May 1915. Woodward was wounded in the leg in January 1916 and, although he survived, his injuries did bring his Chelsea playing days to an end.

Woodward made 116 appearances for the Pensioners, scoring 34 goals, but he missed appearing in the club's first-ever FA Cup final, which was against Sheffield United in 1915. Having been on service in the lead-up to the game, he was released to play in the final, but declined the opportunity as he had not made any appearances in the cup run, insisting his stand-in, Bob Thomson, took his place. Woodward later became a director of the club from 1922 to 1930.

Sadly, seven serving and former Chelsea players died during the Great War. We pay tribute to those who lost their lives over the page.

Chelsea captain Vivian Woodward, above right, shakes hands with Manchester United's George Stacey before kick-off at Stamford Bridge on 20 September 1913

Cover photo courtesy of Coloursport

53

You have been brilliant throughout my 500 games as captain

After leading the team out for the 500th time on Saturday, I want to begin my notes this evening with a big thank you to all of you for your brilliant support throughout my time as captain.

As a 14-year-old boy in the youth team here, I dreamed of captaining Chelsea and I am proud and honoured to have achieved this milestone.

It was important for me to show my appreciation by going over to the travelling fans on Saturday and sharing the moment after another important win.

We were delighted with the performance and the result at Selhurst Park, which is a difficult place to go. From the first minute, I thought we showed our determination to take

Dominic Solanke is just one of the youth players working with the first team

control of the game and make sure we got on the ball and dominated possession. We went in front with a great free-kick from Oscar, who has started the season brilliantly, and Cesc's goal in the second half was brilliant – the passing, the movement and the finish were top class. That wasn't the first time this season we have put together a move like that in the final third and to produce a goal of that quality shows the understanding among this group of players.

I want to mention Dom Solanke, who was among the substitutes on Saturday at the age of 17 and has been working with the first team this season after a brilliant pre-season. He is not the first Chelsea youth player to be named in the squad this season and it is great to see young players who have come through the Academy involved in the first team and getting opportunities.

Now we return to the Champions League and a big match for us as we look to maintain our place at the top of the group. Maribor have drawn both their games so far and it is important we take all three points tonight before travelling to Slovenia for the return match in two weeks' time.

Come on the Chels!

Quality additions help us secure league title number five, 2014/15

Having shown signs of improvement in the Premier League during 2013/14, then adding strength to the squad by bringing back Didier Drogba and signing the likes of Diego Costa and Cesc Fàbregas, the Blues got off to a blistering start in 2014/15. Thibaut Courtois starred in the Schalke programme, having began his first season in the Blues first team after impressing on loan at Atletico Madrid. Our Champions League programme against Maribor discussed John Terry captaining the Blues for the 500th time, while the West Ham programme on Boxing Day remembered Chelsea heroes who had fought in World War One.

Courtois showing determination during a training session, main, and concentration against Swansea, below

Courtois saves from Clint Dempsey in the World Cup round of 16 match between Belgium and the USA

At the start of 2015, the Blues were going for glory in the cup competitions, as well as looking to bring the Premier League trophy back to SW6. Our Champions League programme against Paris Saint-Germain had a unique cover to emphasise the club's stance against discrimination, as well as celebratory pictures after we won our fifth League Cup thanks to a 2-0 win over Tottenham at Wembley. March also saw the club celebrating its 110th birthday and the cover for our Southampton programme harked back to the Chelsea Chronicles of old.

Eden Hazard and Cesar Azpilicueta show their mutual appreciation for each other's efforts in the final by swapping shirts after the game

England international Gary Cahill gets a picture with the trophy in front of a collage of Three Lions legends in the changing room, which is also the one used by the national team for home games

José Mourinho proudly holds his latest piece of silverware in front of a picture in the Wembley changing room of a man he worked under during the early stages of his career, the late Sir Bobby Robson

CHELSEA FOOTBALL CLUB

THE INSIDER SW6

We go inside the Chelsea camp for an exclusive behind-the-scenes look at the boys in blue...

The Chelsea squad celebrate winning the Capital One Cup final by getting a group photo with the trophy in the Wembley Stadium changing room

Didier Drogba gives the trophy a quick polish to keep it looking its gleaming best for the photos

Diego Costa makes sure his team-mates will think twice before interrupting another of his photos, by launching a rolled up sock in their direction

CHELSEA FC

WE ARE ALL BLUE
#EQUALITY

PARIS SAINT-GERMAIN

The CHELSEA F.C.Chronicle
OFFICIAL PROGRAMME

18

SAMSUNG, PROUD SPONSOR OF CHELSEA FC 2005-2015.
Ten successful years, one incredible team.

The Blues sealed the title with three games to spare thanks to a 1-0 win over Crystal Palace at the Bridge. Our third Premier League triumph was marked in the final two programmes of the campaign, against Liverpool and Sunderland, the latter also featuring a unique squad picture courtesy of our shirt sponsor Samsung, whose partnership with the club was coming to an end after 10 years. You can see José Mourinho and John Terry's last notes of a memorable season on page 175.

DIDIER DROGBA

I said when I arrived that I came here because I wanted to win the league again. Every title is very special and the first one I will never forget, but this one is sweet because it is five years since we last won the league. It's a special day. We are the best team in England and we are back again as champions. We did it.

JOHN TERRY

We've worked so hard this year. The first time you win the league is obviously very special, but when you go four or five years without winning it after you've grafted all season and you get nothing, it really hurts – so we're going to enjoy this.

It is even more special when we do it in front of our own fans, for sure. I've been a ball boy here, a mascot, I've painted the stadium and this is what I live for, to give the championship to the fans after five years.

in off the post

Your letters should be of not more than 150 words and addressed to "In off the Post", Chelsea F.C., Fulham Road, London, S.W.6.

FEATURING TONIGHT REPLIES TO OUR REQUEST FOR YOUR ATHENS STORIES

I AM a 16-year-old Chelsea fanatic living in Edinburgh and I made the journey to Athens alone, taking two days off school.

I left Edinburgh by bus at 7.30 p.m. the night before the match and arrived in London at 6.30 a.m. I then made a confusing journey by Underground to Waterloo where I joined the Chelsea party. Another hour and a half coach journey to Stansted Airport followed by a three and a half hour flight to Athens. Boy, was I glad to get there in one piece!

The return journey was similar except I took the overnight train to Edinburgh arriving at seven on Friday morning. Two hours later I was at school, exhausted, telling everybody about my journey. It was the first time I had seen Chelsea and it cost me £47. How's that for a first time? Well done Chelsea!

Adrian Webb.

23 Brighton Place,
Portobello, Edinburgh, 15

THANKS to Dave Sexton and his boys, we were able to spend our first holiday abroad together. Previously, my husband was strictly a U.K. holidaymaker, but for CHELSEA alone he conquered his air-sea sickness and we spent a tremendous holiday at Loutraki, plus the thrill of seeing both matches.

My only chance of a further holiday abroad rests with CHELSEA!

Mrs. Sheila Hadley.

27 Links Avenue,
Morden, Surrey.

*   *   *

ALTHOUGH I am a German girl, I'm a great Chelsea supporter and, of course, I wanted to see Chelsea v. Real Madrid. But this time I attended a boarding school and when we wanted to see a late programme on TV (in Germany the match was shown at 10.30 p.m.) we had to ask our headmistress.

She wasn't very pleased the first time,

JUST TO REMIND YOU

John Dempsey's volley rockets into the net for the first goal of the Athens replay.

16